T0330190

DEVELOPMENT IN AFRICA

Refocusing the lens after the Millennium Development Goals

Edited by

George Kararach, Hany Besada and Timothy M. Shaw

First published in Great Britain in 2015 by

Policy Press
University of Bristol
1-9 Old Park Hill
Bristol
BS2 8BB
UK
t: +44 (0)117 954 5940
pp-info@bristol.ac.uk
www.policypress.co.uk

North America office:
Policy Press
c/o The University of Chicago Press
1427 East 60th Street
Chicago, IL 60637, USA
t: +1 773 702 7700
f: +1 773-702-9756
sales@press.uchicago.edu
www.press.uchicago.edu

British Library Cataloguing in Publication Data
A catalogue record for this book is available from the British Library

Library of Congress Cataloging-in-Publication Data
A catalog record for this book has been requested

ISBN 978 1 44732 853 7 hardcover

The right of George Kararach, Hany Besada and Timothy Shaw to be identified as editors of this work has been asserted by them in accordance with the Copyright, Designs and Patents Act 1988.

The statements and opinions contained within this publication are solely those of the editors and contributors and not of the University of Bristol or Policy Press. The University of Bristol and Policy Press disclaim responsibility for any injury to persons or property resulting from any material published in this publication.

Policy Press works to counter discrimination on grounds of gender, race, disability, age and sexuality.

Cover design by Hayes Design
Front cover image: Getty
Printed and bound in Great Britain by by CPI Group (UK) Ltd, Croydon, CR0 4YY
Policy Press uses environmentally responsible print partners

We would like to dedicate this book to our wives, mothers, brothers and sisters for their unwavering support, persistent encouragement and continual belief in us throughout our careers. This book would not have been possible without their presence in our lives.

GEORGE KARARACH • HANY BESADA • TIMOTHY SHAW

Contents

List of tables and figures

Tables

Figures

Notes on contributors

Professor Manmohan Agarwal is the Reserve Bank of India Chair at the Centre for Development Studies, Thiruvananthapuram, Kerala, India. He retired as Professor from Jawaharlal Nehru University, New Delhi, India after 30 years, and as Adjunct Senior Fellow with the Institute of Chinese Studies. He was Senior Fellow at the Centre for International Governance Innovation (CIGI), Waterloo, Canada, where he worked on issues of the world economy including the G20 and South–South cooperation. He also worked for The World Bank and International Monetary Fund (IMF). His research focused on international and development economics. More recently he worked on the role of current account imbalances in generating the 2008 crisis, the impact of the crisis on developing countries, the G20 and macro coordination, and the role of developing countries in the G20. In development economics, apart from South–South cooperation, he is working on Millennium Development Goals (MDGs) and aid architecture, including Southern development cooperation.

Professor Hany Besada is Regional Adviser, African Mineral Development Centre (AMDC) at the United Nations Economic Commission for Africa (UNECA); Research Professor, Institute of African Studies, Carleton University, Ontario, Canada; Senior Fellow, Centre on Governance, University of Ottawa, Canada; Senior Research Manager, Africa Business Group, a trade and investment consulting firm in Johannesburg, South Africa; and Senior Governance Specialist with ACT-for-Performance in Ottawa, Canada. Until recently, he was Theme Leader, Governance of Natural Resources, North-South Institute in Ottawa, Canada, and Research Specialist on the UN High Level Panel Secretariat Post-2015 Development Agenda, UN Development Programme (UNDP) in New York. He was also Programme Leader and Senior Researcher at the Centre for International Governance Innovation (CIGI), Waterloo, Canada, and Principal Researcher, Business in Africa, South African Institute of International Affairs (SAIIA), Johannesburg, South Africa. He has authored 70 peer-reviewed scholarly papers and over 70 opinion pieces.

Aniket Bhushan is Senior Researcher at the Norman Paterson School of International Affairs (NPSIA), Carleton University, Canada. He has worked with Canada's leading international development policy think-tank, working at the intersection of data, technology and international development. Has over six years' experience in project management, conducting policy analysis, and liaising with international institutions, foundations, civil society and stakeholders in developing countries. He has extensive knowledge and experience in areas including open data standards, social media big data, data management and visualisation platforms and open source software development, and their applications to international development data. His research interests include fiscal mobilisation in developing countries, international finance, the impact of big data and open data on research in international affairs and development. He was, until late 2014, Senior Researcher at the North-South Institute, Ottawa, Canada with the Governance for Equitable Growth programme, and led the Canadian International Development Platform.

Cristina D'Alessandro is currently Professor at the Paris School of International Affairs (Sciences Po), Paris. She holds a PhD in Geography from the Université François-Rabelais de Tours, France, and has more than 15 years' experience in development in Africa. Her teaching, research and publication activity focuses on Sub-Saharan Africa, and more particularly on urban issues, regional integration and regionalisms, natural resource governance, territorial governance, institutional capacity building and leadership. She publishes in French, English and Italian, and is an international scholar with experience in three continents – Africa, Europe and America. She also serves as an adviser and expert for international organisations and institutions working in Africa.

Fatima Denton is Director of the Special Initiatives Division of the United Nations Economic Commission for Africa (UNECA) in Addis Ababa, Ethiopia. She previously led the International Development Research Centre's (IDRC) research on adaptation strategies. Fatima joined IDRC in 2006 after working as a senior energy planner with the UN Environment Programme (UNEP) in Denmark. She also worked with the energy programme of Enda Tiers Monde in Senegal on issues such as sustainable development and climate change vulnerability and adaptation, as well as food security, local governance, water and energy poverty in the Sahel. She has written articles on energy poverty, gender and energy, and climate change adaptation. She is lead author for the Intergovernmental Panel on Climate Change, and was also a member of UNEP's Scientific Technical Advisory Panel. Fatima holds a PhD in Political Science and Development Studies from the University of Birmingham, UK.

Bernadette Dia Kamgnia is Acting Director of the African Development Institute, African Development Bank. Prior to joining the Bank, she was Associate Professor of Economics (Agrégé des Sciences Economiques) at the University of Yaoundé II, Cameroon. She was coordinator of the Master's and PhD training programmes of the new PTCI (Programme de Troisième Cycle Inter Universitaire en Economie) of Conférence des Institutions d'Enseignement et de Recherche Economiques et de Gestion en Afrique (CIEREA), an international non-governmental organisation, based in Ouagadougou, Burkina Faso. Until November 2007, she was manager of the Campus for Francophone Africa of the African Economic Research Consortium (AERC) collaborative PhD programme at the University of Yaounde II, Cameroon, as well as Vice-Dean in charge of the academic affairs of the Faculty of Economics and Management. Since May 2009, she has been involved in the Political Economy and Sectorial Issues Thematic Group of the AERC Research Network. Since 2007 she has also provided reviews for AERC research proposals.

George Kararach is a Ugandan political economist and currently Economic Affairs Officer at the Macroeconomic Policy Division of the United Nations Economic Commission for Africa (UNECE) and Senior Consultant in the Strategy and Operations Policy Department, African Development Bank. He holds a PhD in Economics from Leeds University, UK. Earlier in his career of over 20 years, George worked for the UN Children's Fund (UNICEF), the UN Development Programme (UNDP), and taught economics at Leeds, Middlesex and Luton Universities. He has just published four books: *Macroeconomic policy and the political limits of reform programmes in developing countries* (Africa Research and Resource Forum); *Rethinking development challenges for public policy: Insights from contemporary Africa* (with Kobena Hanson and Timothy Shaw, Palgrave Macmillan); *Economic management in a hyperinflationary environment: The political economy of Zimbabwe, 1980-2008* (with Rapheal Otieno, Oxford University Press); and *Development policy in Africa: Mastering the future?* (Palgrave Macmillan). His other most recent research work includes the development of the Green Growth Index for Africa (GGIA) in collaboration with the Statistics Department of the African Development Bank.

Abbi Mamo Kedir is Economic Affairs Officer in the forecasting section of the Macroeconomic Policy Division of the United Nations Economic Commission for Africa (UNECA). He started working in the Ministry of External Economic Co-operation in Ethiopia after finishing his BA degree in Economics before moving on to teach in the Department of Economics at Addis Ababa University. Before he joined the UNECA, and after finishing his PhD studies, he worked in different capacities in the UK, including as a Research Fellow (University of Nottingham, 2002) and as an Assistant Professor (University of Leicester, 2003-13). In addition, he served as a consultant to The World Bank, Department for International Development (DfID), African Development Bank and USAID. His expertise is in development economics and applied econometrics. He is currently working, *inter alia*, on tax compliance on Africa and development finance, as well as on the empirical link between debt and growth in Africa.

Dr Frannie A. Léautier is Chair and Co-Founding Partner of Mkoba Private Equity, a growth capital fund for small and medium enterprises in Africa. She is former World Bank Vice President and Chief of Staff to the President. She holds several board director positions – PTA Bank, African Economic Research Consortium (AERC), Nelson Mandela Institute for Science & Technology, editorial board of the *Journal of African Trade* (JAT), and UONGOZI Institute. She serves on the Visiting Committees at the Massachusetts Institute of Technology (MIT) Corporation and on the Advisory Board of Women's World Banking. She was Co-Chair for World Economic Forum (WEF) Africa, and is a member of the WEF Global Agenda Councils. She has a Master's and PhD from MIT; a BSc in Civil Engineering from the University of Dar es Salaam; and graduated from Harvard University's Executive Programme. She holds an honorary degree in Humane Letters from North Central College. She was Distinguished Professor at Sciences Po, Paris, and is well published, with several well-acclaimed books, including *Leadership in a globalized world: Complexity, dynamics and risks* (Palgrave Macmillan).

Kemi Medu has a PhD from the Norman Paterson School of International Affairs, Carleton University, Ottawa, Canada.

Victor Murinde is Professor of Development Finance, Birmingham Business School, University of Birmingham, UK. He lectured at Makerere, Cardiff Business School, Bradford University, Loughborough and Manchester Universities. He provides advisory services to governments, companies and international organisations, including The World Bank, United Nations (UN), UN Conference on Trade and Development (UNCTAD), Kuwait Institute of Scientific

Research, African Development Bank and Caribbean Development Bank. He has held the distinguished Hallsworth Senior Research Fellowship at the Institute for Development Policy and Management, University of Manchester, UK, 2001-02, received generous research grants from the European Commission, Department for International Development (DfID), Economic and Social Research Council (ESRC) and the Leverhulme Trust, and been Visiting Professor at the Cardiff Business School and Professor Extraordinary, University of Stellenbosch Business School, South Africa. He was, until recently, Director of the African Development Institute, African Development Bank, Tunis. His current research interests include emerging financial markets, capital structure and dividend policy, bank performance and risk, flow-of-funds, financial development and poverty reduction.

Benjamin O'Bright is a PhD student in Political Science and International Relations at Dalhousie University in Halifax, Canada. His research focuses on the leveraging off-the-shelf consumer technology for achieving human security, successful post-conflict reconstruction, gaps in institutional governance and generalised development. Ben holds a combined BA in Political Science and Legal Studies from Carleton University, Canada, where he studied the pre-Edward Snowden use of digital media sources by intelligence agencies for data collection, and an MSc in the Politics and Government of the European Union (EU) from the London School of Economics and Political Science. His MSc dissertation focused on the reflection of core EU institutional values in member state digital media policies. Between 2007-13 he was a lead researcher with the Landon Pearson Resource Centre for the Study of Childhood and Children's Rights, the London-based Eden Stanley Group, and Junior Researcher at the North-South Institute, Ottawa, Canada.

Natasha Pirzada works with the United Nations Capital Development Fund (UNCDF) LoCAL (Local Climate Adaptive Living) Facility, Bangkok, Thailand. She is excited to be able to contribute towards development in the least developed countries through small infrastructure projects such as the building of roads, bridges and dams that make a dynamic impact on the livelihoods of rural communities. She believes that local economic development and the climate go hand in hand, and that partnerships of the federal government with provincial and local municipal authorities are vital if climate finance is to reach grassroots levels. Natasha has worked, lived and travelled extensively throughout North America, the Middle East and North Africa and South Asia. She holds an MA in Environmental Studies from the University of Waterloo in Canada and a BA in Government from Georgetown University in Washington, DC, US.

Dr Leah McMillan Polonenko is Lecturer at Emirates Aviation University, Dubai, United Arab Emirates. Prior to that she was Assistant Professor of International Development at Tyndale University College and Seminary, Toronto, Canada. Leah received her PhD from Balsillie School of International Affairs, Wilfrid Laurier University, Canada. Her most recent work has looked at the impact of global social policies on local development. Her publication, *The impact of global education policy: Missing out on the 'local' in Southeastern Africa* (Library and Archives Canada: Ottawa), examines the impact of the Education for All policy in Malawi, Tanzania and Zambia, exhibiting her passion to merge international development policy into sustainable practice. She is committed to maintaining research projects that connect research with policy and practice, with the overarching goal of alleviating the challenges of poverty, inequality and under-development. Leah has also researched the possibility for improved socioeconomic and environmental practices in natural resource governance in Sub-Saharan Africa.

Yiagadeesen Samy is Associate Professor and Associate Director (MA programme) at the Norman Paterson School of International Affairs, Carleton University, Ottawa, Canada. He holds a PhD in Economics and his broad research interests are in the areas of international trade and development economics. He has published widely on various issues such as trade and labour standards, foreign direct investment, small island developing states, state fragility, aid effectiveness, domestic resource mobilisation and income inequality. He co-authored a book on fragile states published by Routledge in 2009, and co-edited the 2013 edition of *Canada among nations* on Canada–Africa relations. Some of his recent peer-reviewed publications have appeared or are forthcoming in the *Journal of Conflict Resolution, Canadian Journal of Development Studies, Third World Quarterly* and *International Interactions*.

Timothy M. Shaw is Visiting Research Professor, and for last three years (2012-15), Foundation Director of the PhD in Global Governance and Human Security, McCormack Graduate School, University of Massachusetts, Boston, US, and also Adjunct Professor at both Carleton and Ottawa Universities, Canada. He has been Professor and Director at the Institute of International Relations, University of the West Indies, St Augustine, Trinidad; Associate Research Fellow, United Nations University Comparative Regional Integration Studies, Bruges; and distinguished Research Associate, North-South Institute, Ottawa, Canada. He previously directed the Institute of Commonwealth Studies, University of London, UK, where he remains Professor Emeritus. Since 1 February 2013, he has been an Assigned Professor at the Faculty of Social Science, Aalborg University, Denmark. He is also Visiting Professor at Mbarara and Stellenbosch Universities in Africa, and has received an honorary degree of Doctor of Letters at the University of St Andrews, Scotland. He currently edits an international political economy book series for both Ashgate Publishing and Palgrave Macmillan.

James Wakiaga is currently Senior Economist for the United Nations Development Programme (UNDP), Ethiopia. He previously served in a similar position in Zimbabwe from 2009-13. Prior to this, he worked at Kenya's Ministry of Foreign Affairs and served at the Kenya Embassy in Washington DC, with a liaison role on matters pertaining to The World Bank, International Monetary Fund (IMF), US Congress and the US Treasury Department. He has contributed to several knowledge products on poverty, Millennium Development Goals (MDGs), human development and economic growth, with a focus on Africa. He is also a member of the External Reviewers Group and Strategic Studies Group for the African capacity indicators report.

Karolina Werner is a PhD candidate in Global Governance at Balsillie School of International Affairs, Wilfrid Laurier University, Waterloo, Canada. Prior to entering the PhD programme, Karolina worked as a project manager at the Centre for International Governance Innovation (CIGI) in Ontario, Canada, where she was affiliated with the African Initiative. Before that, she was at the United Nations Industrial Development Organization (UNIDO) and the International Institute for Applied Systems Analysis, both situated in Austria. She has an MA in Peace and Conflict Studies, and an HBSc in Peace and Conflict Studies and Psychology. Karolina's interests lie primarily in conflict issues in Africa, and international conflict mediation and grassroots approaches to conflict transformation.

Kristen Winters was, until October 2014, a Research Assistant at the North-South Institute, Ottawa, Canada.

Acknowledgements

This volume brings together fresh insights from leading scholars and practitioners from both the North and the South on the emerging features of public policy conversations around Africa and the post-2015 development agenda. These consist of old and recurrent problems, for example, the legacy of leadership in African development; issues of agency and political economy – especially the importance of social voice and social inclusion; enhancing governance of all types including that of trans-boundary resources such as water and land; the primacy of resource mobilisation, programme execution and management; and the importance of striking strategic partnerships as well as good management of endowments such as the discovery of new resource wealth.

The completion of this volume has hinged on the support of numerous individuals, whose time and dedication made the compilation process a success. In particular, Kristen Winters, the book project's coordinator, has been instrumental in providing the necessary leadership, critical management and coordination of the entire process from start to finish. The book would not have been possible without her attention to detail, sharp editorial skills, strong research experience and critical project management. She was ultimately responsible for the final touching and compilation of the various chapters, and ensured quality control throughout the entire publication process. The timely assembly of the volume was made possible through the efforts of Ben O'Bright, University of Ottawa researcher, who assisted with some of the editorial work and research that went behind the book.

The book's editors would like to especially acknowledge the contribution of Homi Kharas, Joe Ingram, Caroline Andrew, Eric Champagne, Blair Rutherford, Nicole Rippin, Franklyn Lisk, Stuart Croft, David, Jiajun Xu, Molly Elgin-Cossart, Karina Gerlach, Akopyan, Lisa John, Haroon Bhorat, Anthony Barzey, Amos Cheptoo, Siaka Coulibaly, Gibson Ghuveya, Kobena Hanson, Harry Kojwang, Steve Kayizzi-Mugerwa, John Loxley, Sydney Mabika, Fewstancia Munyaradzi, Takawira Mvuma, Muthuli Ncube, Elias Ngalande, Floribert Ngaruko, Dominique Njinkeu, George Omondi, Michael Plummer, Malcolm Sawyer, John Halligan, Severine Rugumamu and Robert Nantchouang. We thank each of them for their commitment and support.

The project's institutional partners have also been integral players in the creation of this volume. Specifically, the cooperation of the African Development Bank, University of Ottawa Centre on Governance, Carleton University Institute of African Studies and the University of Massachusetts, Boston, facilitated the production process, and without their support, the project may have never gotten off the ground.

Development policy, agency and Africa in the post-2015 development agenda

George Kararach, Hany Besada, Timothy M. Shaw and Kristen Winters

Since 2000, Africa's economic expansion has proceeded with vigorous momentum, maintaining an annual average economic growth rate of 5 per cent or more (IMF, 2013). This robust economic growth is expected to extend beyond 2015, as the continent benefits from opportunities created by a natural resource boom, strong internal demand from its rapidly growing middle class,[1] increased spending on basic infrastructure by both governments and the private sector, adoption and penetration of ICT (for example, mobile telephone penetration has surpassed 90 per cent in urban areas; see The World Bank, 2010), foreign direct and portfolio investments that are projected to reach a record US$80 billion (of which US$57 billion is foreign direct investment, FDI) by the end of 2014, doubling from 2005, and sizeable diaspora remittances, projected to reach US$67.1 billion in 2014 (AfDB, 2014a). However, in 2013, Africa faced major development challenges, some of which had far-reaching implications for the continent. These can be classified as relatively recent (those of yesterday): a rapidly changing demography (youth bulge, urbanisation, horizontal inequalities) and social risks (emerging and re-emerging diseases such as Ebola and Polio, crime, drugs, illicit trade); those of the immediate present (today): transforming agriculture (food security, exports) and global/regional integration (trade, finance, migration, human trafficking, infrastructure); and those of tomorrow: climate change pressures (water and energy insecurity, land shortages/grabs, drought, desertification, coastal populations (McMichael and Butler, 2004)) and technology (UNCTAD, 2012), as well as the business 'model' shocks (economic competition, job creation, and natural resource governance, beneficiation and its distribution).

Africa's economies have need of not only a new dynamism to respond to global competition, but also a strategy that will enhance transformation and socioeconomic achievement beyond the Millennium Development Goals (MDGs), particularly within the context of the post-2015 development framework, and which will include a wide range of development solutions around issues such food and energy security, and enhance service delivery and social inclusion. Africa must work on securing social and political stability and build effective economic governance. This must take the form of a concerted effort in order to enhance national and regional capacity for successful and sustainable development, creating a society that can deal with questions of agency and political economy for quality service delivery, social inclusion and democratic accountability. Policies must be pro-poor and properly sequenced. New alliances must be crafted at the local and regional levels, with adequate governance frameworks anchored on greater civic participation and voice, corporate social responsibility as well as accountability of those in public office.

Challenges remain for the continent in terms of key reforms; policies and legislation need to be designed and implemented to achieve the basic key goals and targets set out in the post-2015 development agenda. The continent needs to accept its proper share of responsibility in accordance with its human, financial and natural resources as well as capabilities, as driven by the five fundamental shifts of the post-2015 development agenda. These include (i) the eradication of extreme poverty in all forms; (ii) inequality and an inclusive economy transformation; (iii) peace and good governance; (iv) forging a new global partnership; and (v) the future of sustainable development given environmental climate change obstacles (UN, 2013).

Some unfinished business for a post-MDG Africa

The continent has a number of challenges that are removing the shine from the 'Africa rising' mantra. According to Akukwe (2013), Africa will have a number of unfinished businesses to conclude well after 2015, including the following:

Achieving participatory democracy: a number of countries continue to have difficulties with the constitution process, as well as in their preparations for elections, including extension or even complete removal of presidential term limits. For example, there were tensions in Kenya following the indictment of President Uhuru Kenyatta by the International Criminal Court (ICC) for alleged complicity in post-election violence in 2007. This only subsided after charges against the President were dropped due to 'lack' of evidence. Zimbabwe remained equally tense in early 2015, with its legacy of disputed elections and polarised politics, as well as crippling international sanctions. The country approved a new constitution, and held fresh elections in 2013, with Zanu-PF reportedly winning a much-disputed landslide victory. Zimbabwe remained at a standstill, waiting to see how this 'victory' would affect the *real politik* in the country after 2015. Any chaos and uncertainty in Kenya has a negative impact on the entire East African economy, affecting the rest of the continent. Equally, violence in Zimbabwe would destabilise the Southern African region, with possibly millions of refugees entering South Africa, adding to the 3 million or so who are already there. Indeed, many 'democratic' governments in Africa continue to struggle with a number of challenges including social exclusion, income inequalities, soaring unemployment, corruption, nepotism and decreasing mineral prices, all of which are having an impact on their economic growth. Power struggles among the elite are rampant in countries including Burkina Faso, Nigeria, South Africa, Ghana, Mali, Senegal, South Sudan, Sudan, Madagascar, Central African Republic, Uganda, Egypt and Tunisia. It remains to be seen whether the continent is taking a backward turn on democracy and the progress it had made prior to 2015 to ensure a transformative developmental trajectory for the foreseeable future and to deliver goals and visions such as Agenda 2063.

Violent conflicts continue to persist: a number of conflicts continue to rage on the continent. For example, the UN Security Council had to approve military intervention in Mali, where the French interceded to regain part of the country captured in 2011 by Islamist groups. Conflict in the eastern Democratic Republic of Congo (DRC) has also persisted, despite the indictment by the ICC of the leader of the M23 rebellion, J.B. Ntanganda, for war crimes. It is likely that the DRC will require major interventions by the international community at the same level as those in Iraq and Afghanistan. In West Africa, Guinea-Bissau remains fragile, due in part to international narcotics trafficking (Akukwe, 2013). In early 2015, the Boko Haram Islamist insurgency in northern Nigeria remained a major source of violence and instability. The Seleka rebel coup of March 2013 in the Central African Republic, following which the country degenerated into a state of wholesale random acts of violence which spilled over the border into Chad and other neighbouring countries, may generate similar actions in other countries, especially where central governments only have nominal control over vast underpopulated territories. And finally, the Somali government has remained dependent on African Union (AU) troops, a situation that might continue long after 2015. Equally, South Sudan saw the end of the MDGs timeline in a state of civil war.

Need for strategic and productive development policies: the continent is yet to develop and implement strategic and productive development policies (for example, granting greater civic voice and participation, effective service delivery, transparency and accountability) – especially those that can tackle corruption, illicit capital flows and the haemorrhaging of state funds. Africa needs to establish stable policy regimes, and as yet, implementing public sector reforms to enhance service delivery remain long-term objectives throughout the continent. Many African countries, including Uganda, Egypt and Zimbabwe, do not even have a fiscally and operationally independent judiciary (Akukwe, 2013). Policies that strategically favour (local) private sector and civil society remain critical yet unattained, due to lack of follow-through. Small and medium-sized enterprises (SMEs) need to benefit from fiscal, policy or logistical incentives from the public sector (Akukwe, 2013). Despite vast mineral resources, there are real concerns over beneficiation and creation of value addition to raw materials that are exported from sectors that form the backbone of many economies across the continent. How do countries transform the mineral and oil/gas sectors into productive sectors that add value to the economy and really benefit the local productive sectors that are required to create decent employment opportunities and lift people out of grinding urban poverty and rural dispossession?

Africa requires a generation of new knowledge and the improved analysis of existing information on beneficiation, value addition and mineral supply chains, which can subsequently inform the design and deployment of effective governance programmes at national and regional levels, public–private partnerships and industrialisation. This can be done by creating and facilitating the meaningful dialogue and co-creation between all engaged actors and levels in Africa's natural resource sectors. Detailed analyses of specific value chains in the interface between mining and manufacturing will identify interventions enhancing domestic capabilities, and bring immediate returns to business, government, communities and society as a whole. This is a step-by-step approach of building national capabilities and practical strategies and solutions, triggering commodity-based industrialisation as an engine of growth and economic transformation for African countries. This effort, enhancing domestic value addition to natural resources, will promote the idea of 'joined-up economies' in Africa, including all relevant state institutions and the private sector, as well as labour and civil society. These policy shortcomings compromised the achievements of the MDGs, and may well undermine future development goals for some time to come.

Trade imbalances with Brazil, Russia, India and China, the Gulf States and traditional markets: in recent times, trade with Brazil, Russia,[2] India and China (BRIC) – largely based around Africa's natural resources – grew to satisfy the rising demands for raw materials necessary for these economies to grow. For example, trade between Africa and China rose from US$9 billion in 2000 to US$160 billion in 2011 (Akukwe, 2013), and surpassed US$200 billion in 2013 (Rotberg, 2014). By 2009, China had become Africa's largest trading partner, importing one-third of its oil from the continent, and some of its investments are tied to resource extraction (Ncube, 2012). At the 2012 Africa-China summit, China pledged US$20 billion in credits by 2015, doubling previous commitments (BBC Online, 2012). President Jacob Zuma of South Africa voiced his concern about 'unsustainable' long-term trade ties with China, and, understandably, African leaders will want the Chinese to import more manufactured goods and services from the continent (Drummond and Xue-Liu, 2013). Equally, trade with the Gulf States – focused significantly on access to food and arable land – rose from US$10 billion in 2002 to US$49 billion in 2011 (Reuters, 2013). But the focus of the Gulf States on agriculture fuels further concerns about unsustainable 'land grabs' in Africa in attempts to enhance the growing of food crops for those foreign markets and to secure their food security.

The land grab is by countries that are running out of arable lands. It has been argued that because 80 per cent of Africa's land is still uncultivated, and 7 per cent of its land is irrigated with low production yields, if they play their cards right, this could benefit African countries as well (Mullin, 2010). Therefore, the real issue becomes ensuring these land deals are structured in a fair and correct manner. International investors need to support development contracts that can benefit African countries, and governments need to be more accountable, transparent and strategic in how they structure deals (Mullin, 2010). There are leaders and African administrations that choose to do what is best for them and their own pockets and that have a total disregard and lack of empathy for the individuals in the country who are suffering as a result of being dislocated from their lands to make way for foreign investments in commercial farming for example. Furthermore, even if the leaders in some African countries are neither self-seeking nor corrupt, they do not necessarily have the tools or infrastructure in place to become more accountable or transparent. These African countries, for the most part, are very poor, and for the administration and leaders it becomes difficult to turn down investments and deals that will essentially give the country money no matter what the long-term repercussions may be. Therefore, although there are economic opportunities for these countries, if during negotiations African leaders push too hard, they could lose the contract as these foreign investors could easily go to another country that is willing to make a deal on these terms. The extraction of natural resources must comply with respect for local human rights, new governance frameworks and encourage beneficiation (ACBF, 2013). Equally, trade balances with the traditional markets of the European Union (EU) and US remain stacked against Africa in 2015. Opportunities for improving the trading fortunes of the continent may exist in other 'emerging' economies such as Mexico, Indonesia and Turkey.

Overcoming tensions in traditional development cooperation: imports between developing countries rose from 35 per cent of all trade in 1995, to 55 per cent (about US$1.5 trillion) in 2010 (WTO, 2010, 2011), a shift away from traditional Western markets punctuated by the recent financial crisis, and consequent attempts to establish new economic partnerships, heralding a new multilateralism and regionalism (Hanson et al, 2012). African exports – especially of natural resources to other countries within the global South – more than doubled between 2010 and 2013 (UNCTAD, 2013). Fellow global South countries such as China, India, Korea and Brazil now account for more than 10 per cent of FDI in Africa, thus providing African leaders with viable alternatives for FDI and economic partnerships. These developments have weakened Western governments' attempts at governance reforms in African countries (Zimbabwe on land reforms and Uganda on anti-gay legislation) by imposing preconditions for any development assistance. Disagreements and tensions have also emerged about what to do about the effects of climate change, and how countries can share the burdens of mitigation and adaptation (CFR, 2013). These trade disagreements will continue well after 2015, especially as Western democracies turn inwards to repair weak domestic economies (Akukwe, 2013) and enhance fiscal consolidation, which will have wide-ranging implications for post-2015 development cooperation as well as broader debates. What sort of alliances should Africa build after 2015? Perhaps strategic South–South cooperation (SSC) will present a viable alternative to a new development cooperation architecture for many African countries. Insomuch as Sino-African relations are shaping the economic trade on the continent, SSC also exists within countries across the continent independently of other countries and regions. In recent years, the opening up of trade systems, particularly in major economic blocs, especially the East African Community (EAC), the South African Development Community, (SADC), the Economic Community of West African States (ECOWAS), and the Common Market for Eastern and Southern Africa (COMESA), has hastened the pace of regional integration. The tripartite free trade area, consisting of the EAC, COMESA and SADC, shows the opportunity for increased free trade across these areas. Some scholars have argued that financial development assistance is not just ineffective, but also damaging to economic growth prospects for the developing country (Easterly, 2001; Prokopijevic, 2006; Leeson, 2008; Coyne and Ryan, 2009; Moyo, 2010). Easterly explains that '568 billion in today's dollars flowed into Africa over the past 42 years, yet per capita growth of the median African nation has been close to zero. The top quarter of aid recipients … received 17 per cent of their GDP in aid over those 42 years, yet also had near-zero per capita growth. Successful cases of development happening due to a large inflow of aid and technical assistance have been hard to find…' (Easterly, 2007, p 4). In addition to the poor track record of aid effectiveness, the aggressive economic growth of non-aid recipient countries is also noteworthy, especially when examining the case of the so-called 'Asian tigers', named such given their aggressive growth.

SSC is, in many ways, an attempt to realise the mantra of 'trade not aid'. The Pacific countries, for example, have heightened their economic connectivity with one another, and lessened their ties with Commonwealth states, including Australia and New Zealand; the latter two may share geographic proximity, but their placement as 'developed countries' removes them from an attempt at collaboration between lesser developed countries. Perhaps the attribute of SSC considered most attractive by least developed states, particularly in Africa, is the horizontal, rather than vertical, form of networking. Slaughter argued in 2004 that the global structure is shifting such that relationships are more horizontal, rather than vertical, in scope. Glennie agrees, asserting that the shift to SSC, inherently a horizontal formation, is the future of international development (Glennie, 2011).

Diseases, counterfeit medicines, access to potable water, food and secure energy: Africa continues to suffer from the negative effects of 'old' diseases such as malaria, as well as new ones like HIV/AIDS, cancer and Ebola.[3] The increasing onslaught of cancer has been largely overlooked and ignored in Africa. According to the World Health Organization (WHO), by 2020, African states will account for over a million new cancer cases per year out of a total of 16 million cases worldwide (WHO, 2011). Africa remains the continent least prepared to cope with the devastating effects of this new pandemic, having only a few cancer care services available. The puzzling question for the world's leading medical practitioners at this stage is how cancer has managed to step outside of its traditional centre point in the West, and set foot in fragile Africa. Some answers could be found in the rising pollution that is affecting an increasing number of African cities across the continent, as well as ongoing economic development and, consequently, increased life expectancy and disposable income, which has resulted in more Africans living in urban areas and adopting Western dietary patterns. All of this has resulted in a gradual increase in cancer cases, particularly breast cancer among women and prostate cancer among men. African men and women are not only more likely to get prostate and breast cancer respectively at a younger age, but are also more likely to be diagnosed at a more developed stage of the disease. The WHO furthermore identified the underlying causes that had resulted in an increase in cancer cases. Principally, steadily ageing populations, high smoking rates, poor nutrition, which is destabilising the immune system, the spreading of a lifestyle rich in fatty foods and lacking exercise, all exacerbated the problem.

In 2011, African health ministers meeting in Brazzaville declared non-communicable diseases a 'significant development challenge', characterised by high morbidity and mortality, and economic burdens (Akukwe, 2013). With high rates of HIV, tuberculosis, malaria and other communicable health conditions (as the 2014 Ebola epidemic in West Africa showed), Africa has high rates of both communicable and non-communicable diseases,[4] remaining at risk from the sale of counterfeit medicines (worth US$46 billion a year). The WHO recently indicated that 35 per cent of malaria medicine samples failed chemical analysis and packaging tests in Africa (WHO, 2011). Most African governments do not have the technical, fiscal and logistical resources to combat the counterfeit medicine business (Akukwe, 2013). Access to safe water remains low across most parts of the continent, despite recent evidence that Africa possesses giant, easily accessible (under)ground water reservoirs (MacDonald et al, 2011). These giant reservoirs predominate in North Africa, which has a difficult geological terrain, with the result that many people will continue to lack access to basic water and sanitation. There is also poor access to energy sources (Besada et al, 2013), as well as food and appropriate nutrients

(Kararach, 2014). These conditions of poor access to basic services are, and will remain, a major source of conflict and state illegitimacy.

Unemployment and the youth bulge as sources of instability: the number of Africans under 30 years of age is estimated to be about 70 per cent of the continent's population (UNECA, 2012). About 60 per cent of the unemployed in Africa are young. About 70 per cent of the youth in Africa thus live below the global poverty line of less than US$2 a day, and in countries such as Nigeria, Ethiopia, Uganda and Zambia, 80 per cent of the youth live in poverty (Akukwe, 2013). Africa's educated and unskilled youth represent a huge risk for the continent's stability. An instance of this was the 2011 uprising by the youth of North Africa against their autocratic, militarised governments. And no country or government in Africa can be immune from potential youth-inspired political uprisings (Akukwe, 2013). A post-2015 development agenda must ensure that any growth generates the requisite jobs to absorb the youth bulge.

Strengthening the engagement of the private sector: it is generally accepted that Africa's transformation is intrinsically linked to the performance of its private sector. For that transformation to happen effectively, the private and public sectors, as well as civil society, need to have constructive engagements to deliver services and open opportunities for continuous economic growth. The private sector is both a potential driver of continental transformation, by using the opportunity from a youth bulge, and a source of conflict if the promise for inclusive growth is squandered through greater inequality (AfDB, 2013, 2014b). The private sector has a critical role in job creation, providing training to optimise the use of African talent, and the provisioning of goods, services and supportive industries, through the sustainable and efficient management and use of Africa's considerable natural resources. For governments on the continent to make substantial progress in attracting foreign investment, they need to reduce business constraints and bottlenecks. Any unnecessary legal, bureaucratic or financial restraint on the transfer of capital does not bode well for the business community. A more engaged private sector will help foster economic recovery and prevent the post-conflict states on the continent from falling back into conflict. National governments need to promote privatisation programmes intended to privatise many state-owned enterprises that could provide greater opportunities that spur development of the private sector. This process represents a cornerstone of governments' overall strategy for national development that will reduce the burden on government coffers, stimulate the economy and provide jobs for the unemployed.

Revitalisation of the private sector should be based on existing programmes in economic reform, decentralisation, infrastructure development and social welfare. Economic reform is underpinned by annual development policy operations. Support for decentralisation aims to go beyond institutional reforms and capacity building; it includes transferring resources to support innovative approaches to decentralised governance together with the use of rapid results initiatives to empower local councils with a view to sustain high economic growth, reduce poverty, generate employment and improve food security. For the sector to be at the forefront of the transformation agenda, there has to be a fundamental change of Africans' thinking over its role as an integral part of development policy. More attention has to be paid to creating enabling environments in the social, political, cultural, institutional, regulatory and legal contexts in which the private sector operates. The roles of governments, private sector and donors have to change to include a variety of organisational strategies, such as strategic planning and performance management, which require skills, institutional and organisational capacities. Corporate governance, peacebuilding and conflict prevention, and regional integration, are some of special areas where Africa needs to invest in capacity building.

Beyond visioning goals in Africa – enhancing implementation: the history of Africa since independence is replete with a myriad of visions and goals such as the Lagos Plan of Action and the Comprehensive Agriculture Action and Development Programme, the MDGs and Maputo Declaration that have had questionable implementation outcomes. It goes without saying that the success of any development process is ultimately dependent on the players who will implement and sustain the process. Investment in people for programme implementation is essential in both the public and private sectors as well as in civil society. This entails developing an in-depth understanding of the nature of local governance and the existing skills within the system, as well as identifying the gaps and areas of capacity weaknesses that need to be rectified in order to enable the institutions to perform effectively by delivering on specified mandates. Projects and programmes need to be properly identified and implemented to meet the very specific needs of the organisation and the individuals within society. With respect to long-term development and strategic business planning, capacity building entails giving vision, leadership and direction to the management of broader development and private sector activities.

Equally, countries need to develop skills and special capacities to translate visions, scenarios and plans into strategies and implementable programmes. It is arguable that many of these key ingredients of transformation were lacking to see the comprehensive delivery of the MDGs by 2015. In this regard, having effective programmes for domestic resource mobilisation (DRM), efficient and prioritised spending as well as rethinking financing development will be critical to ensure the end of aid by 2028 and delivery of Agenda 2063. A symptomatic area of implementation failure is in the delivery of regional integration. Despite being historically core in Africa's development initiatives over the years, integration processes in its various regional economic communities (RECs) have proceeded unevenly, in part due to poor implementation capacity (Kararach, 2014).

Foundations for the future: dealing with agency and political economy issues

At least in the long term, none of the aforementioned challenges are insurmountable, but solutions will require policy cohesion and resilience, creative leadership, careful choice of priorities, prudent management of scarce resources and transparency in public sector operations to allow Africa to 'make aid history' by 2028, as enshrined in the AU Agenda 2063 vision for the continent. They will also require proactive, mutually beneficial engagement with external partners within the context of a new multilateralism and regionalism. The best investment in Africa's development beyond 2015 will be a focus on policies of integration, enhancing incentives, institutions, innovations and a strong infrastructure. Africa's leaders must prioritise inclusive development. These actions require persistent and purposeful governance reforms, paying special attention to political economy questions. The agenda of actions is long, necessitating selectivity and sequencing of activities. New Partnership for Africa's Development (NEPAD) (2009) developed a checklist that includes[5] the following:

- Mobilisation of local own resources by countries with effective and efficient utilisation of financial resources, thus reducing inefficiencies and duplication of efforts.
- Conducive investment climate for local private sector to invest in Africa with incentives, rewards and management systems that effectively utilise African potential, retain African brains, and attract capacity.

- Concerted effort and targeted planning for technical capacity development and human resource development.
- Special efforts to identify, harness and utilise existing capabilities, including underutilised potential, and closing the youth and gender gap at all levels.
- A system of sharing capacities at national, regional and continental levels, and learning from each other.
- Alignment of capacity development/qualification programmes, or new realities and African transformation needs, including strengthening the capacity of those tasked with developing the capacity of others. Any technical assistance should develop and strengthen existing capacity rather than substituting it.
- Organisational reform and collective action of capacity-building institutions to reach a scale that can provide the required specialist knowledge in training and teaching – focusing on performance-enhancing learning approaches as a basic way of operating by capacity development institutions
- Strong focus on managerial skills/soft skills that are essential in the context of the new African agenda to foster professionalism and integrity.
- Networks of communities of experts and practitioners to facilitate exposure, experience sharing, lesson learning and peer support to allow for integration and coordination through a systemic approach addressing 'system failure' and systemic blockages in making a real difference.
- Coordinated and integrated planning of ministries across sectoral boundaries as well as embedding a system of accountability for results/impacts driving integration in alignment with national and local initiatives.
- Continuous monitoring and assessment of performance and impact of development institutions vis-à-vis the 'system failure' and the stated achievements, with intensive feedback and communication between the vertical and horizontal levels.
- Commitment by actors who set up development organisations to follow through and ensure that they are working successfully, including better alignment and coordination of donor assistance that are integrated in national poverty alleviation programmes and development policies.
- Generating jobs and providing equitable access to economic opportunities and broader social inclusion.
- Managing conflict, ensuring security and stability within and across countries.

Outline of the book

The chapters presented in this book have been compiled according to a sense of the outstanding features of public policy conversations that we consider should take place on the continent post-2015. These consist of old and recurrent problems – for example, the legacy of leadership in African development; issues of agency and the political economy (especially the importance of social voice and social inclusion); enhancing governance of all types, including that of trans-boundary resources such as water and land, the primacy of resource mobilisation, programme execution and management; and the importance of striking strategic partnerships as well as good management of endowments such as the discovery of new resource wealth. There are also current issues that include dealing with the youth bulge and unemployment. What should be the nature of policy to make the best of existing resources such as land to create an environment for job-led growth? What is the role of the private sector in economic development in the post-2015 development debate? How does one enhance the potential of intra-Africa trade and cooperation? Can general service delivery be enhanced, and under what conditions? Then there are emerging issues such climate change and the re-emergence of old issues – the speed of disease spread and economic contagion as a consequence of globalisation. What does the rise of BRIC mean for post-2015 African development?

In Chapter One, James Wakiaga provides an overview of the development landscape and discourse. He argues that future development frameworks must be consultative and participate in programme delivery. A post-2015 development agenda must meet the minimum threshold of consensus to galvanise development efforts and guide global and national development priorities. The issue of financing the post-2015 development agenda remains a thorny issue. Chapter One notes that the role of the private sector in partnering for financing and the use of innovative approaches such as capital markets and other financing instruments is worth exploring (Evans, 2013). The Common African Position (CAP) on the issue of financing, for instance, focuses on improving DRM, maximising innovative financing, implementing existing commitments, and promoting quality and predictability of external financing and mutually beneficial partnerships, strengthening partnerships for trade, and establishing partnerships for managing global commons. Wakiaga concludes that the post-2015 development agenda stands at a critical juncture, and it is important to build a global convergence on policy choices and options now, not later.

In Chapter Two, George Kararach argues that a return to developmentalism is critical to allow Africa to grow with transformation, and be in a state to tackle emerging challenges and opportunities such as climate change, food insecurity and the youth bulge. Kararach argues for the need to focus on enablers of development such as infrastructure, regional integration, innovation, social inclusion and human security, and the building of effective institutions. These debates are happening on the back of renewed optimism as a result of a decade-long higher growth trend in Africa as well as Asia and Latin America, where many countries have joined the league of 'emerging' economies. This is also on the backdrop of an apparent return to slower global growth and renewed financial uncertainties in the Organisation for Economic Co-operation and Development (OECD) since 2008, and the eminent shift in the relative economic dynamism of the global North to the global South. Despite this achievement in growth, Africa continues to see the grossly unequal distribution of the benefits of this growth, with most countries having failed to deliver fully on their MDG commitments. The pressures for new alternatives – be they in governance, regionalism or broader economic management – are emerging in Africa, making the notion of a 'developmental' or effective state relevant.

The second decade of the 21st century may be that of Africa's renaissance. As Africa's economic agencies, the United Nations Economic Commission for Africa (UNECA), along with the African Development Bank (AfDB) and the African Union (AU), have come to advocate the adoption of policies leading towards developmental states, so the continent has articulated an African Mining Vision by contrast to other possible strategies for its natural resource governance from assorted global developmental, environmental, financial and industrial agencies. In Chapter Three, Timothy Shaw and Leah McMillan Polonenko begin to identify the background to this quite remarkable shift, and analyse the prospects for its advocacy and adoption by emerging non-state as well as state actors by the end of this decade, both on and off the continent. In so doing, they relate the emerging 'agency' versus 'dependency' debate as a correlate of the continent's recent unprecedented growth. This sets it apart from recent economic difficulties and setbacks in much of the established northern countries of the OECD, especially the Eurozone. In turn, this relates to and resonates with voices such as the UNDP human development report for 2013 that articulates the rise of the global South, including the economic growth of African countries including South Africa, Ghana, Rwanda and Mauritius. The chapter juxtaposes two dominant interrelated strands in the political economy of today's continent: the impact of BRIC, especially China, and episodes of boom and bust, this time with a focus on energy and minerals, but in future, on food, land and water. Shaw and Polonenko also point to a wide variety of novel alternative forms of finance from new donors and foundations, sovereign wealth funds (SWFs), faith-based organisations (FBOs) and global taxes for global public goods/partnerships. All these present Africa with the possibility of the emergence of development states.

Frannie Léautier, in Chapter Four, starts from the premise of the importance of gender and associated agency in development well after 2015. Most analyses of gender in development focus on the role of women or the differentiated impact of development on women. The recent attention of external aid programmes and the rising violence against women in a number of countries, coupled with evidence of disparity in development results when the role of men and women is differentiated, has further clarified the issue by focusing on women and girls. Furthermore, gender has come up as a central issue in the post-2015 identification of priorities following an assessment of the MDGs and efforts to define a new framework for channelling policy attention on a global level, such as through the Sustainable Development Goals (SDGs). Organisations like UN Women have been set up to tackle the obstacles that have an impact on gender equality, women's rights and women's empowerment by supporting the underlying transformation in target areas such as violence against women and girls, inclusion in the distribution of capabilities, services and assets, as well as equality in decision-making power in public and private institutions. This chapter investigates the potential or real negative effect of focusing solely on women, and identifies areas where a focus on men and in particular young men may be beneficial to achieving development results. Léautier argues for a differentiated role of gender in policy design and evaluation, and for gender-disaggregated data to appropriately assess the evidence of critical policies for development with commensurate/requisite reforms.

Indeed, since the early 1980s, African countries have embarked on various forms of 'modern' public sector reforms, with mixed results, and various reasons have been given for these. One of the criticisms is that reforms were undertaken without sufficient data or understanding of the realities on the ground – and thus resultant economic growth is questionable. Until recently there has been no robust, standardised set of indicators to measure the quality of services as experienced by citizens in Africa. Without consistent and accurate information on the quality of services, it is difficult for citizens or politicians (the principal) to assess how service providers (the agent) are performing, and to hold service providers to account. Although the quality of data relating to Africa's public administration has improved over the years by way of indicators (for example, The World Bank's Doing Business or the Country Policy and Institutional Assessment, CPIA), none, so far, has focused on capacity assessment and development. The annual African Capacity Building Foundation (ACBF) Africa capacity indicator reports attempt to change this. These reports, based on a sample of countries, provide both qualitative and quantitative data on several clusters of capacities for development.

In Chapter Five George Kararach discusses the broader context of the developmental state and public service delivery in Africa, debating the notion of capacity, and covering several issues that arise from the use of capacity indicators to understand the nature of the relationships between actors and the beneficiaries of services, namely, accountability, project design and evaluation for a post-2015 development agenda in Africa.

Chapter Six, by Bernadette Kamgnia and Victor Murinde, extends the debate by noticing that any developmental state must prioritise employment creation for the youth in Africa. It notes that the youth in Africa, as in any other country worldwide, have aspirations to become active citizens and to contribute to the development of the continent. Unfortunately, African youth are among the 75 million plus of 15- to 24-year-olds that the International Labour Organization (ILO) indicates are globally looking for a job, and would not be excluded from the 262 million young people that The World Bank surveys describe as economically inactive in emerging economies. As the ILO (2013) neatly puts it, young people face several challenges when entering the labour market, particularly in developing economies. Not only do they need to find a job, and preferably one that corresponds with their level of qualifications, but they also want to develop a foundation for a lasting, stable employment relationship that helps them progress in life. African youth are firmly entrenched in the group of the economically inactive. The main objective of this chapter is to analyse the role of the extractive industries in the creation of jobs for young people in Africa. The structure of youth unemployment is first presented, followed by an analysis of the human resources contradictions in the extractive industries. Strategies to unleash job opportunities in the extractive industries are then outlined, as well as an examination of the nature of industrial policies that can generate job-based growth and transformation for the continent.

But for development to happen, finance remains a critical ingredient. In Chapter Seven, Aniket Bhushan, Yiagadeesen Samy and Kemi Medu argue that domestic resource mobilisation (DRM) must be made a core aspect of financing the post-2015 development agenda in Africa. They note that the debate about what should replace the MDGs provides an opportunity to reflect once again on the Financing for Development (FFD) agenda. A coherent and realistic FFD agenda is thus critical to the success of both the post-2015 process as well as the achievement of new goals and targets. Much like the original MDGs were accompanied by the Monterrey Consensus on FFD, any post-2015 agenda should be accompanied by a new or updated FFD framework. This chapter addresses three main issues. First, the authors summarise ongoing debates about the post-2015 FFD agenda, and situate the implications of the same for African economies. Second, they analyse DRM performance in the region. In particular, they discuss results from their estimation of a *tax effort index* for African countries. Third, and finally, they discuss the implications of these findings, both for the international community (including donors actively engaged in supporting tax capacity building efforts) as well as African governments that are increasingly looking to DRM as a source of financing ambitious post-2015 goals and targets.

In Chapter Eight, Manmohan Agarwal and Natasha Pirzada discuss economic performance and social progress on the continent with a focus on Sub-Saharan Africa, highlighting the effect of least developed countries (LDCs) and fragile states in the region. They explore the extent to which the poor performance of the region is because of the presence of LDCs and failed states. They suggest that the level depends on domestic structures and policies, but the cyclical pattern depends on international forces. However, they find that the LDCs perform better than the non-LDCs, maybe due to a form of convergence, and the fragile states perform better than the non-fragile states. The predominance of LDCs and fragile states in Sub-Saharan Africa does not account for the poor performance of the region. The chapter also raises questions about the usefulness of the differentiation between fragile state and non-fragile state for economic policy-making. The similarity in trends in LDCs, non-LDCs, fragile and non-fragile states suggests that it is more likely that economic performance is strongly influenced by international factors. This conclusion is bolstered by the similarity in economic performance by countries in Latin America and Sub-Saharan Africa by their export orientation. The strong influence of international factors implied by their analysis suggests how important reforms of the major international organisations may be.

Regional integration, regional cooperation, regional coordination, regional harmonisation, regionalism, alternative/new regionalism, pan-Africanism, African unity and related frameworks all are processes, strategies and ideologies aimed at encompassing the current limits, dysfunctions and weaknesses of African states. Their number and diversity show that these attempts have encountered numerous difficulties. This list also underlines that two major levels have emerged that remain crucial today: the continental scale and the macro-regional scale, different not only in their size, but also in their aims and instruments. They also prove that it is problematic to bypass the national scale in Africa. Despite their gaps, African states remain as the central and key stakeholders in the political arena. This debate also revives an ancient implicit questioning about the best scales for development, and consequently, for capacity building. From the local to the regional, and through all intermediate levels, development has been conceived and practised at different levels by different actors during the course of the 20th century.

In Chapter Nine Cristina D'Allessandro investigates macro-regional and continental patterns in Africa, to underline what kind of processes are taking place around the continent, and to establish which of them would be suitable for the future, especially within the context of the post-MDGs agenda. She concludes that achieving the goals of sustainable development, transforming economies, reducing inequalities, improving service delivery, and natural resource management, reducing poverty and improving sensibly people's quality of life requires a global partnership, but also regional adaptations, especially in Africa.

In Africa, The World Bank and AfDB have been the two major players in the arena of multilateral aid. Both have been redefining aid conditionality to the continent since the early 1980s, and into the late 1990s. This has implied a move away from an emphasis on structural adjustment, where finance was provided in return for the promise of policy reforms, to disbursement of funds conditional on reforms already achieved. The new practice is known as *aid 'selectivity' or performance-based allocation* (PBA). The aid literature has been engaged with improving the effectiveness of aid and finding ways of refining the allocation and lending system of major donors such as The World Bank. Whenever aid flows are allocated selectively, donors set conditions or triggers for disbursement according to the achievement of prior policies and institutions. So funds are withheld from countries until they change their policies or institutions to set benchmarks. The World Bank and AfDB base their allocations on an assessment mechanism called the Country Policy and Institutional Assessment (CPIA). In Chapter Ten, George Kararach, Abbi Mamo Kedir, Frannie Léautier and Victor Murinde argue that the use of the CPIA by multilateral banks and other donors have had significant ramifications for Africa to the extent that there is a moral, economic and political imperative for countries to conduct a self-assessment in the event that aid continues to be allocated on the basis of the CPIA. As part of the post-2015 development agenda, therefore, African countries need to have a greater voice on aid allocation policy if they are to be at the 'table' as equal partners.

The MDGs were presented as a blueprint to galvanise governments and private actors towards a substantial reduction in extreme poverty levels by 2015. While the links between poverty and climate change are unsurprisingly complex, academic research and discourse finds itself approaching these two themes, not as interconnected subjects, but rather as variably distinct entities. Cohen et al (1998) argue that even though climate is one symptom of unsustainable development, the two concepts continue to coexist under separate epistemologies, to the extent that climate change has not readily been identified as strongly influencing sustainable development discourse. Indeed, development rarely features in the discussion of indicators for the measurement of climate change and environmental degradation, despite observations that its impacts fall disproportionately on developing countries and the poor. Yet it is increasingly rehearsed in the climate change research that in this interface of climate and development, climate policy goals continue to be missed as a priority for many developing countries, as other issues such as poverty alleviation and energy security remain centre stage on the development agenda. In addition, those most deeply affected by changes in global environmental trends seem less to be the beneficiaries of concentrated efforts towards positive progression but rather appear resigned to be left out in the cold. Targeting the root causes of development stagnation and regression, particularly embodied by climate change, the international community may achieve complementary positive results in both sectors. To do so will require issues of climate change being understood and filtered through the empirical lens of sustainable development priorities, which would support the clarification and simplification of related policy avenues.

In Chapter Eleven, Hany Besada, Fatima Deaton and Benjamin O'Bright follow several avenues of inquiry as a means of unifying research on development issues and related climate change, thereby presenting a critical base on which future study and international action can be undertaken as a post-2015 development agenda. First, using a variety of sources, they provide a six-fold criteria of observable impact areas of climate change on sustainable development. Second, each of the impacts is evaluated in detail, intrinsically demonstrating the potential casual links. Third, they broach parallel subjects and areas of institutional deficit and sustainability, detailing concerns of strategy derailment caused by a lack of stable, organisational foundations. While institutions themselves have the ability to support adaptation and mitigation processes, many of the impacts of climate change on development find their origins in the absence of robust institutional arrangements that will enable and sustain both adaptation and mitigation processes. Last, looking towards the future, several questions are answered in turn, as a means of enabling the coordination of policy and research responses to climate change and sustainable development: what can be done to mitigate observable effects in the immediate future? What policy targets and partnerships must be developed to achieve a reduction in environmental degradation? What are the appropriate avenues for education and awareness in regards to climate change that will promote an engaged public?

Indeed, environmental degradation and other pressures on economic resources will continue to fuel conflict. Karolina Werner starts her discussion in Chapter Twelve by expressing her amazement at the way conflict, peace and security were completely neglected in the discourse that heralded in the MDGs in 2000. She argues that, while drawing up the MDGs in the past was one of first presenting a general vision, then developing targets, and only towards the end addressing the means and tools to achieve them (Domínguez, 2013), the lessons might be to reverse the framework by identifying peace and security as critical 'tools' for development. States must be much more conscious of the practicalities of achieving the ambitious goals while leaving out critical gluing factors in any development agenda, especially knowing the scrutiny future achievements will undergo. Furthermore, one of the criticisms of the MDGs has been that no guidance was provided on how to achieve them, hence, while acknowledging the uniqueness of each case, the new agenda will also attempt to provide some general policy guidelines for accomplishing its targets (UN, 2012). It is therefore imperative that the priorities are both actionable and realistic. Within this general premise of goal selection, human security must feature prominently in any development agenda given the potential impacts of conflict on almost all the economic development aspirations that countries set themselves. Indeed, the failure by some of the countries to meet their MDG targets was partly driven by being marred in conflict and insecurity.

Of course there are dangers of over-simplification when discussing the development challenges and opportunities facing a continent as vast as Africa at a given point in time! Africa is made up of 54 disparate countries in five regions, and is not a single monolithic whole. The 2014 Ebola crisis in three countries in West Africa once again revealed the tendency of those outside the continent to classify it as a distinct entity. Despite the frequent allusion to a new 'scramble for Africa', the continent is planning, managing and starting to finance its own destiny, as it attempts to reclaim the 21st century. Chapter Thirteen forms the conclusion to the book, whereby George Kararach, Hany Besada and Timothy Shaw pull together the major threads of the discussion on post-2015 development and public policy, as Africa anticipates a future that is not just fraught with challenges, but also with opportunities. Africa's vision for the future as it looks beyond the MDGs has been endorsed by heads of states in the name of Agenda 2063, forming the core element for shaping development conversations for the next 50 years or so.

Conclusions

Since the 1990s, Africa has made notable progress in governance, as well as a return to positive growth rates. As noted by McKinsey & Company (2010), Africa's long-term growth will increasingly be driven by 'domestic' social and demographic changes. Key among these will be urbanisation, an expanding labour force and a rising African middle-class consumer. In 1980, about 28 per cent of Africans lived in cities, compared to 40 per cent in 2015. By 2030, this is projected to rise to 50 per cent, and Africa's top 18 cities will have a combined annual spending power of US$1.3 trillion (McKinsey & Company, 2010). Despite its recent success, many development challenges exist in Africa: there is still weak governance and lack of transparency, and the continent's health remains poor.

With increasing globalisation, there is a need to increase regional and national competitiveness, creating more jobs and opportunities for families, while reducing their vulnerability and improving their resilience. Africa needs to strengthen its strategic partnerships, build knowledge and leverage finance to implement effective development/ poverty-oriented programmes in the various countries. Governments' operational quality and results must be improved, along with more work across different strategic sectors, from agriculture to education and health and infrastructure, to enhance service delivery.

References

ACBF (African Capacity Building Foundation) (2013) *Africa capacity indicators 2013: Capacity development for natural resource management*, Harare: ACBF.

AfDB (African Development Bank) (2011) 'The middle of the pyramid: Dynamics of the middle class in Africa', Market brief, 20 April.

AfDB (2013) *Supporting the transformation of the private sector in Africa: Private sector development strategy –2013-2017*, Tunis: AfDB.

AfDB (2014a) *Africa economic outlook* (www.africaneconomicoutlook. org/fileadmin/uploads/aeo/2014/PDF/Pocket_Edition_AEO2014-EN_mail.pdf).

AfDB (2104b) *Ending conflict and building peace – A call for action*, Report of the High Level Panel on Fragile States, Tunis: AfDB.

Akukwe, C. (2013) 'Africa's challenges for 2013', Blog for Think Press Africa (http://thinkafricapress.com/development/africa-2013-development-challenges).

BBC Online (2012) 'China pledges $20bn in credit for Africa at summit', 19 July (www.bbc.com/news/world-asia-china-18897451).

Besada, H. and Ermakov, V. (2008) 'Cancer: Africa's silent killer', *Mail & Guardian*, 10 September (http://mg.co.za/article/2008-09-10-cancer-africas-silent-killer/).

Besada, H., Stevens, Y. and Olender, M. (2013) *Addressing the economic costs of sustainable energy in the global south*, Background Research Paper submitted to the High Level Panel on the Post-2015 Development Agenda.

CFR (Council on Foreign Relations) (2013) 'The global climate change regime', Issue Brief, 19 June (www.cfr.org/climate-change/global-climate-change-regime/p21831).

Cohen, S., Demeritt, D., Robinson, J. and Rothman, D. (1998) 'Climate change and sustainable development: towards dialogue', *Global Environment Change*, vol 8, no 4, pp 341-77.

Cooper, A.F., Kirton, J.J., Lisk, F. and Besada, H. (2013) *Africa's health challenges – Sovereignty, mobility of people and healthcare governance*, Farnham: Ashgate Publishing.

Coyne, C.J. and Ryan, M.E. (2009) 'With friends like these, who needs enemies? Aiding the world's worst dictators', *Independent Review*, vol 14, no 1, pp 26-44.

Domínguez, C. (2013) 'Including security in the post-2015 development goals. Germany could play an active role', *SWP Comments*, December.

Drummond, P. and Xue-Liu, E. (2013) *Africa's rising exposure to China: How large are spillovers through trade?*, IMF Working Paper WP/13/250 (www.imf.org/external/pubs/ft/wp/2013/wp13250.pdf).

Easterly, W. (2001) 'It's not factor accumulation: stylized facts and growth models', *The World Bank Economic Review*, vol 15, no 2, pp 177-219 (http://elibrary.worldbank.org/doi/pdf/10.1093/wber/15.2.177).

Easterly, W. (2007) 'Inequality does cause underdevelopment: insights from a new instrument', *Journal of Development Economics*, vol 84, no 2, pp 755-76.

Evans, A. (2013) *Delivering the post-2015 development agenda: Options for a new partnership*, Policy Brief, November. New York: Center on International Cooperation, New York University.

Glennie, J. (2011) *The role of aid to middle-income countries: A contribution to evolving EU development policy*, Working Paper 331, June, London: Overseas Development Institute (www.odi.org/sites/odi.org.uk/files/odi-assets/publications-opinion-files/7189.pdf).

Hanson, K., Kararach, G. and Shaw, T. (2012) *Rethinking development challenges for public policy: Insights from contemporary Africa*, Basingstoke: Palgrave Macmillan.

ILO (International Labour Organization) (2013) Global employment trends for youth 2013: A generation at risk, Geneva: ILO.

IMF (International Monetary Fund) (2013) *Regional economic outlook – Africa*, Washington DC: IMF.

Kararach, G. (2014) *Development Policy in Africa: Mastering the future?*, Basingstoke: Palgrave Macmillan.

Leeson, P.T. (2008) 'Escaping poverty: foreign aid, private property, and economic development', *The Journal of Private Enterprise*, vol 23, no 2 (www.peterleeson.com/Escaping_Poverty.pdf).

MacDonald, A.M., Bonsor, H.C., Calow, R.C., Taylor, R.G., Lapworth, D.J., Maurice, L., Tucker, J. and O'Dochartaigh, B.E. (2011) *Groundwater resilience to climate change in Africa*, British Geological Survey (http://nora.nerc.ac.uk/15772/1/OR11031.pdf).

McKinsey & Company (2010) 'What's driving Africa's growth' (www.mckinsey.com/insights/economic_studies/whats_driving_africas_growth).

McMichael, A.J. and Butler, C.D. (2004) 'Climate change, health, and Development Goals', *The Lancet*, vol 364, pp 2004-06.

Moyo, D. (2010) *Dead aid: Why aid is not working and how there is another way for Africa*, New York: Farrar, Straus & Giroux.

Mullin, K. (2010) 'African agricultural finance under the spotlight' (http://blogs.reuters.com/world-wrap/2010/08/24/african-agricultural-finance-under-the-spotlight/).

Ncube, M. (2012) 'The expansion of Chinese influence in Africa –
Opportunities and risks', African Development Bank blog, 14 August
(www.afdb.org/en/blogs/afdb-championing-inclusive-growth-
across-africa/post/the-expansion-of-chinese-influence-in-africa-
opportunities-and-risks-9612/).

NEPAD (New Partnership for Africa's Development) (2009) *The
AU/NEPAD Capacity Development Strategic Framework (CDSF)*,
NEPAD Secretariat (www.oecd.org/development/governance-
development/43508787.pdf).

Prokopijevic, M. (2006) *Why foreign aid fails*, International Centre for
Economic Research, Working Paper No 19/2006.

Reuters (2013) 'Wealthy Gulf investors warm to Africa', 2 January
(www.reuters.com/article/2013/01/02/us-gulf-africa-investment-
idUSBRE9010B520130102).

Rotberg, R.I (2014) 'Chinese trade with Africa hits record high',
China-US Focus, 15 March, (www.chinausfocus.com/finance-
economy/chinese-trade-with-africa-hits-record-high/).

Slaughter, A. (2004) *A new world order*, Princeton, NJ: Princeton
University Press.

UN (United Nations) (2012): *Realizing the future we want for all: Report
to the Secretary-General*, New York: UN.

UN (2013) *Shared responsibility and joint accountability: Advancing the post-
2015 development agenda*, High-Level Panel of Eminent Persons on the
Post-2015 Development Agenda 2013 (http://tinyurl.com/p8xrhhj).

UNCTAD (United Nations Conference on Trade and Development)
(2012) *Innovation, technology and South-South collaboration*, Technology
and Innovation Report, Geneva: UNCTAD.

UNCTAD (2013) *World investment report 2013*, Geneva: UNCTAD
(http://unctad.org/en/publicationslibrary/wir2013_en.pdf).

UNECA (United Nations Economic Commission for Africa) (2012)
Africa economic outlook report, Addis Ababa: UNECA.

WHO (World Health Organization) (2011) *Survey of the quality of
selected antimalarial medicines circulating in six countries of sub-Saharan
Africa*, Geneva: WHO (www.who.int/medicines/publications/
WHO_QAMSA_report.pdf).

World Bank, The (2010) *Africa's infrastructure: A time for transformation*,
Washington DC: The World Bank.

WTO (World Trade Organization) (2010) *World trade in 2010*
(wwwwto.org/english/res_e/booksp_e/anrep_e/wtr11-1_e.pdf).

WTO (2011) *World trade report 2011* (www.wto.org/english/res_e/
booksp_e/anrep_e/wtr11-1_e.pdf).

ONE

The post-2015 development agenda: Building a global convergence on policy options

James Wakiaga

Introduction

The international community has been engaged in a post-Millennium Development Goals (MDGs) policy conversation to forge a successor framework that is universally acceptable. The post-2015 development agenda must meet the minimum threshold of the current MDG framework, which successfully helped galvanise development efforts and guide global and national development priorities (ECOSOC, 2011). Multiple stakeholders, ranging from multilateral organisations, civil society and academic institutions, have been debating the form and substance of the post-2015 development agenda (Vandemoortele, 2012). In addition, different forums have been held and publications churned out prescribing the process and substance of the emerging framework. The task of formulating the post-2015 development agenda will not be easy, as it will need to be balanced by a plethora of other global development initiatives that have taken place over the past few years. The Rio+20[1] outcome document, for example, provides good insights for any emerging framework, as does the Busan Global Partnership for Effective Development Cooperation.[2]

The emerging framework must also contend with the dynamics of a fast changing world. The unprecedented shift in global power with the rise of the South, the technological revolution of the last decade, and new challenges caused by climate change all require new thinking and a new approach to human development. This entails a reorientation in development approach through a South-South model as well as a focus on people-centred development. According to Collier (2007), the MDGs have been a major force in addressing the poverty agenda, but the world has changed radically since 2000, when they were first conceived of. The emerging countries of the South, for example, China, India and Brazil, would be expected to play a greater role in shaping the emerging framework based on their own success stories that could be replicated in other developing countries. The IT revolution that marks the advent of innovative tools, such as M-PESA[3] in Kenya, that is promoting financial inclusion, offers an opportunity to leapfrog development. This requires thinking outside the box and moving away from the traditional approaches of addressing development challenges.

Unfortunately, the urgency for a successor framework to the MDGs does not afford the global leadership a luxury of time. The multiple initiatives that have been proposed to drive the post-2015 development agenda are a good indicator to this reality. This includes the United Nations System Task Team (UNTT) established by Secretary-General Ban Ki-moon to support UN system-wide preparations for the post-2015 development agenda; a High Level Panel appointed by the UN Secretary-General to advise him on the post-2015 development agenda; regional and national consultations on the post-2015 development agenda; global thematic consultations; and an intergovernmental Open Working Group to design Sustainable Development Goals (SDGs) as a successor to the MDGs, among other initiatives.

Given the plethora of initiatives, the process of building a global convergence on the emerging post-2015 development agenda shall require the UN to exercise its mandate and play a more assertive role (Vandemoortele, 2012). In this regard, the 2010 High Level Panel Meeting of the General Assembly on the MDGs requested the Secretary-General to initiate discussions on a post-2015 development agenda and to include recommendations in his annual report on efforts to accelerate MDG progress. Furthermore, the appointment of a High Level Panel of Eminent Persons in July 2012 represented a bold step on the part of Mr Ban Ki-moon to provide leadership. The Panel,[4] chaired by the Presidents of Indonesia and Liberia and the Prime Minister of the UK, was tasked to provide guidance and recommendations on the post-2015 development agenda, and has since published its report, discussed later in this chapter.

The emerging framework must demonstrate intrinsic universal appeal and relevance, and be formulated in a way that the goals, targets and indicators resonate with the universal aspirations of human development. They must meet the minimum threshold of the MDGs that are considered simple, measurable and easy to be remembered and understood by the public. According to Vandemoortele (2012), the post-2015 targets must satisfy the conditions of clarity of concept, solidity of indicator and robustness of data. In advancing this argument, Vandemoortele offers three options: (i) retain the current MDGs with minor adjustments; (ii) redefine the architecture; or (iii) develop a completely new framework.

This chapter also takes a look at the African responses to the post-2015 development agenda as articulated in the Common African Position (CAP) on the post-2015 development agenda. The CAP is a consensus document articulating the substantive issues of importance to Africa, and key priorities, concerns and strategies to be considered in the outcomes of the post-2015 negotiation process.

Why a global convergence on policy options?

The changing global dynamics since the adoption of the MDG framework in 2000 calls for a paradigm shift and rethinking in approach. Three issues stand out that could influence the formulation of the new development framework: rising inequality with the potential cost to social and political stability; the impact of climate change and environmental stability; and the rising demand for effective delivery of public goods by the global citizenry.

Rising inequality is a major development challenge that must be addressed in the next dispensation. This is because high inequality hinders economic progress and threatens social cohesion. It has been observed that income inequality in developing countries increased by 11 per cent between 1990 and 2010 (UN, 2013a,b). In addition, the rise in inequality has distorted budgets and political processes, and citizens have become hostage to elite interest (UN, 2013b). Few countries have made significant progress in tackling poverty among the bottom 5 per cent of the poorest segment of our society. Broad globalisation processes as well as domestic policy choices in individual countries have largely driven the inequality. For example, unregulated financial integration and trade liberalisation processes have resulted in unequal distribution of benefits across and within countries. The domestic policy choices such as the scaling down of public investment in critical social sectors like health, education and social protection as part of austerity measures could exacerbate inequality in countries (UN, 2013b). Consequently, thoughts on the post-2015 framework should ensure that the most disadvantaged and vulnerable groups are at the centre of the goals and targets to be formulated. The post-2015 consultations forcefully echo the need to deal with inequality, and this continues to be forcefully voiced by civil society. Stiglitz (2013), for example, posits that in situations or contexts where one interest group holds too much power, it succeeds in getting policies that benefit itself rather than attending to the interest of the whole society.

The second issue that necessitates the need for a global policy convergence on policy options centres on the urgency to deal with the threat of climate change and environmental sustainability. The mismanagement of the environment has severe consequences on livelihoods and the very existence of the planet. The Rio+20 (2012) outcome document acknowledged that 'poverty eradication, changing and promoting sustainable patterns of consumption and production, and protecting and managing the natural resource base of economic and social development are the overarching objectives of and essential requirements for sustainable development' (Rio+20, 2012, p 1). Developing countries, in particular, 'are vulnerable to the adverse impacts of climate change and are already experiencing increased impacts including persistent drought and extreme weather events, sea level rise, coastal erosion and ocean acidification, further threatening food security and efforts to eradicate poverty and achieve sustainable development' (Rio+20, 2012, p 33). For instance, the prolonged droughts in the Horn of Africa have had a tremendous impact on agricultural production and food security. In fact, droughts and the drying of river basins in Southern and Eastern Africa may have induced human migration in search of alternative livelihoods (Lisk, 2009). To protect livelihoods and to ensure food security will therefore require a mix of mitigation and adaptation strategies with a view to limit the overall impact of climate change (FAO, 2012).

Ethiopia provides a good case study of this policy mix through its climate-resilient green growth strategy. The country has been experiencing warming with mean annual temperatures estimated to have increased by 1.3°C between 1960 and 2006, an average rate of 0.28°C per decade. This has brought greater inter-seasonal rainfall variability that has negative effects on the nation's land-based productive sectors and existing urban infrastructure. Hence the nexus between sustainable development and its three dimensions of economic, social and environmental impacts underpinned the call for the development of SDGs in Rio. These are the subject of discussion in the UN Open Working Group, as analysed in later sections of this chapter.

Third, the mass protests experienced during the Arab Spring in 2010 has brought into sharp focus the imperative of addressing the global citizenry demand for accountability and the delivery of public services. Citizens are increasingly putting governments under pressure to be accountable for their actions and to efficiently and effectively deliver on public services. The demand for citizen engagement and public participation in the post-2015 agenda setting has taken centre stage, and this will continue to shape future dialogue on development discourse (UNDESA, 2012, p 1). The call for transparency and accountability to be placed at the centre of development discourse is gaining momentum under the post-2015 development agenda. Some voices have called for efforts to ensure that governance issues are centre stage in the formulation of a global agenda on development through a dedicated stand-alone goal, clearly measurable governance indicators, or at the very least, unequivocal language and references to governance principles such as human rights, political freedoms or democracy (UN, 2013b; Wild and Bergh, 2013). This trend is further manifested by the rise of several global initiatives to promote transparency and accountability including, inter alia, the International Aid Transparency Initiative (IATI), Extractive Industries Transparency Initiative (EITI) and Transparency International (TI).

Fourth is the imperative to build convergence between the North and South divide on the 'common but differentiated roles' towards financing the post-2015 development agenda, as well as the role of South-South cooperation (SSC). The contribution of the South to the aid effectiveness agenda is seen from the prism of the traditional donor frameworks, and the success stories of SSC are not well documented. To narrow this divide it is imperative to consider developing a monitoring and accountability framework that will comprehensively take stock of the contribution of SSC (Besharati, 2013). The SSC will be particularly relevant in the post-2015 development agenda, but should not be viewed as a substitute but rather as complementary to North-South cooperation. Both the High Level Panel on the post-2015 development agenda and the Nairobi outcome document[5] on SSC have outlined ways to strengthen SSC as well as the principles to guide the development cooperation.

Why have the Millennium Development Goals been so important?

In setting an agenda for the post-2015 scenario, it is imperative to understand why the MDGs have been considered important in the development discourse. They have been regarded as essential in building global partnership to address poverty and human progress, and provide concrete numerical benchmarks for tackling extreme poverty in all its dimensions (Hussen, 2013). The MDGs have been credited with providing a framework on which the international community could rally around a common end.

It is important, however, to point out the divergent views held by scholars regarding the MDGs. Howard Friedman (2013), for instance, in a persuasive article, questions whether the MDGs accelerated progress in the reduction of poverty in Sub-Saharan Africa. On the contrary, Jeffrey Sachs (2012) argues that prior to 2000, Sub-Saharan Africa's economic development stalled, coupled with a significant burden of diseases such as malaria and HIV and AIDS taking a toll. In fact, Sachs posits that for developing countries as a whole, economic development was much faster after the adoption of MDGs in 2000, with overall improvement in wellbeing, as illustrated in Table 1.1 below.

Table 1.1 shows that during the period 1990-99, the proportion of the population in Africa living on less than US$1.25 a day kept on rising. However, the rate declined to 1.6 per cent per annum during the period 1999-2010. The under-5 mortality rate also showed a significant decline from 2000 to 2010 (at 3.1 per cent per annum), compared to 1990-2000 (at 1.4 per cent per annum during 1990-2000). In the case of malaria, a dramatic rise of incidences was experienced between 1990 and 2000, and this was a result of declining efficacy of the first and second-line medicines before declining by an estimated rate of 2.1 per cent per annum by 2010.

Some sceptics maintained that the goals are irrelevant and are bound to fail while questioning the top-down nature of goal-setting with a bias towards donor interests and expert views (Khoo, 2005). This sentiment could be true to the extent that the formulation of MDGs was top-down and therefore the views of experts and development partners took precedence. It is within this context that the proponents

Table 1.1: Key indicators reflecting accelerated poverty reduction in Sub-Saharan Africa

	1990	2000	2010	% annual rate of improvement 1990–2000	% annual rate of improvement 2000–10
Poverty rate (proportion of population living on less than $1.25 a day)	56.5	58.0	48.4	−0.3	1.6
Under-5 mortality rate	178	154	109 (2011)	1.4	3.1
Malaria deaths total (000s)	832	1401	1134	−5.3	2.1
Maternal mortality rate	850	740	500	1.4	3.8
Real GDP (1990 = 100)	100	126	219	2.3	5.7

Source: Sachs (2012)

of the post-2015 MDG framework have called for a broader and consultative process.

It is true that the MDGs, however important, have had a fair share of both sceptics and optimists leading to several schools of thought (ACIA, 2011; Bandara, 2012). The optimists, led by influential human development thinkers such as Sachs, Pronk and Vandemoortele, look at the MDGs as ambitious enough to galvanise global support (see Bandara, 2012). The sceptics, such as Clemens and Easterly, regard the MDGs as important in building global awareness but elusive in dealing with the 'how' of achieving these goals. Then we have the radical school of thought comprising the likes of Jolly and Angus who are concerned over the lack of voice for the poor countries in the whole conundrum of the MDG framework. In fact, some have gone further to argue that the preoccupation with targets would lead to the neglect of broader qualitative concerns (Jolly, 2005).

According to the 2012 MDG report (UN, 2012a), however, the framework has been credited for increasing funding through the improved and increased targeting and flow of aid and other investments in development. It is estimated that between 2000 and 2005, total aid to developing countries doubled, from US$60 billion to US$120 billion (Moss, 2010). This was particularly more pronounced in the area of healthcare where assistance more than doubled from US$6.8 billion to US$16.7 billion (Moss, 2010). The MDGs have also been credited for bringing a greater focus on results, which has enabled countries to track and monitor progress based on measurable outcomes. Countries have therefore been able to better reflect their development priorities in national development plans. We have increasingly seen countries linking their medium-term development ambitions to the MDG framework, as in the case of Ethiopia's 2010-15 Growth and Transformation Plan and Zimbabwe's 2011-15 Medium-term Plan. Ethiopia, for instance, is credited with having fully mainstreamed the MDGs to its national development strategy as an overarching development objective. The same applies to several other African countries such as Tanzania that have benchmarked the national development strategies with the attainment of the MDGs in mind and particularly in the context of the Poverty Reduction Strategy Papers (PRSPs) that had become a pre-requisite for World Bank International Development Association (IDA) loans.

The post-2015 development agenda must be viewed within the prism of the performance of the current MDG framework. Despite the criticism of the MDGs framework in its current shape and form, the framework has provided an important basis for tracking development among poor nations. Both the 2012 and 2014 MDG reports (UN, 2012a, 2014) provide candid assessment of the progress in Africa, and highlight some of the impediments that have constrained progress, especially the vulnerabilities to economic and climate shocks.

The 2014 MDG report acknowledges that significant progress has been achieved across all goals, and some of the targets have been met before the 2015 deadline. The most notable has been the dramatic reduction in extreme poverty, where the number of people living in extreme poverty has been reduced by 700 million or 22 per cent by 2010 (UN, 2014). The proportion of people living on less than US$1.25 a day, in Southern, East, Central and West Africa, decreased as a group from 56.5 per cent in 1990 to 48.5 per cent in 2010 (UN, 2014). We have also witnessed the continued increase in the political participation of women across all the four regions of Sub-Saharan Africa and countries, albeit at different levels. There has also been a substantial expansion of malaria interventions, with about 90 per cent or 3 million of averted deaths being children under the age of five living in Sub-Saharan Africa. Between 1990 and 2012, over 2.3 billion people have gained access to an improved source of drinking water, while we have also witnessed a narrowing of gender disparities in school enrolment at all levels of education. Further, the 2014 MDG report (UNDP, 2014) indicates that Sub-Saharan Africa had the highest maternal mortality ratio of developing regions, with 510 deaths per 100,000 live births, compared to the global average of 210 deaths per 100,000 live births. Overall, however, both the 2012 (UN, 2012a) and 2014 Africa MDG reports credit the continent for the progress achieved so far (UNDP, 2014) and Table 1.2 opposite summarises the status.

Based on the information in Table 1.2, it is clear that the framework provided a good measure for tracking progress on MDGs. In addition, regional, national and global MDG reports have provided a good barometer on how well countries are doing. In Africa, however, progress remains uneven, and achievement of MDGs may not be as close, partly due to the unfavourable conditions at the starting point in comparison to other regions (UNDP, 2014). Nevertheless the MDGs have further been credited for showing a greater focus on results. And on this score it can be argued that the framework enabled countries to effectively track and monitor progress based on measurable outcomes. By so doing countries have been able to better reflect their development priorities in their national development plans.

Table 1.2: Summary of the status of millennium development goals in Africa

Goals and targets	Status	Remarks
Goal 1: Eradicate extreme poverty and hunger	Off track	US$1.25 a day poverty in Africa (excluding North Africa) declined from 56.5 to 47.5% during 1990–2008
Goal 2: Achieve universal primary education	On track: net enrolment	On track to meet the primary school enrolment target
		Twenty-five countries have achieved net enrolment ratios of 80% or above, and only 11 have enrolment rates below 75% (UNDP, 2014)
Goal 3: Promote gender equality and empower women	On track	Good progress at primary level but weak parity at secondary and tertiary levels
		High representation in parliament
Goal 4: Reduce child mortality	Off track	Declining, but slowly
Goal 5: Improve maternal health	Off track	MMR reduced from 870 deaths per 100,000 live births in 1990 to 460 in 2013, a 47% reduction between 1990 and 2013 and 2.7% average annual percentage change between 1990 and 2013.
		Despite these achievements, meeting MDG 5 remains unlikely (2014 Africa MDG report (UN, 2014))
Goal 6: Combat HIV/AIDS, malaria and tuberculosis	Off track	HIV/AIDS on the decline especially in Southern Africa, due to behavioural change and use of anti-retroviral therapy
Goal 7: Ensure environmental sustainability	On track: improved water supply	Few countries have reforestation plans
		Emissions minimal for most countries with little increase
		Most countries reduced consumption of ozone-depleting substances by more than 50%
Goal 8: Promote global partnership	Off track	Official development assistance (ODA) from the Development Assistance Committee to Africa declined by 5% between 2011 and 2012 (MDG report 2014 (UN, 2014))

Source: MDR Reports (UN 2012a, 2014)

Post-2015 development debate

The discourse on the post-2015 development agenda has now taken centre stage in the global policy dialogue. The lessons and reflections on the current framework provide a good basis on which to develop the successor global development framework. Vandemoortele (2012, p 6) argues in his paper that 'the architecture of the new agenda will be shaped, in large part, by the process by which it will be formulated.' This lends credence to the approach taken by the UN. In July 2012, the UN Secretary-General appointed a High Level Panel to make recommendations on the development agenda beyond 2015. The High Level Panel used a broad consultative process to develop a report that was later presented to the Secretary-General in May 2013. The formulation of the report benefited from substantive inputs received from national and regional consultations, global thematic consultations as well as consultations held by civil society groups and business associations under the guidance of the UN global compact (UN, 2013a).

The High level Panel report presented a set of recommendations to guide the post-2015 development agenda, and is credited for its wider consultative process in which the UN system supported national consultations in 88 countries, 31 of which are in Africa (UN, 2013a). In addition, there are 11 global thematic consultations, five of which were supported and hosted by an African country. The report galvanised voices in government, the private sector, civil society, women and young people to contribute to the post-2015 development agenda. It is important to look at the reflections emanating from the report, and how these are likely to dominate the discussion on the post-2015 framework. In this regard, the panelists concluded that the post-2015 agenda is a universal agenda that must be driven by five big transformative shifts, as follows (UN, 2013a):

- *Leave no one behind:* this entails keeping the original promise of the MDGs, and now finishing the job. It means moving from reducing to ending extreme poverty, in all its forms, after 2015.
- *Put sustainable development at the core:* this entails advancing the long aspired-to goals of the international community of integrating the social, economic and environmental dimension of sustainability, including green growth, which no county has yet achieved.
- *Transform economies for jobs and inclusive growth:* this calls for structural transformation of economies to create decent jobs and improve livelihoods. It entails a 'shift to sustainable patterns of consumption and production', which could be made possible through adoption

of modern technology, innovation and harnessing of knowledge. It means an expanded role for the private sector to create value and drive inclusive growth.

- *Build peace and effective open and accountable institutions for all:* this calls for a fundamental shift 'to recognise peace and good governance as core elements of wellbeing.' It involves the creation of responsive and legitimate institutions that 'should encourage the rule of law, property rights, freedom of speech and the media, open political choice, access to justice, and accountable government and public institutions.'
- *Forge a new global partnership:* the post-2015 agenda must underpin a transformative shift embedded within the spirit and context of the Paris Declaration, Accra Agenda for Action and Busan commitments, anchored on partnership, mutual accountability and reciprocity, shared humanity and common interests in a fast globalising world.

The High Level Panel report, however, represents only one of the several reports and processes that are ongoing globally. As mentioned earlier, one of the main outcomes of the Rio+20 Conference was the consensus by member states to develop a set of SDGs. These were to build on MDGs and converge with the post-2015 development agenda. As a result, the Open Working Group was established in January 2013 with representation across the global divide. It was supposed to be an inclusive and transparent intergovernmental process, with the responsibility for developing SDGs to be agreed on by the General Assembly. To date, it has conducted eight sessions on various themes identified in Rio+20. Its discussions have also benefited from inputs derived from member states and other stakeholders, especially around poverty eradication and environmental sustainability. Hence, as the Open Working Group embarked on the process of identifying the SDGs, the question remained to what extent these would be synergised with the identified drivers of transformative shifts in the Secretary-General's High Level Panel report (UN, 2013a).

The other notable UN initiative is the establishment of the UN Task Team on the post-2015 development agenda in January 2012. This brings together more than 60 UN agencies and international organisations. It has already published its report, *Realizing the future we want for all* (UN, 2012b), outlining the vision of the UN system in the global development agenda beyond 2015. Its work has centred on global partnership for development, but also supporting the work of the Open Working Group.

The multiple works done under the aegis of the UN is further augmented by regional consultations being spearheaded by the regional economic communities (RECs), and what is certainly emerging is that different regions will come up with different set of priorities depending on the context. For instance, the African consultations being led by the Economic Commission for Africa (ECA), the African Development Bank (AfDB) and the UN Development Programme's (UNDP) Regional Bureau for Africa has focused the agenda on structural economic transformation and inclusive growth; technological transfer, research and development; human development, encompassing health, education, social protection, disaster and risk reduction; gender and women empowerment; access to shelter and water; and financing and partnership.

What does this say about the multiple voices and conversations around the post-2015 development agenda? The stakes are high, and efforts at the global level must be coordinated in order to ensure coherence across the different work streams. While the UN is better placed because of its global mandate, and has put in motion a UN coordination secretariat, linkages with other entities in the private sector and civil society organisations are not clear. This may require organising joint sessions with both the private sector and civil society to take stock of their input. However, the UN system remains the most credible and viable mechanism for bringing coherence to all the ongoing streams of work on the post-2015 global development framework.

The voice of civil society is particularly critical in this process, and global civil societies under the umbrella of Beyond 2015 continue to play this role (see www.beyond2015.org/). This umbrella organisation, comprising membership spread over 100 countries, has strongly voiced support of a framework that is anchored on human rights, poverty eradication, social justice, environmental sustainability and security for all. It is also imperative that the developed countries within the context of the Organisation for Economic Co-operation and Development (OECD) are fully engaged in the consultations, and this seems to be happening. But this does not preclude the fact that so far the countries in the South, where human rights issues, social justice and poverty still prevail, have dominated the consultations process.

Financing for development remains a critical subject for the post-2015 development agenda. The commitments under the Monterrey Consensus and the pledges made by the G8 countries at the Gleneagles Summit are yet to be met. The Make Poverty History summit held at Gleneagles in 2005 pledged to increase aid to Africa by US$25 million per year by 2010. While international aid levels today are higher than they were prior to the 2005 G8 Summit, the Gleneagles commitments are yet to be met. In fact, when the MDGs were adopted, the ODA was already falling, and OECD countries are under increasing pressure to meet the 0.7 per cent ODA-to-GNI (gross national income) target and the 2008 G8 Gleneagles due to the recent financial crisis (Jessee, 2007; The World Bank, 2013). Hollander (2014, p 4) thus posits that 'the overall emphasis on the need for consensus and pragmatism masks the inevitable clash between North and South on the scope of the SDGs as well as post-2015 development agenda.' In essence, he argues of a likelihood of an imminent clash between North and South on a wide array of issues, particularly governance and the right to development principles. For OECD countries, this implies integrating 'goals and targets on good governance, the rule of law, peace, and security' (Hollander, 2014, p 3). The lack of good governance, peace and security is seen as a *raison d'être* of under-development, and must be incorporated into the post-2015 development agenda.

The debate on the post-2015 development agenda in the North centres on the responsibilities for financing the emerging framework. The declining ODA flows, coupled with the global crisis and the increasing importance of emerging donors such as the six-nation Gulf Cooperation Council (Saudi Arabia, United Arab Emirates, Kuwait, Qatar, Oman and Bahrain), BRIC and MINT,[6] will shape the way future goals will be financed. The OECD countries call for shared responsibility, emphasising alternative options and sources of financing to be drawn from private investment, trade and remittances in addition to scaling up the contribution of emerging countries in what has been referred to as the 'new geography of growth' (OECD, 2013). On the other hand, the G77 countries have argued that the new framework should not put an additional burden on developing countries in the form of finances (Hollander, 2014). As expected, the third conference on Financing for Development (FFD), held in July 2015 in Addis Ababa, looked into the financing of the post-2015 development agenda.

The OECD reflections on the post-2015 development agenda are best captured in their policy document entitled *Beyond the Millennium Development Goals: Towards an OECD contribution to the post-2015 agenda* (OECD, 2013) and the OECD Strategy on Development, which outlines 11 elements to guide the crafting of the new framework. In their words, the new framework must be 'global, holistic, measurable and meaningful' (OECD, 2013, p 4). At the global level, the OECD countries would like to see 'a small number of high profile goals and targets' (OECD, 2013, p 1). At the national level, goals, targets and indicators should be defined and tailored to each country's context, capability and priorities. The OECD (2013) position premises on what they refer to as the 'new geography of growth' that looks at the shift in the global economic influence away from OECD countries to the emerging countries. But at the same time, it also recognises a 'new geography of poverty', of which, by 2025, most absolute poverty will be concentrated once again in low-income countries.

For the OECD, the thrust of the debate is that governments and all the stakeholders, including civil society and the private sector, will have to decide whether the new framework will build on existing goals, agree on new ones such as the proposed SDGs, or start from ground zero. In their wisdom, the new framework must be devoid of the North-South divide, and instead focus on a global perspective, be holistic and measurable. The goals should be truly global with shared, but not equal, responsibilities for all countries. They should be holistic by encompassing the poverty and human development agenda of the current MDGs as well as the SDGs. And last, they should be measurable and based on available data and statistics (OECD, 2013).

In summary, the OECD position must be factored into the emerging development framework. These are four 'outcome' elements, including principles underlying future goals, and seven 'tool' elements for achieving existing goals and developing future goals. In a nutshell, the outcome elements shall constitute the imperative of keeping poverty at the centre of development; coming up with a measure on the universality of education success; prioritising gender equality and women empowerment; as well as integrating issues of sustainability in the mainstream of a development agenda (OECD, 2013). The seven 'development enabler' tools are strengthening national statistical systems; building effective institutions and accountability mechanisms; developing and promoting peace and state-building goals; ensuring policy coherence for development; sharing knowledge and engaging in policy dialogue and mutual learning; promoting the global partnership for effective development cooperation; and measuring and monitoring development finance (OECD, 2013).

Africa's position and the post-2015 debate

It is appreciated that Africa bears the brunt of deprivation and under-development. Progress on MDGs has been sluggish, and as of 2010, about 48.5 per cent of the people in Africa are still living on less than US$1.25 a dollar a day (UNDP, 2014). Hence, the continent is an important stakeholder in the outcome of the post-MDG framework. Despite progress achieved in reducing by half the number of poor people in the world ahead of the 2015 timeframe, a significant number still reside in Africa (UNDP, 2014). Sub-Saharan Africa is unlikely to meet the target of eradicating poverty by half by the 2015 deadline – one of the daunting challenges in achieving sustainable development. This has galvanised the African leadership under the auspices of the African Union (AU) to think of new approaches and paradigms for addressing development challenges. The CAP and Agenda 2063 are good examples of recent African initiatives that resonate with the post-2015 development agenda.

The CAP on the post-2015 development agenda was formally endorsed by the Assembly of the heads of state and government of the AU in Addis Ababa, Ethiopia, on 31 January 2014 (AU, 2014). The position builds on all major global efforts and initiatives that have taken place and are being undertaken to draft the agenda, including the role of the UN and the AUC (African Union Commission). The CAP, as a process, was primarily driven by the AU with a view to forge consensus on Africa's key priorities, issues and strategies to be reflected in the post-2015 development agenda. It has consequently encompassed not only the views of the African governments, but also those from the private sector, civil society organisations, youth associations, women groups, trade unions and academia, African multilateral institutions, and selected pertinent UN organisations and agencies (AU, 2014, p 9).

CAP was inspired by the need to stimulate the international commitment for a universal development agenda with due focus on eradication of poverty and exclusion and the pursuit of sustainable and inclusive development, and the political will to back it up (AU, 2014). More importantly, the gap observed in the implementation and outcomes of the MDGs, as manifested by uneven progress in targets and current issues of inequality and inclusivity of economic growth, play a critical role in the drafting of the CAP. It also emanated from the need to assume ownership of the process and to reaffirm common interests as a continent. Hence, it seeks 'to enhance member states' ownership of development; generate the required political will to address the unfinished business of the MDGs; and respond to the emerging issues and gaps in implementation' (AU, 2014, p 10). This is particularly important with regard to data collection and monitoring, missing in the current MDG framework.

The imperative of a rigorous accountability framework for the post-2015 development agenda is the *noblesse oblige* for strengthening statistical capacity in the continent. The UNDP has taken the lead in fostering a common understanding of the concept of a 'data revolution' and the potential roles that governments, development partners and other relevant stakeholders could play and contribute to the development data. The objective in the medium to long term is to galvanise a global partnership for development data and accountability for the post-2015 development agenda. It must be noted, however, that designing an accountability framework for the agenda will be data intensive. Based on the experiences of the MDGs, this remains an important challenge in Africa, and calls for more and better data that is disaggregated, produced more frequently and is more open and more useable. It also requires modernising the national statistical systems in Africa, launching country compacts for better data, and coordinating and harmonising national survey instruments to allow for comparability across countries. The objective of leaving no one behind may be elusive if we are unable to map key indicators and services at relevant political levels.

The Africa regional consultations on developing an accountability framework for the post-2015 development agenda underscored that the process of developing a robust accountability framework could benefit from the UN's collective and proven track record and experience in the field. This could build on the 30 funds, programmes and agencies that constitute the UN Development Group that have been engaged for 15 years in supporting countries to build capacity, expertise and knowledge for the implementation of the MDGs. Their key role in helping member states document their achievements and challenges around the implementation of the new development agenda has been underscored throughout inclusive, participatory and successful multistakeholder consultations carried out in 2013.

It is noteworthy that Africa is also galvanising support for a people-centred development approach in the continent that is anchored on a new development paradigm dubbed Agenda 2063, which is both a vision and an action plan to build a strong and prosperous Africa. The implementation of Agenda 2063 could take a medium and long-term approach with a rolling plan of 25 years, 10 years and 5 years, coupled with a robust monitoring mechanism (AU, 2013, p 5). For the purposes of this chapter, it is important to underscore the synergies that exist between the CAP, Agenda 2063 and the post-2015 development agenda in defining the set ambitions and priorities of bringing the continent to the pathway of sustainable development. Agenda 2063 takes cognisance of the changing global context, where the IT revolution has provided opportunities to leapfrog development.

It builds on the New Partnership for Africa's Development (NEPAD) experience where accountability mechanisms, such as the African Peer Review Mechanism (APRM), has proven effective in monitoring progress, and could be replicated in developing a global instrument for monitoring the post-2015 development agenda.

Turner et al (2014) question whether there are realistic targets for the post-2015 MDGs and Agenda 2063. In a paper prepared for the Institute for Security Studies based in Pretoria, South Africa, they identify eradication of extreme poverty as a major milestone of the post-2015 MDG process as well as Agenda 2063 (Turner et al, 2014). But interestingly, the paper, using the International Futures Forecasting System to explore the goal, finds that many African states are unlikely to meet this target by 2030. Hence it argues in favour of a goal that would see Africa reduce extreme poverty to below 20 per cent by 2030, 10 per cent by 2045 and 3 per cent by 2063 (Turner et al, 2014). In short, for Africa, the post-2015 development framework must embrace critical issues that are indispensable to enhancing human development, and these are articulated both in CAP and Agenda 2063.

It is important to observe that the African region has been the most prepared in articulating its priorities to be factored into the emerging post-2015 development framework. To that extent, the formulation of the 17 SDGs and 169 targets by the UN's Open Working Group were largely influenced by CAP. The African group of negotiators is expected to take up the discussions further to ensure that the African issues articulated in the CAP are embodied in the final SDGs to be adopted by the General Assembly in September 2015. It will also be interesting to see that issues pertaining to governance and security not addressed in the MDGs find space in the post-2015 development framework. To its credit, the CAP dedicated pillar 5 on issues of peace and security by drawing on the nexus between development and peace, security and stability, and this has found space in the SDGs[7] as currently formulated.

Moving the agenda forward

To date, several ideas and suggestions have emerged on the form and substance of the post-2015 development agenda. The consultations and dialogue around the emerging framework have starkly reminded us that the promises made in 2000 have yet to be met. But at the same time, convergence is building on issues that require further consideration. In particular, there is overwhelming concern regarding the vulnerable groups, the poor and other marginalised groups. For example, in the area of education there is convergence on the need to anchor the post-2015 education agenda in a rights-based approach underpinned by the values of universality, non-discrimination and the indivisibility of rights. In the case of health, convergence is building around universality of health coverage, non-communicable diseases, as well as issues of reproductive health and mental disorders. Thus the post-2015 development agenda brings us both opportunities and challenges, such as the systemic and institutional changes in responding to the development challenges, but also an opportunity to invest in new approaches to resolving the global poverty.

Moving forward, it is essential to consolidate the positions of different regions of the world and groupings and multiple stakeholders from civil society, religious groups and the private sector as well as the multilateral organisations. The UN in particular must continue to provide leadership in driving the post-2015 development agenda forward through the various UN initiatives. It is critical that as the consultative process moves towards conclusion, there is an emerging consensus from the OECD, the G8, the G77, as well as middle-income countries, on areas of divergence.

The issue of financing the post-2015 development agenda has not been fully addressed in the consultative stages, and the third conference on FFD to be held in July 2015, in Addis Ababa, Ethiopia, offers an opportunity to deepen and intensify reflections on the financing architecture of the post-2015 development agenda. The role of the private sector in development financing by using innovative approaches such as capital markets and other financing instruments would be worth exploring (Evans, 2013). The CAP on the issue of financing, for instance, focuses on improving domestic resource mobilisation, maximising innovative financing, implementing existing commitments, and promoting quality and predictability of external financing, mutually beneficial partnerships, strengthening partnerships for trade and for managing the global commons.

It is equally important that African countries counter the illicit financial flows that continue to haemorrhage economies. This includes capital flight arising from drug trafficking, smuggling, corruption, tax evasion, as well as fraud. It is estimated that between 2000-06, the developing countries may have lost US$859 million to US$1.06 billion a year through illicit financial flows (Global Financial Integrity, 2008). It is difficult to estimate the figure for Africa due to inadequate data, even though the Global Financial Integrity report does provide estimations based on the International Monetary Fund (IMF) and World Bank calculations over a period of time. Based on the findings of the Global Financial Integrity, Africa may have lost up to US$854 billion over a 39-year period (Global Financial Integrity, 2008, p 10). The financing of the post-2015 development agenda must address this issue as a global common that needs the political will and commitment of both developed and developing countries.

In conclusion, the post-2015 development agenda stands at a critical juncture, and it is important that we build a global convergence on policy choices and options now, and not later. The fact that Africa has taken the lead in developing a CAP on the post-2015 development agenda is laudable, and puts the continent in a strong position to negotiate and influence the outcome of the post-2015 MDG framework. However, the position of other regional groupings, and particularly the OECD countries and emerging donors such as Brazil, Russia, India and China, is critical in building convergence.

The political context will define the positions of both the OECD and emerging donors, particularly in relation to complex underlying issues that need analysis. For instance, most of the high-income countries are less prosperous compared at the time of the launch of MDGs, and have now diverted greater focus on domestic issues. The emerging economies, on the other hand, are far more influential today, but may not be ready to shoulder more responsibility for financing the post-MDG framework. This is the stark reality to face the financing of the SDGs that are far more ambitious compared to the MDGs.

References

ACIA (Advisory Council on International Affairs) (2011) 'The post-2015 development agenda: the Millennium Development Goals', *Perspective*, no 74.

AU (African Union) (2013) *African Union Agenda 2063: A shared strategic framework for inclusive growth and sustainable development*, Background Note, August, Addis Ababa: AU.

AU (2014) *Common African Position on the post-2015 development agenda*, March, Addis Ababa: AU.

Bandara, A. (2012) *Post-2015 global development agenda: A critical assessment of future options*, February (https://post2015.files. wordpress.com/2012/10/post-2015-global-development-agenda-an-assessment-16-02-2012.pdf).

Besharati, N.A. (2013) *Common goals and differential commitments: The role of emerging economies in global development*, Discussion Paper 26/2013, Johannesburg, South Africa: German Development Institute (DIE), in cooperation with South African Institute of International Affairs.

Busan Partnership for Effective Development (2011) *Fourth High Level Forum on aid effectiveness*, Busan, Korea, 29 November-1 December (http://cso-effectiveness.org/IMG/pdf/outcome_document_-_final_en_-2.pdf).

CAFOD (2013) *Post-2015 development agenda: Realizing the convergence of the post-MDG and SDG decision-making processes*, A paper produced by Stakeholder Forum for a Sustainable Future, July (http://www.stakeholderforum.org/fileadmin/files/Post-2015_Development_Agenda_Convergence.pdf)

Collier, P. (2008) 'A measure of hope', *New York Times*, 21 September.

ECOSOC (Economic and Social Council) (2011) 'Millennium development goals and post-2015 development agenda' (http://www.un.org/en/ecosoc/about/mdg.shtml)

Evans, A. (2013) *Delivering the post-2015 development agenda: Options for a new partnership*, Policy Brief, November, New York: Center on International Cooperation, New York University.

FAO (Food and Agriculture Organization) (2012) *Climate change adaptation and mitigation: Challenges and opportunities in the food sector*, Rome: FAO.

Friedman, H.S. (2013). 'Causal inference and the Millennium Development Goals (MDGs): Assessing whether there was an acceleration in MDG development indicators following the MDG Declaration', MPRA Paper No 48793. Munich: Munich Personal RePEc Archive (http://mpra.ub.uni-muenchen.de/48793/1/MPRA_paper_48793.pdf).

Global Financial Integrity (2008) *Illicit financial flows from Africa: Hidden resource for development*, Washington, DC: Global Financial Integrity.

Hollander, S. (2014) 'From stocktaking to negotiation: The final phase of the Open Working Group on Sustainable Development Goals', *The Broker*, March.

Hussen, A. (2013) *Principles of environmental economics and sustainability: An integrated economic and ecological approach*, 3rd edn. Oxford: Routledge.

Jessee, J. (2007) *Gleneagles G8 commitments on debt relief and aid – Two years on*, Research Paper 07/51, London: House of Commons Library, 4 June.

Jolly, R. (2005) 'Global Development Goals: the United Nations experience', *Journal of Human Development*, vol 5, no 1, pp 69-95.

Khoo, S.-M. (2005) 'The Millennium Development Goals: a critical discussion', *Trocaire Development Review*, pp 43-56.

Lisk, F. (2009) 'Overview: The current climate change situation in Africa', in H. Besada and N. Sewankambo (eds) *Climate change in*

Africa: Adaptation, mitigation and governance challenges, CIGI special report, Ontario, Canada: Centre for International Governance Innovation, pp 9-13.

Mas, I. and Radcliffe, D. (2010) 'Mobile payments go viral: M-PESA in Kenya', Seattle, WA: Bill & Melinda Gates Foundation (http://siteresources.worldbank.org/AFRICAEXT/Resources/258643-1271798012256/M-PESA_Kenya.pdf).

Moss, T. (2010) 'What next for the Millennium Development Goals? Suggestions from an MDG sceptic', *Global Policy*, vol 1, no 2, pp 218-20.

OECD (Organisation for Economic Co-operation and Development) (2013) *Beyond the Millennium Development Goals: Towards an OECD contribution to the post-2015 agenda*, Paris: OECD.

Rio+20 (2012) *The future we want*, United Nations Conference on Sustainable Development, 20-22 June, Rio de Janeiro, Brazil (www.uncsd2012.org/content/documents/727The%20Future%20We%20Want%2019%20June%201230pm.pdf).

Sachs, J.D. (2012) 'Post-2015 development framework – reflections and challenges', Speech delivered during an Overseas Development Institute seminar, 10 December.

Stiglitz, J. (2013) *The price of inequality*, London: Penguin.

Turner, S., Cilliers, J. and Hughes, B.B. (2014) *The African futures, Reducing poverty in Africa: Realistic targets for the post-2015 MDGs and Agenda 2063*, August, Pretoria: Institute for Security Studies.

UN (United Nations) (2012a) *The Millennium Development Goals report 2012*. New York: United Nations (www.un.org/millenniumgoals/pdf/MDG%20Report%202012.pdf)

UN (2012b) *Realizing the future we want for all: Report to the Secretary-General*, New York: United Nations (http://www.un.org/millenniumgoals/pdf/Post_2015_UNTTreport.pdf).

UN (2013a) *A new global partnership: Eradicate poverty and transform economies through sustainable development*, Report of the High Level Panel of Eminent Persons on the post-2015 development agenda, New York, March.

UN (2013b) *Humanity divided: Confronting inequality in developing countries*, New York: UNDP.

UN (2014) High-Level Event of the General Assembly, *Contributions of North-South, South-South, triangular cooperation, and ICT for development to the implementation of the post-2015 development agenda*, Background Paper, 20-21 May.

UNDESA (United Nations Department of Economic and Social Affairs) (2012) *Citizen engagement and the post-2015 development agenda: Report of the Expert Group Meeting*.

UNDP (2014) *Assessing progress in Africa toward the Millennium Development Goals, Analysis of the Common African Position on the post-2015 development agenda*, MDG report 2014, New York: UNDP.

Vandemoortele, J. (2012) *Advancing the global development agenda post-2015: Some thoughts, ideas and practical suggestions*, A background paper prepared for the United Nations System Task Team on the post-2015 UN development agenda, April.

Wild, L. and Bergh, G. (2013) 'Are we making progress with building governance into the post 2015 framework?', Overseas Development Institute (ODI) Brief, February. London: ODI (www.odi.org/sites/odi.org.uk/files/odi-assets/publications-opinion-files/8261.pdf)

World Bank, The (2013) *Financing for development post-2015*, Washington, DC, October.

TWO

Debating post-2015 development-oriented reforms in Africa: agendas for action

George Kararach

Introduction

The development history of Africa has been characterised by many twists and turns. Independence in the late 1950s and most of the 1960s was brought about by resistance to colonial sociopolitical and economic relations. For almost 30 years after that, ambitions for a New International Economic Order (NIEO) (a proposal from developing countries to revise the international economic system) was driven by a desire for an autonomous postcolonial development, including in Africa. The debt crisis, by undermining the financial space and tightening the dependence of the developing to the developed world, shattered the unity necessary for the achievement of the NIEO as then conceived (Radice, 2011). Many initiatives and attempts at new alliances were undertaken to try to break what was considered a dependent relationship between the global South and the 'imperial North', including the declaration of economic development as a human right – recognition of the links between rights violations, poverty, exclusion, vulnerability, conflict and failure to achieve development in its multidimensional form. If the 1970s saw a debate of what states could actively do to usher development in Africa, the 1980s saw an attempt to roll back the state. In both cases, the reforms were driven by a sense of limited success in delivering effective development – an environment where the population had a sense of acceptable access to services, voice and self-worth (Sen, 1990). Development was increasingly couched in the context of human freedom and the analysis of poverty put in a multidimensional context.

By 2000, the Millennium Development Goals (MDGs) were born as a global compact to deliver this new vision of development. Today, rapid economic growth has arguably spread from Southeast Asia to

Latin America, and now Africa. While much of the old capitalist industrialist heartland is mired in economic stagnation and fiscal crisis, some of the 'emerging economies' face an investment glut due to increased activities by investors to find new outlets for 'redundant' capital (Radice, 2011). Radice (2011) argues that the current trends in the world economy and global politics provide evidence that the global South has now arrived at 'normal' capitalism (characterised by heightened conflict between labour and capital), at last bringing with it new patterns of uneven development, inequality and injustice. Its newly confident élites, now fully engaged in global circuits of trade, investment and finance, and in global governance too, appear to have left behind their previous colonial-comprador role of serving the interests of 'imperial' capital.[1] He concludes that this trend has brought with it the death of 'developmentalism', the irrelevance of the notion of a developmental state.[2] It is my contention that, looking at the patchy and uneven way the MDGs have been delivered across Africa, and the pressure as well as agency for change that allow for inclusive and sustainable (green) development, the notion of a developmental state remains relevant let alone critical. For our purpose, a developmental state[3] is one that has an ideological orientation to deliver inclusive development à la Mkandawire (2001). In turn it implies the leadership will have the strategic stance to deliver the development vision and objectives anchored on an effective state.

It is our contention that a return to developmentalism is critical to allow Africa to grow with transformation and be in a state to tackle emerging challenges and opportunities, such as climate change, food insecurity and the youth bulge. There is a need to focus on the enablers of development such as the infrastructure, regional integration, innovation, social inclusion and human security, and building effective institutions.

This chapter comprises seven sections, of which this is the first. The following section provides an overview of recent African development experience, arguing that despite the much-celebrated growth performance, there are a number of pending challenges when it comes to the achievement of the MDGs (UNTT, 2012). Some of these are opportunities, while others are challenges. The third section discusses unfinished business, and the fourth summarises the opportunities and challenges. Indeed, there is a need to develop an agenda for practical actions to shape Africa's development post-MDGs. Some of these actions are outlined in the fifth section. The sixth section discusses the post-2105 development priorities, and the last section forms the conclusion.

Context of Africa today: panorama of recent developments and the Millennium Development Goals

Africa is going through its most dynamic growth period in recent times. The continent has achieved growth rates above 6 per cent for most of the past decade, making Africa one of the fastest-growing regions in the world today (The World Bank, 2014). Despite continuing global financial turmoil, Africa is able to continue its outstanding growth performance for a number of reasons. A decade of reform has resulted in better macroeconomic management and a more attractive business climate. The rise of China and other emerging economies is helping to sustain high commodity prices, to the benefit of the resource-rich African continent. Another key factor is the emergence of Africa's middle class, putting more Africans in a position to make consumer choices, and making Africa an increasingly attractive market, for both domestic and foreign investors.

Africa is making progress on a broad range of development frontiers. Poverty rates are falling, the private sector environment is improving rapidly, trade is expanding, and more and more people are becoming connected – to roads, electricity, IT, water and sanitation. Education and health are making steady progress, and the number of fragile states has declined.

The gloom that characterised Africa in the 1980s and 1990s has all but dispersed. From the early 2000s, Africa has seen the longest and most 'sustained' expansion in over 50 years. It has been termed 'lions on the move' (see Figure 2.1). During this period, two very different development experiences have unfolded in tandem (The World Bank, 2012a).

The first version is that GDP growth has been relatively rapid, averaging 5 per cent a year until the 2008-09 global economic crisis, but since 2010, growth has resumed, and is expected to increase to over 5 per cent in 2015 (The World Bank, 2014; UNDESA, 2014). The growth has been widespread: 22 non-oil-importing countries averaged 4 per cent growth or higher for the decade 1998-2008. Africa has been able to attract significant private capital flows, which now exceed foreign aid. Foreign direct investment (FDI) has increased from US$11 billion in 2002 to US$57 billion in 2013 compared to foreign aid increasing from US$18 billion to US$43 billion over this same period (UNCTAD, 2003, 2014). The absolute poverty rate has been falling faster than 1 percentage point a year, and for the first time, between 2005 and 2008, the absolute number of people living on US$1.25 a day fell (by about 9 million) in a number of African

Figure 2.1: Real GDP growth (%) 2005–15

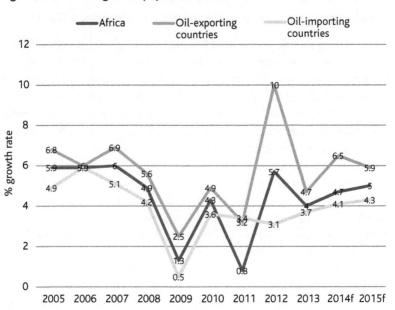

Note: f = forecast.

Source: Based on data from UNECA (2012, 2014) and UN/DESA (2014)

countries with a few exceptions (Zimbabwe and South Sudan, for example) (The World Bank, 2012a). Child mortality has also been declining, and even though a large number of African countries are unlikely to meet the MDGs, about half the 'off track' countries are within 11 per cent of the trajectory to reach the goals (UNDP, 2010).

The second narrative posits that Africa's growth has largely followed commodity prices, and the continent's exports are highly concentrated in primary commodities (coffee, cocoa, cotton, sisal, etc) and few markets (UK, France, US, Italy and Germany). Industry's share of gross domestic product (GDP) is not very different today (28 per cent) as in the 1970s (at 24 per cent) (UNECA, 2014, p 41). With the exception of Mauritius, no African country has achieved significant structural transformation – the reallocation of economic activity (especially through new investment, from low to higher productivity activities leading to higher economy-wide productivity and progressively raising income) across the broad sectors of agriculture, manufacturing and services – necessary for long-term growth (see The World Bank, 2012a). Indeed, some rapidly growing countries such as Burkina Faso, Mozambique and Tanzania have reduced absolute poverty (that is, those on less than US$1.25 a day) only slightly as growth has not translated into increases in new jobs and greater inclusion given the high levels of unemployment of around 60 per cent among young people.

The absolute levels of human development as measured by the Human Development Index are still the lowest in the world. Indicators of service delivery are appalling: teachers in public primary schools in Tanzania are absent 23 per cent of the time; public doctors in Senegal spend a total of 29 minutes a day seeing patients and the rest of the time seeking alternative means to underwrite their incomes (Bold et al, 2011). Such systems are unlikely to be able to deliver at the scale required by Africa's population boom à la Meade et al (1961). Finally, Africa's civil wars may have declined in numbers, but political instability and fragility is still widespread: in Guinea-Bissau and Mali, on the border between South Sudan and Sudan, as well as in eastern Congo, Central Africa Republic and Nigeria. And on any worldwide indicator of corruption, Africa scores the lowest – with countries such as Uganda and Nigeria leading the pack, ranking 140 and 144 of 177 countries rated by Transparency International (TI) in the 2013 Corruption Perception Index respectively (TI, 2103). These figures have not changed much for the continent over the years.

What was the growth performance meant for Africa's ability to meet the MDGs? In 2012, a joint report was published by the UN Economic Commission for Africa (UNECA), the African Union Commission (AUC), the African Development Bank (AfDB) and the United Nations Development Programme (UNDP) Regional Bureau for Africa on assessing MDG progress, both at the indicator and goal level in Africa (UNECA, 2012). A total of 44 MDG indicators were assessed in the following terms: rapid progress, good progress, moderate progress, little progress, slow progress, no progress and no updated data. The outcomes of these assessments have been discussed by James Waikaga in Chapter One of this volume. The question to be answered is whether the adoption of MDG-type goals has been translated into an increased allocation of domestic and international resources to Africa and structural transformation of the continent (UNECA, 2012; AfDB et al, 2013).

Arguably, attempts by countries to deliver the MDGs also highlighted the increasingly important role of the regional (and sub-regional) players in development, including regional integration and intraregional cooperation – especially on issues related to trans-boundary management such as communicable diseases, environmental sustainability and technical cooperation. The UNECA and other

UN agencies, funds and programmes, multilateral organisations and global non-governmental organisations (NGOs) have also provided both technical and financial support to make progress in MDG implementation at the national level. Some other regional institutions supporting the MDG process include the following: AUC and its New Partnership for Africa's Development (NEPAD) programme, Economic Community Of West African States (ECOWAS), the East African Community (EAC), Economic Community for Central African States (ECCAS), the Community of Sahel-Saharan States (CEN SAD), the Common Market for Eastern and Southern Africa (COMESA), the Intergovernmental Authority on Development (IGAD), and the Southern African Development Community (SADC). All these organisations have developed strategic frameworks for pan-African and regional socioeconomic development by focusing on critical challenges facing the continent: poverty and international marginalisation. They also seek to promote cooperation between countries in the regions and with international partners in a number of thematic areas such as agriculture and food security; climate change and natural resource management; regional integration and infrastructure; human development; economic and corporate governance; and cross-cutting issues including gender, capacity development and ICT.

However, the events around the Arab Spring of 2011 and the Ebola crisis of 2014 brought into sharp focus how prepared Africa was to sustain any development momentums gained from the MDGs. Nabli and Ben Hammouda (2014) note that the changes that characterised North Africa after 2010 were an outcome of failure in the social contract and decline into dictatorial states. The Arab Spring was sparked by the Tunisian revolution that in turn got ignited from the self-immolation of Mohamad Bouazizi on 18 December 2010 in protest of police corruption and ill treatment (Fahim, 2011). Poverty, rising food prices, inflation, human rights violation and high unemployment were the main phenomena facing the Arabs. Additionally, there was much corruption of the elites and leaders to generate discontent. The causes of the Arab Spring are not limited to internal causes, however, and may include international factors such as the failure of the War on Terror and the Western strategy of imported democracy in the Middle East. Another possible reason could be the failure of the peace process in the Israeli-Arabic conflict and the existence of Palestine refugees in countries such as Egypt and the wider Middle East. But severe socioeconomic inequality and a heightened sense of injustice drove the populace of North Africa in a renewed demand for change.

Unemployment in the North Africa region remained up to 2015 a major source of economic insecurity and destabilisation of any political system. As noted by Don Tapscott in the UK *Guardian* newspaper, 'twenty-four per cent of young people in the region cannot find jobs' (*The Guardian*, 2011). This percentage of youth unemployment was very high in a region unable to change the situation and to create new jobs, especially after the world financial crises. Equally, political and human rights are fundamental for any society, and citizens in this region were living in a situation of 'bad' political systems based on corruption, state of emergency laws, lack of free elections and freedom of speech, and religious fundamentalism (Sharabi, 1988). The subsequent contagion of the conflict in Egypt, Libya and Tunisia saw the emergence of violent fundamentalist groups such as Al-Qaeda in the Sahel and Boko Haram furthering state fragility in North and part of West Africa in countries such as Mali, Nigeria, Chad and Niger. The question that remains unanswered is whether the Arab Spring-type resistance to ruling elites will gain traction in the rest of Africa, further south of the Sahara.

Equally, the Ebola crisis showed the importance of a regional approach to financing public goods and service delivery. Because of the relatively porous borders in Africa, Ebola was able to quickly spread from Guinea to Sierra Leone and Liberia, with devastating consequences – it could be said that the disease took easy root in countries that were fragile and emerging from years of conflict (Kararach, 2014). Clearly, a number of African countries remained unable to effectively deliver on their own a coherent transformative development agenda, as demanded by the likes of the MDGs.

Africa beyond the euphoria of 'lions on the march': agency and developmentalism

The continent has made some significant strides with respect to growth in the last 10 or so years of MDG implementation. However, Africa's growth has often been concentrated in a few sectors and areas, benefiting only part of the population (AfDB et al, 2013). Hyden (2014) notes that lack of structural transformation has kept what he had called an 'economy of affection' (an informal economy anchored on a familial social protection system) intact for some 35 years. There is thus a need to change the quality of growth, to create more and better jobs and economic opportunities, and to lift more Africans out of poverty while creating a modern formalised economy. Of major concern has been the rise of inequality with economic growth. Africa's

Gini index has widened over the past decade, and is hardly better than it was in 1980.

Social exclusion in Africa exists in several dimensions: geographical (for example, rural poor); social (for example, gender); and economic (for example, unemployment). Recent political upheavals in North Africa have highlighted the plight of Africa's youth. The rapid expansion in education across the continent as part of the drive to meet the MDGs has in its wake many young people largely excluded from the formal economy, creating a clash between expectations and reality that may pose a challenge to social and political stability (AfDB, 2014; Hyden, 2014).

Maintaining the momentum on MDG achievements requires strengthening the role of the private sector in socioeconomic transformation. There is need for more private sector jobs as a strategy for lifting more Africans out of poverty. African countries have to maintain progress in enhancing the environment for business by fostering competition, trade and investment. The average cost of starting a business in Africa has fallen dramatically from US$217 in 2006 to US$77 in 2011, while the average time for setting up a business declined from 58 to 35 days (AfDB et al, 2013). Any room for further improvement must be explored. For example, limited access to finance remains a problem, together with a limited infrastructure and education systems that are sometimes poorly suited to the needs of the labour market – these still hold back small and medium-size businesses (Kararach, 2014).

As noted above, some of the MDG goals needed a regional approach, especially regarding issues such trans-boundary resource management, communicable diseases and development cooperation/partnership. In this regard, regional cooperation and integration is essential for sharing the benefits of growth more broadly and for achieving 'regional inclusion'. Given that many of the countries are small and landlocked, Africa is the most economically fragmented continent, making it difficult to exploit economies of scale and to enhance international competitiveness. Because a high proportion of Africa's poor live in economically marginal and logistically remote areas, they may miss out on the benefits of growth in the more dynamic regions. As a result, African countries need to promote regional integration by simplifying the regional economic architecture including the development of regional infrastructure and enhanced connectivity.

Africa also needs to improve its infrastructure to galvanise productivity and to sustain the recent growth performance. Yet the costs of providing infrastructure can be prohibitive. Less than half of the rural population has access to all-season roads, and the rural electrification rate stands at only 10 per cent (UN, 2013). Population growth has outstripped urban infrastructure development in many countries, and basic services are twice as expensive as in other developing regions. As the MDG progress reports show, improving water and sanitation has been slow (UN, 2013). However, as noted above, Africans are becoming much better connected to information and communications infrastructure – especially regarding expansion in mobile telephony.

Agriculture remains a major sector of Africa's economy, employing 60 per cent of the population, and contributing 30 per cent of GDP. With 16 per cent arable land – the highest of any continent – but only 21 per cent under cultivation, Africa has enormous potential for agricultural development and for ensuring food security (ACBF, 2012). Because population growth has consistently outstripped production, food production per head of population is declining, and food prices are rising at an ever-faster rate. Equally, farm productivity in Africa has failed to improve, and this has worsened a long-term trend of high food prices, leaving rural incomes to stagnate or decline, with negative consequences for the livelihood of the poor (ACBF, 2012).

It is generally acknowledged that Africa has the youngest population, with about two-thirds under 25. Some projections suggest that by 2050, almost 400 million Africans will be between 15 and 24 years of age (AfDB, 2014a). If the energy and creativity of young Africans can be harnessed, this may prove to be Africa's greatest asset. At the same time, 'youth bulge' is already generating pressures and demands for economic opportunities and political voice. If these demands are not met, they could become a source of social and political instability (AfDB, 2014a).

As also noted, conflict and political fragility remain serious inhibitors of Africa's development. A third of African states – with about 200 million people – is still classed as fragile. With 50 per cent higher rates of malnutrition, 20 per cent higher child mortality rates and 18 per cent lower primary completion rates, these countries lag behind developing countries on almost all development indicators. Indeed, no fragile state achieved even a single MDG (AfDB, 2012, 2014b; see also World Bank, 2012b). (Karolina Werner, in Chapter Twelve, takes up in greater depth the issues of conflict and security in influencing the achievement of MDGs.)

Because of deforestation (for farmland expansion and fuel wood) and negative farming practices, environmental degradation in Africa is a serious and growing problem. Some parts of the continent are estimated to be losing 50 tonnes of soil per hectare each year, resulting in stagnating agricultural yields and loss of rural livelihoods (AfDB, 2012, 2014b). Environmental degradation and extreme weather events mostly affect the poor. Climate change is another important challenge threatening to unravel the achievements in some of the MDGs. While Africa has contributed little to the causes of climate change, it is acutely vulnerable to its effects. Paradoxically, however, Africa's low levels of infrastructure development leave it in a unique position to pursue a sustainable development path.

Most African countries have engaged in various forms of public sector reforms since the 1980s in attempts to infuse dynamisms in their economies – especially through liberalisation – with mixed results (Kiggundu, 1997; Owusu, 2012). Devarajan and Fengler (2012, p 4) argue that the growth success is 'mainly due to reforms in economic policies, necessitated by misguided policies of the past', but variations are explained by political economy dynamics with shifting power balances. The development challenges – lack of structural transformation, weak human capital and poor governance – reflect government failures to deliver quality services that are difficult to overcome because they are deeply political and require proactive supporters at various societal levels. Using survey data from Ghana, Owusu (2012), on the other hand, argues for the importance of institutional forms in defining variations in success to deliver quality public services.

Observed data from the real world since independence shows that the African continent experienced highly uneven economic and social performance for whatever reason.[4] Comparisons are usually made with East Asian countries as Africa started from a similar position to most East Asian economies – and in many cases even better – but unlike East Asia, the continent experienced three distinct growth episodes: sluggish growth (1960-75), two lost decades (1976-99), and the 'catch up' (since 2000) (The World Bank, 2012a). Most of the comparisons do not pay much attention to service provision levels, except when treating them as initial conditions (Sachs and Warner, 1997).

The early conceptualisation of policy did not focus on the importance of the human condition as the core development objective (development not being a right) but as a residual to the welfare maximisation objective achieved through the market mechanism by emphasising privatisation and liberalisation (Kararach, 2011). Arguably, the initial poverty reduction strategy for Africa post-independence seemed simple and defined by the widening of the individual's consumption basket subject to available resources based on the neoclassical economic model with one size fitting all. Harrod and Domar (Harrod, 1939; Domar, 1957) defined the growth strategy. Experts believed that Africa just needed transfers of financial resources to close its *development gap* – precisely – *the savings-investment gap*. In neoclassical modelling, investments in services such as roads, schools and clinics did not materialise into higher standards of living and growth as they were conceptualised as inputs into the production functions as opposed to their availability/access being development objectives per se. The discovery of natural resources – particularly oil – across the continent made Africa's exports even more dependent on commodities that saw limited processes of value addition as the oil boom gave a false sense of long-term income. The combination of high and volatile commodity prices and low levels of human development and infrastructure, a lack of competitiveness and weak mobilisation of revenues resulted in Africa's debt crisis beginning in the late 1970s. What followed were two decades of social and economic decline as high-valued products that accompany better service provisions and related governance did not exist across the board (Makoba, 2011).

Indeed, the governance landscape worsened as state legitimacy deteriorated in tandem with poor service provisions. Equally, investments in natural resources and the preoccupation of African governments with natural resources brought about a relaxation of taxation by governments. There was no pressure of governments to invest and strengthen domestic resource mobilisation through taxes as government increased their coffers through commodity-led exports, which in turn helped worsen legitimacy and accountability in government. Governments were not accountable to their population as the general population contributed little to government spending in terms of taxes. By the late 1980s and early 1990s, it became clear that Africa's economic model was not sustainable.

This trend coincided with the ascent of neoliberalism in major donor countries such as the US and UK. Development partners started to argue that aid-financed projects were not productive in a setting where economic policies were distorted by too much state intervention in economic activities. This led to a new era of development thinking, characterised by Structural Adjustment Programmes (SAPs). The problems with the SAPs were not in substance, but in their process. African governments often had little incentive to fully implement SAPs due to principal agent problems, as accountability for the success of the programmes were to 'remote' constituencies outside the continent – mostly the Bretton Woods institutions officials (Besley and Ghatak, 2007) – as it would have hurt their own political interests, and because these policies were imposed from the outside, they could be more easily rejected (The World Bank, 2012a).

The consistent growth for more than a decade has propelled part of Africa to what The World Bank classifies as 'middle income' (Ncube and Shimeles, 2012), or US$1,000 per capita income – and with a 'middle class' of about 350 million people in 48 countries.[5] Ten African countries representing another 200 million people today would become middle income by 2025 if current growth trends continue, or with some modest growth and stabilisation. Another seven countries (70 million people) could reach the same status if they accelerate their economic performance and achieve 7 per cent of uninterrupted growth. Reportedly, 'only ten African countries (230 million people) almost certainly will not reach Middle Income by 2025. Most of them are fragile and conflict affected states' (The World Bank, 2012a).

Economists use a conjuncture of four interrelated factors to explain Africa's 'growth recovery' since 2000, which has become the most sustained expansion since independence, and which was not significantly interrupted by the global financial crisis: policy, demography, geography and technology. However, policy implementation allegedly remains uneven across countries and policy areas. Demographic pressures, urbanisation and technological change are also bringing a number of new challenges of demands for jobs, housing and political voice, which African governments will need to address to sustain the current growth momentum (The World Bank, 2012a). Interestingly, no mention is made of services such as health, education and ICT that help generate positive externalities to support growth.

Economists at both The World Bank and the AfDB argue that the improvement in economic performance has been associated with better policies (Ncube and Shimeles, 2012; The World Bank, 2012a). Over the last decade, Africa allegedly improved its economic and social policies. These reforms occurred mostly because of two main shifts in the region: lessons learned from the structural adjustment period, and subsequent Heavily Indebted Poor Countries (HIPC)/Poverty Reduction Strategy Papers (PRSPs) process that provided debt relief and supported home-grown reform agendas, as anchored in the Lagos Plan of Action,[6] and the end of the Cold War that opened up political and policy space in Africa due to reduced rivalries and interference of the then world superpowers of the US and USSR (The World Bank, 2012a). Even though it did not yet achieve a transformation in governance (because democratic practice was adjusted with a lag), the opening provided voice to many segments of society that had been marginalised. Together with rapid population growth and urbanisation, the demands for better social and economic policies have been growing. In other words, African countries started to experience strong domestically based principal agent-driven adjustments/reforms such as democratisation and devolution based on strong demands for better public service delivery.

The World Bank has now adopted a non-Malthusian view on demographic dynamics, arguing that Africa's economic fortunes have improved at a time when the possibility of a demographic dividend has started to emerge:

> Across the world, demographic dividends are associated with better development results. Since independence, Africa's population grew rapidly from a very low base of below 250 million to 900 million people today. Africa is adding 27 million new people every year and will continue to grow at this speed until 2050. Fertility is expected to come down gradually which will be compensated by people living longer and a larger number of young families (which have fewer children). As a result the most rapidly growing group in Africa are "working adults" (age 16-64) growing by 19 million each year; children (age 0-14) will only continue to grow by 4 million annually. The dependency ratio will keep improving for the next decades and reach a relationship of two working adults per dependent by 2050. (The World Bank, 2012a, p 11)

This analysis ignores the problems created by a huge youth bulge, demanding for more investments in services such as education and the need to create employment to avoid social fracturing and conflict/instability (Kararach et al, 2011). Indeed, a large educated and unemployed youth were at the heart of the conflict that characterised the Arab Spring in North Africa.

Africa has also been urbanising rapidly, with deep implications for social and economic opportunities. World Bank economists argue that:

> … no country has ever reached high income with low urbanization. Today, 41 per cent of Africans live in cities, with a supplementary one per cent being added to cities every two years. By 2033, Africa – like the rest of the world – will be a majority urban continent. Urbanization and development are generally expected to go together. With

a large urban consumer base, firms and customers benefit from scale economies. (The World Bank, 2012a, p 11)

Unfortunately, these kinds of arguments ignore the complexities of cities (Léautier, 2006), and do not consider the need to provide commensurate services such as housing, water and sanitation in a holistic planning framework (D'Alessandro-Scarpari et al, 2016).

The other factor that has arguably played a major role in driving growth in Africa has been the emergence of telephony technology. The mobile revolution is the most visible sign of Africa's emergence, covering a wide range of areas such a mobile banking, e-health, virtual libraries, as well as the usage of the technologies for market intelligence for the agricultural sector and transformation. In 2000, Africans were hardly connected to a typical modern phone network, with the exception of South Africa and a few wealthy individuals. Indeed, there were no affordable cell phones. Yet within the space of a decade, cell phones have become ubiquitous (with the exception of a few countries), and a major tool for communication and wider information exchange (Ghuveya and Léautier, 2010). The figure was put at 735 million subscribers by the end of 2012 (AfDB et al, 2013).

A world post-2015: debating the challenges and opportunities in Africa

Despite the optimism, Africa still faces some development challenges – in fragility, poverty reduction, structural transformation, limited integration, climate change, human development and governance – that may undermine let alone reverse the gains of the last decade or so and undermine service delivery. Some of the issues in relative detail are as follows.

- *Persistent state fragility:* quite a significant number of African countries have been growing much more slowly than the regional average because of being in a fragile state (ACBF, 2011). These are countries where conflict is persistent or socioeconomic governance is weak to the extent that the state is unable to perform its basic functions. Of the 33 fragile states in the world, 20 are in Africa (The World Bank, 2012a, 2014). Excluding the oil-exporting countries, the remaining African fragile states have experienced much slower real GDP growth than their non-fragile counterparts (see Figure 2.1 above). A number of studies show that the slow growth of fragile states is not surprising as these countries suffer from political violence, insecurity and high levels of corruption due to exacerbated struggles over economic rents, resulting in the possibility of the economy getting 'stuck' in a low-level equilibrium trap (Andriamihaja et al, 2012).

- *Fast growth with poverty reduction:* in some of Africa's fast-growing countries, a disturbing number of people are not seeing rapid poverty reduction, and there is a tendency for inequality to also rise (Kararach, 2011; Makoba, 2011). For example, despite years of significant oil revenues, some African countries such as Equatorial Guinea (ranked 136), Nigeria (ranked 153) and Cameroon (ranked 150 out of 177) have posted among the lowest human development indicators in the world as of 2013 (UNDP, 2013). The tragedy is that these countries have not been able to use their oil revenues to significantly improve the welfare of their poor citizens due to weak socioeconomic governance that does not accommodate beneficiation. The reason may be that oil revenues (unlike tax revenues) go directly from oil companies to the government, without passing through the hands of the citizens. This suspicion is confirmed by the persistent complaints and conflict that afflicted the Niger delta over the years over the proceeds from oil production.

- *Inadequate structural transformation:* among those countries that have achieved both rapid growth and poverty reduction, such as Ghana, Rwanda and Ethiopia (for example, poverty here fell from 46 per cent in 1995/96 to 30 per cent in 2011; see Government of Ethiopia, 2012), there has been remarkably little structural transformation in that they are still agricultural commodity dependent. The share of manufacturing in GDP (11 per cent) or employment (8 per cent) is still quite low, and scarcely higher than it was before the growth phase due to limited structural transformation (UNECA, 2014). Arguably, labour intensive manufacturing growth is one of the most effective ways for Africa to absorb the high number/percentage of young people entering the labour force each year by encouraging sectoral diversification, value addition and beneficiation in the extractive as well as non-extractive sectors.

- *Poor infrastructure and connectivity:* many reasons are advanced by commentators as to why competitive development has not taken off in Africa – be it in manufacturing or agriculture or even services – but most of them revolve around the high costs of production and limited market integration on the continent.[7] For example, in transport, immobilisation before loading (in hours) range from 13 hours in Central Africa to 6 hours in East Africa compared with 1.6 hours in France. Payload utilisation, the ratio of the number of kilometres with a payload over the total number of kilometres of a truck, is 75 in Central Africa, 76 in East Africa, compared to 87 in France (Teravaninthorn and Raballand, 2009). A major driver of these high costs and limited market is Africa's huge infrastructure deficit (as given by the Logistics Performance Index, LPI[8]). African exporters arguably face some of the highest transport costs in the world, especially in trying to ship goods from landlocked countries to the ports. Even though the study by Teravaninthorn and Raballand (2009) shows that vehicle operating costs along the four main African transport corridors are no higher than in France, unfortunately, transport prices are among the highest in the world – for example, given the LPI for West Africa (2.19), Central Africa (2.27), East Africa (2.49), Southern Africa (2.73). The difference between transport prices and vehicle operating costs are the profits accruing to trucking companies, some of which are of the order of 100 per cent due to anti-trust behaviours in a collusive transportation market.

- *Business climate:* besides infrastructure, a host of other factors serve to drive up the cost of doing business in Africa. The World Bank's Doing Business indicators consistently rank African countries lowest among all regions of the world in most areas, with Mauritius the best performer ranking 19 out of 187, followed by South Africa in 39th place. There has been some limited progress in reforming business regulations where some countries such as Rwanda and Sao Tome and Principe are among the world's leading reformers in making it easier to undertake a business start-up, reforming the tax regimes. Yet the fact remains that the costs of starting and running a business in Africa are, on average, the highest in the world. For example, Burundi, Cameroon, Central African Republic, Chad, Democratic Republic of Congo (DRC), Kenya and Nigeria ranked 159, 161, 185, 184, 181, 121 and 131 out of 187 assessed in terms of The World Bank's Doing Business 2013 indicators respectively (The World Bank, 2013). It is more costly to rent office space in Lagos than in Manhattan, New York (Mo Ibrahim Foundation, 2012).

- *Persistence of the informal sector or second economy:* the majority of Africans work in smallholder farms and household enterprises where there is limited regulation and protection from poor working conditions – what is often called the informal sector or second economy (Wangwe, 1993). For those low-income countries where there is data, the evidence suggests that the private wage employment sector has been creating jobs at a faster rate than GDP has been growing. However, that growth is from such a low base that it does not come close to absorbing the 7-10 million of new entrants into the labour force every year (The World Bank, 2011). Unfortunately, most young people end up working where their parents do, in smallholder farms and household enterprises, with limited socioeconomic opportunities.

• *Weak human capital:* as noted earlier, despite a decade-and-a-half of economic growth, some poverty reduction and improvement in human capital indicators, Africa still has the lowest levels of human capital in the world. The weak human capital base persists despite the fact that considerable resources – from donors and African taxpayers – have gone into the health and education sectors due to a range of reasons including a brain drain. Take health as an example: achieving the goal of 'Health for All', as embraced in the Alma-Ata[9] about 30 years ago, has proven to be difficult and a mirage, characterised by glaring inequities among socioeconomic groups and classes.[10] Progress in achieving the MDGs was punctuated by the slow progress on meeting the health targets. A good example is the infant mortality rate where progress has been uneven across regions. For example, high infant mortality (ranging from 88-103 per 1,000 live births) in Central African countries could be attributed to political conflict and broader fragility, and the prevalence of malaria in the region (CIA World Factbook, 2014). Taking the DRC, Central Africa Republic and Chad, the malaria mortality rate is above the World Health Organization (WHO) regional average, while in Southern Africa, high HIV prevalence (above 15 per cent) is a determining factor of infant mortality (of 64-88 per 1,000 live births) (CIA World Factbook, 2014). Indeed, a number of diseases such as malaria have persisted, or new ones such as HIV/AIDS have emerged. Poor services have been a result of limited access as well as financing.[11] At least three factors contribute to ineffective public spending and the weak link between service access and quality. First, resources allocated to addressing the problems of poor people do not always reach the front-line service provider due to fiscal leakages and misappropriation. Second, even when resources get to the school or clinic, the provider is often not there – teacher absenteeism rates in Uganda and Tanzania were about 27 and 23 per cent, respectively, because of endemic moonlighting (Bold et al, 2011; The World Bank, 2012a). And third, even when present, the quality of the service is exceedingly poor and, until recently, with limited recourse for citizens to hold providers accountable.

- *Weak regional integration:* it should be highlighted that the economic unions in Africa are each dominated by the economies of a single country, and free movements of people limited to a few countries within each of these unions – Botswana and South Africa in southern Africa, Gabon in central Africa, Côte d'Ivoire and Nigeria in West Africa. Adepoju (2006) claims that migrant labour built the prosperity of these countries – cocoa and coffee plantations in Ghana and Côte d'Ivoire, mines and agriculture in South Africa, and the forestry and oil fields of Gabon. Resource-rich but labour-short countries – such as Botswana, Gabon, Côte d'Ivoire – relied heavily on immigrant labour from neighbouring countries. In that sense, it would pay African countries to have a regional approach to capacity building and skills development. There has been some progress in that most regional integration agreements in Africa include provisions on the free movement of people and the right of residence (Léautier, 2009; Kararach, 2014). Whatever the weaknesses of these provisions, they have led to the easing or abolition of visa requirements for travellers within the integration groups concerned, particularly in western, eastern and southern Africa. However, restrictions remain on employment and the right of residence, with implications for capacity usage and skills development as well as access to public services at a regional level – thus being a major constraint to regional integration. Cristina D'Alessandro takes a deeper look at the issues of integration and regionalism in Chapter Nine of this volume.

- *Availability of data and how accurate they are:* these have weakened strategic planning and the need to accurately time and sequence reforms. The MDG-related and other data have not always been available on time at the national as well as local levels due to weak statistical capacity. If they exist, they have been subject to problems of inconsistency with international standards undermining comparison. Equally, data transmission to and estimates made by international agencies – together with the fact that countries did not produce all the data on MDGs annually (for example, health data in the form of DHS data is generally once every 10 years due to cost of production) – constitute another layer of problems contributing to the observed data gaps. Over the last few years, there have been commendable steps taken by African countries, with the support of international organisations, to obtain data for tracking progress on development such as the MDGs and Agenda 2063. However, a number of challenges persist relating to the production of data in Africa. The low profile of statistics on the continent is due to a number of obstacles, including: inadequate resources allocated to statistical activities; lack of institutional capacity; inadequate coordination of statistical activities; and minimal consideration of African specificities in setting up international standards. The African Statistics System (ASS) is therefore expected to further scale up its efforts toward continental statistical integration to address a continent-wide need for harmonised and quality statistical information. Agencies such as the African Capacity Building Foundation (ACBF), AUC, UNECA and AfDB have embarked on the development of programmes that directly respond to these challenges and improve the statistical capacity of African countries. These include the Africa Symposium for Statistics Development (ASSD), which is an advocacy framework for censuses; the African Charter on Statistics (ACS), constituting a framework for the coordination of statistical activities in the continent; the Strategy for the Harmonisation of Statistics in Africa (SHaSA), which provides guidance on the statistics harmonisation process in Africa; and the new initiative on civil registration and vital statistics as well as the International Comparison Programme (ICP) supported by AfDB and ACBF. A number of countries have adopted strategies for reforming their statistical systems; for example, Uganda and Tanzania have since embarked on national registration programmes resulting in data improvements.

- *Climate change:* the adverse impacts of climate change pose a further threat to the sustainability of MDG achievement and broader African development through heightened risks of extreme weather events such as droughts and floods. Moreover, mitigating climate change presents a significant policy challenge for a region that faces huge energy needs to power its development and industrialisation. The continent must have access to the technology and financing that will enable it to meet those energy needs (currently largely unmet yet rising rapidly with population and economic expansion), but in a way that is consistent – to the extent possible – with climate change mitigation and adaptation. The issue of climate change and adaptation is currently hotly debated (see Bond, 2011; and Nhamo, 2011).

- *Government failure and inaction:* arguably, the above problems are the result of governance or government failure to bring forth pro-poor reforms. Be it that losers are concentrated while winners are diffuse, or that clientelistic/paternalistic politics alter the constraints and incentives facing politicians, the system is in an equilibrium that has no intrinsic force for change or for delivering quality services. Indeed, services are delivered in a principal–agent nexus, whereby politics and representation as well as accountability affect service provision (Easterly and Levine, 1997). Many of these issues have driven the conversations about the presence or lack thereof of a developmental state in Africa (as discussed next).

Building an effective state: some of the agenda for action

So how can development agencies and other partners/players support the building of effective developmental states and forge the engaged societies (The World Bank, 2005) necessary for development in Africa? Below are a few suggestions.

Strengthening economic policy analysis and management: effective economic policy-making (the ability to initiate and maintain necessary reforms) and management is crucial for sustainable development and poverty reduction. The inability of African states to put in place a robust economic policy analysis and management framework in the 1970s and 1980s was partly responsible for the poor economic performance thereof. Inflation and general macroeconomic instability was commonplace. Indeed, the 1980s and 1990s saw a period of radical economic reforms in the name of structural adjustments. While the reforms introduced new ways of economic management, in some instances they speeded up the process of capacity decay and under-utilisation as skilled personnel faced with retrenchment left the public service or the country altogether. It was in this climate that many development agencies started to operationalise their approaches to capacity building, focusing on removing capacity constraints, filling gaps and supporting the development of new capacity in economic policy analysis and management. It was organisationally understood that the government's ability to provide quality goods and services is closely linked to its ability to effectively develop good economic policies and to operationalise them.

Effective public administration and management is at the core of state effectiveness: as noted by ACBF (2002, p 19): '[T]o address the challenges for sustained growth and poverty reduction in sub-Saharan Africa, the public sector must play a significant role. The sector is however barely equipped to do so.... Economic and institutional reforms being undertaken by African countries and the rapid pace with which world economies are becoming integrated, call for a significant shift in the role and the effectiveness of the public sector in sub-Saharan Africa.' The ability of the state to effectively respond to the demands of the citizen depends partly on an effective and efficient public sector. This point is echoed by the World Bank Task Force of 2005 when it noted that: '[A] reality that confronts many governments is that their public services, although large, lack the managerial and professional skills and the service-delivery orientation required to respond to popular pressure for results' (p 35). Building an effective state and forging engagement of the wider society in the development process requires an effective and responsive public administration and management. Ineffective mechanisms for administrative control and the monitoring and evaluation of performance and behaviour accentuate unethical practices that induce weak accountability (UNECA, 1991, pp 13-14).

Without financial management and accountability the state cannot deliver effectively: it is almost common knowledge that many governments in Sub-Saharan Africa have been undermined by allegations of corruption and financial mismanagement. The capacity to plan, budget, use and account for public funds is crucial for the state to deliver on its mandate. Governments need to support initiatives (such as the Transparency and Accountability Initiative) calling for publication and introspection budgetary and spending processes to prevent resource leakages and enhance critical strategic investment. There would thus be a need for greater transparency on how resources are budgeted and utilised, which in turn strengthens accountability and democratic governance as access to critical information is enhanced (Kararach, 2012).

Effective states make policy and programmes on the basis of concrete evidence: to be able to make informed decisions, states and the wider society need reliable and timely information. This means developing an effective national statistical system to provide information to the public, state and business community in the economic, demographic, social and environment arena. Such information is crucial for policy and programme development in the various areas, and for mutual knowledge across states and citizens of the world. Statistics are collated and disseminated to answer burning questions, and in some instances, to allow research questions to be formulated with sufficient precision (UNDESA, 2003, p 45). There have been several initiatives from agencies such as the UN's Systems of National Accounts 93 (SNA93),[12] and the AfDB's ICP[13] to reform how data is collected and interpreted for policy decisions, albeit with some limited success (see Jerven, 2013).

Improving governance through a strong parliamentary framework is crucial for engaging society as well as making states effective: the link between good governance and sustainable development has been known for some time. Good governance encourages social inclusion and the development of social capital and a cohesive and stable society (Jomo and Chowdhury, 2012). The history of governance in African states in the last few decades has been characterised by dictatorship, corruption and nepotism, a society where little demands were made to the state for the provision of basic social services as well as the respect of human rights. In the 1990s a new wave of social transformation – especially democratisation – swept across the continent. Parliamentary elections have been held, and other forms of representative government instituted, especially at the local level. These processes have seen the emergence of more responsive governments and articulate civil groups demanding better social services and an accountable government. Despite the changes, the capacities of both states and civil groups to quickly take advantage of these changes has remained weak. The capacity development support of donors such as ACBF, the Department for International Development (DfID) and the Deutsche Gesellschaft für Internationale Zusammenarbeit (GIZ) to parliament and related institutions is not just to ensure better accountability, but to forge a society that engages the state for better performance on its mandate.

To be effective in their role of watchdog and as participants in policy development and implementation, society acquires skills to articulate its demands on the state: donors over the years have explicitly recognised the need to strengthen the relationship among the public sector, civil society and the private sector through interface interventions – there is an explicit recognition of the equal and mutual importance of state and non-state actors for the development of an inclusive society. Knight et al (2002, pp 161-72) called this approach the 'new consensus' to governance, characterised by building an effective state and an engaged society, deepening democracy and democratic culture, and enlarging the political space for citizens. Many agencies such as UNDP, the UN Population Fund (UNFPA), UN Children's Fund (UNICEF), Oxfam, ACBF and AfDB have continued to support national consultative councils, and to strengthen dialogue between the public sector, private and civil society, with a view to improving good governance, be it corporate or otherwise, and developing a culture of social responsibility. Professionalising the voice of civil society changes the relationship between the state and civil society from one that may be characterised by patronage to one of partnership, with clear principal–agent architecture, by redefining those who are principals (the voters) and agents (the elected officials). A strong civic voice is crucial for quality service delivery (Besley and Ghatak, 2007).

African development after 2015: political economy and keeping the high road

Overall, there are good reasons to be optimistic about Africa's economic prospects. The rise of China and other emerging economies, strong commodity prices, a burgeoning African middle class and the continent's growing appeal to private investors all suggest that the strong growth performance of recent years is likely to continue. Without this growth, sustained poverty reduction would not be possible. Yet it is also clear that the nature of growth in Africa needs to become more inclusive, to provide more opportunities for a wider cross-section of society.

Structural transformation and inclusive growth

The notion of development as industrialisation or structural transformation had, until recently, been abandoned in an exchange of liberalisation and privatisation as the major growth drivers. Neoliberal economists emphasising free markets advised poor African countries to stick with their current primary agriculture and extractives industries, and to 'integrate' into the global economy in terms of comparative advantage (a buzzword for 'as they are'). GDP growth and an increase in trade volumes rose to become euphemisms for successful economic development. Unfortunately, as the recent violent revolts in North Africa have shown, increased growth and trade without social inclusion, jobs and political voice are not development.

The failure to consider structural transformation makes most comparisons of growth in Africa and East Asia spurious. It is not obvious that in the next few decades hundreds of millions of Africans will likely be lifted out of poverty, just as hundreds of millions of Asians were in the past few decades. Indeed, the widened gap between rich and poor in China and India should serve as a warning that inequality could also become a problem as Africa's progress continues, thus undermining any 'demographic' dividend (AfDB, 2014). Without better education and jobs for the young, Africa cannot hope to emulate the Asian miracle.

Despite some improvements in a few countries, the bulk of African countries are either stagnating or moving backwards when it comes to 'industrialisation' of production systems and value addition. The share of manufacturing value-added (MVA) in Africa's GDP fell from 12.8 per cent in 2000 to 10.5 per cent in 2008, while that of developing Asia rose from 22 per cent to 35 per cent over the same period (UNCTAD, 2011). The importance of manufacturing in continental exports also declined, with the share of manufacturing in Africa's total exports falling from 43 per cent in 2000 to 39 per cent in 2008. With respect to manufacturing growth, while most have stagnated, 23 African countries had negative MVA per capita growth during the period 1990-2010, and only five countries achieved an MVA per capita growth above 4 per cent (UNCTAD, 2011).

To highlight the importance of structural transformation, the AfDB recently made a similar point: 'Africa's growth tends to be concentrated on a limited range of commodities and the extractive industries', the report states (AfDB, 2012, p 13). 'These sectors are not generating the employment opportunities that would allow the majority of the population to share in the benefits. This is in marked contrast to the Asian experience, where the growth of labour-intensive manufacturing has helped lift millions of people out of poverty....' (p 13). The Bank went on to note that '[p]romoting inclusive growth means ... broadening the economic base beyond the extractive industries and a handful of primary commodities' (AfDB, 2012, p 21).

Arguably, many African countries need to use heterodox industrial policies, such as temporary trade protection, subsidised credit and publically supported R&D (research and development) with technology and innovation policies if they are ever to get their manufacturing sectors off the ground (Rodrik, 1996; Stiglitz et al, 2013). This is true for all the same reasons that it was true for the UK and other nations that have industrialised successfully (Chang, 2002). To the neoliberal ideologue of free trade and free markets, a number of the common sense and key policies are condemned as 'bad government intervention'. Bilateral and multilateral aid donors also tend to follow suit and advice against such policies, including influencing bilateral investment treaties (BITs) between rich countries and relatively poor African countries.

While critics of industrial policies are correct to cite some historical cases where industrial policies have failed in some African countries, they are often selective (Robinson, 2009) in their criticisms, ignoring those relatively successful cases (Naude, 2010), and leaving unexplained why industrial policies worked in the US, Europe and East Asia while failing so badly in Africa and elsewhere (Amsden, 2003; Naude, 2010). Industrial policy tends to be successful when those with political power who have implemented the policy have either themselves directly wished for industrialisation to succeed, or been forced to act in this way by the incentives generated by political institutions and related agency (Robinson, 2009).

It is arguable that many industrial policies in post-independence Africa failed because they were used inappropriately, with poor sequencing, and were often driven by political considerations or corruption rather than economic analyses or strict efficiency grounds (Kararach, 1997). Industrial policies were often kept for too long, and were too inwardly focused on small domestic markets, neglecting the need to develop regional and international competitiveness. In comparison, the political economies of East Asian countries included institutions that tended to enforce stricter rules for which industries got subsidies and trade protection, and which got cut off from them when they failed to meet specified performance targets (Amsden, 1992). Crucially, this history highlights *how* industrial policies should be implemented and not *if* they should be implemented at all.

African countries need the policy space to adopt industrial and structural policies to keep the momentum, encapsulated in the narrative about 'the rise of Africa'. Notwithstanding the important gains in services industries and per capita incomes, Africa is still not rising, and services alone will not create enough jobs to absorb the millions of unemployed youth in Africa. Indeed, steps must be taken to revise the many trade agreements and BITs currently being negotiated so that Africa has the freedom to adopt the strategic post-2015 policies it needs in order to make genuine progress by building on the achievements of the MDGs.

Innovation, R&D and a knowledge economy

Africa needs to critically understand the importance of innovation and R&D in the modern knowledge economy to steer its transformation and post-2015 agenda. The development of the knowledge economy and its social base depends on the relationships among government, the private sector, civil society and the wider population (Mazzucato, 2013). Due to political-economy factors, it is possible to organise the resources of a country in such a way that the incentives to increase productivity are killed, and the country's economy stagnates, and via off-course its optimal development path. Structural transformation is critical for Africa to diversify and enhance value-addition in most sectors to consolidate the growth seen in recent times and to create necessary jobs. Enhancing value-addition is knowledge-intensive, thus the importance of knowledge management to ensure growth with transformation in Africa.

Service delivery and human development

As noted elsewhere, achieving quality service delivery for the poor requires global action to complement actions by countries and local communities (Kararach, 2013). At the global level, a commitment to this aim has been reflected in wide acceptance of the human development and MDG paradigm, in which people are at the centre of development, bringing about development of the people, by the people and for the people. Essentially, the goals are essentially an agenda for targeted improvements (Vandemoortele, 2010) in the core areas of human development – to be knowledgeable, to have access to essential resources and social services, to acquire a decent standard of living and to be able to participate in the life of the community. Effective service delivery has been critical in realising the MDGs. As an example, to achieve the MDG on poverty and hunger, African governments needed to come up with holistic approaches to be incorporated into their national development plans. Specific interventions such as rolling out carefully targeted and sustainable social cash transfers, support for raising smallholder farm productivity, business development services, small grants, microfinance for poverty reduction, the promotion of livestock productivity and employment in labour-intensive sectors were thus required (UNDP, 2011). A post-2015 African development agenda must keep service delivery at its core!

Innovative financing and smart partnerships

There is evidence that Africa's development efforts – including an estimated 70 per cent of Africa's approximately 50 million micro, small and medium enterprises (MSMEs) – are constrained by poor access to the finance necessary to create a dynamic economy and delivery of essential services (Beck et al, 2011, 2014). This has led to significant under-investment, particularly in capital goods, services and R&D, with serious implications for innovation, productivity and competitiveness (Gebreeyesus, 2009; Onyeiwu, 2011; AfDB et al, 2013). Policies as well as financial resources should be targeted at easing supply-side constraints in transportation, storage, communications and the access of local entrepreneurs to open markets, particularly for agricultural produce and enhancing beneficiation in the natural resource sector. Actions must be taken to expand the domestic revenue base through effective taxation policy and ensuring its full administration is critical, as the official development assistance (ODA) shows greater volatility, and may even decline in coming years. Equally, leakages and capital 'flight' must be tackled to abate the flow of necessary resources out of the continent (Ndikumana and Boyce, 2011). Deploying the fiscal space for increased investments in human development is a strategy used effectively by countries that show significant progress on human development.

Africa needs to deal with the reality that cooperating partners have also been slow in meeting the agreed ODA target of 0.7 per cent of their GDP to support the achievement of the MDGs by 2015. As a result, strategic and long-term solutions to the challenges of access to medium- and long-term capital in Africa needs to incorporate all available instruments, including lines of credit, equity and related instruments, agency lines, risk-sharing, guarantees and technical assistance that accommodates innovative efforts and approaches.

Sustaining the momentum of the achievements beyond 2015

Africa needs to design mechanisms to foster economic transformation as well as inclusive and equitable growth as a core undertaking for the post-2015 development. It has to develop productive capacities and create decent employment and promote sustained economic growth, social development, environmental protection, democracy, good governance and the rule of law at national and continental levels. It is also critical that an enabling environment for doing business be created to spur private sector development as a major ingredient for enhancing livelihoods, and eradicating poverty and hunger. Given the ever-changing aid architecture with new donors and multilateralism, Africa needs to rethink how it strengthens international cooperation to address the persistent challenges related to sustainable development for all, in particular, in order to remove obstacles and constraints, strengthen support and meet the special needs of people living in areas affected by complex humanitarian emergencies such as South Sudan and the DRC, and in areas affected by terrorism like Somalia and Nigeria. Enhancing human security must thus be put as a major pillar of a post-2015 African development agenda.

We have also noted that service delivery must be enhanced; this means strengthening national governance mechanisms, institutions and capacity. African countries also need to develop capacities in science, technology and innovation to cut themselves a niche in an ever-changing and competitive world economy. To sustain the momentum gathered during the implementation of the MDGs, the continent needs to develop a resource framework broader than aid, which would include the mobilisation of investment (foreign and domestic), remittances and innovative financing for development, and promote 'enablers', including peace and security, and infrastructure development. Addressing issues of climate change mitigation, adaptation and financing, disaster risk reduction and the effects of climate change on rural-urban migration must also be top of the agenda, including the development of climate smart agriculture.

While fighting terrorism and fostering global security is important, it is equally critical to ensure that security considerations do not crowd out development goals as the two objectives are intertwined! Africa must be a strong partner for improved global and regional governance, coordination and partnerships including regional integration. Africa has to sustain the momentum of the MDGs by adopting creative and strategic interventions and implementation modalities. As Table 2.1 shows, African countries need to know the variations and similarities of what other developing countries want to set as their priorities in order to make strategic choices and alliances to influence their own post-2015 agenda.

Conclusions

There has been some sense of renewed optimism as a result of a decade-long higher growth trend in Africa as well as Asia and Latin America, where many countries have joined the league of 'emerging' economies. This is also on the backdrop of an apparent return to slower global growth and renewed financial uncertainties in the OECD since 2008, and the eminent shift in the relative economic dynamism of the North to the global South. Despite this achievement in growth, Africa continues to see the grossly unequal distribution of the benefits of this growth, with most countries failing to deliver their MDGs commitments. For Radice (2011), what we are seeing in Africa

Table 2.1: African versus other regional priorities for the post-2015 development agenda

	Economic sustainability	Social sustainability	Environmental sustainability	Governance and institutions
Africa	Economic growth and transformation; poverty reduction; employment, especially youth employment; food security; trade, investment and technology; income inequality	Education; health; gender equality and women's empowerment; social protection	Climate change; disaster risk reduction; desertification; biodiversity; urbanisation	Democracy and the rule of law; affective institutions; conflict resolution and citizen security; global governance
Latin America and the Caribbean	Economic growth and diversification; employment; trade, investment and technology; income inequality	Education; health; gender equality and women's empowerment; social protection	Climate change; biodiversity; disaster risk reduction; urbanisation	Democracy and the rule of law; effective institutions; armed violence and citizen security; global governance
Asia and the Pacific	Economic growth; poverty reduction; employment; food security; trade, investment and technology; income inequality	Education; health; gender equality and women's empowerment; social protection	Climate change disaster risk reduction; biodiversity; urbanisation	Democracy and the rule of law; effective institutions; citizen security; global governance
Western Asia	Inclusive growth and diversification; adequate mapping and reduction of poverty; employment, especially youth and women; trade, investment and technology; regional cooperation and integration	Education; health; gender equality and women's empowerment; social protection; social justice	Climate change; water and food security; desertification; urbanisation	Democracy and the rule of law; effective institutions; rights and freedoms; conflict resolution and self determination; global and regional governance
Europe and Central Asia	Full employment; reduction of the informal sector; income and wealth inequality; regional cooperation and economic integration	Education; health; gender equality; social protection; equitable pensions systems	Climate change; disaster risk reduction; biodiversity; food security; urbanisation	Democracy, free press and the rule of law; effective institutions; citizen security; global governance

Source: UN (2013)

and the wider global South is the death of developmentalism and the birth of 'normal' capitalism. As he put it:

> For normal capitalism is not the capitalism of the post-war "golden age", or of the developmental ambitions of the 1960s and 1970s. It is an economic system prone to destructive booms and slumps, to financial crises that wipe out household savings and government fiscal strategies alike, to polar extremes of wealth and poverty, and to a continuing reckless consumption of the global commons. It is also a political order constituted first and foremost on the defence of private property, in which the reach of democratic and electoral accountability stops at the entrance to the gated communities and tax havens of the super-rich, whether they hail from Omaha or Beijing. In the Davos World Economic Forum, the Bilderberg meetings and the Group of Thirty (set up in 1978 as a think tank of top bankers and finance experts), the eager and willing servants of the super-rich figure out how to manage the affairs of the rest of us, so as to keep the global "middle classes" onside and the rest too fascinated by the possibility of prosperity and too terrified of exclusion from it, to contemplate a real and sustainable alternative. (Radice, 2011, p 31)

We argued elsewhere (Kararach et al, 2011) that pressures for new alternatives – be it in governance, regionalism and broader economic management – are emerging in Africa, making the notion of a 'developmental' or effective state relevant. Today, African society expects that those citizens (including the diaspora) who possess the necessary knowledge will analyse and expose the workings of neocolonialism, and do even more to develop an alternative order based on equality and social justice. The attempt to have a sense of a new compact post-2015 is anchored on the reality that the present crisis in the North may not signal an end to neoliberalism, but it should certainly signal the urgency of this task and a reconfiguration of the political economy dynamics in Africa for a developmental state.

It is also generally accepted that the Millennium Declaration was meant to be a compact between the world's rich and poor countries. African nations, as much as other poor countries, committed to refocus their development efforts, while rich countries pledged to support them with finance, technology and access to their markets. But oddly, of the eight goals, only the last one dealt with 'global partnership', or what rich countries could and should do. Unfortunately, the MDGs contained no numerical target and accountability framework for financial aid or any other aspect of rich countries' assistance, in contrast to the highly specific poverty-related targets set for developing countries. The unasked question with respect to Africa must be why we need a global effort to convince African countries to do what is good for them! Given the importance of service delivery as related to issues of agency, poverty reduction and human development should be the first order of business for African governments, with or without the MDGs or any such goals.

Despite the growth-linked optimism, Africa still faces a number of development challenges including setting carbon taxes and other measures to ameliorate climate change; more work visas to allow flexible migration flows from poor countries; strict controls on arms sales to developing nations to enhance human security; reducing support for repressive regimes; and improved sharing of financial information to reduce money laundering, illicit flows and tax avoidance. Africa needs to prioritise those agendas that will build on the achievement of the MDGs, but also put it on a transformative growth trajectory to allow for greater social inclusion and sustainable development.

References

ACBF (African Capacity Building Foundation) (2002) *Helping Africa make the 21st century – A new horizon in capacity building – Consolidated strategic medium-term plan, 2002-2006*, Harare: ACBF Secretariat.

ACBF (2011) *Africa capacity indicators – Capacity development in fragile states*, Harare: ACBF.

ACBF (2012) *Africa capacity indicators – Capacity development for agricultural transformation and food security*, Harare: ACBF.

Adepoju, A. (2006) 'Leading issues in international migration in Sub-Saharan Africa', in C. Cross, D. Gelderblom, N. Roux and J. Mafukidze (eds) *Views on migration in Sub-Saharan Africa: Proceedings of an African Migration Alliance Workshop*, Pretoria: Human Sciences Research Council, pp 25-47.

AfDB (African Development Bank) (2012) *Annual development effectiveness review 2012: Growing African economies inclusively*, Tunis: AfDB.

AfDB (2013) *Annual development effectiveness review 2013: Towards sustainable growth for Africa*, Tunis: AfDB (www.afdb.org/fileadmin/uploads/afdb/Documents/Project-and-Operations/ADER-%20 Annual%20Development%20Effectiveness%20Review%202013.pdf).

AfDB (2014a) *Ending conflict and building peace in Africa: A call to action – Report of the High Level Panel on fragile states*, Tunis: AfDB.

AfDB (2014b) *Tracking progress in figures*, Tunis: AfDB (www.afdb-org.jp/file/news-and-pressrelease/Tracking_Africafs_Progress_in_Figures-3.pdf).

AfDB, OECD (Organisation for Economic Co-operation and Development), UNDP (United Nations Development Programme), UNECA (United Nations Economic Commission for Africa) (2013) *African economic outlook 2013, Structural transformation and natural resources*, Addis Ababa: UNECA.

Amsden, A.H. (1992) *Asia's next giant: South Korea and late industrialization*, Oxford: Oxford University Press.

Amsden, A.H. (2003) *The rise of 'the rest': Challenges to the West from late-industrializing economies*, New York: Oxford University Press.

Andriamihaja, N., Cinyabuguma, M. and Devarajan, S. (2012) *Avoiding the fragility trap in Africa*, Policy Research Working Paper No. 5884. World Bank, Washington, D.C.

Beck, T., Lin, C. and Ma, Y. (2014) 'Why do firms evade taxes? The role of information sharing and financial sector outreach', *Journal of Finance*, vol 69, no 2 (April), pp 763-817.

Beck, T., Maimbo, S.M., Faye, I. and Triki, T. (2011) *Financing Africa: Through the crisis and beyond*, Washington, DC: The World Bank.

Besley, T. and Ghatak, M. (2007) 'Reforming public service delivery', *Journal of African Economies*, vol 16, AERC Supplement 1.

Bold, T., Svensson, J., Gauthier, B., Mæstad, O. and Wane, W. (2011) *Service delivery indicators: Pilot in education and health care in Africa*, CMI Report, no 8. Bergen: Chr. Michelsen Institute.

Bond, P. (2011) *Politics of climate justice: Paralysis above, movement below*, Pietermaritzburg, South Africa: University of KwaZulu-Natal Press.

Chang, H. (2002) 'Breaking the mould. An institutionalist political economy alternative to the neo-liberal theory of the market and the state', *Cambridge Journal of Economics*, vol 26, no 5, pp 539-59.

CIA World Factbook (2014) (www.cia.gov/library/publications/the-world-factbook/rankorder/2091rank.html).

D'Alessandro-Scarpari, C., Hanson, K. and Kararach, G. (2016) 'Peri-urban agriculture in southern Africa: miracle or mirage?', *African Geographical Review* (forthcoming).

Devarajan, S. and Fengler, W. (2012) 'Is Africa's recent growth sustainable?', Mimeo, Institut français des relations internationals (IFRI).

Domar, E. (1957) *Essays in the theory of economic growth*, New York: Oxford University Press.

Easterly, W. and Levine, R. (1997) 'Africa's growth tragedy: policies and ethnic divisions', *Quarterly Journal of Economics*, vol 112.

Fahim, K. (2011) 'Slap to a man's pride set off tumult in Tunisia', *New York Times*, 21 January (www.nytimes.com/2011/01/22/world/africa/22sidi.html?pagewanted=all).

Guardian, The (2011) 'Egyptian protesters break into Israeli embassy in Cairo', 10 September (www.theguardian.com/world/2011/sep/10/egyptian-protesters-israeli-embassy-cairo).

Gebreeyesus, M. (2009) *Innovation and microenterprises growth in Ethiopia*, UNU-WIDER Research Paper No 2009/51, Helsinki: United Nations University-World Institute for Development Economics Research.

Government of Ethiopia (2012) *Ethiopia MDGs report 2012: Assessing progress towards the Millennium Development Goals*, Addis Ababa: Ministry of Finance and Economic Development (MOFED).

Guvheya, G. and Léautier, F. (2010) *Using information communication technology (ICT) to enhance socio-economic development – Implications for capacity development in Africa*, ACBF Working Paper 20, Harare: ACBF.

Harrod, R.F. (1939) 'An essay in dynamic theory', *Economic Journal*.

Hyden, G. (2014) 'The economy of affection in Tanzania – Important as ever', Nordic Africa Institute Forum, 18 June (http://naiforum.org/2014/06/the-economy-of-affection-in-tanzania).

Jerven, M. (2013) *Poor numbers: How we are misled by African development statistics and what to do about it*, Ithaca, NY: Cornell University Press.

Jomo, K.S. and Chowdhury, A. (eds) (2012) *Is good governance good for development?*, London and New York: United Nations and Bloomsbury Academic.

Kararach, G. (1997) 'Ideology of development and sector-led growth in Tanzania: An essay in the reconstruction of economic theory', PhD thesis, University of Leeds.

Kararach, G. (2011) *Macroeconomic policy and the political limits of reform programmes in developing countries*, Nairobi: African Research and Resource Forum.

Kararach, G. (2012) 'Effective states and capacity development for financial governance in Africa: case and agenda for operationalization', *Capacity Focus*, vol 2, no 1.

Kararach, G. (2013) 'Service oriented government: debating the developmental state and service delivery in Africa: are capacity indicators important?', in A. Rosenbaum and W. Liqun (eds) *Studies in administrative reform: Building service-oriented government and performance evaluation systems*, Beijing: Chinese Academy of Governance Press, pp 25-60.

Kararach, G. (2014) *Development policy in Africa: Mastering the future?*, Basingstoke: Palgrave Macmillan.

Kararach, G., Hanson, K. and Léautier, F. (2011) 'Regional integration policies to support job creation for Africa's burgeoning youth population', *World Journal of Entrepreurship, Management and Sustainable Development*, vol 7, no 2/3/4, pp 177-215.

Kiggundu, M.N. (1997) *Retrenchment programs in Sub-Saharan Africa: Lessons for demobilization*, Bonn: Bonn International Center for Conversion, July.

Knight, B., Chigudu, H. and Tandon, R. (2002) *Reviving democracy: Citizens at the heart of governance*, London: Earthscan.

Léautier, F. (2006) 'Understanding cities in a globalizing world', in F. Léautier (ed) *Cities in a globalizing world: Governance, performance and sustainability*, Washington, DC: The World Bank, pp 1-8.

Léautier, F. (2009) 'Leadership in a globalized world: complexity, dynamics and risk', Lecture PPT Notes, The Fezembat Group, 26 February.

Makoba, J.W. (2011) *Rethinking development strategies in Africa – The triple partnership as an alternative approach – The case of Uganda*, Oxford: Peter Lang.

Mazzucato, M. (2013) *The entrepreneurial state: Debunking public vs private sector myths*, New York: Anthem Press.

Meade, J.E. (1961) *A neo-classical theory of economic growth*, New York: Oxford University Press.

Mkandawire, T. (2001) 'Thinking about developmental states in Africa', *Cambridge Journal of Economics*, vol 25, no 3, pp 289-313.

Mo Ibrahim Foundation (2012) *2012 index of African governance* (http://ayyaantuu.com/wp-content/uploads/2012/10/2012-IIAG-summary-report.pdf).

Nabli, M.K. and Ben Hammouda, H. (2014) 'The political economy of the new Arab awakening', in C. Monga and J. Yifu Lin (eds) *The Oxford handbook of Africa and economics: Context and concepts*, Oxford: Oxford University Press, pp 700-720.

Naude, W. (2010) *Industrial policy: Old and new issues*, UNU-WIDER Working Paper No 2010/106, Helsinki: United Nations University-World Institute for Development Economics Research.

Ncube, M. and Shimeles, A. (2012) *The making of the middle class in Africa*, AfDB Research Department Working Paper, Tunis: African Development Bank.

Ndikumana, L. and Boyce, J.K. (2011) *Africa's odious debt: How foreign loans and capital flight bled a continent*, London: Zed Books.

Nhamo, G. (2011) 'REDD(+) and the global climate negotiating regimes: challenges and opportunities for Africa', *South African Journal of International Affairs*, vol 18, no 3.

Onyeiwu, S. (2011) *Does the lack of innovation and absorptive capacity retard economic growth in Africa?*, UNU-WIDER Working Paper No 2011/19, Helsinki: United Nations University-World Institute for Development Economics Research.

Owusu, F. (2012) 'Organizational culture and public sector reforms in a post-Washington consensus era: lessons from Ghana's good reformers', *Progress in Development Studies*, vol 12, nos 2-3, pp 135-51.

Radice, H. (2011) 'The crisis and the global south: from development to capitalism', *Economic and Political Weekly*, vol 46, no 48, pp 27-31.

Robinson, J. (2009) 'Industrial policy and development: a political economy perspective', Paper prepared for the 2009 World Bank Annual Bank Conference on Development Economics (ABCDE) Conference in Seoul, 22-24 June.

Rodrik, D. (1996) 'Understanding economic policy reform', *Journal of Economic Literature*, vol 34, no 1, p 941.

Sachs, J. and Warner, A.M. (1997) 'Source of slow growth in African economies', *Journal of African Economies*, vol 6, no 3.

Sen, A. (1990) *Development as freedom*. Oxford: Oxford University Press.

Sharabi, H. (1988) *A theory of distorted change in Arab society*, New York: Oxford University Press.

Stiglitz, J.E., Lin, J.Y., Patel, E. and Esteban, J. (2013) *The industrial policy revolution II: Africa in the twenty-first century*, Basingstoke: Palgrave Macmillan.

Teravaninthorn, S. and Raballand, G. (2009) *Transport prices and costs in Africa: A review of the international corridors*, Washington, DC: The World Bank.

TI (Transparency International) (2013) *Corruption Perception Index*, Berlin: TI.

UN (United Nations) (2013) *A regional perspective on the post-2015 United Nations development agenda*, New York: UN.

UNCTAD (United Nations Conference on Trade and Development) (2003) *World investment report 2003: FDI policies for development: National and international perspectives*, Geneva: UNCTAD (http://unctad.org/en/docs/wir2003light_en.pdf).

UNCTAD (2011) *Economic development Africa report 2011: Fostering industrial development in Africa in the new global environment*, Geneva: UNCTAD (http://unctad.org/en/docs/aldcafrica2011_en.pdf).

UNCTAD (2014) *World investment report 2014: Investing in the SDGs – An action plan*, Geneva: UNCTAD (http://unctad.org/en/PublicationsLibrary/wir2014_en.pdf).

UNDESA (United Nations Department of Economic and Social Affairs) (2003) *Handbook of statistical organization*, New York: UN.

UNDESA (2014) *World economic situations and prospects*, New York: UN.

UNDP (United Nations Development Programme) (2010) *2010/2011 human development report – Sustainability and equity: A better future for all*, New York: UN.

UNDP (2011) *Zambia human development report 2011: Service delivery for sustainable human development*, Lusaka: UNDP.

UNDP (2013) *2013 human development report – The rise of the south: Human progress in a diverse world*, New York: UNDP.

UNECA (United Nations Economic Commission for Africa) (1991) *Ethics and accountability in African public services*, Addis Ababa: UNECA.

UNECA (2012) *Assessing progress in Africa toward the Millennium Development Goals*, MDG report 2012, Addis Ababa: UNECA.

UNECA (2014) *Economic report on Africa 2014 – Dynamic industrial policy in Africa: Innovative institutions, effective processes and flexible mechanisms*, Addis Ababa: UNECA.

UNTT (United Nations System Task Team) (2012) *Realizing the future we want for all. Report to the Secretary-General*, New York: UNTT.

Vandemoortele, J. (2010) *Changing the discourse of MDGs by changing the discourse*, Real Instituto Elcano, No 132.

Wangwe, S. (1993) 'Small and micro enterprise promotion and technology policy implications', in A.H.J. Helmsing and T. Kolste (ed) *Small enterprises and changing policies*, London: Intermediate Technology Publications.

World Bank, The (2005) *Building effective states and engaged societies*, Report of the World Bank Task Force on Capacity Development, Washington, DC: The World Bank.

World Bank, The (2011) *Africa's Pulse: An analysis of issues shaping Africa's economic future*, vol 4, September.

World Bank, The (2012a) *Africa's Pulse: An analysis of issues shaping Africa's economic future*, vol 6, October.

World Bank, The (2012b) *Global monitoring report 2012: Food prices, nutrition, and the Millennium Development Goals*, Washington, DC: The World Bank.

World Bank, The (2013) *Doing business report 2013*, Washington, DC: The World Bank.

World Bank, The (2014) *Africa's Pulse: An analysis of issues shaping Africa's economic future*, vol 10, October (www-wds.worldbank.org/external/default/WDSContentServer/WDSP/IB/2014/10/23/000470435_20141023112521/Rendered/PDF/912070REVISED00ct20140vol100v120web.pdf).

THREE

Public diplomacy for developmental states: implementing the African Mining Vision

Timothy M. Shaw and Leah McMillan Polonenko

Introduction

The second decade of the 21st century may be that of Africa's renaissance. As Africa's economic agencies, the United Nations Economic Commission for Africa (UNECA) along with the African Development Bank (AfDB) and the African Union (AU) have come to advocate the adoption of policies leading towards developmental states, so the continent has articulated an African Mining Vision (AMV; see www.africaminingvision.org) (AMV, 2009, 2011a, 2011b) by contrast to other possible strategies for its natural resource governance (Florini and Dubash, 2011) from assorted global developmental, environmental, financial and industrial agencies.

This chapter begins to identify the background to this quite remarkable shift, analysing the prospects for its advocacy and adoption by emerging non-state as well as state actors by the end of this decade, both on and off the continent. In so doing, we relate to the emerging 'agency' versus 'dependency' debate (Brown, 2012; Brown and Harman, 2013; Harman and Brown, 2013; Lorenz and Rempe, 2013) as a correlate of the continent's recent unprecedented growth. This sets it apart from recent economic difficulties and setbacks in much of the established North of the Organisation for Economic Co-operation and Development (OECD), especially the Eurozone. In turn, this relates to and resonates with the latest UN Development Programme (UNDP) human development report for 2013 that articulates the rise of the global South, including the economic growth of the African countries South Africa, Ghana, Rwanda and Mauritius (UNDP, 2013).

This chapter juxtaposes two dominant interrelated strands in the political economy of today's continent: the impact of BRICS,[1] especially China (Xing, 2013), and the return of a commodities boom, this time with a focus on energy and minerals, but in future, on food, land and water. Indeed, while these commodities have experienced a downturn over the last decade, the presented expected boom will occur over the coming decades. In turn, it notes the difficulties of the Euro's PIIGS (Portugal, Italy, Ireland, Greece and Spain),[2] and the declining salience of the European Union (EU) symbolised by the stalling of the Economic Partnership Agreement (EPA) project. A wide variety of novel alternative forms of finance are appearing from new donors and foundations, sovereign wealth funds, faith-based organisations (FBOs) and global taxes for global public goods/partnerships. For example, we explore alternative forms of taxation, including 'the Carbon Tax, Aviation Tax, Currency Transaction Tax (CTT) or Tobin Tax, World Trade Tax, International Arms Trade Tax' (Accuosto and Johnson, 2004, p 23) as alternative mechanisms for taxation that give financing for global public partnerships.

User fees can also be added as an alternative form of financing. In fact, 'organizations like the ITU [International Telecommunication Union] and UNESCO [United Nations Education, Science, and Cultural Organization] have at different moments considered the possibility that a percentage of the resources generated by international telecommunications be used to promote the development of more equitable communications systems' (Accuosto and Johnson, 2004, p 24). The use of special drawing rights (SDRs) (an exchange of one's rights for currencies held by the International Monetary Fund [IMF]) is another example of alternative financing (Lamb, 2002). Lamb suggests leveraging development assistance for governments to properly fund projects oriented towards global development initiatives. He argues that the more affluent taxpayers from the global North could be inclined to add to development funding if improved financing for initiatives was seen to overcome global priorities.

The majority of these new forms of financing are still channelled through African governments. For example, the reliance on official development assistance (ODA) or taxes of any kind is still assumed at state level. Thus, while the forms of financing might be new, the local financiers are not. These alternative forms still rely on the predictability, transparency and accountability of governments to use this financing to improve the global issues identified, including the HIV/AIDS crisis, climate change and education. The need for improved governance at government level is still pressing.

African development post-2015

Half of the dozen fastest growing countries identified in *The Economist*'s 'World in 2010' were African (*The Economist*, 2010a,b; 2011), from Ghana, the best-case example of democratic development, to Angola, the new 'oil giant'. However, this does not take into account that these economic improvements are often not realised by local citizens within the countries; thus, these measures of economic growth do not account for local realities. The mining sector in particular has been criticised for not providing socioeconomic benefits to the surrounding community (Westphalen, 2012).

And the unexpected conclusion of the commodities boom mid-decade with myriad difficulties in the BRICS and other 'emerging markets' has forced Africa to rethink its growth through its exports strategy, especially imminent 'new' oil and gas producers like Ghana, Mozambique and Uganda, and even South Sudan. How should such countries aspire to becoming 'developmental' rather than 'fragile' states post-2015 as commodity (especially oil) prices decline along with some currencies, such as South Africa's rand? But as already indicated, the range of new actors engaged with the continent gives Africa unheard-of choices regarding sources of finance, technology, partnerships and so on (Shaw, 2015a, 2015b).

It has been argued that such growth and associated changes in the nature of 'governance' inside the continent may expand the possibility and reach of 'agency' of African countries and communities (Brown, 2012; Brown and Harman, 2013; Lorenz and Rempe, 2013): the ability of a range of African state and non-state actors to have an impact on decisions and directions at a variety of levels can be seen by expanding their room for manoeuvre (Africa Progress Panel, 2012). However, the extent to which African non-state actors have real agency is debatable. Particularly in mining communities, the ability for non-state actors to possess real agency is rare.

This unanticipated possibility is not just a function of continuing growth courtesy of the BRICS, especially China (Xing, 2013). It also results from global rebalancing as the initial trans-Atlantic crisis at the end of the first decade spills over into the PIIGS of the Eurozone (Overbeek and Apeldoorn, 2012) with ODA from the OECD countries becoming less central and salient to African states (Sumner and Mallett, 2012; vom Hau et al, 2012). It may also incorporate analytic shifts that transcend such perspectives in other regions, especially in the ebullient global South (Hanson et al, 2012; UNDP, 2013). In short, established assumptions about inherited 'dependency' on the supposedly ubiquitous external needs to be reconsidered, especially if the latter now includes burgeoning transnational diasporas (Ratha et al, 2011; The World Bank, 2011b). The African diaspora's financial contributions are considerable – between 2008 and 2009, The World Bank documents that US$22 billion remittances were sent to Sub-Saharan Africa per annum (The World Bank, 2014). Recent initiatives like the African Diaspora Program of The World Bank are attempting to entice African diasporas to contribute in terms of skills and infrastructure to their native African state (The World Bank, 2011a, 2011b). However, the African brain drain is real and has been well documented. For example, more African-trained medical graduates born or trained in Sub-Saharan Africa work in the US than in 'Ethiopia, Ghana, Liberia, Tanzania, Uganda, Zambia, and Zimbabwe combined' (Jack, 2013).

A rather optimistic projection reflects the 2011 declaration from the UNECA (2011, pp 7-9, 95-111) that the continent should adopt a 'developmental state' strategy, which has led to some significant state and non-state expressions of agency that would have been unimaginable in previous 'neoliberal' decades. Practically, non-state actors should create partnerships with governments and business actors to ensure that they have agency at all levels of decision-making processes. Given the shift towards global governance forms of power, it is imperative that non-state actors pursue alternative forms of representation to maintain agency. These actors include human rights organisations, FBOs, non-governmental organisations (NGOs) and advocacy groups.

As the UNECA declaration (2011, p 2) further indicates, '... global developments have significant implications for African countries, though the direction and magnitude of impact naturally vary among countries. On the whole, African economies have recovered from the crisis better than expected', perhaps owing to significant economic growth, particularly with heightened forms of South-South cooperation (SSC) across the continent (Koehane, 1984; Kliman and Fontaine, 2012). For example, the growing relations between India and Africa, and China and Africa, continue to improve economic performance, even in the wake of the financial crisis and its immediate aftermath. This unanticipated, unprecedented courageous departure from the discredited and disappearing 'Washington Consensus' has since been followed up by a 2012 edition (UNECA, 2012) entitled *Unleashing Africa's potential as a pole of global growth*, and parallel reports from UNDP (2012) (the first human development report for the continent) and from the African Development Bank (AfDB) et al (2012). Apart from economic growth, Africa's resurgence and agency can be noted through its quick pace of industrialisation, the scale of growth of employment, infrastructural development and the inclusion of the local. For example, the discovery of offshore mining in Ghana in 2007 has propelled the country into growth accounted for not only in economic terms, but also in terms of infrastructural growth, growth of its tourism sector and improved employment opportunities.

As the contributions to two imminent, innovative volumes suggest (Brown and Harman, 2013; Lorenz and Rempe, 2013), agency around regional development in Sub-Saharan Africa constitutes a dramatic divergence from established dependency assumptions and perspectives (Africa Progress Panel, 2012; Hanson et al, 2012; Shaw, 2012): to policy-maker from policy-taker. The movement towards regional agency has been particularly relevant given the increased focus on SSC. As African countries continue to experience difficulties in terms of monocropping and smaller economies, regionalism has provided an alternative form of economic growth and agency throughout the globe. Given the importance of regionalism in the wake of globalisation (Pieterse and Rehbein, 2009), heightened regions, including the East African Community (EAC), Common Market for Eastern and Southern Africa (COMESA), South African Development Community (SADC) and Economic Community of West African States (ECOWAS) has only improved Africa's agency globally.

The African Mining Vision as African agency?

The most dramatic example of this transformation in the policy landscape to date is the articulation of an AMV at the turn of the decade, itself a synthesis of the ongoing redefinition of energy and resource governance with the African developmental state. The AMV has been reformulated in a variety of regions and sectors by Florini and Dubash (2011), Goldthau and Witte (2010), Kuzemko et al (2012), building on common notions of transnational private governance. And it has been advocated by the continent's inter-state agencies, reflecting its newfound resilience, particularly given its heightened agency and economic growth (Shaw, 2012). But it faces serious competition from several other alternatives, from regional to global, uni- to multisectoral, and uni- to multistakeholder.

The AMV was preceded at the start of the century by the Intergovernmental Forum on Mining (IFM) to be joined by the Natural Resource Charter (NRC)[3] in terms of resource governance, but challenged by the Extractive Industries Transparency Initiative (EITI; see www.eiti.org) in terms of financial arrangements, for example, by ensuring that governments pay their dues as set out in EITI guidelines. Meanwhile, a US federal agency – the US Securities and Exchange Commission (SEC) – is imposing new norms and public rankings of corporate compliance around conflict metals out of the Congo in association with a regional African interstate institution – the International Conference on the Great Lakes Region (ICGLR) – orchestrating high-tech multinational corporations (MNCs) and a range of local to global, minor to major NGOs. Together, the two organisations have been working towards imposing Dodd Franks Section 1502,[4] ensuring that the supply chain of all mining companies is documented. To this end, the ICGLR and SEC are working together with numerous NGOs and business actors to improve the monitoring of mining. Moreover, the corporate sector's own agency International Council on Mining and Minerals (ICMM), inter-state northern OECD and non-state global World Economic Forum (WEF) have generated their own rules for natural resource governance (NRG) entitled 'Resource endowment initiative', 'Due diligence guidance for responsive supply chain of minerals from conflict-affected and high risk areas' and 'Vision on responsible mineral development', respectively.

The AMV was developed towards the end of the first decade of the present century to advocate sustainable development towards industrialisation. It is based on a comprehensive and informed report by an International Study Group entitled *Minerals and Africa's development* (AWV, 2011a), which attempted to lay out the several steps and challenges ahead. Building on the Lagos Plan of Action,[5] and seeking to achieve MDGs, it focused on a mix of established and novel issues: environment, artisanal and small-scale mining), corporate social responsibility (CSR), maximisation and management of revenues and sustainability via backwards and forwards linkages to maximise benefits, and recognising the imperatives of governance and regional dimensions.

This chapter situates the development of such a vision in terms of the continent's regional development that is related to the emergence of varieties of capitalism – from North Atlantic and Japanese to Brazilian, Chinese, Indian and South African (Goldstein, 2007). But to situate the articulation of and prospects for the AMV, we also explore a couple of the primary features of the AMV 2011 report: the proliferation of varieties of finance and the range of new regionalisms.

However, by way of caution or proportion, the late-2012 Chatham House report, *Resources futures* (Lee et al, 2012), only recognises one African country, Nigeria, in its proposed set of R30 (Resource Thirty).[6] However, Nigeria's advocacy of 'collaborative governance' is otherwise persuasive.

The political economy of natural resources is increasingly shaped by the large, structural shifts under way in the world. The world must now contend, not just with growing environmental threats such as climate change and water scarcities, but also with the shift in consumer power from West to East, the concentration of resource ownership, and the rise of state capitalism. All these moving pieces are changing the rules of the resources game (Lee et al, 2012, p 8). For example, state capitalism in Tanzania can be seen through the country's energy supplier. TANESCO, the Tanzania Electric Supply Company, is the largest energy supplier in the country. It is also government-owned. The ownership of this resource by the state illustrates a turn towards state ownership of resources – a push away from the neoliberal privatisation model.

Varieties of 'transnational' governance

In a post-bipolar era, the mix of fragile/failed states (ACBF, 2011; Brock et al, 2012), proliferating 'global' issues and pressures for democratisation/accountability/sustainability have generated some innovative forms of 'transnational' (Brown, 2011) or 'private' (Dingwerth, 2008) governance around the continent, symbolised by the early Ottawa and Kimberley Processes (KP),[7] now augmented by the Forest Stewardship Council/Marine Stewardship Council (FCS/MCS) (for the last decade, part of the expanding ISEAL Alliance (www.isealalliance.org)[8] and the UN Collaborative Programme on Reducing Emissions from Deforestation and Forest Degradation in Developing Countries (UN-REDD).[9] These may not yet be authoritative and their scope still fails to reach continuing scourges like small arms and light weapons, despite progress towards an Arms Trade Treaty, but they are transforming the governance landscape. And they constitute the backdrop to the AMV and parallel initiatives around NRG in Africa and elsewhere, with the KP[10] being the organic predecessor of SEC rules in response to Dodd-Frank.

Recent comprehensive innovations for decreasing deforestation and improving environmental sustainability include the industry-supported FCS and the parallel MCS, foundation stones for the burgeoning ISEAL Alliance. But for Africa, aside from the AMV, the four compelling schemes are:

i.   the pioneering, decade-old Intergovernmental Forum on Mining, Minerals, Metals, and Sustainable Development,[11] which has now articulated a Mining Policy Framework (MPF) (see www. globaldialogue.info).

ii. the International Financial Institution (IFI)-endorsed NRC (see www.naturalresourcecharter.org) – analysts and others discussing desiderata for the sector;

iii. the G8-supported multi-stakeholder EITI (see www.eiti.org), the latter being particularly timely given the dangers of the 'resource curse' and windfall profits around BRICS, if not BRICS' demand for energy and minerals; and

iv. the latest, which is both unilateral and regional with global reach, US derived for the Great Lakes Region on 'conflict minerals': Dodd-Frank instructed SEC Section 1502 on the 3Ts (tin, tantalum and tungsten) and gold from Congo with inter-state ICGLR and local to global NGOs including Partnership Africa Canada in Ottawa and Global Witness as well as the Enough Project (see www.enoughproject.org).

Each of these initiatives calls for transparency from mining companies and offering options for consumers to educate themselves on companies that abide by sustainable and ethical principles. For example, the Partnership Africa Canada Diamond Watchlist advises consumers which companies are still on the watchlist for including conflict minerals in part of their supply chain. Advocacy organisations can improve their functionality through these initiatives by having reliable sources for determining which companies need to be persuaded, and by providing opportunities for businesses to sign up for standards to improve their practices.

Its rules, defined in late 2012, stretch to over 350 pages with over 900 footnotes for implementation in 2013 with reporting by MNCs on any use of conflict metals by May (US SEC, 2014).[12]

Each of these five transnational NRG networks – AMV, EITI, IGF, NRC and SEC – entails different assumptions, emphases and preferences. Is an agreeable/productive/sustainable division of labour among them desirable, let alone possible? In terms of geographic scope, SEC is the most regional and narrowest in target, AMV, the most continental, and the NRC, the most global. In terms of types of actors, the Intergovernmental Forum is the most state-centric as well as green, followed by AMV, which is driven by intergovernmental agencies including some established OECD donors, whereas SEC presents challenges for MNCs. In terms of sectoral focus, the SEC is focused on selected high-tech minerals, EITI is preoccupied by finance (Campbell, 2013), with the NRC being animated by academics mainly from the global North (its Technical Advisory Group includes Paul Collier, Peter Eigen, Michael Spence and Jose Ocampo), constituting something of an 'epistemic community'. They have identified a dozen precepts for good NRG that their board, led by the likes of Zedillo and Ibrahim, seek to effect. In relation to corruption, the EITI is hegemonic. EITI and the NRC are the most endorsed by OECD donors; the AMV least so, with some G20 mainly mining countries most supportive of the Intergovernmental Forum; and the SEC is US-centric, with implications for major IT corporations in Asia and elsewhere. Twenty-two of the 37 countries in EITI are African, just under half (10) being compliant, the rest candidates seeking validation; one (Madagascar) has been suspended. EITI is an extensive multistakeholder network of companies, civil societies (for example, Global Witness, Open Society/Publish What You Pay, Oxfam, Revenue Watch, Transparency International [TI]), partners (mainly OECD donors) and investors such as finance companies, pensions funds and sovereign wealth funds.

This fivesome indicates the heterogeneous and dynamic range of governance arrangements, but together such regional initiatives indicate enhanced prospects for African agency in the new decade, more so in some fora than others. The KP and SEC processes are indicative of how some agencies just keep on going: Partnership Africa Canada and Global Witness were among the initiators of the campaign against blood diamonds; they are now integral to the ICGLR-SEC nexus.

Varieties of African agency

We base this analysis on five major developments in agency, especially at the regional level, that suggest above all that the character of regional development is very much in flux on the continent (Shaw, 2012). First, African regions have generated a series of innovations, from the Maputo Corridor[13] to trans-frontier peace parks or the Tripartite Free Trade Agreement (T-FTA)[14] between the SADC, EAC (Hansohm, 2013) and COMESA (Hartzenberg, 2012). Second, as suggested in (i) above, African stakeholders have been central to a set of innovations in transnational governance however problematic, from the KP to the EITI. In both these initiatives, African businesses and NGOs were actively involved in supplying information to ensure these processes could function. In the case of the KP in particular, African governments played host to the initiative, enabling its inception in 2000 in southern Africa. South Africa, Botswana, the Democratic Republic of Congo (DRC) and Namibia have all acted as chairs for the initiative. Third, South Africa has been elevated and recognised as the fifth member of BRICS. This raises questions about the emphasis or priority of the second largest economy on the continent and its leadership aspirations on the regional, continental and/or global level (Jordaan, 2003; Flemes, 2010; Nel and Nolte, 2010; Nel et al, 2012). South Africa is perceived globally as being a strong economy and trade partner, particularly with its key role in BRICS. It was asked to join BRICS in 2010, a noteworthy accomplishment recognising its reputation as a strong economy. According to President Zuma, South Africa is not just representing its own country on the regional bloc, but the interests of the entire continent (Besada et al, 2013).

Fourth, if we expand our purview from the continent itself to its diasporas concentrated in Europe and North America, agency through remittances is likely to become even more influential in the years ahead (Ratha et al, 2011; AU, nd). The UN Conference on Trade and Development (UNCTAD) assesses that 33 African countries benefit annually from remittances sent from the African diaspora, which is not surprising given 3 per cent of Africa's population lives outside the continent. Remittances have grown in importance to the continent and have 'more than quadrupled since 1990, reaching US$40 billion in 2010. This represents about three per cent of Africa's total GDP' (AfDB, 2013, p 1).

And finally, albeit controversially, if we go beyond the 'formal and legal' to 'gangs and guns' we can discover novel forms of African agency particularly in de facto regional conflict zones like the Great Lakes, the Horn of Africa and the Sahel, and in the energy and minerals sectors (Besada, 2010; Bagayoko, 2012; Klare, 2012; Nathan, 2012). In short, we need not only to appreciate and to include such agency; we need to redefine it to reflect Africa in the new millennium as a burgeoning part of the global South (UNECA, 2011, 2012; UNDP, 2013).

In a series of recent reports, the Centre for Global Development (CGD) in Washington, DC now suggests that 17 African countries are 'leading the way' (Radelet, 2010); McKinsey & Company laud the growth of the African lions (McKinsey & Company, 2010); and the Boston Consulting Group (BCG) (2010) has identified 40 African corporations as global 'challengers' based on diversification of corporations and their reach across the continent.

In addition to dynamic and heterogeneous varieties of private/ transnational governance (see (ii) above), Africa also needs to advance network diplomacy (that is, diplomacy between global networks) rather than more traditional forms of diplomacy, involving civil society and private companies as well as states and intergovernmental agencies (Heine, 2006), using new technologies/media, including social media. The AMV is one variety focused on states and donors, but the Intergovernmental Forum on Mining, Minerals, Metals and Sustainable Development is more global than continental, the NRC more academic in orientation and EITI the most extensive multistakeholder.

The take-up of the AMV from mining ministries and African institutions seems limited to date: minimal response from either the mining industry or civil society on or off the continent, potentially because the AMV continues to be viewed as a state-centric initiative, stemming from the pan-African roots of the African Union (AU). And forms of evaluation to plot the progress of the AMV seem lacking thus far: a variety of heterogeneous diplomacies may be required to advance let alone sustain NRG, such as the creation of epistemic communities and emerging networks between corporations and non-state actors. But the Intergovernmental Forum did consider a comparative analysis of its established MPF and the AMV in late 2012.

As the early bird of African mining regulations, the Intergovernmental Forum, which started life as a Global Dialogue on Mining, Metals and Sustainable Development, just marked its first decade. It resulted from a Canadian and South African initiative arising from the Johannesburg summit on sustainable development in 2002, although it was only formally instituted in 2005: a partnership within the UN Commission on Sustainable Development (UNCSD). It is more focused on sustainable development, and its membership of 43 states is less exclusively African than the AMV: less than 50 per cent. It tracks the UNCSD timetable and treats a range of industry, social, environmental and related issues such as communities and small-scale mining, EITI and KP. Meanwhile, an unlikely source of enlightened regulations – the US SEC – has enacted the Dodd-Frank Megabill including Section 1502 on conflict minerals involving ranking the supply-chains of MNCs who consume them: this empowers the ICGLR and subsequent NGOs, along with the OECD.

This chapter has four interrelated parts that stake out paths to a brighter future for the continent centred on its regional innovations, including its myriad diasporas. First, the focus of both an imminent collection (Lorenz and Rempe, 2013), Africa has generated an innovative range of 'new regionalisms' involving a range of non-state actors: from the Maputo Corridor and Kgalagadi trans-frontier peace park to the Nile Basin Initiative/Dialogue; and from the ICGLR to corporate supply chains, and now onto the grand scheme for the T-FTA (Hartzenberg, 2012). Alex Warleigh-Lack et al (2011) have begun to recognise the relevance of such new regional relationships for comparative studies of the EU, especially as it confronts its own financial crisis around the Euro (Acharya, 2012; Fioramonti, 2012). While the success of these initiatives is yet to be determined, their existence is one step further towards sound regional governance of the mining sector. Moreover, their existence demonstrates that African regions are recognising the necessity for creating their own initiatives for improving transparency and accountability in the natural resource sector.

Second, there is growing articulation in the present century of 'new multilateralisms' or 'transnational governance' with African dimensions – African agency. These are dynamic and span several emerging sectors, including the International Campaign to Ban Landmines with the Ottawa Process, the KP, and Partnership Africa Canada. Global Witness, the Diamond Development Initiative, and the EITI, FSC and MSC are all processes that have created treaties and regulations in their respective areas of expertise (for example, marine regulations for the MSC) (Cadman, 2011; Gale and Haward, 2011).

In terms of human security, regulators including include the International Action Network on Small Arms and the Arms Trade Treaty,[15] debated inconclusively in mid-2012 in New York, yet coalitions over small arms and light weapons and children and women's security are stalled due to US vetoes. However, the focus of this chapter, developing out of such learning experiences, is that the continent is defining its own AMV by contrast to the Paul Collier/ World Bank NRC The ICGLR nexus, including Global Witness and Partnership Africa Canada, enables it to put its own spin on the SEC Section 1502 rules. Together, these initiatives have given more avenues for corporations to improve transparency, and opportunities for advocacy by NGOs have also expanded, as there is more evidence of which corporations do, and which do not, abide by standards set.

Third, post-Washington Consensus, ODA from the OECD is of declining importance or attraction (vom Hau et al, 2012; Sumner and Mallett, 2013). Rather, a range of 'innovative sources of finance' are being identified, encouraged by the 'Leading Group',[16] as indicated in the next section: a global solidarity fund, currency transaction tax, carbon taxes/trading, climate change funds, controls on money laundering and remittance taxes, as well as emerging donors like the BRICS and Gulf States (Mawdsley, 2012; Besada and Kindornay, 2013; Gray and Murphy, 2013), some with Sovereign Wealth Funds; FBOs; and new private foundations such as The Bill & Melinda Gates Foundation, The Clinton Foundation and The Mo Ibrahim Foundation, leading to the African Green Revolution Forum and the Global Alliance for Vaccines and Immunisation (GAVI). These initiatives have been particularly useful for providing the necessary awareness and funding for environmental sustainability and the provision of medical vaccinations, and are particularly vital in Africa, where diseases including malaria, HIV/AIDS, guinea worm and tuberculosis continue to take lives each year (for example, according to the WHO, just under 500,000 children under five years old died of malaria in 2012; WHO, 2013).

And finally, what are the implications of this trio of novel directions and players – African agency – for our analyses and policies, state and non-state? Who are the 'drivers' or agents, innovators and animators in the AMV? What is the balance between state and capital, especially within state-owned enterprises (SOEs) and between indigenous and international capital? In short, how can regional cooperation be maximised and regional conflict minimised?

Informed by contemporary international relations (Dunn and Shaw, 2001; Cornelissen et al, 2012), and development studies perspectives in particular, this chapter identifies emerging opportunities as well as challenges for African agency at the start of the second decade of the 21st century. It especially focuses on whether the emergence of the BRICS/'second world' (Khanna, 2009), now including South Africa and the MINT (Mexico, Indonesia, Nigeria and Turkey), presents unanticipated possibilities (Shaw, 2010) or threats to a heterogeneous continent, one that includes burgeoning 'developmental' as well as 'fragile' or 'failed' states (ACBF, 2011); hence the timeliness of the China case study in Harman and Brown (2013).

What has Africa learned and what can it adapt after its first half-century, given the significantly transformed global context at the turn of the decade is a major question for policy-leaders: divergent regional incidences of and responses to the 'global' financial crisis, with the global South being much less negatively affected than the established trans-Atlantic core in both 'old' and 'new' worlds (Pieterse, 2011)? And can African agency seize the opportunity to become the primary driver of regional development in the second decade of the 21st century (Brown, 2012; Brown and Harman, 2013; Lorenz and Rempe, 2013)?

Varieties of innovative sources of finance

Even before the end of the 2010 'global' financial crisis, there was a looming gap in funding for African development if it was to even aspire to realise the MDGs in 2015; hence the current preoccupation with post-2015 development directions. In response to such deficiencies as well as the slowness of the 'Monterrey Consensus'[17] to have an impact on ODA effectiveness – from Accra and Paris to Busan at the end of 2011 – France animated a 'Leading Group' of states to suggest other means to advance global public goods. In association with major international NGOs in a Forum on the Future of Aid, a Taskforce on International Financial Transactions and Development came to advance the notion of 'taxation for the governing of globalisation' at the decade's end. This purpose of this Leading Group was to improve financing and mechanisms for global public goods. This connects with the post-2015 debate of improving financing systems for development goals. These forums and taskforces provide opportunities for better understanding of the concept of development and how to drive initiatives moving forward. Alternative forms of financing, including taxation, play a large part in this dialogue.

Other alternatives included ODA from new members of the EU and the BRIC/BRICS as 'emerging donors' (Sumner and Mallett, 2013), the latter reflected in the Forum on China-Africa Cooperation, which discussed the need for development assistance from China to Africa (Taylor, 2011), for example. Despite this call, Sino-African relations are still heavily influenced by infrastructural development. New private foundations have emerged around the turn of the century to parallel established ones like the Carnegie Foundation, the Ford Foundation and the Rockefeller Foundation, notably the Gates Foundation, but now also ones such as the Tony Blair Faith Foundation, The Clinton Foundation and the Mo Ibrahim Foundation (Besada and Kindornay, 2013). Similarly, FBOs increasingly span many religions, particularly the more pragmatic, mainstream dominations (for example, Aga Khan Foundation, Catholic Relief Services, Islamic Relief, Lutheran World Relief and World Vision). Faith-based organisations continue to play a vital role in non-governmental development assistance across the continent. For example, 40-50 per cent of health services on the continent are provided by FBOs (Olarinmoye, 2012, p 2). With new as well as established private foundations, they increasingly form partnerships with international organisations such as, for example, the Alliance for a Green Revolution in Africa, and GAVI (Rushton and Williams, 2011).

Among the dozen or so global levies, mainly on ubiquitous financial flows, proposed by the Taskforce to advance global public goods, were the following:

• Global Solidarity Fund for global public goods which aim to contract the digital divide;

- Currency Transaction Tax (along the lines of the original Tobin Tax), which broadens the base of global taxation for development on each transaction;
- airline ticket levies already being implemented by some governments in the North like Spain and Korea, with revenues going for anti-AIDS, tuberculosis and malaria (ATM) vaccines in association with the Clinton and Gates Foundations;
- carbon taxes/trading, a not uncontroversial set of measures encouraged by the UN Intergovernmental Panel on Climate Change (IPCC) and set of climate change summits, such as COP15 in Copenhagen 2009, COP16 in Cancun 2010 and COP17 in Durban in 2011, related to the Clean Development Mechanism (CDM), which provides credits for reducing emissions as part of the Kyoto Protocol;
- climate change funds such as the International Bank for Reconstruction and Development (IBRD) Global Environmental Facility and UN-REDD;
- Digital Solidarity Fund established in Geneva, which works to reduce the digital divide through financing, mobilisation and SSC;
- UNITAID, an international drug purchase facility to advance access to ATMs, now with broad inter- and non-state participation;
- controls on money laundering encouraged by the OECD and G8 – capital flight estimated at some US$500 billion? – including (global and Caribbean) Financial Action Taskforces on off-shore financial centres over two decades, leading to Publish What You Pay and EITI; and
- remittance taxes on North-South flows that have blossomed to over US$300 billion pa (Ratha et al, 2011; The World Bank, 2011), larger for some states like Nigeria or Lesotho than ODA.

But getting from conceptualisation to policies/politics is problematic, which is where varieties of regionalisms come in to engage in such public, open diplomacy (Shaw et al, 2011; Fanta et al, 2013). Hence the imperative of animating a timely, extensive coalition to redefine and revive the continent's direction at the turn of the decade, as suggested in the conclusions below (Africa Progress Panel, 2012).

Varieties of 'new regionalisms'

Reflective of its more than 50 states, already Africa has been the leading region in the South to advance regional innovations and institutions, even if it has received less analytic attention – both in terms of economic theory and social study – than, for example, Asia (Shaw et al, 2011). In the initial one-party nationalist period, reflective of jealousy surrounding newly realised independence, these were typically 'old' intergovernmental arrangements. But in the post-bipolar era, such regionalisms became less exclusively state and economic, and more inclusive around emerging issues like ecology, energy, security, water and so on (Shaw et al, 2011). Indeed, while regional economic integration does exist, including regional economic communities (RECs), these are equally, if not more, interested in larger outcomes of emerging issues (ECDPM, 2012). And now, regional development is increasingly focused on new resources such as corridors for supplies (SID, 2012), and pipelines and valleys for energy and water (Fanta et al, 2013), symbolised by the new eastern Africa as a rising energy region (*The Economist*, 2012). Hence the relevance of TradeMark in Southern and East Africa (TMSA and TMEA), which intends to improve market availability and production in South East Africa through partnerships with corporations, governments and non-state actors,[18] facilitating regional infrastructures, networks and supply-chains (SID, 2012).

Nevertheless, first, the revived, redefined EAC is emblematic of 'new' African regionalisms: five rather than the initial trio of members (and onto a half-dozen, with South Sudan in 2013) (Hansohm, 2013), with innovative civil society, media, parliamentary and security dimensions (SID, 2012), qualifying as an instance of 'new regionalisms' (Shaw et al, 2011). Given the scale and resilience of regional conflict on the continent, several attempts have been made at regional peace-building, from Dafur to Côte d'Ivoire, especially around ECOWAS, Greater Lakes Region and Horn, such as the ongoing process around the ICGLR, reinforced and publicised by SEC Section 1502 on conflict metals. These increasingly involve a fluid range of actors in a heterogeneous coalition (Leonard, 2013), from international NGOs to MNCs, as such conflicts are always about 'greed' as well as 'grief'; so resource extraction and accumulation proceeding in tandem with violence, all too often targeting women and children as successive UN documents on the Congo have revealed.[19] And as security is increasingly privatised, so such coalitions become ever more problematic, as there is a disconnect between private and public interests and needs. This is particularly so around energy and mineral extraction and supply-chains as their products attract the attention of transnational as well as local criminal networks. Shorter-term peace-making is typically tied to longer-term norm creation to advance sustainable development by regulating the flow of 3T conflict metals and minerals like coltan, diamonds and gold, as already indicated in (i) above (see www.enoughproject.org).

Second, in the new century, regionalisms on the continent have come to cover the spectrum of levels – macro/meso/micro (Grant and Soderbaum, 2003; Soderbaum and Taylor, 2008; Teiku, 2011) – and sectors – civil society, corporate networks, security etc. While Export-Processing Zones (EPZs) are associated with Asia and gas pipelines with Central Europe (Kuzemko et al, 2012), development corridors and peace parks are largely a function of Southern Africa's distinctive political economy – functions that warrant further study to examine their success (Ramutsindela, 2011). Similarly, Africa has its share of river valley organisations – for example, Congo, Niger, Nile, Zambezi etc – and other cross-border networks which are more or less formal micro-regions. The Maputo Corridor, an established trade border between South Africa and Mozambique, has advanced growth in Southern Mozambique as well as the eastern Witwatersrand, reinforcing the cross-border dimensions of the Lesotho highlands water project for electricity and water; the latter was informed by the only global commission to be based outside the North (in Cape Town), which also included MNCs as well as NGOs and states in its membership (Khagram, 2004): the World Commission on Dams. Reflective of growing concern for the environment, Southern Africa (in Mozambique, South Africa, Zimbabwe and Swaziland) is the centre of the trans-frontier peace parks movement that has led to the recognition of several such cross-border parks in the region; these may evolve from designated elephant corridors to multipurpose functional arrangements for renewable energy and water resources.

Third, encouraged by the growing recognition of climate change (the development of IBSA [India, Brazil and South Africa] into BASIC [Brazil, South Africa, India and China] around COP15 in Copenhagen at the end of 2009 and beyond), the continent's river basins are beginning to receive exponential attention as centres of biodiversity, energy, food and water as well as conflict: the Congo River and the Zambezi; the Nile Basin Initiative and Dialogue is arguably the most advanced to date, given its inter-dialogue approach that encompasses a multistakeholder analysis and contribution. The Nile Basin is challenging given the great number of countries, businesses, local communities and other actors invested in the water body. The Initiative and Dialogue has done well to attempt to bring together all these voices in a multistakeholder mechanism.

Fourth, symptomatic of emerging tensions and possibilities is the discovery of oil (Shaxson, 2007; Singh and Bourgouin, 2012) around the rift valley lakes in northwest Uganda along the border with Congo; such oil production may propel Uganda into the ranks of the developmental states, but it may endanger some of its environment and wildlife, let alone local communities.[20] In early 2012, new discoveries of oil and gas were announced in northern Kenya and southern Ethiopia and in northern Mozambique and southern Tanzania by a series of global energy players (*The Economist*, 2012): an emerging energy exporting region of growing importance for the AMV. The first East Africa Oil and Gas Summit was held in Nairobi in November 2012 to discuss pipelines from Juba to Lamu and Mtwara to Dar es Salaam and Mombasa as well as a refinery in northern Uganda. Some of the 50 global energy companies involved in this new Eastern Africa include CNPC and CNOOC from China, Anardarko and ExxonMobil from the US and BG Group, and ENI, Statoil and Tullow from Europe.

Fifth, the continent's pattern of inter-regional relationships (Fawn, 2009) is in flux, from classic, inherited North-South dependencies towards a novel South-East axis around China and India, but also Japan and Korea along with athletics, film and music. Symbolically, Africa's regions' reluctance to sign EPAs with the EU at the turn of the decade, despite a mix of pressures and incentives, may mark a turning point as global rebalancing continues: Europe of the Eurozone crisis around the PIIGS and Asia of the BRICS transforms policy options and calculations for the continent, as suggested in Cheru and Obi (2010), advancing the prospects for African agency. Indeed, Cheru and Obi suggest a wide range of options for Africa given the continuing and often competitive interests of China and India. The tone of annual Forum on China-Africa Cooperation palavers (Taylor, 2011) can be contrasted to that at the third EU-Africa summit in Tunis in November 2010. Iberia increasingly relies on investment from and emigration to Angola, Brazil, Mexico and Mozambique. These examples indicate that Africa is shifting its relations from North-South to South-South, particularly with the BRICS and Gulf Region.

Finally, sixth, given its numerous landlocked states, Africa has always experienced informal cross-border migration and trade, some now in illegal goods like drugs and small arms (there are approximately 8 million small arms migrating through West Africa, for example; see Religions for Peace, nd). And as MNCs, now from China and India as well as South Africa (hence the transition from IBSA to BRICS), have increased their investments in energy and minerals, franchises and shopping malls, so their logistics and supply chains have come to successfully define their own regional networks (Power et al, 2012).

Exponential infrastructural development will further new regionalisms on the continent in the second decade of the 21st century, symbolised by the mobile phone revolution and the roles of MTN and Celtel/Bharti, including the Mo Ibrahim Foundation.

Varieties of innovative analyses/policies

Burgeoning varieties of NRG, finance and regionalisms reinforce prospects for public policy in and around the continent (Hanson et al, 2012), such as the AMV. They also present challenges to African and related analyses – from dependency to agency (Brown, 2012; Cooper and Shaw, 2012; Brown and Harman, 2013; Cooper and Flemes, 2013; Lorenz and Rempe, 2013; Grant et al, 2014) – as they demand 'innovative' perspectives and policies, both state and non-state, including civil societies, private companies and media, both print and social. Simultaneously, the focus of regional development is shifting from older intergovernmental paradigms (Acharya, 2012) around the formal economy to newer technologies and sectors such as energy and water, pipelines and refineries (Cornelissen et al, 2012; Shaw et al, 2011).

Africa at the turn of the second decade of the 21st century is, then, at a crossroads in terms of governance for development, as symbolised by the AMV: can it seize its second chance and transcend its somewhat lacklustre first half-century to advance developmental states (UNECA, 2011, 2012)? In turn, can African interests advance inclusive public or network diplomacy of non-state as well as state actors for the most marginalised continent in the global South using new medias/technologies, as suggested in the transition from KP to ICGLR? Africa's place at the centre of innovative sources of finance and styles of governance leads to optimism (UNECA, 2009; Hanson et al, 2012) while the number of continuing conflicts and persistent fragile/failed states leads to scepticism, and even pessimism (Brock et al, 2012): what balance can be achieved by 2020 and beyond? In turn, in Africa, as elsewhere in the global South (UNDP, 2013), what is the balance between regional conflict and regional development (Fanta et al, 2013)? As Brown (2012, p 1889) has proposed:

> ... future work on African agency would be able to engage seriously with the continent's role in international politics in a way that presents Africa as actor not just acted upon, historical agent not just history's recipient.

Conclusions

To be sure, there has been a shift in both agency and political economy dynamics on the African continent. The post-2015 policy agenda must consider these changes, and look for ways to better incorporate and empower Africa's newly forming distinct level of 'agency' in future development and economic conversations. Conversations pertaining to NRG in particular are not situated within the AU's landscape – the AMV as a clear indication of a shift toward more Africa-centric planning. Although the dream of African-led planning has been ongoing since independence (particularly with the pan-African philosophy originating with thinkers like Presidents Nkrumah [Ghana], Selassie [Ethiopia] and Touré [Senegal]), it is the current economic growth of Sub-Saharan Africa that makes this ability for true African initiatives now a true reality.

There are a variety of reasons for this shift to a more nuanced African agency. As shown throughout this chapter, the growth of Africa's role in the global sphere is intensifying, given both Africa's growing economic influence and its position in forms of SSC. South Africa's invitation to join BRICS is a noteworthy example of the growing influence the continent is having globally. President Zuma has articulated his belief that South Africa represents all of Africa in this bloc. Indeed, it has greatly signified the shift toward Africa as a major player in the global economic system.

The role of China in Africa's influence also cannot go unnoticed when analysing Africa's changing agency. China's growing on the continent is well known, as is the Chinese hands-off policy approach. Unlike Western donors whose assistance has traditionally been accompanied by mandatory policy measures, China does not seek ideological political endeavours. While China has received much criticism for this approach (and rightfully so, particularly in areas of human rights abuses), Africa has been able to use the stark differences between China and the West to leverage both parties, particularly the latter. If Africa disagrees with the policy implications of the prospective donor, it can threaten to simply get assistance from another donor. Unlike in the past, Africa has options other than the West, and has used this as a leveraging tactic.

The changing forms of regionalism on the continent are also noteworthy (Grant and Soderbaum, 2003; Iheduru, 2011). As described throughout this chapter, new modes of cooperation and participation between and within states enables Africa to improve its functionality through a variety of methods and geographical locales. Although regionalism is not new, the variety of cooperations available is. The recent growth of global civil societies and cross-continental networks, for example, enables the growth of influence in public spheres, including policy. Citizens previously underrepresented now have larger civil society organisations, for example, working alongside them for change. This has increased the availability of power to smaller and more local bodies, enabling even the most marginalised voices to be heard.

There is much optimism regarding Africa's role in the post-2015 world. New levels of governance, exemplified in the AMV, showcase the opportunity for the continent to continue to grow, both economically and politically. Africa's new political forms, particularly with the heightening influence of regional governance, has captured global attention, and can offer new modes of policy that can be used in other emerging regions, including Latin America and Southeast Asia.

The growth is apparent and the optimism is great. If Africa continues to exhibit levels of economic and political growth, including as an emerging leader in forms of SSC, the future for the continent is bright. The post-2015 agenda can learn a lot from the recent past of Africa, and recognise that African agency must be carefully considered if a new form of the MDGs is to emerge.

References

ACBF (African Capacity Building Foundation) (2011) *African capacity building indicators 2011: Capacity development in fragile states*, Harare: ACBF.

Acharya, A. (2012) 'Comparative regionalism: a field whose time has come?', *International Spectator*, vol 47, no 1, March, pp 3-15.

Accuosto, P. and Johnson, N. (2004) 'Financing the information society in the south: A global public goods perspective', Prepared for the Association for Progressive Communications (APC) by the Instituto del Tercer Mundo, Montevideo, Uruguay, June.

AfDB (African Development Bank) (2011) *The middle of the pyramid: Dynamics of the middle class in Africa*, Tunis, April.

AfDB (2013) 'Harnessing remittances for Africa's development' (www. afdb.org/en/blogs/afdb-championing-inclusive-growth-across-africa/post/harnessing-remittances-for-africas-development-11565/).

AfDB, OECD (Organisation for Economic Co-operation and Development), UNDP (United Nations Development Programme) and UNECA (United Nations Economic Commission for Africa) (2012) *African economic outlook 2012: Promoting youth employment* (www.africaneconomicoutlook.org).

Africa Progress Panel (2012) *Report 2012*, Geneva (www. africaprogresspanel.org/homepage/).

AU (African Union) (nd) *Remittances* (http://pages.au.int/remittance/ about).

AMV (African Mining Vision) (2009) *African Mining Vision*, February, Addis Ababa: AMV.

AMV (2011a) *Minerals and Africa's development: International Study Group report on Africa's mineral regimes*, Addis Ababa: AMV.

AMV (2011b) *Addis Ababa Declaration on building a sustainable future for Africa's extractive industry: From vision to action*, December, Addis Ababa: AMV.

Bagayoko, N. (2012) 'Introduction: hybrid security governance in Africa', *IDS Bulletin*, vol 43, no 4, July, pp 1-13.

BCG (Boston Consulting Group) (2010) *The African challengers: Global competitors emerge from the overlooked continent*, Boston: BCG.

Besada, H. (ed) (2010) *Crafting an African security architecture: Addressing regional peace and conflict in the 21st century*, Farnham: Ashgate.

Besada, H. and Kindornay, S. (eds) (2013) *The future of multilateral development cooperation in a changing global order*, London: Palgrave Macmillan.

Besada, H., Tok, E. and Winters, K. (2013) *South Africa in the BRICS: Opportunities, challenges and prospects*, Ottawa: North-South Institute (www.nsi-ins.ca/wp-content/uploads/2013/10/2013-South-Africa-in-the-BRICS.pdf).

Brock, L., Holm, H.-H., Sorensen, G. and Stohl, M. (2012) *Fragile states: Violence and the failure of intervention*, Cambridge: Polity Press.

Brown, S. (ed) (2011) *Transnational transfers and global development*, London: Palgrave Macmillan.

Brown, W. (2012) 'A question of agency: Africa in international politics', *Third World Quarterly*, vol 33, no 10, pp 1889-908.

Brown, W. and Harman, S. (eds) (2013) *African agency and international relations*, Abingdon: Routledge.

Cadman, T. (2011) *Quality and legitimacy of global governance: Case lessons from forestry*, London: Palgrave Macmillan.

Campbell, B. (ed) (2013) *Modes of governance and revenue flows in African mining* (International Political Economy Series). Basingstoke: Palgrave Macmillan.

Cheru, F. and Obi, C. (eds) (2010) *The rise of China and India in Africa*, London: Zed for NAI.

Cooper, A.F. and Flemes, D. (eds) (2013) 'Special Issue: emerging powers in global governance', *Third World Quarterly*, vol 34, no 6, pp 943-1144.

Cooper, A.F. and Shaw, T.M. (eds) (2012) *The diplomacies of small states: Between vulnerability and resilience?* (2nd edn), London: Palgrave Macmillan.

Cornelissen, S., Cheru, F. and Shaw, T.M. (eds) (2011) *Africa and international relations in the twenty-first century*, London: Palgrave Macmillan.

Dingwerth, K. (2008) 'Private transnational governance and the developing world', *International Studies Quarterly*, vol 52, no 3, pp 607-34.

Dunn, K.C. and Shaw, T.M. (eds) (2001) *Africa's challenge to international relations theory* (updated paperback edn), London: Palgrave.

ECDPM (European Centre for Development Policy Management) (2012) 'Regional integration', *GREAT Insights*, vol 1, no 9, November (www.ecdpm.org).

Economist, The (2010a) *The world in 2010: 25th anniversary edition.*

Economist, The (2010b) 'Lights, camera, Africa', vol 397, no 8713, 18 December, pp 85-7.

Economist, The (2011) 'The Lion Kings?', vol 398, no 8715, 8 January, pp 72-3.

Economist, The (2012) 'African energy: eastern el dorado?', 7 April.

Fanta, E., Shaw, T.M. and Tang, V. (eds) (2013) *Comparative regionalisms for development in the 21st century: Insights from the global south*, Farnham: Ashgate for NETRIS.

Fawn, R. (ed) (2009) 'Special Issue: globalising the regional, regionalising the global', *Review of International Studies*, vol 35, February, pp 1-261.

Fioramonti, L. (ed) (2012) *Regions and crises: New challenges for contemporary regionalisms*, London: Palgrave Macmillan.

Flemes, D. (ed) (2010) *Regional leadership in the global system: Ideas, interests and strategies of regional powers*, Farnham: Ashgate.

Florini, A. and Dubash, N.K. (2011) 'Special Issue: global energy governance', *Global Policy*, vol 2, September, pp 1-154.

Gale, F. and Haward, M. (2011) *Global commodity governance: State responses to sustainable forest and fisheries certification*, London: Palgrave Macmillan.

Goldstein, A. (2007) *Multinational companies from emerging economies*, London: Palgrave Macmillan.

Goldthau, A. and Witte, J.M. (eds) (2010) *Global energy governance: The new rules of the game*, Washington, DC: Brookings Institution.

Grant, J.A. and Soderbaum, F. (eds) (2003) *The new regionalism in Africa*, Aldershot: Ashgate.

Grant, J.A., Nadège Compaoré, W.R. and Mitchell, M.I. (eds) (2014) *New approaches to the governance of natural resources: Insights from Africa*, London: Palgrave Macmillan.

Gray, K. and Murphy, C. (eds) (2013) 'Special Issue: rising powers and the future of global governance', *Third World Quarterly*, vol 34, no 2, pp 1360-2241.

Greenpeace (2012) *Guide to greener electronics*, November (www.greenpeace.org/international/en/Guide-to-Greener-Electronics/18th-Edition/).

Hansohm, D. (2013) *South Sudan, Sudan and the East African community: Potential of enhanced relationships*, Working Papers W-2013/4, Bruges: United Nations University-Comparative Regional Integration Studies.

Hanson, K.T., Kararach, G. and Shaw, T.M. (eds) (2012) *Rethinking development challenges for public policy: Insights from contemporary Africa*, London: Palgrave Macmillan.

Harman, S. and Brown, W. (2013) 'In from the margins? The changing place of African international relations', *International Affairs*, January, vol 89, no 1, pp 69-87.

Hartzenberg, T. (2012) *The tripartite free trade area: Towards a new African integration paradigm?*, Stellenbosch: Tralac.

Heine, J. (2006) *On the manner of practising the new diplomacy*, Working Paper #11, Waterloo: Centre for International Governance Innovation.

Iheduru, O.C. (2011) 'The new ECOWAS: implications for the study of regional integration', in T.M. Shaw, A. Grant and S. Cornelissen (eds) *The Ashgate research companion to regionalisms*, Aldershot: Ashgate, pp 213-39.

Jack, A. (2013) 'Study highlights scale of African doctor "brain drain"', *Financial Times*, 18 September (www.ft.com/intl/cms/s/0/9647519c-207a-11e3-b8c6-00144feab7de.html#axzz3I7R7tQ7H).

Jordaan, E. (2003) 'The concept of a middle power in IR: distinguishing between emerging and traditional middle powers', *Politikon*, November, vol 30, no 2, pp 165-81.

Keohane, R. (1984) *After hegemony: Cooperation and discord in the world political economy*, Princeton, NJ: Princeton University Press.

Klare, M.T. (2012) *The race for what's left: The global scramble for the world's last resources*, New York: Metropolitan.

Khagram, S. (2004) *Dams and development: Transnational strategies for water and power*, Ithaca, NY: Cornell University Press.

Khanna, P. (2009) *The second world: How emerging powers are redefining global competition in the twenty-first century*, New York: Random House.

Kliman, D.M. and Fontaine, R. (2012) *Global swing states: Brazil, India, Indonesia, Turkey and the future of international order*, Washington, DC: German Marshall Fund.

Kuzemko, C., Belyi, A.V., Goldthau, A. and Keating, M.F. (eds) (2012) *Dynamics of energy governance in Europe and Russia*, London: Palgrave Macmillan.

Lamb, G. (2002) 'Synergies between aid and the financing of global public goods', in I. Kaul, K. Le Goulven, M Schnupf (eds), *Global public goods financing: New tools for new challenges*, New York: UNDP (www.bvsde.paho.org/texcom/cd050853/lambsyne.pdf).

Lee, B. et al (2012) *Resources futures*, London: Chatham House, December.

Leonard, D. (ed) (2013) 'Special Issue: social contracts, networks and security in tropical Africa', *IDS Bulletin*, vol 44, no 1, January.

Lorenz, U. and Rempe, M. (eds) (2013) *Mapping agency: Comparing regionalisms in Africa*, Farnham: Ashgate.

McKinsey & Company (2010) *McKinsey on Africa: A continent on the move*, New York, June.

Mawdsley, E. (2012) *From recipients to donors: Emerging powers and the changing development landscape*, London: Zed.

Nathan, L. (2012) *Community of insecurity: SADC's struggle for peace and security in Southern Africa*, Farnham: Ashgate.

Nel, P. and Nolte, D. (eds) (2010) 'Regional powers in a changing global order', *Review of International Studies*, vol 36, no 4, October, pp 877-974.

Nel, P., Nabers, D. and Hanif, M. (eds) (2012) 'Special Issue: regional powers and global redistribution', *Global Society*, vol 26, no 3, pp 279-405.

Olarinmoye, O.O. (2012) 'Faith-based organizations and development: prospects and constraints', *Transformation: An International Journal of Holistic Mission Studies*, vol 29, no 1.

Overbeek, H. and van Apeldoorn, B. (eds) (2012) *Neoliberalism in crisis*, London: Palgrave Macmillan.

Pieterse, J.N. (2011) 'Global rebalancing: crisis and the East-South turn', *Development and Change*, vol 42, no 1, pp 22-48.

Pieterse, J.N. and Rehbein, B. (eds) (2009) *Globalization and emerging societies: Development and inequality*, London: Palgrave Macmillan.

Power, M., Mohan, G. and Tan-Mullins, M. (2012) *China's resource diplomacy in Africa: Powering development?*, London: Palgrave Macmillan.

Radelet, S. (2010) *Emerging Africa: How 17 countries are leading the way*, Washington, DC: Center for Global Dialogue.

Ramutsindela, M. (2011) 'Transfrontier conservation and the spaces of regionalisms', in T.M. Shaw, A. Grant and S. Cornelissen (eds) *The Ashgate research companion to regionalisms*, Aldershot: Ashgate, pp 361-73.

Ratha, D. et al (2011) *Leveraging remittances for Africa: Remittances, skills and investments*, Washington, DC: The World Bank and African Development Bank.

Religions for Peace (nd) *Small arms and light weapons: Africa. A resource guide for Religions for Peace* (www.un.org/disarmament/education/docs/SALW_Africa.pdf).

Rushton, S. and Williams, O.D. (eds) (2011) *Partnerships and foundations in global health governance*, London: Palgrave Macmillan.

Shaw, T.M. (2010) 'Can the BRICs become a bloc?', in 'The emerging politics of the emerging powers: the BRICs and the global south', *China Monitor*, vol 52, June, pp 4-6.

Shaw, T.M. (2012) 'Africa's quest for developmental states: "renaissance" for whom?', *Third World Quarterly*, vol 33, no 5, pp 837-51.

Shaw, T.M. (2015a) 'African agency: Africa, South Africa and the BRICS', *International Politics*, vol 52.

Shaw, T.M. (2015b) 'From post-BRICS decade to post-2015: insights from global governance and comparative regionalisms', *Palgrave Communications*, vol 1, no 1, January.

Shaw, T.M., Grant, J.A. and Cornelissen, S. (eds) (2011) *The Ashgate research companion to regionalisms*, Farnham: Ashgate.

Shaxson, N. (2007) *Poisoned wells: The dirty politics of African oil*, New York: Palgrave Macmillan.

SID (Society for International Development) (2012) *State of East Africa 2012: Deepening integration, intensifying challenges*, Nairobi for TMEA.

Singh, J.N. and Bourgouin, F. (eds) (2013) *Resource governance and developmental states in the global south: Critical international political economy perspectives*, London: Palgrave Macmillan.

Soderbaum, F. and Taylor, I. (eds) (2008) *Afro-regions: The dynamics of cross-border macro-regionalism in Africa*, Uppsala: Nordic Africa Institute.

Sumner, A. and Mallett, R. (2013) *The future of foreign aid: Development cooperation and the new geography of global poverty*, London: Palgrave Macmillan.

Taylor, I.C. (2011) *The Forum on China-Africa Cooperation (FOCAC)*, Abingdon: Routledge.

UNDP (United Nations Development Programme) (2012) *African human development report 2012: Towards a food secure future*, New York (www.afhdr.org).

UNDP (2013) *Human development report 2013: The rise of the South: Human progress in a diverse world*, New York, March.

UNECA (United Nations Economic Commission for Africa) (2009) *African governance report II*, Addis Ababa: UNECA (www.uneca.org/sites/default/files/PublicationFiles/agr2-english.pdf).

UNECA (2011) *Economic report on Africa 2011: Governing development in Africa – The role of the state in economic transformation*, Addis Ababa: UNECA.

UNECA (2012) *Economic report on Africa 2012: Unleashing Africa's potential as a pole of global growth*, Addis Ababa: UNECA.

UNECA (2013) *African governance report III 2012: Elections and the management of diversity in Africa*, New York: Oxford University Press.

US SEC (Securities and Exchange Commission) (2014) (www.sec.gov/)

vom Hau, M., Scott, J. and Hulme, D. (2012) 'Beyond the BRICs: alternative strategies of influence in the global politics of development', *European Journal of Development Research*, vol 24, no 2, April, pp 187-204.

Warleigh-Lack, A., Robinson, N. and Rosamond, B. (eds) (2011) *New regionalism and the EU: Dialogues, comparisons and research directions*, Abingdon: Routledge.

Westphalen, L.G. (2012) *Corporate social responsibility in the mining sector*, ssources Future: Canada: Co-operation and Development (www.fraserinstitute.org/uploadedFiles/fraser-ca/Content/research-news/research/articles/corporate-social-responsibility-in-mining-sector-CSR.pdf).

WHO (World Health Organization) (2013) *Malaria: Factsheet on the world malaria report 2013* (www.who.int/malaria/media/world_malaria_report_2013/en/).

World Bank, The (2011a) *Africa's future and The World Bank's support to it*, March, Washington, DC: The World Bank.

World Bank, The (2011b) *Migration and remittances factbook 2011* (2nd edn), Washington, DC: The World Bank.

Xing, L. (ed) (2013) *China-Africa relations: The past, the present and the future*, Farnham: Ashgate.

Useful websites

African Development Bank: www.afdb.org
Africa Human Development Report 2012: www.afhdr.org
www.africaneconomicoutlook.org
Boston Consulting Group: www.bcg.com
Center for Global Development: www.cgdev.org
International Conference on the Great Lakes Region: www.icglr.org
ISEAL Alliance: www.isealalliance.org
McKinsey & Company: www.mckinsey.com
United Nations Economic Commission for Africa: www.uneca.org

Organisation for Economic Co-operation and Development: www.oecd.org

Partnership Africa Canada: www.pacweb.org

Resources Futures: www.resourcesfutures.org

FOUR

The role of gender in development: where do boys count?

Frannie A. Léautier

Introduction

Most analyses of gender in development focus on the role of women or the differentiated impact of the development on women. Recent attention of external aid programmes and the rising violence against women in a number of countries, coupled with evidence of disparity in development results when the role of men and women is differentiated, has further clarified the issue by focusing on women and girls. Furthermore, gender has come up as a central issue in the post-2015 identification of priorities following an assessment of the Millennium Development Goals (MDGs) and efforts to define a new framework for channelling policy attention on a global level, such as through the Sustainable Development Goals (UN Women, 2013).

Gender inequalities have been extensively identified as underpinning the five clusters of the MDGs, namely, poverty and sustainable development; access to services; care and care giving; voice and agency; and international partnerships and accountability (Jones et al, 2010). It has long been argued that it is important to address the structural causes of gender-based discrimination. Organisations like UN Women have been set up to tackle the obstacles that have an impact on gender equality, women's rights and women's empowerment by supporting the underlying transformation in target areas such as violence against women and girls, inclusion in distribution of capabilities, services and assets, as well as equality in decision-making power in public and private institutions (UN Women, 2013). Attention to implementation has led policy-makers to look for practical ways to address gender-based violence as well as equality in access to resources such as finance (see, for example, Kim et al, 2007).

This chapter investigates the potential or real negative effects of a focus solely on women, and identifies areas where a focus on men, and in particular young men, may be beneficial to achieving development results. Arguments are presented for a differentiated role of gender in policy design and evaluation and for gender-disaggregated data to appropriately assess the evidence of critical policies for development. Five selected issues are investigated. The first relates to the shifting perspectives on the role of gender in development. Second is consideration of the role of globalisation on the quality of life and status of women. Third, the role of men and boys in development is explored. Fourth, some examples of development in practice, including the role of gender in development, particularly in advancing the MDGs and the post-2015 development agenda, are provided. The chapter concludes with the question of gender and culture and the main elements to achieve a real transformation of people's lives through the lever of gender.

Changing perspectives on gender

Gender has been shown to have an impact on development through three main pathways – fear and risk taking; uneven capabilities; and unequal decision-making power (UN Women, 2013). The first pathway of fear is visible in terms of conditioning behaviour that fear and experience of violence plays in debilitating women and girls from taking action to attain sustaining livelihoods. The second pathway of capabilities is mainly seen in the stubborn, multigenerational inequalities that emanate from the uneven distribution of knowledge, health services, land, finance, decent work and pay, all that culminate to maintain poor development outcomes from mother to daughter and granddaughter. Finally, inequality in decision-making power – in public and private institutions, national parliaments and local councils, media and civil society, the management and governance of firms, but also in communities and families – prevents large-scale changes in status from occurring in one or two generations. Decision-making power deficits put women and adolescent girls in a structural disadvantage that is difficult to overcome over short periods of time, lessening the sharpness of public policies to address inequality.

There has been a changing perspective on the role of gender in development over the past quarter of a century (for a good overview, see Tinker, 1990). Economic analysis and policy application from the 1950s and several decades afterwards focused on the household unit, with little differentiation on the role of women; thereby missing the contribution of women to the economy, particularly in subsistence economies. During the 1990s the main concern related to the persistence of inequalities in the face of development, and encouraged a partnership between men and women to obtain important development results. Attention went to community-level interventions to improve agriculture, educate rural populations in health and sanitation and raise literacy levels. The definition of the MDGs brought attention to the channels by which gender affects development, leading to innovation in the approaches to designing and implementing development programmes. The role played by technology and education, as well as the work of women inside and outside the home, got the attention of researchers during this period. Gender analysis became an accepted practice in most development institutions to such an extent that 'gender mainstreaming'[1] entered the lexicon of development programmes (Moser, 1993). A lot of interest also went into the work of women in export factories, some of which has gained importance due to recent issues related to worker safety and the ethics of purchasing agreements in the wake of the female worker-dominated garment industry in Bangladesh and the building collapse that killed 1,127 and injured 2,500 in April 2013 (Uddin, 2013).

Perspectives on the role of gender in the 2000s had anticipated the type of issues in the Bangladesh building collapse, but debate was more focused on the need for taking joint responsibility for gender outcomes, asking for men to be more implicated in the outcomes related to women. For example, the Grameen Bank, started by a man, Mohammed Yunus, gave credit mostly to women, some of whom used the credit to buy equipment or other means of production (rickshaws, three-wheeler motorbikes) for their husbands or their sons, leading to criticism of the impact such access to credit had even when it was targeted at women (Tinker, 1990). Success of women in these cases depended on the behaviour of the husbands and sons – a cultural channel on the status of women.

Other criticisms were targeted towards corporations, imploring them to be more mindful of conditions of work and business ethics in general. For example, a critical review of the rise of the Bangladeshi garment industry by Ahmed (2004) gives responsibility for safety and fairness in the workplace to the millionaire industrialists who provide employment opportunities for women. Ahmed (2004) recognises that women who work for the garment industry would otherwise not be employed, but that the industry owners provide little voice and security. The role of international firms in formulating, implementing and adhering to ethical business principles, such as codes of conduct, also garnered attention during the period of the 2000s.

Codes of conduct in the sporting goods industry were among the early areas of reform due to pressure from international non-governmental organisations (NGOs) armed with more information about sourcing strategies and business practices of firms such as Nike (van Tulder and Kolk, 2001). The sporting industry – a large employer of women in manufacturing – was subjected to rapid changes in its business practices as the pressure for application of universal moral norms and fundamental rights came into contact with national traditions, cultures and regulatory practices, including on the issues related to the safety and security of workers in factories in developing countries (van Tulder and Kolk, 2001). Examples include the response by companies such as Nike to the public relations nightmares of the 1980s involving underpaid workers in Indonesia, child labour in Cambodia and Pakistan, and poor working conditions in China and Vietnam. Nike managers went from being defensive at first, to formulating a code of conduct for its suppliers that was applied on a global scale, requiring their suppliers to observe universal norms of labour, environment and safety standards (Locke et al, 2007).

A decade later, and particularly as the result of the so-called Arab Spring, treatment of gender issues leaned towards a specification with a considered role of boys and men in horizontal equality, particularly as it relates to power distribution among men and women in transforming societal norms (for the theoretical underpinnings of power relations in politics, see Cornwall et al, 2011). During the Arab Spring, a series of demonstrations, protests and civil unrest and wars were directed against existing regimes, starting with Tunisia, and spreading throughout much of the Arab world. Young women were involved along with young men directly in leading and organising protests physically or virtually through social media. Following the outcome of the revolutions, large numbers of Tunisian women were elected to the Constituent Assembly and participated in the drafting of the new constitution (Hatem, 2013).

Similarly, more attention has gone to the role of men and women in shaping gender inequalities (Ghannam, 2013). The Arab Spring illustrates how previous horizontal inequalities – social, economic or power related – could be reduced when excluded groups (youth and women) coming from similar social and economic backgrounds push against forced inequalities between them.

Treatment of the role of boys and men in gender analysis builds on the seminal work of Connell (2003) that brought in the role of education and institutions to shape boys' gender development for achieving gender equality. The work of Cornwall et al (2011) calls for renewed engagement in efforts to challenge and change stereotypes of men so as to dismantle structural barriers to gender equality and to mobilise men to build new alliances with women and social and gender justice in general. Such engagement is to be led by fathers and husbands (a cultural channel), as well as the organisations that support development programmes (a policy channel), and leaders in positions of authority in the public and private sector (a leadership channel).

The timeline of change in Figure 4.1 shows an increasing demand and dependence by policy-makers on the role of men and boys to achieve the development outcomes of women and girls. Such changes have been mainly driven by the realisation that for change to take place, especially where cultural norms are important in day-to-day decisions, it is no longer helpful to focus on only one part of the equation. The 1990s focused on encouraging partnership between men and women. By the 2000s there was a shift of focus to ensuring men and women took joint responsibility in gender outcomes. A decade later saw a deeper understanding that boys and men have a role in achieving horizontal equality, where men and women in similar situations are expected to be treated equally (in earnings, responsibilities, and so on). The evolution shows that to get change in the lives of women and girls, the channel of change is cultural and the agent of change may have to be men and boys. By 2015, a review of the achievements of the MDGs indicates the interdependency of the role of men and women for sustainable development.

Figure 4.1: Shifting perspectives on the role of men and boys

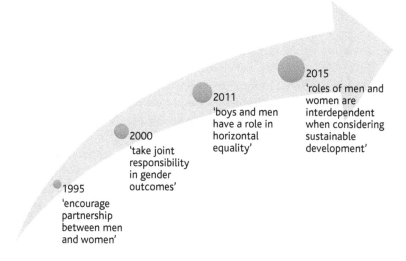

2015
'roles of men and women are interdependent when considering sustainable development'

2011
'boys and men have a role in horizontal equality'

2000
'take joint responsibility in gender outcomes'

1995
'encourage partnership between men and women'

Role of globalisation in determining gender perspectives

Globalisation as measured by increased travel, interaction and exchanges between societies has also had an impact on the quality of life and status of women. Becker (1957/1971) theorised that increased competition in the product market, such as the kind that has evolved as a result of competition by firms in increased geographical spaces and markets, would reduce the discrimination of women and minorities in the long run. Indeed, increased global sourcing, combined with competition in manufacturing, has been seen to reduce the ability of firms to discriminate between the wages of men and women, thus leading to an importation of equality on gender dimensions (Black and Brainerd, 2004). Such findings support the idea that more globalisation would lead to more equality across the genders, particularly in industries that are affected by global trade. Black and Brainerd (2004) find that non-concentrated industries, like apparel and accessories and knitting mills, were affected by trade, and hence subject to the phenomenon of 'importation of equality' across the genders. The challenges of safety seen in the case of the apparel industry in Bangladesh come about from local horizontal inequalities that relegate jobs in apparel factories to women with little voice and few exit options (Ahmed, 2004), hence maintaining inequalities in society.

Globalisation has another channel by which it has an impact on horizontal inequalities – the channel of communication and interaction. The norms and roles of women that are deeply embedded in culture have been shifting as a result of exchanges in the areas of film, television, music and fashion, from the advanced economies to the developing countries. Movie-goers mimic the portrayed roles of women in film and fashion on a global scale, with young women showing preferences for attire, for example, that makes young women dress almost universally alike across a wide range of countries and cultures. In other instances, young women could seek to become leaders in their societies because of what they have seen in the movies or on television.

Increased levels of tourism have brought different ways of behaving and being that women in other cultures have adapted and embraced. Studies such as those by Guilamo-Ramos et al (2011) have shown the influence of alcohol and sexual behaviours in tourism areas on the use of alcohol and the sexual practices of adolescents living close to the tourist areas, for example. More women in Western Africa ride motorcycles – solving their access to markets problem – even in cultures where that was not acceptable previously, as they have seen women in neighbouring countries do so. Changes in the role of women have at times been superficial, with gender roles changing only in a few spheres, such as driving a car or riding a motorcycle, and have not been accompanied by changes in the critical institutions supporting gender equality in broader economic or social spheres. For example, some countries have gone on to embrace majorities of women in parliament and women heads of state, but have done little to change the status of women in society as the elite have acceded to these positions with limited impact on the average woman.

Six African countries top the world in female representation in parliament, with some like Rwanda being number one, at 56 per cent of seats in parliament held by women (Olopade, 2012), showing tremendous change in the political status of women. However, the same result is not visible across the board in countries that have women leaders, as the condition of women remains challenging despite having women acceding to top political positions. The presence of women politicians, like President Ellen Johnson-Sirleaf in Liberia and former president Joyce Banda in Malawi, has been shown to diversify the policy agenda and promote equity and justice (Olopade, 2012). The results in concrete terms are many times slow to follow.

A television series like Borgen from Denmark, which portrays a powerful woman prime minister who came to power unexpectedly and who runs a minority government, has been a topic of much discussion around the world, as women and men discuss the challenges of leadership across different cultures. Some have used the series to explain trends in leadership in Australia in speculating on Julia Gillard's real prime ministerial experience in Australia compared to that of fictional Danish Prime Minister Birgitte Nyborg (Murphy, 2013).

A key question that needs to be evaluated is whether women's rights and gender equality in decision-making and politics have led to improved development outcomes in these African states. A survey by the World Economic Forum (WEF) in a report by Hausmann et al (2012) showed that the Nordic countries have done better in closing the gender gap in political power (Iceland claimed number one position four years in a row, followed by Finland, Norway and Sweden), but the changes globally are very slow. Evidence is still weak in addressing this question, despite the excellent report by Hausmann et al, where they show a faster closing of the gender gap in access to health and education (96 per cent of differences between men and women have disappeared). Political empowerment remains challenging even in advanced economies, as does economic power, where there are significant wage differences, and gaps in leadership by women in business remain.

Globalisation has also instituted changes in domestic traditions of countries to a varying degree depending on the openness of cultures to international influence. In some cases, there have been significant endogenous changes in cultural norms – such as having a woman crowned king of the village of Otuam in Ghana – that have captured foreign reporters' attention and that have further emphasised the global impact of information access through television and social media (Quist-Arcton, 2010; Sesay and Kermellotis, 2013). In the case of Ghana, the woman who became king had lived for many years in America and brought a different approach to decision-making when she inherited the throne, with attention to accountability and effectiveness to her people, without changing the title of her role to 'queen', preferring to keep the title 'king', even though the society did not previously anticipate a woman in that role.

Other changes coming as a result of globalisation relate to the sharing of successful evidence-based policy and the adoption of holistic approaches to dealing with cultural challenges that have gender dimensions. A good example is the evaluated success of the use of micro-finance interventions in South Africa as a means to generate sources of sustainable livelihood, empower women and reduce intimate partner violence (Kim et al, 2007), which was successfully transferred to other countries such as Côte d'Ivoire (Hossain et al, 2014) and Bangladesh (Dalal et al, 2013).

There is, however, another dimension relating to the differentiated impact of globalisation on outcomes for women. Life expectancy has improved due to better access to healthcare, including from mobile solutions for advice and supervision of treatments, to the increased use of telemedicine (Johnston et al, 2004). Countries in Eastern Africa are a good illustration of this point. Female life expectancy improved by four years in nearly every country in Eastern African between 2008 and 2012 (see Table 4.1). This period coincided with the growth in access to mobile phones which have been used not only for banking, but also for sending important information on health, and in particular, women's health. In Kenya, for example, which had a female life expectancy in 2012 of 63, up from 59 in 2008, subscribers to Safaricom got access to health experts at two cents per minute (Talbot, 2011). In 2010, m4RH (mobile for reproductive health) was launched as a pilot project in Kenya and Tanzania by the non-profit human development organisation IFHI 360, which was then adapted for Rwanda in an effort to improve access to sexual and reproductive health information for young people (IFHI 360, 2013).

Table 4.1: Female life expectancy at birth and the role of technology

Country	Female life expectancy at birth in years in 2012	Change in female life expectancy at Birth in years between 2008–2012	Change in mobile cellular subscriptions per 100 people between 2008–2012
Burundi	56	3	22
Ethiopia	65	4	20
Kenya	63	4	29
Rwanda	65	4	37
Tanzania	62	4	26
Uganda	60	4	18

Source: The World Bank (2012)

Women have also participated more in the global economy through trade. Evidence shows a strong correlation between increased international trade and increases in female employment and an increase in exports and higher wages for women in export-oriented economies (ITC, 2014). A good example is the selling of Rwandan baskets to Hollywood and Saks Fifth Avenue through Gahaya Links (Ellis and Leposo, 2012).

As mentioned earlier, women have also increased their political participation as heads of state, ministers of key ministries, heads of regional and continental organisations and as members of parliament, largely because of the speedier sharing of ideas across the world. There are several networks that have been created, such as The Women's Leadership Network, Global Women's Leadership Network, Asia-Pacific Economic Cooperation (APEC) Women Leaders Network and Young Women's Leadership Network, all aimed at speeding up learning and knowledge sharing, and increasing participation of women in decision-making, among other objectives.

Globalisation processes work at the cultural level as well as functioning as a sort of speeded-up transmission belt for norms on the roles of women, thereby creating a space for easier networking and benchmarking of institutions supporting gender equality. Practices across the globe and the resultant benchmarking that is done, pressured by the networking of agents across the world with an interest in gender issues, comes into contact with national and local realities. Consider, for example, the APEC Women Leaders Network, which functions similarly to the other global women leaders networks, but incorporates features that are unique to the Asian context, such as a focus on science and technology issues.

Domestic cultures embedded in the observed national and local realities determine the degree of openness to international influence, and the speed and depth at which endogenous changes in cultural norms are possible. When the interactions between global and local work well, they have positive impacts. Such impacts are many times visible in local health systems that can benefit from ideas in solving challenges in other contexts, such as HIV and AIDS approaches in South Africa that have been useful for Côte d'Ivoire (Hossain et al, 2014). Other examples include the interdisciplinary approaches to solving environmental challenges in the Amazonian ecosystem that have been learned from other contexts outside of Brazil and integrated intensely local issues that are of importance to the peoples of the Amazonian forest (Foller, 2001).

Outcomes for women when globalisation works well could be improved life expectancy, literacy, participation in the economy and political inclusion. The change model on the role of globalisation on the quality of life and status of women pictured above in Figure 4.2 helps us develop and test a set of hypotheses, as shown in the following section. These hypotheses include the impact of globalisation on women's economic participation, access to opportunities that came about as a result of easier connections to the outside world and across women networks, and changes in women's political rights as a result of being integrated in global political processes.

Figure 4.2: Change model on the role of globalisation on quality of life and status of women

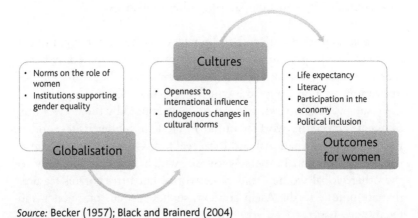

Source: Becker (1957); Black and Brainerd (2004)

Globalisation and gender: what are the hypotheses?

There are a number of channels by which globalisation has an impact on the issues of gender and the differentiated role of men and women. Cho (2012) looks at globalisation as the spread of economic, political, social, cultural and technological interactions across countries; that is, the spreading of ideas, information, values and flows of people, goods, capital, services and market exchanges. As such, when there is a differentiated role or reaction to these flows across gender lines, the spread of such interactions would also be expected to follow gender lines.

Three hypotheses can be defined on the role of globalisation on gender: economic globalisation, social globalisation and political globalisation. Hypotheses can be formulated along the following lines:

- *Economic globalisation:* does economic globalisation improve women's economic rights in the form of employment and wages, and if so, what is the role of men in the process?
- *Social globalisation:* does globalisation provide women with more opportunities to communicate and form networks? Does increased networking lead to increasing women's freedom of expression and civil association? Does globalisation result in changes in institutions, attitudes and values affecting women, and if so, what is the role of men in the process?
- *Political globalisation:* does globalisation have an impact on women's political rights including political representation and female participation in political processes?

Using data from existing sources, this section proposes a set of evidence that can be used to examine these three hypotheses. For the first hypothesis, the trends of female ownership of firms across countries in Africa are considered. Jones (2012) investigated the effects of female ownership on firm performance using evidence from Ghana, and found that, on average, female-owned firms are about 25 per cent less productive than male-owned firms, after controlling for time-invariant factors like sector, location and union status. The lower productivity could be as a result of many factors including constraints in accessing capital, weak capacity to develop effective business plans and lower access to markets. Jones (2012) finds these constraints to be binding to female-owned firms as they have a lower survival rate because of lower productivity. In a globalised world, where competition weeds out lower productivity firms, we should expect to see fewer female-owned firms except in locations where female-owned companies have succeeded in improving productivity, or where there are strong networks of support that allow female-owned firms to succeed.

Looking at data from The World Bank's Doing Business indicators (The World Bank, 2014), globalisation has had a differential effect on the role of women in enterprises. Consider, for example, that between 2005 and 2010, the depth of female ownership in domestically listed companies was less than 50 per cent in all but three countries (Côte d'Ivoire, Liberia and Madagascar) (see Table 4.2). The availability of strong networks of women traders who then go on to form companies and enterprises that generate jobs and exports is one of the distinguishing features of these three countries.

Other economic dimensions of globalisation can be seen in the positive effects it has had in raising incomes for all families. However, globalisation has not eroded gender disparities (Giugale, 2011). Women found more employment opportunities in societies that opened up more to the outside world but remained 'occupationally segregated', according to Giugale (2011). There are also some negative effects as a result of globalisation, such as women being stuck in subsistence farming in societies with low manufacturing capabilities. Women have not enjoyed employment in the booming extractive industries of oil, gas and mining, and hence stand to lose out even more, with the new discoveries of oil and gas and rich minerals in Africa.

Table 4.2: Firms with female participation in ownership (2005–10)

Depth of female ownership (%)	Countries	Share of countries (%)
No data	Central African Republic, Comoros, Djibouti, Equatorial Guinea, Libya, Sao Tome & Principe, Somalia, Sudan, Tunisia, Zimbabwe	19
0–10	Eritrea, Sierra Leone	4
11–20	Algeria, **Burkina Faso**, **Cameroon**, Guinea Bissau, Lesotho, Mali, Mauritania, Mauritius, Morocco, Niger, Nigeria	21
21–30	Angola, Gambia (The), Guinea, Malawi, Mozambique, Senegal, South Africa, Swaziland	15
31–40	Burundi, **Cape Verde**, Congo DR, Congo, Egypt, Ethiopia, Gabon, Kenya, Namibia, Tanzania, Togo, Uganda, Zambia	25
41–50	Benin, Botswana, Chad, Ghana, Rwanda	10
>50	Côte d'Ivoire, Liberia, Madagascar	6

Note: Countries in bold type have seen significant changes.

Therefore, supporting the first hypothesis, evidence shows that, while there are positive impacts of globalisation on the role of women in owning companies and also on their income status, there are frictions that need to be catered for (see Table 4.3). These include supporting the productivity improvements of female-owned companies by having them learn, partner or merge with male-owned companies. Other actions could include making deliberate efforts to pair up women with men in the sectors like oil, gas and mining, and encouraging girls at an early age to be interested in science and technology. Within the agriculture sector, deliberate efforts to use the access to ideas that has been made easier as a result of globalisation, in order to bring productivity improvements to the agricultural practices of women, could also go a long way to addressing the apparent negative effects of women being stuck in subsistence farming. Rwanda is a country that has used these ideas to further the productivity gains from agriculture, and to bring the positive impacts of global knowledge to bear on the performance of activities led by women. This is especially visible in the 'one cow one family' programme (Ntanyoma, 2010), where the government provided support for families to have access to a cow. Milk production levels not only went up, but the welfare of households did as well. Governments can therefore play a very important role in ensuring access to knowledge and ideas, in addition to capital and technology, to change economic outcomes across gender dimensions. Ensuring access to land and titles for women could also go a long way to eradicating some of the productivity-related challenges. Women who do not hold a title would not have as much incentive to invest in the future, fearing risk of loss of that investment should a husband or father die.

For the second hypothesis on social globalisation, there is evidence of differential effects on men and women in Africa. Positive effects relate to the progress made on the ratification of the Committee

Table 4.3: Globalisation and its differential effects on men and women in Africa: economic dimensions

Positive effects	Negative effects
• *Globalisation raised incomes for all families but did not address the gender disparities* • *Women found more employment opportunities in societies that opened up more to the outside world but remained 'occupationally segregated'*	• Women remained stuck in subsistence farming in societies with low manufacturing capabilities • Women have not enjoyed employment in the booming extractive industry sectors – oil, gas, mining

Source: Giugale (2011); Cho (2012)

on the Elimination of Discrimination Against Women (CEDAW),[2] which has increased literacy levels, participation in the economy and representation in parliament. Changes in institutions that come about from participation in international organisations and declarations can alter culture and result in changes in attitudes and values of concern to women's equality (Gray et al, 2006). As women engage internationally with other women, they learn about different ways of practising, and bring these practices to their home countries, thereby changing practices in their local environment. A good example is what has happened in the area of female genital mutilation, where international and regional pressure has come to bear in changing practices at the local level in a number of countries.

Negative effects have been around the issue of trade, where international trade has been seen to erode traditional and local economies or to degrade the environment. This has consequences for both men and women who suffer when their surroundings deteriorate (Gray et al, 2006). Other negative effects have to do with the weak bargaining capabilities of local societies that expose them (women in particular) to risks of diminishing opportunities from globalisation (Gray et al, 2006). An example is what has happened to the land tilled by women when rich minerals have been discovered underneath and they have been dispossessed of the land for mining purposes, as has happened in Zimbabwe and Zambia. It is clear from looking at data on trade that this is an area that could benefit from having both men and women improve their skills in trade negotiation and bargaining capacities. Achievements on the trade front at the country and regional level is likely to help both men and women, and efforts should go there, rather than to the differential role of men and women in trade. As countries join international institutions such as the World Trade Organization (WTO) and other international institutions, one could expect positive effects for changes in culture, attitudes and values concerning women's equality (see Table 4.4).

Evidence for the third hypothesis, on whether globalisation has an impact on women's political rights including political representation and female participation in political processes, is more difficult to establish. This is mainly because in some ways Africa is more advanced than other regions of the world in terms of women in important political positions. The continent boasted four women heads of state as of 2013 – Liberia, where President Ellen Johnston-Sirleaf won a second term and was still in office in 2013; Malawi, where President Joyce Banda was sworn in following the death of the former president, served for one term and lost at the elections; Mauritius,

Table 4.4: Globalisation and its differential effects on men and women in Africa: social dimensions

Positive effects	Negative effects
• *Ratification of CEDAW has increased female levels of literacy, participation in the economy, and representation in parliament* • *Changes in institutions that come about from participation in international organisations and declarations can alter culture and result in changes in attitudes and values of concern to women's equality*	• Where international trade erodes traditional local economies or degrades the environment, women as well as men suffer • Weak bargaining capabilities of local societies expose them (women in particular) to risks of diminishing opportunities from globalisation

Source: Gray et al (2006)

where Monique Ohsan Bellpeau was President for a few months in 2012 and then assumed the position of Vice President; and the Central African Republic, where Catherine Samba-Panza had been acting as President since January 2014. Having a woman as head of state does not always lead to positive outcomes, as has been seen in the case of Liberia and Malawi, where critics have noted increased corruption and other social ills plaguing both countries. There are also many more women in parliament in Rwanda than in many other countries in the world. The examples from practice shared next provide some insights into the reasons for such success, and the lessons learned for other areas of partnership between the genders to get better results.

Examples from practice

There are a number of examples that can be used to see how the issue of gender and the specific role of men and boys feature in development questions. Looking at cultural factors, Marin et al (1997) show the pathways through which culture has an effect on the efficacy of social policies. The cultural effects have been assessed with respect to condom use. Traditional gender role attitudes shape the reaction women would have towards condom use, which leads to two main potential outcomes – arguments about sexual comfort and coercive sexual behaviour which limits the use of condoms. Affected by social norms around condom use and any perceived failure in the self-efficacy of condoms, the norms combine to limit the actual use of condoms. There will be no change in the use of condoms unless there are changes in the perceptions around sexual comfort and the attitude towards women and the degree of coercion in sexual behaviour. Improvements in the technology of condoms could also have an influence in raising the degree of condom use, and hence the outcomes on sexually transmitted diseases in society and on women and girls.

On the political side, we look at the role of men in supporting women in politics. We investigate two types of changes – those that are driven by changes in the constitution and those that come from instituting quotas – in the expected role of women in politics. The case of Rwanda is one where quotas were instituted resulting in a 63.8 per cent of women in parliament following the elections of September 2011, which is more than four times higher than the world average (Inter-Parliamentary Union, 2013). South Africa chose the constitutional route, and has seen a steady increase in the numbers of women in local government since 1995, with women holding 40.8 per cent of seats following the elections in May 2014. In both cases, it means that men would have had to vote for women to have them in parliament or local government. The changes in perception could have come about as a result of seeing women in positions of power, and gaining confidence that they can play the role. The changing role of men and women thus has an impact on attitudes and subsequent political outcomes (see Figure 4.3).

Another important factor in investigating the issue of gender in political leadership has to do with the role men play in supporting women in politics. In Liberia, Ellen Johnson-Sirleaf was elected President with a large support from men. In Mauritius, Monique Ohsan-Bellepeau succeeded into the role of acting President in March 2012 with support from men in large numbers. In Malawi, Joyce Banda succeeded peacefully into the presidency in April 2012. All these political successes happened largely because of the support these candidates had from women, but not exclusively, as they needed men to support them to attain majorities, and indeed, to govern.

Gender and culture

The role of men and boys in development varies by culture, as can be seen in the case of condom use among Latino men in Los Angeles (Harvey and Henderson, 2006). The effects of globalisation described earlier have also been functioning on cultural levels, with specific impacts on local norms around the role of women. The apparel sector and trade have been particularly important in shaping the access of women to economic production channels in a number of countries.

Figure 4.3: Role of men in supporting women in politics: quotas versus constitutions

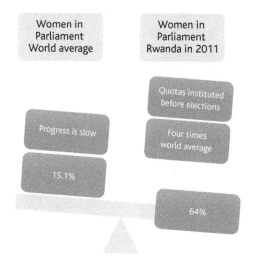

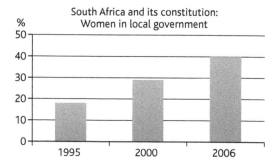

Source: Beall (2004); EISA (2009); Inter-Parliamentary Union (2015)

However, culture can also have a distorting effect on trade and economic activity. A particularly telling case study to illustrate this point is the global trade in used clothing in Africa. Used underwear sparked a sensitive debate on culture in Africa, which brings to bear many of the arguments made so far on the role of culture on gender and its related effects. A number of organisations, including charities, have been selling used clothing in Africa, including used undergarments. On 10 January 2012, Zimbabwe banned the sale of used underwear in an effort to maintain health standards and to protect the domestic textile industry. The ban came from legislation introduced by the finance minister, Tendai Biti, who was reportedly appalled to find out many of the country's flea markets were selling used, and sometimes soiled, undergarments to impoverished customers (*Christian Post Africa*, 2012). The *Zimbabwe Mail* (9/1/2012) quoted the minister as saying, 'If you are a husband and you see your wife buying underwear from the flea market, you would have failed', adding 'If I was your in-law, I would take my daughter and urge you to first put your house in order if you still want her back.' The arguments of personal hygiene and self-esteem were debated across the spectrum of comments in social media in Africa.

Conclusions

This chapter has provided the causal pathways that need to be considered when designing effective policies. Evidence has been provided that when such causality is well understood and integrated into development policy and decision-making, the outcomes for women, adolescent girls and society as a whole are better. Understanding the role men and boys can play in getting transformational change in society is critical for the attainment of the Millennium Development Goals (MDGs), and even more important in light of the post-2015 debate in Africa. Such comprehension is critical, whether looking at issues of security, economic and social wellbeing, or participation in political and business decision-making.

Questions of women's security – whether personal in terms of freedom from fear of being attacked at home, within the community or as they go about their economic activities – are intricately tied to the role, attitudes, perceptions and behaviour of men. There cannot be a peace and security agenda that does not include women and adolescent girls, and there cannot be good outcomes for women when men and boys are not included.

The inclusion of women in economic transformation, whether domestic or global, is critical for the development of countries. When women have access to land, jobs and finance, they are able to contribute to their own and their families' improvement and wellbeing. It is, however, critical to be mindful of the blockers to the economic access channels that are related to culture – the differentiated role of men and women in finance, access to land and access to certain types of jobs and positions of authority. Lack of attention to cultural factors could render inclusion policies less effective, as shown in the case of safety in the workplace in global manufacturing value chains.

Women's capacity to generate sustainable livelihoods and to have access to knowledge and ideas, as well as the resources they need to succeed – whether education and training, land, finance or title – are also intricately linked to the attitudes and behaviours of men around educating girls, providing credit to women, endowing women with land when inheritance is decided, and respecting land and property titles when women hold them. Little progress can be attained in economic outcomes for women without considering the role men play in determining access to critical factors of production.

Enacting policies that are appropriate for development requires them to be effective in dealing with challenges of exclusion, including exclusion of women. Such policies can only come about when women are engaged in processes of political decision-making, policy design and investment prioritisation. All these are important priorities for the post-2015 development agenda, and as they, too, are intricately linked to the role men play in social, economic and political spheres, the understanding of these intricate linkages is critical for an effective post-2015 development agenda.

In conclusion, there are a number of areas where support from boys and men is needed in order to get positive outcomes in the welfare of women and girls. Such areas include policies that require a change in behaviour that goes at deeply routed norms and practices – as in the case of access to finance, safety in the workplace, access to the market, including a safe means of transport, and reproductive health issues. Other instances are when change requires a deep transformation that can only succeed if the whole of society is engaged and is benefiting – such as in the bargaining power for trade and access under globalisation, actions to control negative effects on the ecosystem, or inclusive and effective political systems. Yet other examples relate to when transformation can only happen when men join in the process of change – as in electing women political leaders, educating the girl child, and building effective and sustainable businesses. Finally, men and boys' support can be elicited to get change in other critical areas by tapping into their cultural functions and standing in society – as in the access to land and land titles. All these illustrations support the theoretical underpinnings of the role of men and boys in generating outcomes from policy changes relating to women and girls.

References

Ahmed, F.E. (2004) 'The rise of the Bangladesh garment industry: globalization, women workers, and voice', *Feminist Formations*, vol 16, no 2, pp 34-5.

Beall, J. (2005) *Decentralizing government and centralizing gender in southern Africa: Lessons from South African experience.* United Nations Research

Institute For Social Development (UNRISD) Occasional Paper 8. New York: United Nations.

Becker, G. (1957/1971) *The economics of discrimination*, Chicago, IL: University of Chicago Press.

Black, S.E. and Brainerd, E. (2004) 'Importing equality? The impact of globalization on gender discrimination', *Industrial and Labor Relations Review*, vol 57, no 4.

Cho, S.Y. (2012) *Integrating equality – Globalization, women's rights, and human trafficking*, Economics of Security Working Paper 69, Berlin: German Institute for Economic Research (DIW).

Christian Post Africa (2012) 'Zimbabwe bans sale of used underwear the poor are often forced to buy', 10 January.

Connell, R.W. (2003) *The role of men and boys in achieving gender equality*, Report submitted to the Expert Group Meeting on 'The role of men and boys in achieving gender equality' held in Brasilia, Brazil from 21 to 24 October by the United Nations Division for the Advanced of Women (DAW) in collaboration with ILO, UNAIDS and UNDP (www.un.org/womenwatch/daw/egm/men-boys2003/Connell-bp.pdf).

Cornwall, A., Edström, J. and Greig, A. (2011) *Men and development: Politicizing masculinities*, London: Zed Books.

Dalal, K., Dahlström, Ö. and Timpka, T. (2013) 'Interactions between microfinance programmes and non-economic empowerment of women associated with intimate partner violence in Bangladesh: a cross-sectional study', *British Medical Journal*, vol 3, no 12 (www.ncbi.nlm.nih.gov/pmc/articles/PMC3855592/).

EISA (2009) *Election Update South Africa: February–July, 2009*, Johannesburg: EISA.

Ellis, J. and Leposo, L. (2012) 'Rwandan basketmakers weave their way into Macy's', *African Voices*, CNN, 22 June.

Foller, M. (2001) 'Interactions between global processes and local health problems. A human ecology approach to indigenous groups in the Amazon', *Cadernos de Saúde Publica*, vol 17, Supplement Rio de Janeiro.

Ghannam, F. (2013) *Live and die like a man: Gender dynamics in urban Egypt*, Stanford, CA: Stanford University Press.

Giugale, M. (2011) 'Globalization: has it helped or hurt women?', *Huffington Post*, 16 December.

Gray, M.M., Caul Kittilson, M. and Sandholtz, W. (2006) 'Women and globalization: a study of 180 countries, 1975-2000', *International Organization*, vol 60, no 2, pp 293-333.

Guilamo-Ramos, V., Jaccard, J., Lushin, V., Martinez, R., Gonzalez, B. and McCarthy, K. (2011) 'HIV risk behavior among youth in the Dominican Republic: the role of alcohol and drugs', *Journal of the International Association of Providers of AIDS Care*, vol 10, no 6, pp 388-95.

Harvey, S.M. and Henderson, J.T. (2006) 'Correlates of condom use intentions and behaviours among a community-based sample of Latino men in Los Angeles', *Journal of Urban Health*, July, vol 83, no 4, pp 558-74.

Hatem, M.F. (2013) 'The Arab Spring: youth and gender in the debate on gender and revolution', *Turkish Review*, 1 March (www.turkishreview.org).

Hausmann, R., Tyson, L.D. and Zahidi, S. (2012) *The global gender gap report 2012*, Geneva: World Economic Forum (www3.weforum.org/docs/WEF_GenderGap_Report_2012.pdf).

Hossain, M., Zimmerman, C., Kiss, L., Abramsky, T., Kone, D., Bakayoko-Toposlska, M., Annan, J., Lehmann, H. and Watts, C. (2014) 'Working with men to prevent intimate partner violence in a conflict-affected setting: a pilot cluster randomized controlled trial in rural Côte d'Ivoire', *BMC Public Health*, vol 14 (www.ncbi.nlm.nih.gov/pmc/articles/PMC4007144/).

IFHI 360 (2013) 'Mobile for reproductive health project: Rwanda', Program Brief, IFHI 360, The Science for Improving Health (www.fhi360.org/sites/default/files/media/documents/m4rh-rwanda-brief.pdf).

Inter-Parliamentary Union (2015) 'Sluggish progress on women in politics will hamper development'. Press release (www.ipu.org/press-e/pressrelease201503101.htm).

ITC (International Trade Centre) (2014) 'Women and trade', Women and Trade Programme, ITC (www.intracen.org/itc/projects/women-and-trade/).

Johnston, K., Kennedy, C., Murdoch, I., Taylor, P. and Cook, C. (2004) 'The cost-effectiveness of technology transfer using telemedicine', *Health and Policy Planning*, vol 19, pp 302-9.

Jones, N., Holmes, R. and Espey, J. (2010) 'Progressing gender equality post-2015: harnessing the multiple effects of existing achievements', *IDS Bulletin, Special Issue: The MDGs and Beyond*, vol 41, no 1, pp 113-22.

Jones, P. (2012) 'Identifying the effects of female ownership on firm performance: evidence from Ghana', *Journal of Economic Literature* (https://editorialexpress.com/cgi-bin/conference/download.cgi?db_name=CSAE2012&paper_id=433).

Kim, J.C., Watts, C.H., Hargreaves, J.R., Ndhlovu, L.X., Phetla, G., Morison, L.A., Busza, J., Porter, J.D.H. and Pronyk, P. (2007) 'Understanding the impact of a micro-finance-based intervention on women's empowerment and the reduction of intimate partner violence in South Africa', *American Journal of Public Health*, October, vol 97, no 10, pp 1-10 (www.ncbi.nlm.nih.gov/pmc/articles/PMC1994170/).

Locke, R.M., Qin, F. and Brause, A. (2007) 'Does monitoring improve labor standards? Lessons from Nike', *ILR Review*, vol 61, no 1.

Marin, B., VanOss Gomez, C.A., Tschann, J.M. and Gregorich, S.E. (1997) 'Condom use in unmarried Latino men: a test of cultural constructs', *Health Psychology*, vol 16, no 5, pp 458-67.

Moser, C. (1993) *Gender planning and development: Theory, practice and training*, New York: Routledge.

Murphy, K. (2013) 'What Borgen's prime minister tells us about Julia Gillard', Australia Culture Blog, *The Guardian*, 13 June.

Ntanyoma, R.D. (2010) 'The effect of livestock production on poor and small holder farmers' income in Rwanda: case of one cow one family program', Research paper presented in partial fulfillment of the requirements for obtaining a Masters of Arts in Development Studies, The Hague, The Netherlands.

Olopade, D. (2012) 'The fairer leaders, views from around the world', *New York Times*, 10 July.

Quist-Arcton, O. (2010) 'In Ghanaian village, American woman reigns as king', NPR Special Series: 'Hidden world of girls', 11 November.

Sesay, I. and Kermellotis, T. (2013) 'The American secretary who became king: a woman's journey to royalty', *African Voices*, CNN, 1 February.

Talbot, D. (2011) 'Kenya has mobile health app fever', *MIT Technology Review: Communications News*, 16 December (www.technologyreview.com/news/426378/kenya-has-mobile-health-app-fever/).

Tinker, I (1990) *Persistent inequalities: Women and world development*, New York: Oxford University Press.

Uddin, S. (2013) 'Bangladesh factory collapse: why women endure danger to make clothes for the West', NBC News, World News on NBCNEWS.com, 26 May.

UN (United Nations) Women (2013) *A transformative stand-alone goal on achieving gender equality, women's rights and women's empowerment: Imperatives and key components*, UN Women Policy Division, Position Papers, p 42 (www.unwomen.org/en/digital-library/publications/2013/7/post-2015-long-paper).

van Tulder, R. and Kolk, A. (2001) 'Multinationality and corporate ethics: codes of conduct in the sporting goods industry', *Journal of International Business Studies*, vol 32, no 2, pp 267-83.

World Bank, The (2012) *World development indicators 2012*, Washington, DC: The World Bank (http://data.worldbank.org/products/wdi).

World Bank, The (2014) *Doing Business Indicators 2014: Understanding regulations for small and medium size enterprises*, Washington, DC: The World Bank (www.doingbusiness.org/reports/global-reports/doing-business-2014).

Zimbabwe Mail (9/1/2012)

FIVE

Service-oriented government: the developmental state and service delivery in Africa after 2015 – are capacity indicators important?

George Kararach

Introduction

A service-oriented government has a social contract to deliver services to its population, thereby winning trust and legitimacy (Besley and Ghatak, 2007). Since the early 1980s, African countries have embarked on various forms of 'modern' public sector reforms, with mixed results, and various reasons have been given for these. One of the criticisms is that reforms were undertaken without sufficient data or understanding of the realities on the ground, and thus resultant economic growth is questionable (Jerven, 2011). By the 1990s, the debate had moved to whether or not the African civil service was too big ('bloated'), cost too much and needed to be reduced (see, for example, Kiggundu, 1992; see also World Bank, 1993, 1997, 2000). Indeed, the 'development' community often argues that what African countries need is not so much building new capacities as discovering and implementing more strategic and effective utilisation of existing indigenous ones (The World Bank, 2005).

In order to utilise capacity better and accelerate progress toward the Millennium Development Goals (MDGs), African governments, donors and non-governmental organisations (NGOs) have committed to increase resources to improve service delivery. Unfortunately, budget allocations alone do not determine outcomes (Besley and Ghatak, 2007), and are poor indicators of the true quality of services in countries with weak institutions (Svensson, 2012). Moreover, when service delivery failures are systematic, relying exclusively on the public sector to address them may not be realistic (UNECA, 1991), requiring an approach that may incorporate the private and voluntary sectors (Besley and Ghatak, 2007; Makoba, 2011). It is necessary to empower citizens and civil society actors to put pressure on governments to improve performance (Besley et al, 2005). For this to be realised, citizens must have access to information on service delivery performance as well as quality.[1]

Until recently, there has been no robust, standardised set of indicators to measure the quality of services as experienced by citizens in Africa. Existing indicators tended to be fragmented, focusing either on final outcomes or inputs, rather than on the underlying systems (ACBF, 2011; The World Bank, 2012). Efforts such as the African Peer Review Mechanism (APRM) did not make much headway because of its voluntary nature,[2] and the tendency of governments to restrict the cohort studied as well as being inadequately self-critical (Jordaan, 2006; Boyle, 2008). Without consistent and accurate information on the quality of services, it is difficult for citizens or politicians (the principal) to assess how service providers (the agent) are performing and to hold service providers to account. Although the quality of data relating to Africa's public administration has improved over the years by way of indicators (for example, The World Bank's Doing Business or the Country Policy and Institutional Assessment, CPIA), none has so far focused on capacity assessment and development. The annual African Capacity Building Foundation (ACBF) Africa capacity indicators reports attempt to change this. These reports, based on a sample of countries, provide both qualitative and quantitative data on several clusters of capacities for development and a widened cohort of respondents.

The purpose of this chapter is to contextualise and review ACBF's work relating to the 2011 and 2012 Africa capacity indicators reports, their relevance for public service reform, and to discuss possible implications for more specified and targeted capacity development interventions for different countries such as fragile states (the focus of the 2011 report), sectors such as agriculture (the focus of the 2012 report), and the overall modernisation of the African public service, including local governance and development.

The chapter discusses the broader context of the developmental state and public service delivery in Africa, debating the notion of capacity, and covering several issues that arise from the use of capacity indicators to understand the nature of the relationships between actors and the beneficiaries of services, namely, accountability, project design and evaluation.

Debating the developmental state and service delivery in Africa

Africa's post-independence development experience gave rise to a debate about the state in social transformation, and comparisons were made with the Southeast Asian experience (World Bank, 1993, 1997). Post-independence development paradigms were based on the idea of a strong central government that would secure 'social justice' for all citizens, and an economic programme characterised by nationalisation and attempts at import-substitution industrialisation. However, from this emerged non-democratic regimes and highly centralised and monolithic states. The new regimes and central governments were considered as facilitators of wealth redistribution, whereas the people's sense of duty, responsibility and identity remained centred on local concerns, within ethnic groups, the village and the family – with devastating consequences for service delivery (Easterly and Levine, 1997).

This resulted in social conflicts and led many national armies or civil groups to forcibly seize power. From around 1963, Africa found itself mired in a spiral of political, social and ethnic conflict. Most of the military regimes adopted new constitutions in order to guarantee freedom and human rights for all citizens. But the political and socioeconomic conditions of Africa that underpinned the demands for reform had not improved. Reforms were needed that ensured that citizens were not treated as subjects (Mamdani, 1996).

By the 1980s and 1990s, both domestic and external forces started to exert considerable pressure on African governments to 'liberalise' the political and economic space – redefining the role of the state. Consequently, various attempts at systems were embarked on that entailed ambitious programmes of political, institutional and economic reform. The major objectives of these reforms were changing the role of government (World Bank, 2000), creating an enabling environment for the private sector and civil society to flourish, and establishing an effective civil service by increasing its competence, efficiency, fairness and quality of services. Some of the reforms came in the guise of New Public Management (NPM). Unfortunately, governance in Africa has been marked by authoritarianism and state privatisation for the benefit of the ruling elite, resulting in institutional disintegration rather than development and effective service delivery (Besley and Ghatak, 2007).

The success of state-led economic development in the 1970s and 1980s in East Asia (Amsden, 1989) gave rise to the emergence of a new perspective in the development discourse, namely, the developmental state (Amsden, 1989; Rapley, 1996, pp 118-19; Woo-Cumings, 1999, p 63; Boyd and Ngo, 2005, p 1). Initial studies concentrated on understanding the political, economic, financial and institutional factors and configurations that led to the successful development outcomes witnessed in the East Asian region (Woo-Cumings, 1999). Inquiries focused on identifying the necessary ingredients through growth diagnostics – governance, economic and social conditions – that would make the implementation of the developmental state approach feasible in non-East Asian regions under current global political and economic conditions (see, for example, Robinson and White 1998; Rodrik, 1996; Woo-Cumings, 1999; Mkandawire, 2001; Weiss, 2003; Chang, 2006; Acemoglu, 2008).

Chalmers Johnson pioneered the conversation on the developmental state, focusing on Japan's very rapid and highly successful postwar reconstruction and industrialisation process from 1925 to 1975 (Johnson, 1982). He argued that the origin of Japan's developmental state is best understood not in cultural terms, but rather by examining the specific events that shaped the country's history – especially the efforts aimed at coping with an international order dominated by the Western developed countries. Johnson locates Japan's motivation in two major contexts: (i) being a late developer striving to catch up; and (ii) within East Asian revolutionary nationalism (Johnson, 1982, pp 11, 25, 1999, p 44).

Johnson contends that markets do not exist in isolation, but that they are a creation of the state, and politics set the necessary operational boundaries between a plan-rational and a market-rational arrangement. He posits that, 'observers coming from a market-rational system often misunderstand the plan-rational system because they fail to appreciate that it has a political and not an economic basis' (Johnson, 1982, p 24). The most crucial element of the developmental state is not its economic policy, but its ability to mobilise the nation around economic development within a capitalist system (Johnson, 1982, pp 302-10). He argues that a developmental state is characterised by a small but inexpensive, professional and efficient state bureaucracy (Johnson, 1982, pp 314-20). A 'developmental' or 'plan-rational state' is one that is determined to influence the direction and pace of economic development by directly intervening in the development process, rather than relying on the uncoordinated influence of the market to allocate economic resources (Johnson, 1982, pp 319-20).

Evans (1989, 1995) introduced the concept of 'embedded autonomy' to illustrate his argument that developmental outcomes are largely conditioned by the form taken by state organisation – the bureaucratic elements as well as the nature of its ties with dominant societal interests. The state is autonomous insofar as its bureaucracy cannot be instrumentally manipulated and agency-captured by powerful rent-seekers, and is embedded insofar as it is able to maintain close contact with dominant interests in society for the purpose of negotiating and soliciting necessary resource inputs required in the transformation process (Evans, 1995, p 12). There are two salient features that characterise and combine autonomy and 'embeddedness' (Evans, 1995, p 164). First, the state bureaucracy is in a relatively privileged position held by a single pilot agency (Evans, 1995, pp 156, 157). Second, these bureaucracies are capable of binding the behaviour of both the incumbent public officials and the private sector to the pursuit of collective ends (Evans, 1995, pp 164-5). Effective state capacity in respect of the relationship between the state and private enterprise is critical in determining the developmental role of the state (Evans, 1995, pp 13-16, 58, 70-81, 209-10). The state may never fully manage to escape the dangers of particularistic interests and is not and cannot be static. It tends to progressively transform itself into 'its own gravedigger' (Evans, 1992, p 165). The state is able to shift positions along the continuum of 'predatory–developmental states' suggested in the embedded autonomy thesis (Evans, 1992, p 157), and when it is constructed under extremely challenging and in conducive conditions (Evans, 1992, p 164).

Adrian Leftwich introduced a theory and model of the developmental state premised purely on political considerations (Leftwich, 2000, p 4). The emergence and consolidation of a developmental state is conditioned by five major factors (Leftwich, 2000, pp 160-5): (i) a political elite which is developmentally oriented and which demonstrates high levels of commitment and will in attaining economic growth and possessing sufficient capacity to influence, direct and set the terms of operation for private capital (Leftwich, 2000, pp 163-4); (ii) the creation of a powerful, professional, highly competent, insulated and career-based bureaucracy; (iii) the existence of a social context in which civil society has been weak, to allow for easy moulding by the political elite; (iv) the existence of high levels of capacity for the effective economic management of both domestic and foreign private economic interests; and (v) a record of a mix of repression and poor human rights adherence or limited space for dialogue and policy debate. This gives rise to the question of whether there is need for democracy before development, or vice versa (Leftwich, 2000, p 174). Leftwich concedes that the development performance of a particular country is not a function of the regime type, but rather, it is decisively influenced by the 'character of the state and its associated politics' (Leftwich, 1993, p 614). Thus developmental states do not arise from formulae devised in Western capitals or think tanks (Leftwich, 2000, p 168). Such states can only come about through indigenous processes of capacity building and public sector performance improvements (ACBF 2002; Kararach, 2012). This is a welcome conclusion if human development and service delivery is the focus.

The IPE, or institutional political economy, approach posits an alternative theory of state intervention, and provides an alternative framework to the neoliberal paradigm (Chang, 1999, pp 185-7, 2002b, 2003c, p 3, 2003d, pp 50-2). IPE delineates four crucial elements of neoliberalism, namely, the state, the market, institutions and politics (Chang, 2002b, p 542). IPE asserts that the state has an important role to play, not only in regulating the market system, but also in actually constructing and directly influencing the operation of the markets beyond the limits allowed by the neoliberal orthodoxy espoused under the Washington Consensus (Chang, 2002b, pp 547-8, 2003d). The policies of successful East Asian states often significantly diverted from the Washington Consensus (Chang, 2006, p 2). Indeed, most developing countries that have placed great faith in the primacy and total freedom of the market have attained unsatisfactory development outcomes (Chang, 2002b, p 548). Second, there is no such thing as a 'free' market as they are all created and must be regulated (Chang, 2002b, p 544). The conventional market versus institutions dichotomy is thus misleading as markets themselves are also institutions (Chang, 2006, p 50; see also Chang, 2002a, 2003a,b, 2007). In fact, the emergence of the market order derives from an active role of the state (Chang, 2003d, p 50). In most successful economic experiences, it is the state and not the market that has demonstrated effective capacity to coordinate investment, make economic decisions, finance industry, discipline recipients of state-created rents and provide a development vision (Chang, 1999, pp 182, 194). These roles of the state become even more important in the case of developing countries (Chang, 2006, p 28). Markets are fundamentally political constructs, and therefore it is not possible or even desirable to completely depoliticise them (Chang, 2002b, p 555). The construction of markets and the process of defining 'endowments' for market participants is a highly political exercise (Chang, 2002b, p 559; Kararach, 2011). The role of politics in the market must be seen as a process through which people with different, and equally legitimate, views on the contestability of the existing rights–obligations structure vie with each other depending on principal–agent relations (Chang, 2002b, pp 555-6).

Linda Weiss asks the question: has globalisation rendered the developmental state approach irrelevant (Weiss, 2000)? Globalisation has resulted in two important tendencies: fragmentation and the emergence of global value chains. Fragmentation describes a situation where various components are produced in different countries (Feenstra, 1998). This process is sometimes referred to as 'vertical specialisation'. te Velde et al (2006) report that world trade in parts and components in the manufacturing sector stands at about 30 per cent. Campa and Goldberg (1997), using an input-output methodology, find that fragmentation as measured by the share of imports in total inputs used in production has risen considerably over the years. Developing countries have, to some extent, benefited from these dynamics.

In global value chains, trade is based on networks of firms across national borders. A value chain describes the range of activities needed to bring a product or service from conception, through the processes of production, into finalisation for consumers and disposal after use (Kaplinsky, 2000). To appreciate the complexity of these processes, one needs to understand the typology of governance in value chains and the effects of these (te Velde, 2010). Of concern here is the way developing countries participate in global value chains – especially the nature of the capacity and skills required for them to benefit from such engagements with rich country importers and retailers.

So what are the defining features of the developmental state in Africa?

Development-oriented political leadership: a development-orientated political leadership and a powerful economic and political ideology focused on development are essential (Amsden, 1989; Wade, 1990; Woo-Cumings, 1999; Beeson, 2003). It is generally argued that the East Asian developmental states had political elites that were able to devise functional state institutions heralding both political stability and economic development (Waldner, 1999, p 1). The bureaucracy had sufficient scope to take the initiative and to act authoritatively in pursuit of the desired development goals (Wade, 1990; Weiss, 2003, p 24). The East Asian states' unique capacity was rooted in political alliances, domestic authoritarian rule and effective economic institutions (Deyo, 1987). However, with respect to Africa, Mkandawire's (2001) argument that development was a central preoccupation for most first-generation leaders in Africa may be exaggerated, although it can be held to apply to a number of them, such as Kaunda in Zambia, Nyerere in Tanzania or Nkrumah in Ghana. In these cases, the developmental state's ambitions were pursued after independence with a focus on achieving continent-wide political 'liberation'. The development project was not supported by visions of development that extended to ensuring adequate public services. There was an overbearing statist intervention in the economy without the supportive productive services such as education, health and communication. Supported initially by primary sector export income, poorly performing state-owned enterprises were subsidised by the treasury, becoming a major drain on scarce foreign exchange reserves, and were a source of macroeconomic instability. This excessive 'statism' encouraged rent-seeking that diverted economic actors from productive activities (Bates, 1981, pp 11-14). Eventually these 'development' projects had to be abandoned. One can cautiously argue that the recent turn-around in Africa's fortunes may be related to reforms that put governance and people first (The World Bank, 2012), as other drivers of growth such as commodity prices and access to new markets remain unstable and unpredictable.

Autonomous and effective bureaucracy: with respect to the autonomy, capability and effectiveness of the bureaucracy, the East Asian developmental states have arguably been outstanding (Woo-Cumings, 1991; Clapham, 1996, p 162; Booth, 1999, p 305; Wong, 2004). Although the postcolonial state in Africa assumed a huge economic role, it did not have the manpower or regulatory and administrative capacity to efficiently manage the tasks at hand (Englebert, 2000; van de Walle, 2001; Nissanke and Aryeetey, 2003, p 4). The bureaucracy in postcolonial Africa also lacked the autonomy deemed necessary in a developmental state, as it fractured into ethno-linguistic interests, becoming susceptible to predatory behaviour (corruption, rent-seeking, abuse of public resources) and a basic lack of accountability (Easterly and Levine, 1997; Olukoshi, 2004). This, in turn, had detrimental effects on the performance of the bureaucracy, particularly with regard to policy-making and implementation and service delivery (Besley and Ghatak, 2007).

Production-oriented private sector: a production-oriented private sector has been critical for the rapid progress of industrialisation and modernisation that occurred in the East Asian developmental states (Aküyz et al, 1999, p 1; Booth, 1999, p 306). Their development goal was high economic performance with speed and flexibility through the creation of a suitable business environment (Amsden, 1989, p 316; Westphal, 2002). State intervention in the East Asian developmental states denoted a different type of capitalism, where the primary purpose of intervention was to promote the private sector by creating conditions for capital accumulation and productivity improvement (Amsden, 1989). The state utilised a wide range of policy and institutional instruments to allow firms to meet domestic and international business standards, productivity levels and organisational and technical capacities. Such instruments included selective and strategic use of protectionism, provision of industrial subsidies and programmes tied to performance standards and targets, as well as the creation of business coalitions among industrial and financial capital and the state (Wong, 2004, p 350) The state was not only able to secure the ability of the private sector to compete at any level but, more crucially, was also able to 'create' and 'reward' in addition to 'picking' good performers and 'punishing' bad ones (Amsden, 1989, p 16; Wade, 1990).[3] Effectively, the state promoted long-term investment among the industrial elites that resulted in sustained industrial development (Low, 2004, p 5). In Africa, the private sector is yet to play a significant role in the national development process. Until recently, the state in postcolonial Africa was instinctively opposed to private sector development, and did not recognise it as a crucial development player or partner (Stein, 2000, p 18). There was a lack of incentive mechanisms to encourage private investment. State dominance of the economy led to the neglect and crowding-out of the private sector from the economic arena, and worse, to the creation of rent-seeking business elites. To be successful businesspeople depended heavily on political connections rather than performance (Mamdani, 1976). Such state–business relations encouraged corrupt practices and negatively affected business efficiency and productivity as well as service delivery (Besley and Ghatak, 2007).

Performance-oriented governance: developmental states are arguably sensitive to principal–agent relationships, and are found to enjoy the support of their constituencies because these states promote rapid economic growth and provide economic benefits to both the ruling elites and the general citizenry (Weiss, 2000, p 26; Leftwich, 2002, p 270; Chang, 2003d). This approach to development is 'pro-poor', requiring a democratic governance orientation with important consequences for service delivery. First, the ruling elites demonstrate high levels of commitment to poverty reduction as well as addressing equity concerns from the early stages of the socioeconomic transformation process (Aküyz et al, 1999, p 43; Booth, 1999, p 304; Hort and Kuhlne, 2000, pp 167-8). Rapid industrial growth in East Asia was paralleled by a favourable pattern of income equality, low unemployment and the near elimination of grinding poverty (Deyo, 1987, p 2); and second, successful economic performance is the primary source of political legitimacy (Koo and Kim, 1992, p 125; Kwon, 1999; Yang, 2000; Kim, 2007, p 120). Rapid economic development generated a broad 'growth coalition' and supportive policies sustained an institutional and political framework (Haggard, 1989, 1990). Unfortunately, most postcolonial African states opted for one-party systems that were autocratic and intolerant to dissent. This approach was allegedly appropriate for the dual tasks of nation-building and socioeconomic development, but had the unintended consequence of bolstering the ruling elites' power, and facilitated their self-enrichment; in short, it established predatory rule (Ake, 1996) without a focus on performance-oriented governance. The ruling elites depended on the distribution of spoils to stay in power, and diverted huge amounts of public resources for patronage, thus detracting from genuine development efforts (Englebert, 2000; Goldsmith, 2004, p 91; Acemoglu, 2005).

Knowledge, openness and monitoring of performance: it is also critical to add that the developmental state put high premiums to the usage of information and knowledge to allow the wider society to engage in development initiatives. In this regard, the role of the media in shaping and enhancing the flow of information, as well as facilitating policy dialogue and programme monitoring, becomes critical. Other institutions supporting accountability/transparency such as academia, parliament, anti-corruption courts, supreme audits and inspectorates of government are all key to ensure successful service delivery. The history of African countries enhancing knowledge utilisation and freedom of information is varied and chequered. Nabli and Ben Hamouda (2014) argue that the decay in the social contract that had allowed openness and huge investments in social programmes such as education and health in post-independent North Africa was a major driver of the Arab Spring of 2011 and subsequent revolutions. The importance of knowledge in a modern African economy is increasingly being recognised, resulting in a plethora of policy think tanks and knowledge networks to strengthen knowledge generation, storage and dissemination since the 1990s (Hanson and Kararach, 2011). The capacity to adapt or transfer technology will remain a critical element of this drive for transformation (Simpson, 2006) and the need to enhance service delivery. The inability to quickly adopt and adapt available knowledge as well as wider state capacity to deliver critical services was poignantly brought home by the Ebola outbreak in the three West African countries of Guinea, Liberia and Sierra Leone. Indeed, the outbreak raised deeper questions about the ability of Africa to cope with shocks and rebound to a transformative developmental trajectory.

Developmentalism in Africa in the 1960s and 1970s was characterised by weak state capacity and ineffective policy intervention in the national economy; the neglect of production-oriented private business; and excessive forms of autocratic and predatory governance as well as poor service delivery. These features undermined the initial efforts by some nationalist leaders to establish developmental states. From the late 1980s, the debate on good governance and its requirements provided an impetus for new approaches to public sector management reforms. Some of the changes that have taken place have been aimed at tackling some of the worst forms of governance abuses and failures in Africa: the personalised nature of rule in which key political actors exercise unlimited power; systemic clientelism; misuse of state resources and institutionalised corruption; opaque government; the breakdown of the public realm; the lack of delegation of power; and the withdrawal of the masses from governance (Bratton and van de Walle, 1992; Hyden and Bratton, 1992; Hyden et al, 2000).

Good public management and administration, with an emphasis on accountability and responsiveness to customer needs, has been seen as an aspect of good governance by donor agencies supporting reforms in developing countries (Léautier, 2009). To The World Bank, good governance consists of a public service that is efficient, a judicial system that is reliable, and an administration that is accountable to the public. The World Bank lists four elements of good governance (The World Bank, 1989, 1992):

1. Public sector management, emphasising the need for effective financial and human resource management through improved budgeting, accounting and reporting, and rooting out inefficiency, particularly in public enterprises.
2. Accountability in public services, including effective accounting, auditing and decentralisation, and generally making public officials responsible for their actions and responsive to consumers.
3. A predictable legal framework with rules known in advance; a reliable and independent judiciary and law enforcement mechanisms.
4. Availability of information and transparency in order to enhance policy analysis, promote public debate and reduce the risk of corruption.

In all the good governance prescriptions, public management reforms are a key component pointing towards market and private sector approaches to public sector management, under the guise of NPM.

In the literature, the 'developmental state' has two components: one *ideological*, one *structural*. It is this *ideology–structure nexus* that distinguishes developmental states. Such a state is essentially one whose ideological underpinning is 'developmentalist' in that it conceives its 'mission' as that of ensuring economic development, usually interpreted to mean high rates of accumulation and industrialisation. Such a state 'establishes as its principle of legitimacy its ability to promote sustained development, understanding by development the steady high rates of economic growth and structural change in the productive system, both domestically and in its relationship to the international economy' (Castells, 1992, p 55). At this ideational level, the élite must be able to establish an 'ideological hegemony', so that its developmental project becomes, in a Gramscian sense, a 'hegemonic' project to which key actors in the nation adhere voluntarily. The *state-structure* side of the definition of the developmental state emphasises *capacity* to implement economic policies sagaciously and effectively. Such a capacity is determined by various other related capacities: institutional, technical, administrative and political. Undergirding all these is the *autonomy* of the state from social forces so that it can use these capacities to devise long-term economic policies unencumbered by claims of myopic private interests. The quest for a 'strong state' in the development process was a feature of the 'modernisation' literature. Such a state was contrasted to what Myrdal (1968) referred to as the 'soft state' that had neither the administrative capacity nor the political wherewithal to push through its developmental project. And finally, the state must have some social anchoring that prevents it from using its autonomy in a predatory manner and enables it to gain adhesion of key social actors.

The importance of capacity in the development process has come to the fore, especially with respect to service delivery. Even though information is not yet available to delineate the precise impact of the economic crises on MDG achievement, we know that many African countries were sharply affected by these shocks. However, with support from their international development partners, including the African Development Bank (AfDB) and the United Nations Development Programme (UNDP), African countries have taken a series of measures aimed at stemming the adverse effects. The emerging picture of Africa portrays a continent that has secured progress in key areas such as net primary enrolment, gender parity in primary education, political empowerment of women, access to safe drinking water, and stemming the spread of HIV/AIDS. On the economic front, growth has begun to pick up. Policy innovations in Africa are facilitating progress toward attainment of the Millennium Development Goals (MDGs). These include new and expanded social protection programmes that were once thought to be unaffordable to most poor countries but are now embraced as important additional interventions to secure progress on key human development indicators. In addition, countries have used the MDGs as a framework for development planning, strengthening and coordination. Most African countries, however, lack three key political governance preconditions for a developmental state, namely, a viable state, secure legitimate political order and sufficient national authority (Diamond, 1999; Joseph, 1999; Gyimah-Boadi, 2004; Bratton and Chang, 2006, pp 1059, 1066).

Understanding the role of capacity in Africa's development

By the 1980s, much debate arose as to how Africa's continuing economic crisis could be alleviated and development spurred. A seminal work in this regard was the report *Sub-Sahara Africa: From crisis to sustainable growth – A long-term perspective study (LTPS)*, produced by the Africa Region of The World Bank (The World Bank, 1989). This report marked a shift from state-led development to neoliberalism. No deliberate actions were required, except in special cases to correct market failure, to build/develop capacities!

It was argued earlier that deficiencies in state capacity represent a significant weakness in the postcolonial development experience in Africa, not only in the developmentalist phase, but also under subsequent market-oriented Structural Adjustment Programmes (SAPs). Mkandawire (2001) levels strong criticism against international agencies, principally The World Bank and International Monetary Fund (IMF), arguing that these two agencies have played an important role in reducing the capacity of the civil service in many African countries by imposing SAPs. These agencies, according to Mkandawire, more often than not 'suggested that public expenditure in Africa is too high largely because of a bloated bureaucracy that drains the state coffers. The standard policy prescription was retrenchment of the civil service' (Mkandawire, 2001, p 307).

During the 1980s and 1990s, public sector reforms were conceived in the context of the SAPs – or NPM – characterised by an attempt to apply 'core' private sector operational principles to the public sector. The framework entailed four broad 'principles': (i) slowing down or reversing government growth; (ii) privatisation and quasi-privatisation; (iii) automation in the production and distribution of public services; and (iv) an international agenda in public sector reforms (Kiggundu, 1998).

Hood (1991, pp 4-5) argued that there are several key doctrinal components of NPM: (i) heads-on professional management; (ii) explicit standards and measures of performance; (iii) greater emphasis on output controls; (iv) disaggregation of units in the public sector; (v) greater competition in the public sector; (vi) private sector styles of management practice; and (vii) greater discipline and parsimony in resource use.

To Owusu and Ohemeng (2012), NPM entails the employment of market-type arrangements such as performance contracts, the creation of 'politically independent' agencies, contracting out, internal markets and citizens' charters. It is also associated with measures to reduce the public sector, namely, privatisation and retrenchment (Pollitt, 1993, cited in Owusu and Ohemeng, 2012. Manning (2001), however, views NPM as an ideology or bundle of particular management approaches and techniques (borrowed from the private for-profit sector). Joseph Ayee argues that NPM 'shifts the emphasis from traditional public administration to public management and pushes the state towards managerialism or "enterprise culture"' (Ayee, 2012, p 97).

Inadvertently, NPM considered the issue of capacity. In this framework, capacity represents an organisation's 'ability to perform work' or deliver on its mandate (Yu-Lee, 2002, p 1). With respect to the public sector, organisational capacity is synonymous with 'government's ability to marshal, develop, direct and control its financial, human, physical and information resources' (Ingraham et al, 2003, p 15), and, in the non-profit sector, as a set of management practices, processes or attributes that help an organisation to fulfil its mission (Letts et al, 1999; Eisinger, 2002, p 117).

Over the years, the notion of capacity has faced competing definitions and metrics for measurement have equally varied. For example, there seems to be some confusion between the meaning of capacity and terms such as capability and ability, and that of capacity building (Gargan, 1981; Honadle, 1981; Chaskin, 2001; Lopes, 2002; Cairns et al, 2005). Eisinger (2002, p 117) notes a disagreement in the literature as to whether organisational capacity has latent universal characteristics for most institutions, or is rather a set of attributes unique to each organisation or is multidimensional (Ingraham et al, 2003).

Capacity has been used at times to describe both the ends (effectiveness of organisation) and the means to an end (ability to deliver a mandate by an agency) (Honadle, 1981). For some scholars, the lack of capacity or presence thereof encompasses any quality that can 'impede or promote success' in achieving organisational objectives (Chaskin, 2001, p 292). Many define capacity as a purely internal organisational quality, comprising human and capital resources, and at other times as a concept with both internal and external aspects (for example, external financial support, networks of supportive relationships or partnerships, sources of training, political support, ICT, etc) to provide the supportive environment (Brinkerhoff, 2005; Forbes and Lynn, 2006). Capacity also has both tangible and intangible, or quantitative and qualitative dimensions, including not only the number of staff but also their specialised skills, and the strength or quality of organisational leadership (Glickman and Servon, 1998; Chaskin, 2001; Eisinger, 2002; Lopes, 2002; Sowa et al, 2004). Ingraham et al (2003, p 15) note, for example, that 'capacity ... rests on the quality of managers and systems.'

One could argue that much of the difficulty in conceptualising organisational capacity is related to its multiple qualities, as an input and an output/outcome, a resource as well as a process (Christensen and Gazley, 2008). Capacity development entails not just processes but also structures with qualitative and quantitative characteristics (Sowa et al, 2004) – thus the need for objective measures. Ingraham et al (2003, pp 15-22) identify four operational 'levers' driving capacity: the quality, characteristics or extent of management systems, leadership, alignment across systems and a 'results focus' to give the concept programmatic relevance. These levers are based on feedback loops that allow public managers to obtain performance information and adjust approaches accordingly. Honadle (1981, p 577) argues that although 'inputs' in the form of resources (for example, personnel, revenue, information or community support) are 'grist for capable organisations', the real institutional strengths lie in the less tangible abilities of an organisation to proactively attract, absorb and utilise resources. Capacity is different from capacity building, whereby the former describes the means to performance, while the latter is linked to efforts to improve organisational means (Polidano, 2001).

The ACBF (2011, pp 30-1) expresses capacity as:

> ... the ability of people, organizations, and society as a whole to manage their affairs successfully; and that it is the process by which people, organizations, and society as a whole unleash, strengthen, create, adapt, and maintain capacity over time. Capacity is also better conceptualized

when answering the question: capacity for what? Capacity for individuals, organizations, and societies to set goals and achieve them; to budget resources and use them for agreed purposes; and to manage the complex processes and interactions that typify a working political and economic system. Capacity is most tangibly and effectively developed in the context of specific development objectives such as delivering services to poor people; instituting education, public service, and health care reform; improving the investment climate for small and medium enterprises; empowering local communities to better participate in public decision making processes; and promoting peace and resolving conflict.

This definition is in agreement with the approach taken by the African Union (AU)/ New Partnership for Africa's Development (NEPAD) in the Capacity Development Strategic Framework (CDSF) adopted by African heads of state in 2003. The CDSF is designed to guide countries and institutions to (i) deeply analyse the fundamental capacity challenges confronting them; (ii) promote the adoption of innovative, appropriate and effective solutions to capacity development that take into account local needs, priorities and context; and (iii) encourage the application of integrated, comprehensive and sustainable solutions. The ACBF's framework appears to offer a more holistic approach to defining capacity and its associated attributes than, say, that of the AU's APRM or CDSF. One is therefore able to frame capacity not only in a multidimensional manner, but also subdivide it into distinct functional categories such as resources, effective leadership, skilled and sufficient staff, institutionalisation and external linkages (Eisinger, 2002).

Public service delivery is key because it works to cement the social contract and enhance state legitimacy. Increasingly, many governments are adapting new technology to bring services nearer to the people through e-governance. E-government is expected to improve the effectiveness, efficiency and productivity of a government's service provision. With computerisation, government becomes the largest public information owner, and manages vast resources of data, resulting into effective governance.

Using capacity indicators as a service delivery tool in Africa

Capacity has been identified as one of the missing links in Africa's development story. Traditional technical assistance to Africa had not produced the desired results (Easterly's 2006 'white man's burden'). Arguably, the requirements of agencies supporting technical assistance (sometimes dubbed capacity building) in Africa, including the existing development finance institutions, did not offer the opportunity for the kind of effective and flexible partnership between Africans and donors that was necessary to deal appropriately and adequately with the critical issues surrounding capacity building. The African Capacity Building Initiative was born under the auspice of the AfDB, World Bank and UNDP (Ofosu-Amaah, 2011). The founding of ACBF was part of the drive to sort out what was considered Africa's growth/development malaise with a number of public sector reform initiatives.

The Africa Capacity Index (ACI) is intended to highlight key determinants and components of capacity for development. The methodology used by ACBF for calculating the indicators is based on three levels of capacity: (i) institutional level; (ii) organisational level; and (iii) individual level. The enabling environment – whether in terms of policy or institutions – refers to the system beyond the organisation, including the tone set by leadership. It encompasses the broader system within which individuals and organisations function, thus influencing their performance outcomes. The role of leadership is to set the vision, tone and stage by which activities are undertaken or implemented (ACBF, 2012). Additionally, the ACI also contextualises capacity development using four clusters: *policy environment, processes for policy implementation, development results at country level,* and *capacity development outcomes* at three levels: enabling environment, organisational and the individual. In addition to overall scores, the reports provide data for each of the capacity clusters of the participating countries, and rank them from very high to very low. For the two consecutive reports, none of the participating countries scored very high. This mirrors the findings of recent studies that call for enhanced reforms (Ayee, 2012; Owusu and Ohemeng, 2012).

At the core of the methodology is an exploratory approach. The ACI is a composite index computed from four sub-indices,[4] each of which is an aggregated measure that is calculated on the basis of both a quantitative and a qualitative assessment of various components that form a cluster. The clusters are obtained to underpin the dimensions (ACBF, 2011, p 36). Table 5.1 summarises the results of the performance of 42 African countries along the three levels of capacity: enabling environment/institutions, organisations, and individual. The results show that most of the countries score low or very low capacity at the organisational and individual levels.

Table 5.1: Capacity dimensions in 2012 (% of countries by level)

Level	Enabling environment	Organisational level	Individual level
Very low	0.0	4.8	
Low	0.0	23.8	19.0
Medium	40.5	4.8	9.5
High	57.1	35.7	0.0
Very high	2.4	31.0	0.0
Total	100	100	100

Source: ACBF (2012)

The organisational level of capacity comprises the internal policies, arrangements, procedures and frameworks that allow organisations to operate effectively, accommodating the integration and consolidation of individual capacities for specified goals. The individual level assesses the skills, experience and knowledge that are vested in people. Leadership enters at the individual level in the values that determine accountability and results, thus enabling individuals to transform the work environment to generate results.

The ACI clusters are made of the following dimensions: policy environment; processes for implementation; development results at country level; and capacity development outcome (see Table 5.2).

The policy environment underpins what makes development possible, with particular emphasis on effective and development-oriented organisational and institutional frameworks. It is focused on (i) the existence of national strategies for development and their level of legitimacy; (ii) national levels of commitment to achieving development and poverty reduction objectives such as the MDGs, Sustainable Development Goals (SDGs); Sustainable Energy for All (SEFA) and so on; (iii) country-level awareness and the need for better utilisation of

Table 5.2: Pattern of African Capacity Index 2012 results

Level	ACI 2012 (% of countries)	Policy environ-ment	Processes for implementation	Development results at country level	Capacity develop-ment outcome
Very low		0.0	0.0	0.0	
Low	52.4	0.0	0.0	19.0	23.8
Medium	31.0	2.4	33.3	66.7	4.8
High	2.4	23.8	50.0	11.9	0.0
Very high	0.0	73.8	16.7	2.4	0.0
Total	100	100	100	100	100

Source: ACBF (2012)

limited resources for capacity development prescribed by policies for aid effectiveness; and (iv) the degree of social stability and inclusion – indeed, broad participation and good governance underpin this measure. Strong leadership is again crucial for nurturing the development of strategy and incorporating it into vision-driven activities.

Processes for implementation anchor the extent to which African countries are prepared to deliver results and outcomes. This dimension of the ACI scans the creation of an environment that motivates and supports individuals: the capacity to manage stakeholder partnerships inclusively and constructively; and the capacity to establish appropriate mechanisms for managing policies, strategies, programmes and projects. Of equal importance are processes for designing, implementing, monitoring and evaluating, and managing national development strategies to produce socially inclusive and poverty-reducing development outcomes. Development results are tangible outputs that permit development in a sustainable way. The primary scope covered by this cluster are the coordination of aid support to capacity development; the level of creativity and innovation in sectoral policies; achievements in the implementation of the Paris Declaration on Aid Effectiveness; and achievement in gender equality and social inclusion as well as in partnering for capacity development.

The 'capacity development outcomes' are captured mainly through the financial commitment to capacity development; the actual achievement of specified development goals; gender and broader social equity; and the achievements in the implementation of sectoral policies, among other measures. Leadership is given prominence in the dynamic aspects of human and organisational capacity.

The 2011 African capacity indicators report compares capacity development in fragile and non-fragile states, and finds that, as expected, the capacity for delivering development outputs and outcomes in fragile states is very low, but a careful look at the data shows that the fragile states have more capacity at organisation level, politics, power and incentives (ACBF, 2011, pp 65-7). This finding has implications for designing the mix of capacity interventions for different types of countries, choosing among different interventions – resources (for example, budget support), skills and knowledge (for example, training), organisation (for example, ICT, decentralisation), politics and power (for example, development of national political parties), or incentives (for example, sectoral policy reforms and regulations). These results imply that capacity-building initiatives in fragile states should focus on improving service delivery for development outcomes for the majority of citizens.

The two capacity indicators reports also find that for almost all countries surveyed, capacities for development at the *individual* level were the lowest, followed by organisation level (ACBF, 2011, pp 226-7). This finding is particularly disturbing for at least two reasons. First, over the past 30 years or so, most of the capacity-building initiatives in Africa have focused on human resource development, in the form of education, training, study tours and technology transfer, as well as organisational interventions such as restructuring, twinning arrangements, equipment (for example, computers, internet, etc) and leadership training. It is practically impossible to achieve development results and deliver quality services to citizens if the public service is weak at the individual and organisation levels. It is important to go beyond the numbers of the indicators and investigate the deeper causes of capacity weaknesses at these operating levels – again, highlighting the importance of data. Some of the causes of capacity weakness are discussed below.

Capacity for implementation: it is generally accepted that most reforms in government fail (Polidano, 2001) due to weakness in capacity for implementation (ACBF, 2011, 2012). This may also cause reforms to be blocked outright by resistant forces/groups or be put into effect in a tokenistic and half-hearted fashion. There may also be cases of policy reversal due to political economy reasons (Rodrik, 1996). As Piñera (1994, p 231) put it, 'good policy is good politics.' The two reports show that Africa does not have a very high level of implementation, despite being strong in the policy environment (see Table 5.1 above). These results point to the need to better understand the role organisations play as mechanisms for the effective implementation of development initiatives (see, for example, Kiggundu, 1998).

Leadership: Polidano (2001) argued that the reforms of the 1980s and 1990s in countries such as the UK, New Zealand and Australia succeeded because they were vigorously implemented. He noted that there was an exceptionally high degree of political backing for reform in these countries. These kinds of leadership appear to be absent in other parts of the world where the implementation record has been dismal (Caiden, 1991; Kiggundu, 1998). For example, in the cooperative movement, Kamoche (1997, p 270) gives lack of dynamic leadership as the cause of African failures. The African capacity indicators report advocates a new model of reforms (see Ayee, 2012; Owusu and Ohemeng, 2012) characterised by transformational capacity development, incorporating all institutions of governance, including civil society and the private sector. Leadership is crucial in providing direction, especially to donor-supported interventions/ reforms. Such reforms, according to Ayee (2012, pp 90-1), require a 'commitment to establish a more professional civil service with a stronger emphasis on performance....' Ownership of reform must be diffused widely *within* the government through better coordination (Knight et al, 2002). Because government is not a monolithic whole, reform must have a sustained focus on end results, such as greater efficiency, quicker or more equitable service delivery, and reduced corruption. Reform must also transcend the administrative concerns of central agencies, even though it may be under the leadership of these same agencies.

Donor coordination: it is acknowledged that donor agencies wield significant influence (Mosley et al, 1991; Wood, 2006). Donors provide much of the funding for reform initiatives, particularly in Africa. The history of SAPs has been littered with various cases of donor-influence peddling (Campbell and Stein, 1992; Wood, 2006). This power over funding has led donor agencies to select and define reform projects well beyond the limits of their authority (Polidano and Hulme, 1999). Donors should respond to needs identified by client governments according to the Paris Declaration and the Busan High Level Forum on aid effectiveness. If governments refuse to succumb to the whim of donors, this may result in the suspension of assistance (Hirschmann, 1993, p 126). The Africa capacity indicators reports reveal the very limited extent of support by donors to capacity development, and a less than desirable aid coordination mechanism (ACBF, 2011, 2012). Essentially, the commitments around Paris and Busan need to be revisited.

Ownership: lack of local ownership of development interventions remains a critical issue in many African countries, even after Busan. Donors recognise this glaring malpractice, but they do not always see the link with their own way of doing business (Birdsall, 2004). The donor community tends to see lack of ownership as a problem of project management that can be resolved by holding seminars and consultation meetings with local officials. The gap between donor and beneficiary also limits input to project design (Polidano and Hulme, 1999). Aid dependency may undermine sovereign and democratic decision-making, resulting in huge problems of project coordination within the host country. In some instances, aid funds may be misappropriated or allocated to non-priority issues (Wescott,

1999). The capacity indicators reports provide baselines for tracking levels of ownership of policy reforms and processes.

Participation: in the context of public sector reform, participation involves either decentralisation or devolution to allow citizenry/ stakeholder inputs in decision-making. Participation affords interested parties less need for coordination and control, more effective utilisation of human resources, greater commitment to organisational objectives, and public intervention in shaping the activities needed for effective service provision (Peters, 1992; Turner and Hulme, 1997; Barima and Farhad, 2010). However, representation or participation does not automatically guarantee ownership, and that is why it is crucial to have champions and leaders of reform.

Transparency and accountability: citizens want to know what is being done on their behalf. Once the reform process is transparent, the official implementing the reform can be held accountable. Paul (1991, p 5) argues that accountability is the 'driving force generating the pressure for key actors involved to be responsible for and to ensure good public service performance.' In Africa, where there have been considerable concerns over corruption and kleptocracy, transparency and accountability become important tools to combat resource waste. Accountability helps in tackling corruption and improves public sector performance, effectiveness, efficiency, achievement of goals, probity and regularity on the part of public officials who are naturally expected to be compliant of the formal rules and regulations of the agencies in which they work. The Africa capacity indicators reports survey the state of accountability in the development processes on the continent. Of the 42 countries surveyed for the 2012 report, 16 countries (about 38 per cent) reported having in place institutions designed to promote transparency, accountability and to combat corruption in the public sector.

Financial commitment for reform and capacity development: there is a tendency in Africa for donor agencies to push through public sector reform – especially privatisation and commercialisation, co-production and deregulation of the economy. They also encourage public–private sector partnership in the provision of social welfare, public goods and services as alternative methods of enhancing public sector efficiency à la NPM. Some scholars argue that any such partnerships are meant to create fiscal space for governments and to improve citizen access to services. Equally, enhanced competition in service provision is expected to encourage quality institutions and improve social welfare

(Batley, 1994, 1997; Collins, 2000). The levels of commitment to reform can be gauged through budgetary allocations.

Training as an important tool: improving an individual's skills according to operational job requirements is an important element in the management of expertise. The Africa capacity indicators reports assess the amount of resources spent on training programmes to support skills development for Africa by agencies such as the ACBF. However, in the literature, there is debate about the nature and value of training, and in particular, its ability to lead to improvements in individual and organisational performance (Montgomery, 1986; Collins and Wallis, 1990; Jones, 1990; Kiggundu, 1998). It could be said that the value of training is realised if the training goes beyond filling gaps in current skill levels. Evaluation of any reform programme should determine whether the acquired skills have led to any noteworthy improvements in performance and productivity following a training event (Kamoche, 1997; Ayee, 2008). The Africa capacity indicators report makes a case for systematic evaluation of training programmes on the continent using ACBF experience as a basis (ACBF, 2011, 2012). ACBF also supports the 'drivers of change' approach – something that scholars like Booth et al (2005) strongly recommend – to map out how change occurs, the 'power relations at stake and the structural and institutional factors underlying the "lack of political will" behind the reform process' (Owusu and Ohemeng, 2012, p 136).

Citizenship and citizen engagement: public service reform is not only about political leaders and public servants. More importantly, it is about citizens and the communities where they live and work. When citizens are organised and have the capacity and willingness to interact with all levels of government, they tend to receive better public services. Evidence from the anti-poverty and progressive social change literature (see, for example, Kiggundu, 2002, 2012), suggests that when the population develops a strong sense of citizenship and civic engagement, it also develops the capacity to interact with governments and voices its legitimate demand for quality public services. This is particularly so at the local level. The Africa capacity indicators report findings, that for most African countries capacity at the individual level is low or very low, have implications for public service reforms as they relate to ordinary African citizens. In addition to building individual capacities for public servants in formal public agencies, there is an urgent need to build capacities for informed, responsible and responsive citizenship and associative civic engagement in the local communities.

Conclusions

It is essential to realise that combating corruption is no panacea (Besley and Ghatak, 2007) as there are other priorities. There is a need to pay close attention to existing institutions and enforcement mechanisms as well as unwritten rules that can hinder or further public service provision. Effective and quality service delivery must be tailored to local circumstances. This requires a sound evidence base and 'public policy' reasoning. Policy-makers must learn from their own experiences as well as others. Effective policy in Africa depends on expanding the evidence base, which presupposes good data collection and analysis. The Africa capacity indicators reports contribute to a wider understanding of the principles of good policy-making in service delivery in Africa. A critical look at the reports (ACBF, 2011, 2012) shows that there are enormous gaps in capacity or effective public sector reforms in Africa.

It has been noted in this chapter that successful reforms depend on commitment by political leaders and bureaucrats, and the establishment of values and frameworks that do not allow waste of public resources. In this regard, the reports, and its component indicator, the ACI, are a vital addition to the conceptual, methodological and diagnostic tools available for Africa's capacity development and public sector reform. The key findings of these reports allow for more focused and targeted public service reforms in different types of countries, and at different levels. These kinds of reports give practitioners room to test the adequacy of development agencies' operational definitions of capacity development, and their appropriateness for modernising Africa's public services in light of the increasing demands of citizens and the current dynamic and complex global economy and global society. The baselines being developed are crucial tools for the formulation, benchmarking and implementation of a developmental public service in Africa.

References

Acemoglu, D. (2005) *Politics and economics in weak and strong states*, NBER Working Paper No W11275, April, Cambridge, MA: Massachusetts Institute of Technology, Department of Economics.

Acemoglu, D. (2008) 'Interactions between governance and growth: what World Bank economists need to know', in *Governance, growth, and development*, Washington, DC: The World Bank.

ACBF (African Capacity Building Foundation) (2002) *Helping Africa make the 21st century – A new horizon in capacity building – Consolidated strategic medium-term plan, 2002-2006*, Harare: ACBF Secretariat.

ACBF (2011) *Africa capacity indicators – Capacity development in fragile states*, Harare: ACBF.

ACBF (2012) *Africa capacity indicators – Capacity development for agricultural transformation and food security*, Harare: ACBF.

Ake, C. (1996) *Democracy and development in Africa*, Washington, DC: The Brookings Institution.

Aküyz, Y., Chang, H.-J. and Kozul-Wright, R. (1999) 'New perspectives on East Asian development', in Y. Aküyz (ed) *East Asian development. New perspectives*, London: Routledge, pp 4-36.

Amsden, A. (1989) *Asia's next giant. South Korea and late industrialization*, New York: Oxford University Press.

Ayee, J.R.A. (2008) *Reforming the African public sector: Retrospect and prospects*, Dakar: CODESERIA.

Ayee, J.R.A. (2012) 'Improving the effectiveness of the public sector in Africa through the quality of public administration', in K.T. Hanson et al (eds) *Rethinking development challenges for public policy*, Houndsmill, Basingstoke: Palgrave Macmillan, pp 83-115.

Barima, A.K. and Farhad, A. (2010) 'Challenges of making donor-driven public sector reform in Sub-Saharan Africa sustainable: some experiences from Ghana', *International Journal of Public Administration*, vol 33, nos 12-13, pp 635-47.

Bates, R.H. (1981) *Markets and state in tropical Africa*, Berkeley, CA: University of California Press.

Batley, R. (1994) 'The consolidation of adjustment: implications for public administration', *Public Administration and Development*, vol 14, pp 489-505.

Batley, R. (1997) *A research framework for analysing capacity to undertake the 'new roles' of government*, Role of Government in Adjusting Economies Paper 23, Birmingham: Development Administration Group, The University of Birmingham.

Beeson, M. (2003) 'Sovereignty under siege. Globalisation and the state in Southeast Asia', *Third World Quarterly*, vol 24, no 2, pp 357-74.

Besley, T. and Ghatak, M. (2007) 'Reforming public service delivery', *Journal of African Economies*, vol 16, AERC Supplement 1.

Besley, T., Persson, T. and Sturm, D. (2005) *Political competition and economic performance: Theory and evidence from the United States*, NBER Working Paper No 11484, Cambridge, MA: National Bureau of Economic Research.

Birdsall, N. (2004) *Seven deadly sins: reflections on donor failings*, CGD Working Paper no 50, London: Center for Global Development.

Booth, A. (1999) 'Initial conditions and miraculous growth. Why is South East Asia different from Taiwan and South Korea?', *World Development*, vol 27, no 2, pp 301-21.

Booth, D., Crook, R., Gyimah-Boadi, E., Killick, K., Luckham, R. and Boateng, N. (2005) 'What are the drivers of change in Ghana?', Policy Briefings on Drivers of Change in Ghana 1-5, Centre for Democratic Development/Overseas Development Institute (www.odi.org.uk/resources/details.asp?id=1322&title=drivers-change-ghana).

Boyd, R. and Ngo, T.W. (2005) *Asian states. Beyond the developmental perspective*, New York: Routledge.

Boyle, B. (2008) *Making the news: Why the African Peer Review Mechanism didn't*, SAIIA Occasional Paper Number 12, September, Johannesburg, South Africa: South African Institute of International Affairs.

Bratton, M. and Chang, E.C.C. (2006) 'State building and democratization in Sub-Saharan Africa. Forwards, backwards, or together?', *Comparative Political Studies*, vol 39, no 9, pp 1059-83.

Bratton, M. and van de Walle, N. (1992) 'Towards governance in Africa: popular demands and state responses', in G. Hyden and M. Bratton (eds) *Governance and politics in Africa*, Boulder, CO: Lynne Rienner, pp 27-56.

Brinkerhoff, D.W. (2005) *Organisational legitimacy, capacity and capacity development*, ECDPM Discussion Paper 58A, Maastricht: European Centre for Development Policy Management.

Caiden, G.E. (1991) *Administrative reform comes of age*, Berlin: Walter de Gruyter.

Cairns, B., Harris, M. and Young, P. (2005) 'Building the capacity of the voluntary non-profit sector: challenges of theory and practice', *International Journal of International Public Administration*, vol 28, pp 869-85.

Campa, J. and Goldberg, L. (1997) *The evolving external orientation of manufacturing industries: Evidence from four countries*, NBER Working Paper 5919, Cambridge, MA: National Bureau for Economic Research.

Campbell, H. and Stein, H. (eds) (1992) *Tanzania and the IMF: The dynamics of liberalization*, Boulder, CO: Westview Press.

Corrigan, T. (2015) 'Why the African Peer Review Mechanism must remain voluntary', SAIIA Policy Briefing 130, March, Johannesburg, South Africa: South African Institute of International Affairs.

Castells, M. (1992) 'Four Asian tigers with a dragon head. A comparative analysis of the state, economy and society in the Asian Pacific Rim', in R.P. Applebaum and J. Henderson (eds) *States and development in the Asian Pacific Rim*, London: Sage, pp 176-98.

Chang, H.-J. (1999) 'The economic theory of the developmental state', in M. Woo-Cumings (ed) *The developmental state*, New York: Cornell University Press, pp 182-99.

Chang, H.-J. (2002a) 'Breaking the mould. An institutionalist political economy alternative to the neo-liberal theory of the market and the state', *Cambridge Journal of Economics*, vol 26, no 5, pp 539-59.

Chang, H.-J. (2002b) *Kicking away the ladder. Development strategy in historical perspective*, London: Anthem Books.

Chang, H.-J. (2003a) *Globalisation, economic development and the role of the state*, London: Zed Books.

Chang, H.-J. (2003b) 'Kicking away the ladder. Infant industry promotion in historical perspective', *Oxford Development Studies*, vol 31, no 1, pp 21-32.

Chang, H.-J. (ed) (2003c) *Rethinking development economics*, London: Anthem Press.

Chang, H.-J. (2003d) 'The market, the state and institutions in economic development', in H.-J. Chang (ed) *Rethinking development economics*, London: Anthem Press, pp 41-60.

Chang, H.J. (2006) *The East Asian development experience. The miracle, the crisis and the future*, London: Zed Books.

Chang, H.J. (2007) *Bad Samaritans. Rich nations, poor policies, and the threat to the developing world*, London: Random House.

Chaskin, R.J. (2001) 'Building community capacity: a definitional framework and case studies from a comprehensive community initiative', *Urban Affairs Review*, vol 36, no 3, pp 291-323.

Christensen, R.K., and Gazley, B. (2008) 'Capacity for public administration. Analysis of meaning and measurement', *Public Administration and Development*, vol 28, pp 265-79.

Clapham, C. (1996) *Africa in the international system. The politics of state survival*, Cambridge: Cambridge University Press.

Collins, P. (2000) 'State, market and civil society: towards partnership?', in P. Collins (ed) *Applying public administration in development: Guideposts to the future*, Chichester: Wiley, pp 69-78.

Collins, P. and Wallis, M. (1990) 'Privatization, regulation and development: some questions of training strategy', *Public Administration and Development*, vol 10, pp 375-88.

Deyo, F.C. (ed) (1987) *The political economy of the New Asian industrialism*, Ithaca, NY: Cornell University Press.

Diamond, L. (1999) *Developing democracy. Toward consolidation*, Baltimore, MD: Johns Hopkins University Press.

Easterly, W. (2006) *The white man's burden: Why the West's efforts to aid the rest have done so much ill and so little good*, New York: The Penguin Press.

Easterly, W. and Levine, R. (1997) 'Africa's growth tragedy: policies and ethnic divisions', *Quarterly Journal of Economics*, vol 112, pp 1203-50.

Eisinger, P. (2002) 'Organizational capacity and organizational effectiveness among street-level food assistance programs', *Non-profit and Voluntary Sector Quarterly*, vol 31, no 1, pp 115-30.

Englebert, P. (2000) 'Pre-colonial institutions, post-colonial states, and economic development in tropical Africa', *Political Research Quarterly*, vol 53, no 1, pp 1-30.

Evans, P.B. (1989) 'Predatory, developmental and other state-apparatuses. A comparative political economy perspective on the third world state', *Sociological Forum*, vol 4, no 4, pp 561-87.

Evans, P.B. (1992) 'The state as a problem and solution. Embedded autonomy and structural change', in S. Haggard and R. Kaufman (eds) *The politics of structural adjustment. International constraints, distributive conflicts and the state*, Princeton, NJ: Princeton University Press, pp 139-81.

Evans, P.B. (1995) *Embedded autonomy: States and industrial transformation*, Princeton, NJ: Princeton University Press.

Feenstra, R.C. (1998) 'Integration and disintegration in the global economy', *Journal of Economic Perspectives*, Fall, pp 31-50.

Forbes, M. and Lynn, L.E. Jr (2006) 'Organizational effectiveness and government performance: a new look at the empirical literature', Paper presented at the Determinants of Performance in Public Organizations Conference, University of Hong Kong, 7-10 December.

Gargan, J. (1981) 'Consideration of local government capacity', *Public Administration of Review*, vol 41, no 6, pp 649-58.

Glickman, N. and Servon, L.J. (1998) *More than bricks and sticks: Five components of CDC capacity*, New Brunswick, NJ: Rutgers Center for Urban Policy Research.

Goldsmith, A.A. (2004) 'Predatory versus developmental rule in Africa', *Democratization*, vol 11, no 3, pp 88-110.

Gyimah-Boadi, E. (ed) (2004) *Democratic reform in Africa. The quality of progress*, London: Lynne Rienner.

Haggard, S. (1989) 'The East Asian NICs in comparative perspective', *Annals of the American Academy of Political and Social Science*, vol 505, pp 129-41.

Haggard, S. (1990) *Pathways from the periphery: The politics of growth in the newly industrializing countries*, Ithaca, NY: Cornell University Press.

Hanson, K. and Kararach, G. (2011) The challenges of knowledge harvesting and the promotion of sustainable *development for the achievement of the MDGs in Africa*, ACBF Occasional Paper no 12, Harare: ACBF.

Hirschmann, D. (1993) 'Institutional development in the era of economic policy reform: concerns, contradictions, and illustrations from Malawi', *Public Administration and Development*, vol 13, no 2, pp 113-28.

Honadle, B.W. (1981) 'A capacity-building framework – a search for concept and purpose', *Public Administration Review*, vol 41, no 5, pp 575-80.

Hood, C. (1991) 'A public management for all seasons', *Public Administration*, vol 69, no 1, pp 3-19.

Hort, S.E.O. and Kuhnle, S. (2000) 'The coming of East and South-East Asian welfare states', *Journal of European Social Policy*, vol 10, no 2, pp 162-84.

Hyden, G. and Bratton, M. (eds) (1992) *Governance and politics in Africa*, Boulder, CO: Lynne Rienner.

Hyden, G., Olowu, C and Okoth-ogendo, W. (eds) (2000) *African perspectives on governance*, Trenton: African World Press.

Ingraham, P.W., Joyce, P.G. and Donahue, A.K. (2003) *Government performance: Why management matters*, Baltimore, MD: Johns Hopkins University Press.

Jerven, M. (2011) 'The quest for the African dummy: explaining African post-colonial economic performance revisited', *Journal of International Development*, vol 23, no 2, pp 288-307.

Johnson, C. (1982) *MITI and the Japanese miracle. The growth of industrial policy, 1925-1975*, Stanford, CA: Stanford University Press.

Johnson, C. (1999) 'The developmental state. Odyssey of a concept', in M. Woo-Cumings (ed) *The developmental state*, New York: Cornell University Press, pp 32-60.

Jones, M. (1990) 'Efficiency and effectiveness in an African public administration context', *International Journal of Public Sector Management*, vol 3, pp 58-64.

Jordaan, E. (2006) 'Inadequately self-critical: Rwanda's self-assessment for the African peer review mechanism', *African Affairs*, vol 105, no 420, pp 331-51.

Joseph, R. (ed) (1999) *State, conflict and democracy in Africa*, Boulder, CO: Lynne Rienner.

Kamoche, K. (1997) 'Competence-creation in the African public sector', *International Journal of Public Sector Management*, vol 10, no 4, pp 268-78.

Kaplinksy, R. (2000) Globalization and unequalization: what can be learned from value chain analysis?', *Journal of Development Studies*, vol 37, no 2, pp 117-46.

Kararach, G. (2011) *Macroeconomic policy and the political limits of reforms in developing countries*, Nairobi: African Research and Resource Forum.

Kararach, G. (2012) 'Effective states and capacity development for financial governance in Africa: case and agenda for operationalisation', *Capacity Focus*, vol 2, no 1.

Kiggundu, M.N. (1992) *Size and cost of the civil service: Reform programmes in Africa*, United Nations Department of Economic and Social Development, DESD/SEM.92/1 INT-90-R78, New York.

Kiggundu, M.N. (1998) 'Civil service reforms: limping into the twenty-first century', in M. Minogue, C. Polidano and D. Hulme (eds) *Beyond the new public management: Changing ideas and practices in governance*, Cheltenham: Edward Elgar, pp 155-71.

Kiggundu, M. (2002) 'Bureaucracy and administrative reform in developing countries', in C. Kirkpatrick et al (eds) *Handbook on development policy and management*, Cheltenham: Edward Elgar, pp 291-302.

Kiggundu, M.N. (2012) 'Anti-poverty and progressive social change in Brazil: lessons for other emerging economies', *International Review of Administrative Science*, vol 78, no 4, pp 733-56.

Kim, S. (2007) 'Consolidating the authoritarian developmental state in the 1970s Korea. Chosen strategies', *International Review of Public Administration*, vol 12, no 1, pp 119-32.

Knight, B., Chigudu, H. and Tandon, R. (2002) *Reviving democracy: Citizens at the heart of governance*, London: Earthscan.

Koo, H. and Kim, E. (1992) 'The developmental state and capital accumulation in South Korea', in R.P. Appelbaum and J. Henderson (eds) *States and development in the Asian Pacific Rim*, London: Sage Publications, pp 121-49.

Kwon, H. (1999) *The welfare state in Korea. The politics of legitimation*, Basingstoke: Macmillan.

Léautier, F. (2009) 'Leadership in a globalized world: complexity, dynamics and risk', Lecture PPT Notes, The Fezembat Group, 26 February.

Leftwich, A. (1993) 'Governance, democracy and development in the third world', *Third World Quarterly*, vol 14, no 3, pp 605-24.

Leftwich, A. (2000) *States of development. On the primacy of politics in development*, Cambridge: Polity Press.

Leftwich, A. (2002) 'Forms of the Democratic Developmental State — Democratic Practices and Development Capacity', in M. Robinson and G White (eds) *The democratic developmental state: Politics and institutional design*, Oxford: Oxford University Press.

Letts, C., Ryan, W.P and Grossman, A. (1999) *High performance non-profit organizations*, New York: John Wiley.

Lopes, C. (2002) 'Should we mind the gap?' in Sakiko Fukuda-Parr, Carlos Lopes and Khalid Malik (eds), *Capacity for development: New solutions to old problems*, London: Earthscan.

Low, L. (ed) (2004) *Developmental states. Relevant, redundant or reconfigured?*, New York: Nova Science Publishers.

Makoba, J.W. (2011) *Rethinking development strategies in Africa – The triple partnership as an alternative approach – The case of Uganda*, Oxford: Peter Lang.

Mamdani, M. (1976) *Politics and class formation in Uganda*, New York: Monthly Review Press.

Mamdani, M. (1996) *Citizen and subject: Contemporary Africa and the legacy of late colonialism*, Princeton, NJ: Princeton University Press.

Manning, N. (2001) 'The legacy of the new public management in developing countries', *International Review of Administrative Sciences*, vol 67, no 2, pp 197-312.

Mkandawire, T. (2001) 'Thinking about developmental states in Africa', *Cambridge Journal of Economics*, vol 25, no 3, pp 289-313.

Montgomery, J.D. (1986) 'Levels of managerial leadership in Southern Africa', *Journal of Developing Areas*, vol 21, pp 15-30.

Mosley, P., Harrigan, J. and Toye, J. (1991) *Aid and power: The world bank and policy-based lending* (2 vols), London: Routledge.

Myrdal, G. (1968) *Asian drama. An inquiry into the poverty of nations*, 3 vols, New York: Pantheon.

Nabli, M.K. and Ben Hammouda, H. (2014) 'The political economy of the new Arab awakening', in C. Monga and J. Yifu Lin (eds) *The Oxford handbook of Africa and economics: Context and concepts*, Oxford: Oxford University Press, pp 700-35.

Nissanke, M. and Aryeetey, E. (eds) (2003) *Comparative development experiences in East Asia and Sub-Sahara Africa. An institutional approach*, Aldershot: Ashgate.

Ofosu-Amaah, W.P. (2011) *The African Capacity Building Foundation: Rising to the challenge of capacity through a unique and innovative framework*, ACBF Development Memoir no 7, Harare: ACBF.

Olukoshi, A.O. (2004) 'Democratisation, globalisation and policy making in Africa', in C.S. Soludo, O. Ogbu and H.-J. Chang (eds) *The politics of trade and industrial policy in Africa. Forced consensus?*, Trenton/Ottawa: Africa World Press/IDRC, pp 43-74.

Owusu, F. and Ohemeng, F.L.K. (2012) 'The public sector and development in Africa: the case for a development public service', in K.T. Hanson et al (eds) *Rethinking development challenges for public policy*, Houndsmill, Basingstoke: Palgrave Macmillan, pp 117-54.

Paul, S. (1992) 'Accountability in public service: exit, voice and control', *World Development*, vol 20, no 7, pp 1047-61.

Peters, B.G. (1992) 'Government reorganization: a theoretical analysis', *International Political Science Review*, vol 13, no 2, pp 199-217.

Piñera, J. (1994) 'Chile', in J. Williamson (ed) *The political economy of policy reform*, Washington, DC: Institute of International Economics.

Polidano, C. (2001) 'Why civil service reforms fail', *Public Management Review*, vol 3, no 3, pp 345-61.

Polidano, C. and Hulme, D. (1999) 'Public management reform in developing Countries: issues and outcomes', *Public Management*, vol 1, no 1, pp 121-32.

Pollitt, C. (1993) *Managerialism and public services*. Oxford: Blackwell.

Rapley, J. (1996) *Understanding development. Theory and practice in the third world*, London: Lynne Rienner.

Robinson, M. and White, G. (eds) (1998) *The democratic developmental state politics and institutional design*, Oxford: Oxford University Press.

Rodrik, D. (1996) 'Understanding economic policy reform', *Journal of Economic Literature*, vol 34, pp 9-41.

Simpson, B.M. (2006) 'The transfer and dissemination of agricultural technologies: issues, lessons and opportunities', *African Technology Development Forum Journal*, vol 3, no 1, pp 10-17.

Sowa, J.E., Selden, S.C. and Sandfort, J.R. (2004) 'No longer unmeasurable? A multidimensional integrated model of non-profit organizational effectiveness', *Non-profit and Voluntary Sector Quarterly*, vol 33, no 4, pp 711-28.

Stein, H. (2000) *The development of the developmental state in Africa: a theoretical inquiry*, Centre of African Studies, University of Copenhagen.

Subramanian, A. and Roy, D. (2003) 'Who can explain the Mauritian miracle: Meade, Romer, Sachs, or Rodrik?', in D. Rodrik (ed.) *In search of prosperity: Analytic narratives on economic growth*. Princeton, NJ: Princeton University Press.

Svensson, J. (2012) 'Service delivery indicators', Presentation delivered at The World Bank, Washington, DC, January.

te Velde, D.W. (2010) 'Global Financial Crisis Discussion Series. Paper 23: Methodological note: update for phase 2 studies', London: ODI.

te Velde, D.W., Rushton, J., Schreckenberg, K., Marshall, E., Edouard, F., Newton, A. and Arancbia, E. (2006) 'Entrepreneurship in value chains of non-timber forest products', *Forest Policy and Economics*, vol 8, pp 725-41.

Turner, M. and Hulme, D. (1997) *Governance, administration and development: Making the state work*, New York: Palgrave.

UNECA (United Nations Economic Commission for Africa) (1991) *Ethics and accountability in African public services*, Addis Ababa: UNECA.

van de Walle, N. (2001) *African economies and the politics of permanent crisis, 1979-1999*, Cambridge: Cambridge University Press.

Wade, R. (1990) *Governing the market. Economic theory and the role of government in East Asian industrialisation*, Princeton, NJ: Princeton University Press.

Waldner, D. (1999) *State building and late development*, Ithaca, N.Y.: Cornell University Press.

Weiss, L. (2000) 'Developmental states in transition. Adapting, dismantling, innovating, not "Normalising"', *The Pacific Review*, vol 13, no 1, pp 21-55.

Weiss, L. (ed) (2003) *States in the global economy. Bringing the domestic institutions back in*, Cambridge: Cambridge University Press.

Wescott, C. (1999) 'Guiding principles on civil service reform in Africa: an empirical review', *International Journal of Public Sector Management*, vol 12, no 2, pp 145-70.

Westphal, L.E. (2002) 'Technology strategies for economic development in a fast changing global economy', *Economics of Innovation and New Technology*, vol 11, nos 4, 5, pp 275-320.

Wong, J. (2004) 'The adaptive developmental state in East Asia', *Journal of East Asian Studies*, vol 4, no 3, pp 345-62.

Woo-Cumings, M. (1991) *Race to the swift. State and finance in Korean industrialisation*, New York: Columbia University Press.

Woo-Cumings, M. (ed) (1999) *The developmental state*, Ithaca, NY: Cornell University Press.

Wood, A. (2006) 'Looking ahead optimally in allocating aid'. Paper presented at UNU-WIDER Conference on Aid: Principles and Performance, Helsinki.

World Bank, The (1989) *Sub-Sahara Africa: From crisis to sustainable growth – A long-term perspective study (LTPS)*, Washington, DC: The World Bank.

World Bank, The (1992): *Governance and development*, Washington, DC: The World Bank.

World Bank, The (1993) *The East Asian miracle. Economic growth and public policy*, New York: Oxford University Press.

World Bank, The (1997) *World development report. The state in a changing world*, New York: Cambridge University Press.

World Bank, The (2000) *Reforming public institutions and strengthening governance. A World Bank strategy*, Washington, DC: The World Bank.

World Bank, The (2005) *Building effective states and forging engaged societies: Report of the Task Force on capacity development in Africa*, Washington, DC: The World Bank.

World Bank, The (2012) *Africa's Pulse, volume 6*, Africa Chief Economist Office, Washington, DC.

Yang, J.J. (2000) 'The rise of the Korea welfare state amid economic crisis, 1997-99: implications for the globalisation debate', *Development Policy Review*, vol 18, no 3, pp 235-56.

Yu-Lee, R.T. (2002) *Essentials of capacity management*, New York: John Wiley & Sons.

SIX

Employment creation for youth in Africa: the role of extractive industries

Bernadette Dia Kamgnia and Victor Murinde

Introduction

Singular among the economic challenges facing African countries today is the issue of youth unemployment. Almost 200 million of the population in Africa, equivalent to approximately 17 per cent of the population in 2015, is in the age range of between 15 and 24 years old (AfDB, 2013a). Essentially, in the majority of African countries, young people represent a significant proportion of the total national population. Unfortunately, they constitute the bulk of the unemployed in Africa, irrespective of their school qualifications. And young women are the most likely to be out of the labour market in many African countries, due to entrenched gender biases.

There are many causes of youth unemployment. It is attributed either to the lack of prioritisation of job creation in development policies, or to the socioeconomic environment, without ignoring the negative impact of the structure of African economies and the educational system.

But African economies have been growing healthier since the late 1990s, with an increasing number of African countries engaging or upgrading in global value chains such as agriculture, tourism and manufacturing. Interestingly, governments have been firmly engaging in affirmative actions in favour of youth employment.

The contention in this chapter is that in the current supportive economic environment, Africa must leverage opportunities in the extractive industries[1] by enhancing value addition and converting these into jobs for its growing youth. Indeed, the extractive industries sector suffers from a skills shortage and an apparent low capacity for job generation.

This chapter is structured into five sections. The next section highlights the key aspects of the youth unemployment challenge in Africa. The third section reviews the African heads of states' Declaration of Intent on the Joint Youth Employment Initiative for Africa (JYEIA), pointing to the need to give due consideration to a keen blend of policy, direct actions and knowledge production. Evidence on the booming of the extractive sector is highlighted in the fourth section. The fifth section examines the means for mobilising partnerships in catalysing opportunities in the extractive industries into youth employment in Africa, and some policy recommendations are offered.

Youth employment: a dire challenge in Africa

As noted earlier, Africa has the youngest population in the world, and it is critical to invest strategically in order to reap the demographic dividend.

Young people constitute the bulk of the unemployed in Africa

It is largely believed that with a population growth of 2.2 per cent per year and a fertility rate of 5.2 children per woman, the highest in the world, the number of young people in Africa will double, to constitute 29 per cent of the total world youth population by 2050 (AfDB, 2011; AfDB et al, 2012; ILO, 2012a).

According to the United Nations (UN) Focal Point on Youth, close to 75 million young people worldwide were unemployed in 2012, which is 12.6 per cent, three times the global adult unemployment rate of 4.5 per cent (ILO, 2012a,b, 2013).[2] Youth unemployment has become a challenging issue globally, but remains a greater barrier for the economic and social development of the African continent. As reported by the International Labour Organization (ILO) (2013, p 116), North Africa records the highest youth unemployment rate, whereas the rate remained around 12 per cent in Sub-Saharan Africa since 2005, well above their 2000 levels of 13.3 per cent, as shown in Figure 6.1. Nevertheless, irrespective of the region, the youth unemployment rate has been consistently twice that of adults from 2000 to 2012.

These rates are even higher in some countries. Indeed, the 2013 ILO report indicates that in South Africa, the rates are much higher than the regional average, and over half of the young people in the labour force were unemployed in the first three quarters of 2012. In Namibia, youth unemployment was 58.9 per cent in 2008, and in Réunion, it was 58.6 per cent in 2011 (ILO, 2013). Beyond country

Figure 6.1: Unemployment rate for youth and adults in Africa (%)

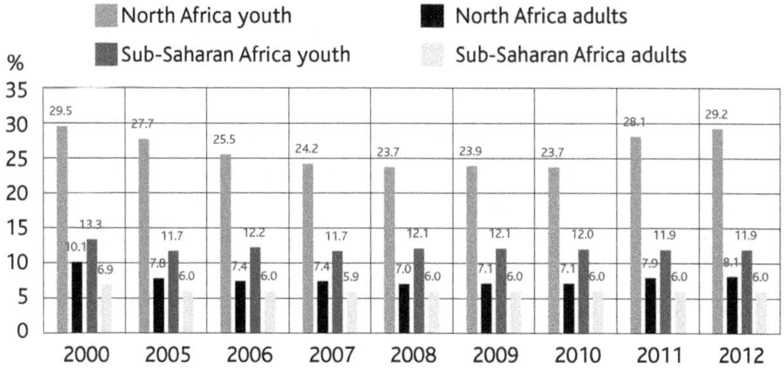

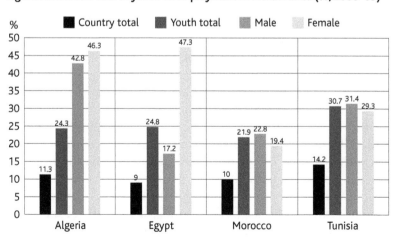

Source: Constructed based on data from Table A3 of ILO (2014, p 120)

specificities, the gender structure of youth unemployment merits some close consideration.

Young women are the most likely to be unemployed in Africa

Using a gender lens, the youth unemployment rates for males and females in Morocco were fairly close in 2011: 18.1 per cent for young men and 17.4 per cent for young women (ILO, 2013). This was also the case in the 2000s (see Figure 6.2). In Tunisia, young women were slightly better off than those in Algeria and Egypt in the 2000s, but in

Figure 6.2: Gender lens of youth unemployment in North Africa (%, 2000–09)

Source: Constructed based on data from Table 9.3 of The World Bank (2011, p 102)

the same period, Egyptian young women were far more likely to be unemployed than young men, as revealed by Figure 6.2. This structure was also reported for Algeria in 2010, which had an unemployment rate of 37.5 per cent for young women compared to 18.7 per cent for young men.

The unemployment rate was generally high in Sub-Saharan African countries such as South Africa, Namibia, Ethiopia and Botswana (see Figure 6.3), but the gender bias towards young women was relatively lower in Sub-Saharan Africa than in North Africa, as shown in Figure 6.3.

In terms of individuals out of the labour force, The World Bank (2009a) reports that young women's labour participation rates were likely to be the most affected in Sub-Saharan Africa by unemployment in the early 2000s, with a regional mean of 58.0 per cent for young women and 52.3 per cent for young men, as depicted in Figure 6.4.

As can be seen from Figure 6.4, the distribution of young men and women according to job status in the 14 countries surveyed by The World Bank (2009a) follows a similar pattern to the regional mean. But Kenya, Mozambique, Mauritania, Malawi, Nigeria and Uganda revealed the greatest number of young people out of the labour force, whereas Sao Tomé and Principe had the largest gender unemployment gap. Following this World Bank survey analysis, a number of facts 'conspire' to keep female youth out of the labour force in Sub-Saharan Africa. These factors are related to the type of the jobs available, the skills of the jobseekers, or to the marital status of the individuals in the two groups. The survey results demonstrate that even though women tend to work more hours than males, they are more likely to engage in non-market activities.

The survey also revealed that young women had lower levels of school attainment and school enrolment, which is rather common to African countries. For instance, in 2005, the male and female net school enrolment ratios in Africa were 71 and 65 per cent in primary education and 28 and 23 per cent in secondary education respectively, whereas the male gross school enrolment ratio in tertiary education was 6 per cent, while that of women was 4 per cent (The World Bank, 2009b). Indeed, in many African countries, most female youth have already been married before the age of 24, and the majority of them prioritise motherhood at the expense of education and participation in the labour force. All these factors merely define women in the vulnerable working group, irrespective of their age. McKinsey & Company (2012) further underscore that, even when women own businesses and become job creators, the numerous

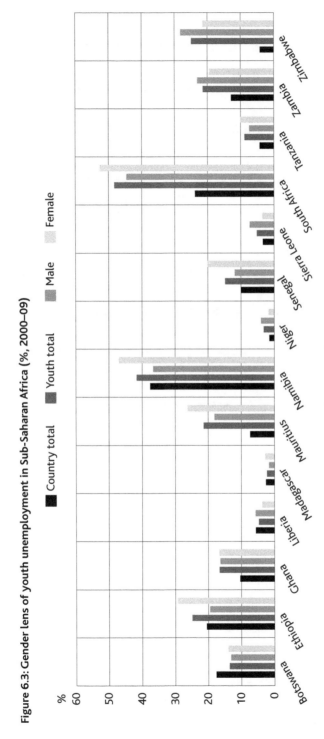

Figure 6.3: Gender lens of youth unemployment in Sub-Saharan Africa (%, 2000–09)

Source: Constructed based on data from Table 9.3 of The World Bank (2011, p 102)

Figure 6.4: Distribution of young men and women by job status (%)

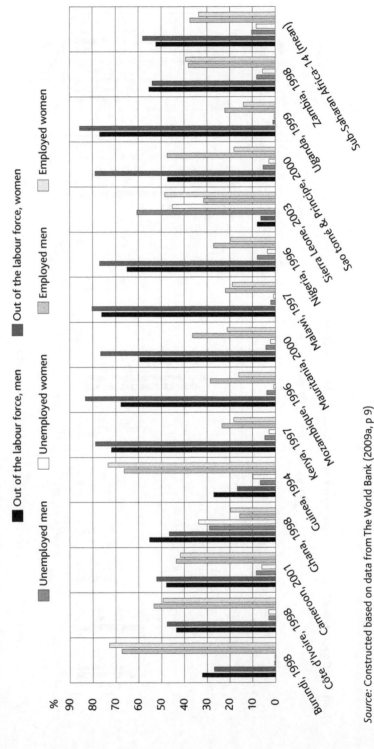

Source: Constructed based on data from The World Bank (2009a, p 9)

constraints they face – such as access to capital and land, and a low level of education – leave female-led small businesses on the low productivity side.

The debates about the roles of the extractive sector come at a moment when Africa is seeking its rapid transformation, and envisions driving an industrial revolution using local people. In this regard, the challenges of youth unemployment must be part of the larger agenda. Indeed, a number of affirmative actions are being explored to support effective youth employment interventions.

Affirmative actions for youth employment

In the face of the current favourable economic growth conditions in Africa, and the commitments governments are adopting at their summits (for example, the Common African Position [CAP] on the post-2015 agenda), policy, direct actions and knowledge production must be best blended and entrenched for sustaining job creation for young people in Africa.

Favourable economic environment for youth employment creation in Africa

The causes of youth unemployment are numerous, ranging from lack of prioritisation of job creation in development policies to the socioeconomic environment, through to the structure of African economies and educational systems. Job creation schemes either remain non-existent or were not activated by development policies. The majority of African economies are dominated by a multifaceted informal sector. In some Sub-Saharan African countries, the informal sector comprises as much as 90 per cent of non-agricultural employment. This tends to be the case for at least two reasons. First, it is believed that African university graduates barely meet labour market demands in a number of African countries due to a skills mismatch. Second, in many cases socioeconomic environments are flecked by tensions and conflicts, and are thus likely to push active populations into the informal sector. Fortunately, a great number of African economies have been growing healthier since the late 1990s.

Indeed, it is widely admitted that six of the ten fastest growing economies in the period 2001-10 were in Africa: Angola, Nigeria, Ethiopia, Chad, Mozambique and Rwanda. Moreover, the prospective views on Africa's growth from 2011 to 2015 brought into the growth outlook countries such as Tanzania (7.2 per cent), Democratic

Republic of Congo (DRC) (7 per cent), Ghana (7 per cent) and Zambia (6.9 per cent), while Ethiopia (8 per cent), Mozambique (7.9 per cent) and Nigeria (6.8 per cent) (The World Bank, 2011). On a regional stand, West Africa and East Africa are forecast to maintain their ranking at the top of the continental growth array, with 7.1 and 6.2 per cent in 2015 respectively (AfDB et al, 2014). More interestingly, while the growing diversification of African economies shelters them against external shocks, growth episodes are getting longer in Africa.

African economies have also been integrating into global value chains that best map the continent's resource endowment, with some cases as presented in Table 6.1, below.

Extractive industries, tourism, services and agriculture have the largest share of integrated economies, as shown in Figure 6.5. Should agriculture be conceived on a more aggregate view to include horticulture, then the agriculture value chain would also be one of the well-integrated value channels in Africa.

Biofuel value chains are also expanding on the continent. Kenya, Uganda and Ethiopia are upgrading their horticulture value chain, whereas the value chains of palm nuts for vegetable oil and soap must be nurtured in countries such as Côte d'Ivoire and Cameroon. Other agricultural value chain experiences are sorghum for the production of

Table 6.1: Participation of selected African countries in GVCs

	Extractive industries	Agriculture	Horticulture	Fishing	Construction/ manufacturing	Textile	Animal husbandry/ leather	Tourism	Services
South Africa	✓				✓				✓
Botswana	✓					✓	✓	✓	✓
Kenya			✓			✓	✓	✓	
Nigeria	✓	✓							✓
Morocco					✓			✓	
Senegal		✓							
Uganda			✓	✓					✓
Mozambique	✓							✓	
Zambia	✓								
Madagascar	✓	✓						✓	✓

Source: Constructed using value chain participation information in country notes in AfDB et al (2014)

Figure 6.5: Degree of integration of some value chains in Africa

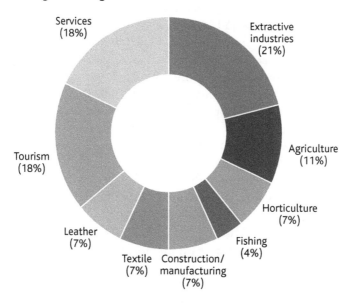

Source: Constructed based on the information in Table 1 (AfDB et al, 2014)

beer, bananas to make drinks, and exports of mangoes, garlic, onion, tomatoes, pineapples and avocados.

Essentially, the extractive sector has economic potential for creating new jobs and ultimately for reducing poverty. Development partners and governments in Africa are joining their planning and financing efforts to tackle the problem of youth unemployment on the continent.

Targeted actions for youth employment in Africa

On 12 September 2013, the African Union Commission (AUC), the African Development Bank (AfDB), the United Nations Economic Commission for Africa (UNECA) and the ILO signed a Declaration of Intent on the Joint Youth Employment Initiative for Africa (JYEIA). This spells out the duties of the four parties in the creation of employment to accelerate youth development and empowerment, underscoring three areas of intervention: policy-level intervention, direct intervention and knowledge production. Direct action provides hands-on solutions to the problem, and a sound policy ensures the sustainability of the interventions, whereas success stories are disseminated through knowledge produced.

Many more actions have been launched since the mid-2000s, in support of effective employment interventions. In 2006,[3] the AU heads of states endorsed the JYEIA Charter geared towards strengthening, reinforcing and consolidating continental and regional partnerships and relations. It entered into force on 8 August 2010, having been signed by 37 countries and ratified by 21. Equally, the Assembly of heads of states and governments of the AU[4] declared 2009-18 as the Decade on Youth Development in Africa as well as approving a plan of action in line with international consensus on the International Year of Youth 2010 (ILO, 2012b). As a follow-up, at their July 2011 summit in Malabo, the deliberation of the AU heads of states led to the declaration to advance the youth agenda by adopting policies and mechanisms for the creation of safe, decent and competitive employment opportunities (ILO, 2012b).

The ILO (2012b, p 105) recorded a number of these programmatic interventions for creating youth employment in Africa in terms of their geographic distributions, thematic areas, milieus of residence in specific countries, strategic approaches and implementation modalities, partnerships in implementation, modes of financing, targeted beneficiaries and special priorities, notably young women, and disabled and unemployed young people. Unemployment programmes are scattered over the regions, mapping almost all the 54 countries. Overall, these interventions included as thematic areas employment creation, skills development, employment services, integrated services and others, but employment creation and skills development were given the highest priority across the continent. Moreover, interventions were developed in due recognition of the unemployment gap between the rural and urban areas of Africa. In effect, unemployed and under-employed youth are not only in a greater number in rural Africa, but rural youth also face more acute challenges in accessing job opportunities. In their implementation, the interventions pull together as many development partners as possible, but without advocating for a one-size-fits-all solution to the youth employment challenge (ILO, 2012b, p 68).

Governments in Africa are going beyond declarations adopted at their various summits. Some are mainstreaming employment in their national employment policies and national development frameworks in an attempt to address concerns for youth employment. For instance, the Ethiopian national development Growth and Transformation Plan for the period 2010-15 set employment creation as a priority, with a firm commitment to mainstream women and youth issues across all development plans – women and youth empowerment and equity is one of the pillars of the strategy. Others put in place frameworks to elaborate shared programmes, with UN agencies and/ or multilateral development banks. Examples include the ILO (2012b) joint programme that emphasised community participation either in the identification, design and/or implementation, as in Côte d'Ivoire, Liberia, Zimbabwe and Mozambique.

In sum, either for youth or for adults, Africa has upheld the urgent need to create jobs for its growing population in the last decade or so. Agriculture, household enterprise and services (either wage or hospitality) have generated the bulk of jobs in Africa, and are expected to lead in the creation of new jobs. The question is to know what contribution the extractive industries could make. Could the extractive industries, in their expansion in Africa, be part of the solution for youth employment?

Potential for youth employment in the extractive industries

Africa must leverage opportunities in the extractive industries to create productive and decent jobs.[5] Certainly, relevant partnerships could unleash job opportunities in the extractive sector.

Extractive industries, a booming sector

More than 250 million Africans live in countries where natural resources account for more than 80 per cent of exports, and in some cases, more than 50 per cent of government revenues (The World Bank et al, 2010). In the specific case of the extractive industry, the investment projects implemented by large multinational and national companies are growing exponentially, encouraged by the numerous recent natural resource discoveries and increasing demands. According to Ramdoo (2012), Africa has about 30 per cent of the world's extractive resources, and produces over 60 different types of metals, ores and minerals.

The boom and bust of gold-mining projects in a number of West African countries is noteworthy, particularly in Ghana, Burkina Faso, Mali, Mauritania, Liberia and Sierra Leone, where a significant rise in gold prices between 2007-12 stimulated further exploration and development of projects in these countries over the five years, and the reverse happened when prices decreased in 2011.

For oil, it is believed that over 10 per cent of the world's reserves are in Africa, which constitutes over 12 per cent of the global market.

Ramdoo (2012) highlights that new discoveries of hydrocarbons show that Sub-Saharan Africa is home to some 115 billion barrels of oil, of which 75 per cent are offshore in the Atlantic Ocean. The same estimates portrayed Africa as hosting some 744 trillion cubic feet of gas, most of it stacked offshore off East Africa, mainly in Tanzania, Mozambique, Madagascar and Seychelles. Of course, the persistent upward shift in oil supply coupled with the sluggish global economic recovery, including in the European Union (EU), and the lower than expected growth in China and other emerging countries, has pushed the price of crude oil down to a historic five-year low, as at December 2014. Over the first quarter of 2015, oil prices lunged even deeper, at levels lower than the 2009 rates, rising slightly to around US$60 per barrel by late April of 2015 (*Global Finance Magazine*, 2015). The anticipated negative impacts of this price downturn might slow down oil exploitations and decelerate ongoing explorations.

Beyond oil, Africa has the largest reserve of bauxite, cobalt, industrial diamonds, manganese, phosphate rock and platinum (Ramdoo, 2012). The trends in mineral discoveries set the extractive sector as a firm driver for Africa's transformation. Strategies and appropriate policies must therefore be designed and put in place in order to unleash job opportunities in the sector.

Diverse job opportunities in the extractive industries, with specific skills requirements

Globally, three major categories of activities shape the extractive industry: (i) activities pertaining to the extraction of raw materials from the earth; (ii) the processing of extracted minerals for sale or commercial use in construction, building, road or manufacturing works; and (iii) transport and storage, which ensure overall connections within the industry. Extractive-related activities involve exploration, development and mining. Processing activities comprise beneficiation, smelting and refining, without omitting other added value activities (Antonio, 2012). Each industry node calls for the intervention of specific professionals, which in the case of oil and gas, Sigam and Garcia (2012) group into three categories: (i) technical jobs; (ii) operational jobs and (iii) support positions, as defined in Table 6.2.

Exploration globally centres on project appraisal. At exploration, one seeks to know (i) if the required resource is economically feasible to develop; and (ii) what the environmental impact of the project could be and what environmental impact strategy to put in place. Economists in general, and environmental economists in particular,

Table 6.2: Professionals required in the oil and gas industry

Professional required	Exploration	Production	Transportation	Refining	Distribution	Marketing
Technical job	Geo-scientists	Petroleum engineers	Mechanical engineers	Chemical engineers	Industrial engineers	Analysts and traders
Operational job	Oil drillers and seismic crews	Oilfield workers	Pipeline workers	Plant operators	Terminal operators and truckers	Service station attendants
Support position	Landmen	Petroleum attorneys	Petroleum accountants	Human resources	Information technology	Administrative assistants

Source: Sigam and Garcia (2012)

undertake tasks (i) and (ii) above. Production is technically preceded by the construction of facilities and staff housing, but the required professionals are either engineers or operational workers or staff such as attorneys. Transportation, refining and the marketing of the specific minerals requires technical, operational and support jobs. Overall, careers in the extractive industry are as diverse as engineering, finance, law, design, IT, environmental management, customer support, sales and health and safety.

Of course, extractive industries are believed to be highly capital-intensive and make a limited direct contribution to employment. The World Bank (2013) supports this assertion with some evidence as presented in Table 6.3.

This gives a broad basis for comparison over countries and types of mining worldwide, pulling together examples from Africa, Latin America and Asia. The liquid natural gas project in Papua New Guinea appears as a typical example of extractive industries that is highly capital-intensive, with a limited contribution to employment. In effect, in Papua Guinea, the investment cost of the project exceeded twice the country's GDP at project start-up, and generated around 9,300 jobs during construction, but it is unlikely to generate more than 1,000 direct jobs in the longer term. Interestingly, however, the gold-mining project in Peru required an investment of only 2.6 per cent of GDP, but it was projected to generate 6,000 jobs during construction and sustain one-third of these jobs in the longer term. Coal mining in Mozambique is expected to increase its employment creation from 150 to 4,500 in the longer term of a decade or so, with an investment requirement of only 13.9 per cent of 2010 GDP. Overall, some extractive activities may have different capacities for generating a notable amount of jobs, even for young people, provided the appropriate policies are put in place to unleash them.

Table 6.3: Jobs creation in the extractive industries

Country	Project (sector or resource)	Investment (% of GDP, 2010)	Direct employment number
Papua New Guinea	LNG Project (liquid natural gas)	237.0	9,300 during construction; 1,000 afterward
Mongolia	Oyu Tolgoi (copper, gold)	74.2	14,800 during construction; 3,000 to 4,000 afterward
Botswana	Jwaneng Cut 8 Project (diamonds)	20.2	1,000
Papua New Guinea	Ramu Mine (nickel)	19.0	5,000 during construction; 2,000 afterward
Mozambique	Benga Mining (coal)	13.6	Currently 150; 4,500 afterward
Tanzania	Mchuchuma (coal)	12.2	5,000
Namibia	Husab Mine (uranium)	11.9	5,200 during construction; 1,200 afterward
Zambia	Lumwana Mine (copper)	9.3	4,700 during construction
Pakistan	Reko Diq Mining (copper, gold)	4.0	2,500 during construction; 200 afterward
Peru	Conga Mine (gold)	2.6	6,000 during construction; 1,700 afterward

Source: The World Bank (2013, p 200).

Sigam and Garcia's analysis (2012) is noteworthy for highlighting the potential for jobs creation in the extractive industries. They argue that at the local level, large-scale extractive projects can have significant employment effects. However, the net impact depends on how these projects affect employment in pre-existing activities, such as agriculture or small-scale mining. At best, communities can capture a number of benefits depending on their qualification for the available jobs opportunities, or their ability to indirectly participate in the supporting activities of the wider value chain. This point is also advanced by USAID (2008),[6] which specifically points to the role that artisanal and small-scale mining could play in local employment, notably in poor countries. Unfortunately, the contribution of artisanal and small-scale mining to the economy is oftentimes difficult to estimate for at least two reasons. First, artisanal and small-scale mining are typically informal activities, and second, in many cases, these activities are performed either in remote locations and are therefore difficult to observe, or they are conducted during periods of seasonal agricultural inactivity or under-employment, hence as part-time occupations.

But it is important to appreciate job opportunities in the extractive industries with respect to their specific skill requirements. Some jobs require just a high school diploma – for example, the assay technician who collects samples from the mine, splits, dries, crushes, splits again and pulverises the samples to the consistency of talcum powder. Or the environmental technician who conducts water, soil and air monitoring activities, who enters the industry with a high school degree (see Mining Information Institute, 2013, or visit www.mineralseducationcoalition.org/sites/default/files/uploads/rolesinminingppt6.pdf). Indeed, many more jobs in the extractive industry require college degrees (Mining Information Institute, 2013). This is especially the case for geologists, mineralogists, geophysicists, geophysical engineers and geotechnical engineers. Young men and women in Africa can access some of the available jobs if their skills match the requirements of this labour sub-market.

Catalysing opportunities in the extractive industries into youth employment in Africa: partnerships matter

The specificity of existing jobs in the extractive industries and the associated huge investment gap requires public–private partnership schemes as innovative sources of funding for catalysing job opportunities into youth employment in Africa.

Partnership in skills development for the extractive industries

Job opportunities in the extractive industries are notable, but skills constraints remain tight. For instance, Sigam and Garcia (2012) contend that rising skills shortages have become one of the main problems facing the oil industry throughout the world. Skills shortages leave many producers unable to meet their schedules. Hence, delays in the implementation of projects are increasing, whereas some contracts have to be renegotiated in order to meet the skills constraint. The unfortunate fact is that even job advertisements with promises of high pay are insufficient to secure enough qualified personnel.

The causes of skills shortages, irrespective of the economic sectors in developing countries, are numerous, but five may be considered as critical in the case of Sub-Saharan Africa: (i) scarce educational facilities; (ii) weak vocational and technical training; (iii) lack of school accreditation; (iv) increasing demand for higher skilled workers in the industry; and (v) attrition during the search for more productive sectors and/or regions. In short, the skills mismatch extends to various economic sectors in Africa including manufacturing and mining. For example, the African Mineral Skills Initiative (AMSI, 2013) indicates that the Mozambique government requires around 300 staff members with at least an undergraduate-level education just to fill the current vacancies, whereas one of the numerous resource companies such as BHP Billiton or Anadarko Petroleum operating in Mozambique foresee the need for almost 700 professionally trained staff by the end of 2015 (an increase of almost 500 from 2013), and for 9,314 semi-skilled and unskilled mine workers over the same period. In Ghana, however, trained professionals are leaving the country to apply their skills in other West African countries, as well as in Australia, Canada and South Africa, hence creating a significant vacuum in the country for the capacity to replace such professionals. In Guinea, weak local expertise in key areas such as taxation, community relations, contract negotiations and mine administration highly constrains the mining reform process[7] that has been launched (Ministère des Mines et de la Géologie, 2011).

Some extractive industries provide on-the-job training, but a given position must be filled before the individual can have access to such training: individuals must first qualify for the available jobs. UNESCO's report on Education for All (2010) stresses that governments, trade unions and employers must develop effective vocational education to give young people the skills for effectiveness in employment. This calls on mutually reliant interactions among educational systems, institutions and industries – in this case, the extractive sector. In the extractive industries, effective and trustworthy institutions are not only a prerequisite for business, but also for the implementation of local contents[8] to support education and skill needs, among others. But educated citizens develop good institutions and skill that bridge the quality of interaction between the educational systems and extractive sectors. Figure 6.6 highlights the envisioned interactions.

The success of technical and vocational education programmes is highly variable, and also depends on conditions outside the education sector. A number of African countries have been relying on technical and vocational training since the 1970s, with the aim of creating a class of young professionals. But on completing training, the scarcity of corresponding job opportunities often lowered the expectations of degree earners to attain work in their field. Rather,

Figure 6.6: Interactions among educational, institutional and economic stakeholders

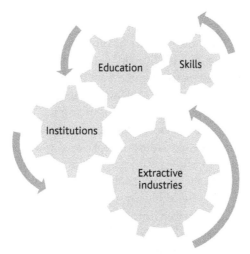

Source: Adapted from Gao (2010)

they join universities, mostly schools of economics, and management departments in particular, whose degrees allow a number of young people to enter the informal sector and to undertake activities such as petty trade. This has been the case in Francophone African countries such as Cameroon, Côte d'Ivoire and Burkina Faso.

Fortunately, some models have produced good results. As a means of enriching the discussion and reforming skills development schemes, the same UNESCO report proposes (i) reinforcing the links between the education sector and the labour market; (ii) recognising that past achievements are no guarantee of future success, and that governments must adapt and renew vocational programmes in light of changing circumstances; (iii) avoiding the separation of vocational education from general education based on rigid tracking into vocational streams, especially at an early age; (iv) developing a capability-based national qualification systems involving the private sector, that allows training to be used for transferable credits into technical and general education; and (v) integrating vocational programmes into national skills strategies, aligned with the needs of high-growth sectors. In the search for strategies to reduce the skills constraint, we may give a special tribute to model (iv) as a precursor of public–private partnerships in education for labour markets.

Coordinating training, work experience and labour market services in the extractive industries: are public–private partnerships in education a viable solution?

In its analysis of the collaboration of the private and public sector in education, The World Bank (2009b, p 15) refers to these schemes as modern public–private partnerships. In such partnerships, governments contract with private providers to deliver a range of inputs and services with the expectation that they will introduce new pedagogical skills and management efficiencies that the public sector lacks, thus generating alternatives to traditional forms of public education. Of the seven forms of public–private partnerships in education analysed by The World Bank, facility availability and education services could be harnessed to solve the skills gap problem in the extractive sector. The considered partnership implies 'governments contracting the same private firm, not only to build the facility, but also to undertake all of the activities associated with delivering education and related services' (The World Bank, 2009b). The private sector, in this case, the extractive sector, would engage in the educational system in the area of curriculum design and delivery. The expected results are educational outcomes that best suit the labour market.

The ILO (2012b) compiled some ideal cases for combining training, work experience and labour market services from a number of countries in Sub-Saharan Africa. These fall under either one of two broad views: (i) promote youth entrepreneurship and practical skills training in partnership with employers, based on labour market needs, or (ii) adopt a combination of apprenticeships, internships, work placements and industrial attachments. In regard to the first group of views, the majority Zimbabwean perception is that the government and its partners should commit to financing entrepreneurship, training and skills development for young people using informal and formal channels of training. Zambians were in favour of rehabilitating the infrastructure and upgrading equipment and other training aids in all the vocational training and/or youth resource centres by government, so as to create a favourable training environment and to provide relevant skills to young women and men (ILO, 2012b). Under view (ii), the perception from Madagascar is for a system that encourages employers to recruit young people without experience and from more marginalised groups. These views are shared by people interviewed in South Africa – underpinned by the social compact between the government and the private sector as a way to place young people in internship programmes. Government and the private sector should take part equally in providing such work experience places. In Zambia, however, it is believed that a sound model is based on creating incentives for employers to take on young people as interns and apprentices to promote more formal and informal apprenticeships and work-related exposure (ILO, 2012b). As incentives, the government could offer subsidies to employers or establish a youth employment quota system.

Introducing new pedagogical skills and management efficiencies in the African educational system is of the utmost importance to sustain the development of youth employment in the extractive industries for two reasons in particular. First, jobs in this sector are very specific and young people need the appropriate training and skills. The participation of the extractive industries in the design and delivery of training courses should significantly reduce the skills gap in the sector. And second, the boom of the extractive sector makes it a viable niche for solving the problem of youth unemployment on the continent, provided, of course, they have the right skills.

Partnerships between the extractive industries and governments are best spelt out in local contents. Such strategies are essential for overcoming the financial and resource constraints in the education sector, among others. For instance, companies' local content agreements on training and employment for nationals and their preference for local suppliers could be better aligned with public policies for human capital development, job creation and technology transfer. In Guinea, for example, Article 108 of the Mining Code[9] stipulates that 'Any holder of an exploitation permit or a mining concession shall design during the development phase, and present to the Ministry in charge of Professional Training and to the Mining Administration, a training plan for Guinean managers enabling them to develop the requisite knowledge and skills in order to take management positions in the first five years as from the starting date of commercial production' (Ministère des Mines et de la Géologie, 2011). In that regard, one would advocate for local contents that allow countries to apply hiring quotas or targets for training local workers. But targeting specialised staff such as mining engineers would work best. These arrangements will be the most effective if policies are complemented with training programmes supported by the extractive industries and intended to ensure the availability of skilled workers.

An example of public–private partnerships in training for the extractive industries is Sierra Leone's Peace Diamonds Alliance initiative. The government of Sierra Leone, large-scale diamond corporations such as DeBeers and Rapaport, and several international development organisations and non-governmental organisations

(NGOs) collaborated to create the Peace Diamonds Alliance. This advocates for an integrated and transparent approach to diamond management. Examples of the services it provides are developing competitive buying schemes, training miners to recognise the value of their products, tracking diamonds from earth to export, providing credit to miners, and ensuring that communities benefit from the mining that takes place in their localities. Among other skills, the Alliance trained 209 individuals on valuation techniques, as reported by Wise and Shtylla (2007, p 52).

Sigam (2012, p 11) notes that several resource-rich countries have applied hiring quotas or targets for training local workers in order to increase local staffing in the extractive industries. Sigam further argues that even having had to comply with targets of participation, oil companies in countries such as Nigeria and Angola have encountered difficulties in achieving these targets, especially for the more specialised staff. In effect, this revealed that two conditions are necessary to ensure the effectiveness of schemes of hiring quotas or targets for training of local workers: (i) such policies must be complemented with training programmes supported by the extractive industries, and (ii) the supported training programmes are intended to ensure the availability of skilled workers in accordance with the sector's changing requirements. As reported by Sigam (2012), support measures to local entrepreneurs and special preferences in terms of participation and training in Trinidad and Tobago were applied for a certain period for local capabilities development, business opportunities and diversification.

In short, an ideal public–private partnership in education for the extractive industries would function such that young people who are inexperienced would be accorded the first opportunity to acquire the necessary exposure and skills needed in the sector. Inexperienced young people are, for example, new graduates in mineral engineering and related technical fields who may not yet have the same practical skills as their counterparts who graduated a few years earlier and who have gained some experience and are gainfully employed. A necessary condition for effective first job opportunities for new graduates is partnerships in education for which industries commit themselves to take new graduates as interns and apprentices to create apprenticeships and work-related exposures that fit the sector's needs.

Conclusions

Africa must address the urgent need to create jobs for its growing population. Agriculture, household enterprise and services have generated the bulk of jobs in Africa, and are expected to lead in the creation of new jobs. The key argument of this chapter is that policies should be put in place to create opportunities in the booming extractive sector for youth employment. Public–private partnerships in education to develop the necessary capacities/skills in young people are perceived as a viable solution, and such partnerships are best spelt out in local contents. Local content strategies provide the framework for negotiating such partnerships between companies and governments. The efficacy of these partnerships relies on the alignment of public economic policies with priorities for industrial development, private sector development, investment promotion and competitiveness. More specifically, we advocate for local contents that allow countries to apply hiring quotas or targets for training local workers. These arrangements will be the most effective if policies are complemented with training programmes supported by the extractive industries and intended to ensure the availability of skilled workers. Another version of partnership that is likely to lead to youth employment is a partnership to allow young people who are inexperienced to be accorded the first opportunity to acquire the necessary experience and skills needed in the sector.

References

AfDB (African Development Bank) (2011) *Accelerating the AfDB's response to the youth unemployment crisis in Africa*, OSHD/EDRE Working Paper, Tunis: AfDB.

AfDB (2013a) 'Youth employment in Africa: a brief overview and the AfDB's response', AfDB Partnerships Forum 2012, PowerPoint presentation by Stijn Broecke, EDRE2 (Division 2 of the Research Department of the African Development Bank) Amadou B. Diallo, OSHD1 (Division 1 of the Human Development Department of the AfDB).

AfDB (2013b) *From fragility to resilience: Managing natural resources in African fragile states*, Draft document for review, March.

AfDB, OECD (Organisation for Economic Co-operation and Development), UNDP (United Nations Development Programme) and UNECA (United Nations Economic Commission for Africa) (2012) *African Economic Outlook*, Issy les Moulineaux, Chapter 6 (http://www.africaneconomicoutlook.org/en/).

AfDB, OECD and UNDP (2014) *African economic outlook 2014: Global value chains and Africa's industrialisation* (http://dx.doi.org/10.1787/aeo-2014-en).

AMSI (African Mineral Skills Initiative) (2013) *Business plan*, Addis Ababa: UNECA.

Antonio, M.A. (2012) 'The Africa Mining Vision: towards shared benefits and economic transformation', *GREAT Insights*, vol 1, issue 5, July.

Gao, R. (2010) *Education and corporate social responsibility*, Social Business/Enterprise and Poverty Certificate, HEC Chair, Paris: HEC (Hautes Ecoles de Commerce).

Global Finance Magazine (2015) 'US oil prices rise above $60 a barrel', 5 May (www.gfmag.com/topics/syndicate/34310674-us-oil-prices-rise-above-60-a-barrel).

ILO (International Labour Organization) (2009) *The informal economy in Africa: Promoting transition to formality: Challenges and strategies*, Geneva: ILO, Employment Sector and Social Protection Sector (www.ilo.org/wcmsp5/groups/public/@ed_emp/@emp_policy/documents/publication/wcms_127814.pdf).

ILO (2012a) *Africa's response to the youth employment crisis: Synthesis of key issues and outcomes from eleven national events on youth employment in the African region*, Regional report, CH-1211, Geneva: ILO (www.ilo.org/publns).

ILO (2012b) *Youth employment interventions in Africa: A mapping report of the employment and labour sub-cluster of the Regional Coordination Mechanism (RCM) for Africa*, Geneva: ILO (www.ilo.org/wcmsp5/groups/public/---africa/documents/publication/wcms_206325.pdf).

ILO (2013) *Global employment trends for youth 2013: A generation at risk*, Geneva: ILO.

ILO (2014) *Global employment trends for youth 2014: Risk of a jobless recovery?*, Geneva: ILO.

McKinsey & Company (2012) *Africa at work: Job creation and inclusive growth*, August (www.mckinsey.com/insights/africa/africa_at_work).

Mining Information Institute (2013) *Mining careers* (www.mineralsed.ca/i/pdf/MII%20Careers%20in%20Mining.pdf).

Ministère des Mines et de la Géologie (2011) 'Code minier de la République de Guinée', République de Guinée (http://itie-guinee.org/codes_miniers/Code_Minier_2011.pdf).

Population Reference Bureau (2012) *World population data sheet*, Washington, DC (www.prb.org/pdf12/2012-population-data-sheet_eng.pdf).

Ramdoo, I. (2012) 'Treasure hunt: do extractive resources work for development?', *GREAT Insights*, vol 1, issue 5, July.

Sigam, C. (2012) 'Human capacity problems in developing countries and local content requirements in the extractive industries', *GREAT Insights*, vol 1, issue 5, July.

Sigam, C. and Garcia, L. (2012) *Extractive industries: Optimizing value retention in host countries*, Geneva: United Nations Conference on Trade and Development.

UNESCO (United Nations Educational, Scientific and Cultural Organization) (2010) *Education for All global monitoring report: Reaching the marginalized: A summary*, Paris: UNESCO (http://unesdoc.unesco.org/images/0018/001865/186525E.pdf).

UN (United Nations) (2012) *World youth report 2012: The UN focal point for youth 2012*, New York: UN.

USAID (United States Agency for International Development) (2008) *Partnering with extractive industries for the conservation of biodiversity in Africa: A guide for USAID engagement*, Biodiversity Assessment and Technical Support Program (BATS), Task Order 02, November (http://pdf.usaid.gov/pdf_docs/Pnadn726.pdf).

Wise, H. and Shtylla, S. (2007) *The role of the extractive sector in expanding economic opportunity*, Economic Opportunity Series, Corporate Social Responsibility Initiative Report No 18, Cambridge, MA: Kennedy School of Government, Harvard University.

World Bank, The (2009a) *Africa development indicators 2008/09, Youth and employment in Africa: The potential, the problem, the promise*, Washington, DC: The World Bank.

World Bank, The (2009b) *The role and impact of public–private partnerships in education*, Washington, DC: International Bank for Reconstruction and Development and The World Bank.

World Bank, The (2011) *Africa development indicators 2011*, Washington, DC: The World Bank.

World Bank, The (2013) *World development report: Jobs*, Washington, DC: The World Bank.

World Bank, The, World Bank Institute and AfDB (African Development Bank) (2010) 'Governance for extractive industries', PowerPoint presentation, March (www.mmdaproject.org/presentations/GEI%20Update%20March%202010%20external.pdf).

SEVEN

Financing the post-2015 development agenda: domestic revenue mobilisation in Africa

Aniket Bhushan,[1] Yiagadeesen Samy and Kemi Medu

Introduction

The debate about what should replace the Millennium Development Goals (MDGs), come 2015, provides an opportunity to reflect once again on the Financing for Development (FFD) agenda. It also comes on the back of dramatic reductions in global poverty in the last decade, and when many of the so-called fragile and conflict-affected states – many of which are located in Sub-Saharan Africa – are the least likely to meet any of the MDGs. Poverty remains stubbornly high in Sub-Saharan Africa – despite a fall in poverty rates, the number of people living on less than US$1.25 per day has increased from 205 million in 1981 to 414 million in 2010 (data from PovcalNet, The World Bank). A coherent and realistic FFD agenda is thus critical to the success of both the post-2015 process as well as the achievement of new goals and targets. Much like the original MDGs were accompanied by the Monterrey Consensus on FFD (UN, 2003), the post-2015 agenda will likely be accompanied by a new or updated FFD framework.

The Monterrey Consensus outlined six leading actions to meet the challenge of financing the MDGs. The first among these was domestic resource mobilisation (DRM).[2] DRM, as outlined in the Monterrey Consensus, comprised fiscal revenue mobilisation (that is, tax and non-tax revenue mobilisation), but also strengthening the domestic financial sector in developing countries by encouraging the orderly development of capital markets, sound banking systems and increasing financial inclusion. For the purposes of this chapter we limit our analysis of DRM to domestic *revenue* mobilisation, that is, issues related to taxation and revenue mobilisation, with an emphasis on DRM in Africa.

The Third International Conference on FFD took place on 13–16 July 2015 in Addis Ababa, Ethiopia (UN, 2015a). This follows prior FFD conferences, beginning with the landmark Monterrey Consensus (see above) in 2002 and the Doha follow-up conference in 2008. DRM, which has been recast as 'domestic public finance', again emerges as a top priority. Recent discussions highlight important progress since Monterrey. Developing countries on average have achieved revenue increases of 2 to 3 per cent of GDP, with some achieving increases of up to 5 per cent (UN, 2015a). Despite this, there are several challenges. Domestic revenues are insufficient, and tax and expenditure policies are regressive and have negative consequences for inequality in many countries. Sub-national entities in general do not have access to sufficient resources, harmful tax competition persists both across and within countries, revenue and expenditure decisions rarely take sustainable development criteria into account, and budget processes lack transparency and participation. These generalisations hold true with very few exceptions (UN, 2015a).

The prevailing mood in several donor countries is to move away from traditional grant-heavy ODA in favour of other kinds of 'blended' financing. Donors are highlighting the relative decline of ODA compared to other financial sources such as foreign direct and portfolio investment, the growth of private grants (from foundations), remittances and internal resources mobilised in the form of tax and non-tax revenue (UN, 2015b). Expectations surrounding the ability of developing countries to mobilise DRM in this context are further heightened.

This chapter addresses three main issues. First, we summarise ongoing debates about the post-2015 FFD agenda, and situate the implications of the same for African economies. Second, we analyse recent DRM performance in the region. In particular, we discuss results from our estimation of a *tax effort index* for African countries. Third, we discuss the implications of these findings, both, for the international community (including donors actively engaged in supporting tax capacity building efforts) as well as African governments that are increasingly looking to DRM as a source of financing ambitious post-2015 goals and targets. A concluding section recaps findings and the main messages.

Development goals and the Financing for Development agenda

DRM is again gaining prominence in discussions surrounding the 'post-2015' agenda (Bhushan, 2013). However, until the Monterrey

Consensus, which accompanied and followed the MDGs, DRM had received relatively little attention as a development financing strategy, especially in poorer regions such as Sub-Saharan Africa (Culpeper and Bhushan, 2008, 2009, 2010).

Monterrey served to highlight and focus attention on DRM even in the poorest regions. More recently, the international community has begun to acknowledge the importance of DRM, as evidenced by support for initiatives such as the African Tax Administration Forum (ATAF) established in 2009, and the European Commission Communication on Tax and Development from 2010. Notwithstanding this recent interest, regional and multilateral institutions such as The World Bank, International Monetary Fund (IMF) (through regional technical assistance centres) and the African Development Bank (AfDB) have been working on supporting tax capacity building in Africa for decades. So a legitimate question is, what is different in the case for enhancing DRM? There are at least three important reasons to re-emphasise DRM now.

First, most donor countries have failed to live up to the long-standing commitment to deliver 0.7 per cent of GNI (gross national income) as aid, even in good times. In 2013, only 5 of the 28 Development Assistance Committee (DAC) member countries met that commitment, and the unweighted average country effort was 0.40 per cent (OECD, 2014). Donors have also fallen far short of the 2005 G8 Gleneagles commitment to raise the volume of aid and to double aid to Africa by 2010.[3] Beyond the numbers there is also a sense that donor views on the purpose of aid are constantly shifting, and there is increasing scepticism about the utility of aid given over decades and development results achieved. Moreover, the recent global economic crisis has brought aid budgets in many countries under pressure. After years of sustained increases, OECD-DAC aid has fallen by 6 per cent in real terms during 2013-15. We know from past crises in donor countries that aid budgets decline, bottoming out over several years, and may not return to pre-crisis levels at all (Roodman, 2008; Dang et al, 2009). This makes enhancing alternative sources, including but not limited to domestic revenue, a matter of urgency for many developing countries.

Second, the experience of more successful developing countries has served to highlight the importance of building strong domestic fiscal and financial systems. The experience of China, India and East Asian economies has been seminal for other developing regions. As the Commission on Growth and Development (The World Bank, 2008, p 54) that examined the experience of 13 high-growth developing economies since 1950 concludes, 'there is no case of a high investment path not backed up by high domestic savings.' In principle, countries could rely on foreign capital to finance investment, but capital inflows to developing and emerging economies over the past several decades have been very volatile. Moreover, effective fiscal systems are critical not only to public sector savings mobilisation, but to state building more generally. Political scientists have long emphasised the fact that taxation is fundamental to state building (Tilly, 1975; Herbst, 2000) and forms the foundation of the social contract between the state and citizens. Without taxation there can be no viable state (OECD and AfDB, 2010).

Recent research has refocused attention on the critical importance of domestic taxation to state building and state–citizen relations in the African context (Brautigam, 2008). There is growing concern that heavy reliance on resources other than broad-based domestic taxation can be a disincentive to develop institutional capacity and accountability to citizens, and ultimately promoting prosperity. Governments that derive the bulk of their resources from donors, for instance, may be more responsive to donor than domestic priorities (where the two differ). Indeed, the undermining of good governance and political accountability may be the most important reason to be concerned about high levels of aid dependence.

Third, it is now widely accepted that external resources will not be enough to meet financing needs, not only to achieve the MDGs, but also to sustain developmental performance beyond 2015. Aid in most countries simply will not be sufficient. Financing gaps to meet the proposed post-2015 goals are of relatively significant orders of magnitude, and have been estimated at US$38 billion in the education sector, US$37 billion in heath, US$26.7 billion in water and sanitation, and over US$50 billion in food and agriculture, on an annualised basis (Greenhill and Ali, 2013). These estimates place the total post-2015 development financing gap at around US$186 billion annually (by comparison, total net ODA by DAC donors was US$134.8 billion in 2013; see OECD, 2014). Similarly the cost of (theoretically) eliminating poverty at the US$2/day level through perfect transfers to those living below this income threshold has been estimated at US$289 billion in 2010 (our calculation based on the Kaufmann et al [2012] database; for estimates, see also Kharas and Rogerson, 2012).[4] Recent OECD estimates place the financing cost of achieving the first six MDGs at US$120 billion, more than half of which would be needed in 20 low-income countries (Atisophon et al, 2011). How do these gap estimates compare with what we know about the role played by foreign aid? Meeting the MDG financing cost of US$120 billion would require more than a doubling of the current annual level of country programmable aid (or the share of aid that is actually received by countries and over which they have meaningful control). If the global community wished to eliminate US$2/day poverty around the world, and was prepared to target all country programmable aid (CPA) in just this one area, we would still end up with a shortfall of over US$200 billion (our calculation for 2010 based on the Kaufmann et al [2012] database, and OECD-DAC CPA database). Clearly, external resources such as aid will not be enough to meet the financing needs of an ambitious post-2015 agenda.[5] Domestically mobilised resources, through taxes and non-tax revenues, will be expected to play an increasingly important role.

Post-2015 development framework and implications for Africa

This section summarises the status of ongoing discussions on the post-2015 development framework.[6] It draws on two initiatives. First is the final report of the High Level Panel of Eminent Persons on the Post-2015 Development Agenda (UN, 2013), appointed by the UN Secretary General, and co-chaired by the Prime Minister of the UK, President of Liberia and President of Indonesia. Second, it also draws on ongoing research on the emerging post-2015 agenda that has been conducted at the North-South Institute in Ottawa, Canada, including the post-2015 tracking tool (CIDP, 2013; Higgins, 2013; Higgins and Bond, 2013).

The final report of the High Level Panel, which is meant to inform further debates on the ultimate framework that will be adopted in September 2015, emphasises the need for a universal agenda driven by five big transformational shifts: leave no one behind; put sustainable development at the core; transform economies for jobs and inclusive growth; build peaceful and effective, open and accountable institutions; and forge a new global partnership.

These 'transformative shifts' can be interpreted in light of current global circumstances and the shortcomings of the original MDGs. The call to 'leave no one behind' is an implicit acceptance of a key shortcoming of the original MDGs. The MDGs over-emphasised first, global, and second, national-level progress, even if this meant unequal progress across race, ethnicity, geography, gender or income groups. The need to respond to a lack of attention to distributional issues in the original MDGs can be seen in the transformative shifts that underpin the emerging post-2015 framework. Similarly, the emphasis on sustainable development is recognition of the fact that more serious effort is needed at the global level to address climate change than is being made in ongoing intractable climate debates. It is also an attempt to bridge the post-2015 agenda with the SDGs process. The emphasis on jobs and inclusive growth is not new, even compared to the original MDGs, and therefore hardly a transformative shift, but is more a reflection of the current malaise in the global economy. The emphasis on peace, security and accountable institutions is in response to the fact that these issues received inadequate attention in the original MDGs, as pointed out repeatedly by the G7+ group of fragile states, which have argued that the special circumstances of fragile states meant that they were set up to fail on the original MDGs. The call to forge a new global partnership is again neither new nor transformative. MDG 8 was centred on this very issue, and it is also one of the areas where least progress has been made. Its inclusion in the post-2015 debate is both recognition of the unfinished task and the inadequacy of MDG 8.

It is worth noting that the High Level Panel report is more a starting point for further debate than an authoritative consensus on a new agenda. This is clear from the 12 proposed illustrative goals and targets (see Table 7.1 below). The majority of these can be interpreted as extensions of the original MDGs. For instance, while MDG 1 called for halving over 25 years the share of people living in extreme poverty, defined as below US$1.25/day, the High Level Panel proposal targets bringing this number down to 'zero'. Goals around women's empowerment and gender equality, education, health, food security and nutrition, water and sanitation, energy, employment, and an enabling global environment, all have precursors in the MDGs.

However, there are important differences between the High Level Panel's proposal and the original MDGs. Unlike the original MDGs, which were framed as 'global' goals, to which each country contributes, the High Level Panel proposal envisions only 'global minimum standards' around certain goals, and leaves the specifics of target setting to individual national determination.[7] In all, 54 specific sub-goals are proposed in the 12 areas in Table 7.1, but 'global standards' are only proposed for 26 of these. The High Level Panel report recognises that the majority of the proposed goals and targets require further technical work to find appropriate indicators that are sufficiently disaggregated (UN, 2013).

How and where are taxation and revenue mobilisation addressed in the proposed High Level Panel agenda? The main area where

Table 7.1: High level panel's illustrative goals for the post-2015 agenda

1. End poverty.
2. Empower girls and women and achieve gender equality.
3. Provide quality education and lifelong learning.
4. Ensure healthy lives.
5. Ensure food security and good nutrition.
6. Achieve universal access to water and sanitation.
7. Secure sustainable energy.
8. Create jobs, sustainable livelihoods and equitable growth.
9. Manage natural resource assets sustainably.
10. Ensure good governance and effective institutions.
11. Ensure stable and peaceful societies.
12. Create a global enabling environment and catalyse long-term finance.

Source: UN (2013)

taxation is explicitly referenced in the High Level Panel proposal is with regard to goal 12 on creating a global enabling environment and catalysing long-term finance. The emphasis here is on reducing illicit flows and tax evasion, and increasing stolen asset recovery. Tax incentives and subsidies are also referenced as a means for financing investment in sustainable energy. Explicit reference is also made to the need for developed countries to pay more attention to exchanging tax information and combating evasion. The link between DRM in developing countries and international tax regulation is recognised. The Panel calls for continued investment in building stronger tax systems and broadening domestic tax bases, especially in low and middle-income countries. It is noteworthy that while the High Level Panel proposal calls for 'universal domestic resource targets' based on the tax/GDP ratio, it falls short of specifying what the targets or indicators should be, or how they should be applied (for example, if there should be a global minimum).

The High Level Panel proposal is only one of several proposals on the post-2015 agenda that have been put forth. For an analysis of how taxation and resource mobilisation issues are addressed in other proposals, we refer to the North-South Institute's post-2015 tracking tool project (CIDP, 2013). As of the July 2013 update, 69 proposals, encompassing 1,111 goals targets and indicators, have been surveyed and coded in the North-South Institute's tracking tool. Of these, six proposals make explicit reference to taxation as a key issue. Proposals address taxation from the perspective of reducing evasion and illicit flows, reducing tax competition, levying new progressive eco-taxes, raising taxes on the wealthiest, removing taxes on remittance transfers and intensifying global transparency and tax information sharing. However, most proposals fall short of proposing specific indicators by which to measure progress.

It is clear from the above that even where the emerging post-2015 framework is not that different from the MDGs, its objectives (such as 'ending poverty') are ambitious. A serious implication for African countries is that while the new formulation of 'nationally determined targets' increases the level of agency African countries may have (compared to the MDGs), the proposed global minimum standards may actually require disproportionately greater effort by these countries (as they are further off the proposed minimum). In fact, most areas where a global minimum standard approach is proposed apply largely to developing countries and not advanced economies. Reaching proposed global minimum standards – such as ending poverty, ending child marriage, ensuring completion of primary education, ending preventable infant deaths, ending hunger, ensuring access to safe drinking water – will require proportionately greater effort to get to that standard by the poorer countries. Meanwhile, in other areas – such as creating an enabling environment for long-term finance, delivering foreign aid and technical assistance in accordance with agreed aid effectiveness principles, developing country access to export markets and climate change – curiously, no minimum standards are proposed.

It can also be concluded that the discussion around taxation and revenue mobilisation as it relates to post-2015 goals and targets remains undeveloped. Much of the emphasis is on international aspects such as tax evasion, capital flight and tax havens, while the treatment of domestic tax systems, tax policy and administrative reforms receives lesser attention. To the extent that aid flows alone will not be enough to finance poverty reduction as well as other needs such as infrastructure, and the fact that in a post-crisis environment donor countries want to ensure that their aid does not discourage revenue-raising efforts, African countries, through regional and multilateral forums, could make further effort to elevate the treatment of DRM within the post-2015 framework, especially around the need to catalyse long-term finance.

Emerging Financing for Development agenda and implications for Africa

How does the emerging post-2015 FFD agenda compare with the original Monterrey Consensus FFD agenda? What are the main differences and similarities, and what are the implications of the same for African countries? These questions are briefly taken up in this section.

A general observation about the emerging post-2015 FFD agenda is that the role of foreign aid and the international donor community is being decisively downplayed, whereas the role of domestic financing and international private capital is being strongly emphasised. The High Level Panel report, for instance, believes that the majority of the money to finance post-2015 goals will come from domestic sources in light of the fact that low- and middle-income countries have made a lot of progress in raising domestic revenues. The report further notes that even where developing countries require substantial external resources, the main part of this will *not* be aid from developed countries, but that the most important source of long-term finance will be private capital such as FDI and portfolio investment from pension funds as well as investment from sovereign wealth funds and development banks (UN, 2013).

This is a substantial change from the tenor of the Monterrey Consensus that followed the MDGs. While Monterrey always recognised the importance of private capital, the broader emphasis was still on foreign aid commitments and the role played by international donors. The ultimate 'consensus' was very much a compromise embedded in the 'donor–recipient' paradigm, which the post-2015 debates and emerging FFD agenda seek to change. There is a rapidly emerging consensus that private capital will play a far greater role in the emerging FFD agenda than it did in Monterrey (Cutter, 2013; ECOSOC, 2013; European Commission, 2013; Mohieldin, 2013; Prizzon, 2013; Sheng, 2013; UNTT, 2013).

A second important difference is the timing of the formal FFD process. The Monterrey conference on FFD took place two years after the MDGs were in place. Since the third FFD conference will take place in July before the September 2015 summit, it could potentially send a strong signal that the post-2015 agenda will be backed by hard financial commitments (Evans and David, 2013; Prizzon, 2013; UN, 2013). The parameters of what the FFD consensus should cover have also expanded compared to Monterrey and the MDGs. The UN (2013) argues that the aim of the conference should be to 'discuss how to integrate development, sustainable development and environmental financing streams', and that 'a single agenda should have a coherent overall financing structure'.

These developments have important implications for Africa, especially poorer countries in the region that are still some of the most aid-reliant in the world, and find it difficult to attract sustainable foreign private capital. On the surface, the post-2015 FFD agenda may be very similar to the Monterrey Consensus. The High Level Panel report recognises that the vision for how to fund the post-2015 agenda has already been agreed at Monterrey (UN, 2013). However, even as a vision may have been laid out, donors have repeatedly failed to live up to aid commitments. A new or updated agenda that de-emphasises aid could increase the financing burden on developing countries, including low-income countries in Africa. And yet these discussions are entirely devoid of any realistic assessment of the financing potential of domestic taxation, non-tax revenue mobilisation or other alternative financing options. While such analyses are rare, one study that looked at the potential for enhanced tax collection in developing countries found that there is a limit to how much can be expected from DRM in the foreseeable future. In the context of financing the MDGs, most countries that can improve revenue collection were found to be already well on their way to achieving the MDGs. Moreover, there is a stark contrast between the relative ease with which upper-middle-income countries can enhance tax collection and the challenge that low and lower-middle-income countries face. While upper-middle-income countries could raise tax collection by over 3 per cent of GDP, potentially raising an additional $US60 billion, low-income countries would be expected to raise around 2.5 per cent of GDP, yielding only US$3 billion (Atisophon et al, 2011). African countries should push for a more realistic approach and one that is prefaced by a systematic estimation of the untapped domestic revenue potential across Africa.

Another important implication is that while integrating development and environmental financing agendas sounds good on paper, in reality, estimating costs in these areas is anything but straightforward. Adding environmental costs to the FFD agenda changes the scale of the financing discussions dramatically. The only available estimate of the post-2015 agenda places the financing gap at US$186 billion. Adding costs related to renewable energy takes the gap figure to over US$1 trillion (Greenhill and Ali, 2013).[8] When gap estimates get so large, they may alienate stakeholders and risk making the entire discussion unrealistic and unproductive. Even if this scale of financing could be mobilised, arguably, the disbursement, monitoring and evaluation structures required to ensure effective expenditure are not in place. While it makes sense for climate financing to be part of the same FFD agenda, African countries should play a stronger role in further defining and limiting the parameters of the discussion to a realistic, accountable and productive FFD agenda.

Most FFD discussions are preoccupied with estimates of financing gaps (Greenhill and Ali, 2013). Gap estimates, while useful in providing a sense of the scale involved, make assumptions that do not hold in the real world; hence these estimates cannot be totally accurate. Gap estimates assume mobilised financing can be perfectly transferred to beneficiaries. For instance, estimates surrounding the cost of closing the theoretical poverty gap (discussed above) assume those living in absolute poverty can be identified and targeted without cost and without leakage. These assumptions do not hold in reality. Second, gap estimates typically do not take into account spillover effects of financing. For instance, expenditure on basic education probably has a complex but important impact on estimated health financing costs, as education affects health outcomes and the demand for healthcare. Third, and most importantly, gap estimates assume that lack of financing is the 'binding' constraint, in that without removing this particular constraint further progress cannot be made, for example, through more efficient spending or better policies and programmes. This is a key weakness. The emerging FFD agenda, much like the Monterrey Consensus before it, pays insufficient or no attention at all to the efficiency and effectiveness of public expenditure in developing countries. Doing so would entail an important shift in focus as this area is beset by major data challenges despite significant donor investment in developing country statistical systems.[9] A systematic assessment of potential gains through more efficient and effective public expenditure may even bring down financing gap estimates in some contexts. To the extent that domestic resources will be increasingly relied on for development finance, the efficiency and effectiveness of public expenditure should be a priority. However, the orders of magnitude involved are so large that all options – increased domestic and external financing, innovative financing and expenditure efficiency – will need to be considered.

The emerging post-2015 FFD agenda has set high expectations surrounding developing country DRM efforts and DRM's contribution to financing ambitious post-2015 goals. Indeed, during recent outreach missions, both by The World Bank President and the Chair of the High Level Panel secretariat, one of the main reasons given for being optimistic about delivering on the ambitious post-2015 agenda and goals such as 'ending poverty' was that more countries are now more able to rely on their own resources to finance their own development (Higgins and Bond, 2013; North–South Institute, 2013). Given this backdrop, the remainder of this chapter analyses whether DRM expectations, especially as they relate to Africa, are reasonable.

To do so we analyse trends in revenue mobilisation, institutional performance and tax effort.

Recent trends in domestic resource mobilisation in Africa

The definition of DRM or domestic revenue mobilisation, for the purposes of the analysis here, is restricted to tax and non-tax revenues (unless otherwise specified). The first important point to note regards data coverage and quality. Most analyses of taxation tend to rely on data from The World Bank's World Development Indicators (WDI) database, which is one of the most widely used data sources in development research. Our primary interest for the analysis here is in the 51 countries in the African region over a relatively recent 15-year time period, from 1996 to 2010. Relying on WDI for the tax/GDP ratio data would give us, at most, 264 out of a possible 765 (country, year) observations. Clearly, coverage of tax data in the WDI is inadequate.[10] Furthermore, data in the WDI tends to be lagged, often by about two years.[11] Data is also insufficiently disaggregated, such as by the composition of tax types.

For these reasons, and in order to provide a more comprehensive picture, we use two alternative data sources in the analysis here: the African Economic Outlook's fiscal database (African Economic Outlook, 2012) and USAID's Collecting Taxes database (USAID, 2012). For African countries, using African Economic Outlook (2012), we are able to extend observations to 751 (out of 765). The African Economic Outlook database also disaggregates mobilised revenues into detailed tax types, which allows us to analyse which revenue sources are driving overall performance. USAID (2012) in addition provides data for over 200 countries across 31 indicators including tax structure, administration and performance, productivity, and efficiency metrics. This data is useful in comparing African countries with other developing regions.

Tax collection has been rising in Africa and crossed over the 20 per cent of regional GDP mark in 2009. However, the ratio is less than 17 per cent in half of African countries (African Economic Outlook, 2010; Atisophon et al, 2011). More recent data indicates that the (unweighted) average tax/GDP ratio for Sub-Saharan African countries in 2011–12 was below 17 per cent.

Figure 7.1 provides a comparison of the tax/GDP ratio across select regions. The data show a declining trend in the tax/GDP ratio in recent years across most regions, and a likely reason for this is that most regions are still recovering from the global financial crisis. The

Figure 7.1: Tax/GDP ratio across regions

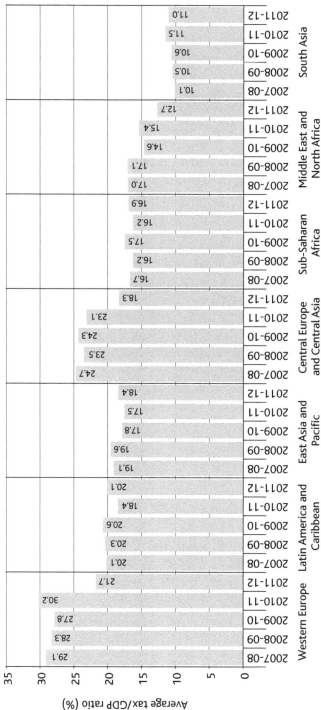

Source: CIPD (2013); Higgins et al (2013)

crisis both dampened economic activity, and also affected revenue mobilisation as most governments undertook fiscal stimulus measures (including tax cuts) to respond to the crisis and revive growth.

The tax/GDP ratio tends to be positively correlated with per capita incomes. The ability of countries to mobilise revenues increases with income levels, and is positively correlated with economic structure indicators such as trade openness, but negatively correlated with the share of agriculture, which is typically a hard-to-tax sector (Bhushan and Samy, 2012). Figure 7.1 shows the highest tax ratios are in more advanced regions such as Western Europe, Central Europe and Central Asia, while the lowest ratios tend to be in poorer regions such as South Asia. As Figure 7.2 shows, the ratio rises as we move from low-income to middle-income and high-income countries.

Sub-Saharan Africa does *not* have the lowest tax/GDP ratio, even across developing regions. At around 16 per cent in recent years, the ratio is lower than Latin America, slightly lower than East Asia, but far higher than South Asia. The ratio is also higher than the average for low-income countries.[12]

Figure 7.3 provides further details for individual countries in the Sub-Saharan region. As can be seen, the regional average is driven up by a handful of countries; most countries in the region have tax/GDP ratios below the regional average.[13]

While the above data are useful in providing a general sense of recent trends in tax mobilisation and how Africa compares with other regions, it does not provide a sense of the factors driving these trends. For this

Figure 7.2: Tax/GDP ratio across income groups

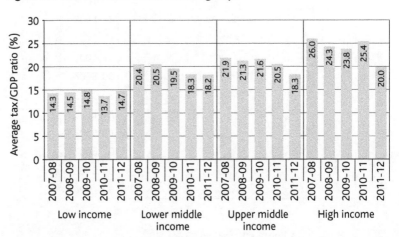

Source: CIPD (2013); Higgins et al (2013)

Figure 7.3: Tax/GDP ratio across Sub-Saharan Africa

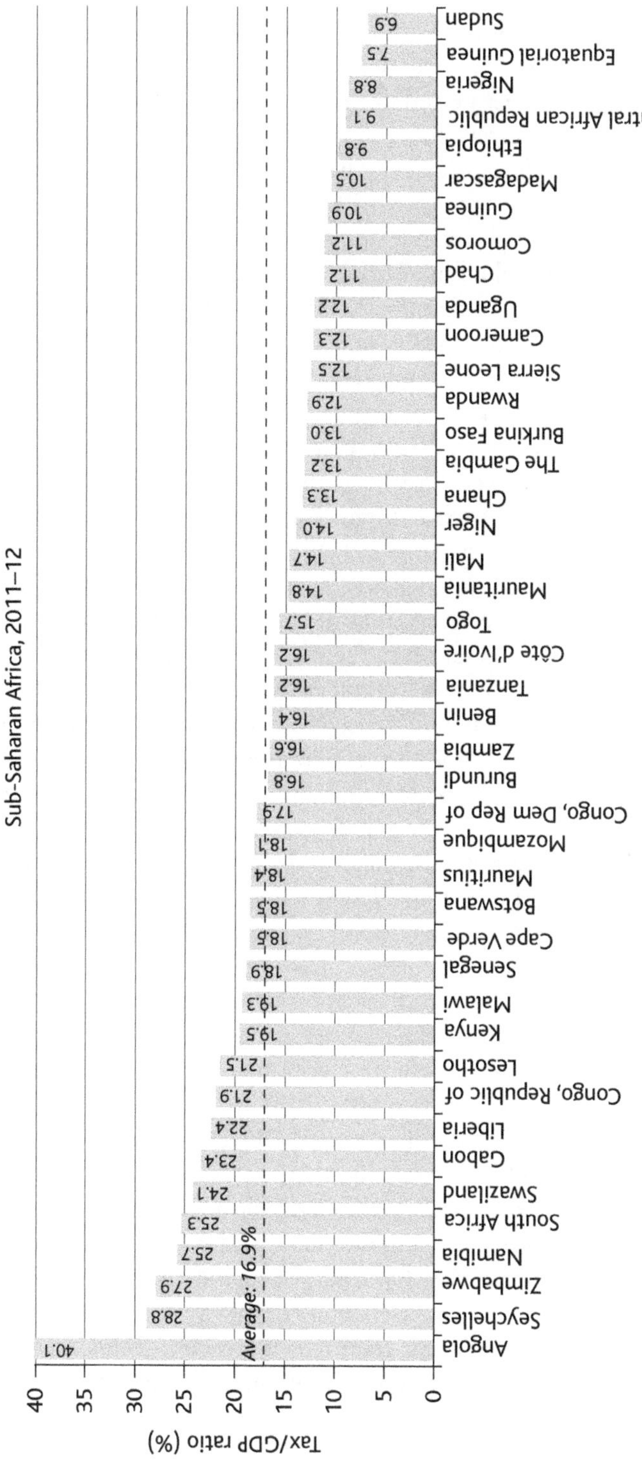

Sub-Saharan Africa, 2011–12

Country	Tax/GDP ratio (%)
Angola	40.1
Seychelles	28.8
Zimbabwe	27.9
Namibia	25.7
South Africa	25.3
Swaziland	24.1
Gabon	23.4
Liberia	22.4
Congo, Republic of	21.9
Lesotho	21.5
Kenya	19.5
Malawi	19.3
Senegal	18.9
Cape Verde	18.5
Botswana	18.5
Mauritius	18.4
Mozambique	18.1
Congo, Dem Rep of	17.9
Burundi	16.8
Zambia	16.6
Benin	16.4
Tanzania	16.2
Côte d'Ivoire	16.2
Togo	15.7
Mauritania	14.8
Mali	14.7
Niger	14.0
Ghana	13.3
The Gambia	13.2
Burkina Faso	13.0
Rwanda	12.9
Sierra Leone	12.5
Cameroon	12.3
Uganda	12.2
Chad	11.2
Comoros	11.2
Guinea	10.9
Madagascar	10.5
Ethiopia	9.8
Central African Republic	9.1
Nigeria	8.8
Equatorial Guinea	7.5
Sudan	6.9

Average: 16.9%

Source: CIPD (2013); Higgins et al (2013)

we turn to the African Economic Outlook fiscal database. Figure 7.4 provides a sense of the dynamics underlying DRM performance across Africa over a 15-year period from 1996 to 2010. Two points are worth emphasising. First, revenue mobilisation has started to increase in the region relatively recently, since the early 2000s, which coincides with the point in time when growth started to pick up for many African countries. Total tax revenue mobilisation was nearly stagnant from 1996 to 2002, but then increased from around US$137 billion in 2002 to a high of US$497 billion in 2008, representing a compound annual growth rate of nearly 24 per cent.

This performance also coincides to some extent with major reforms to tax policy, administration and tax structures across many countries in the African region. The two main areas of recent donor supported tax reforms in Africa have been the introduction of Value Added Tax (VAT) and the establishment of autonomous revenue authorities (ARAs) (Bhushan and Samy, 2012).[14]

Second, and more importantly, as can be seen from the two graphs below the overall revenue trend in Figure 7.4, the majority of the increase in tax mobilisation in the region has been driven by revenue mobilised from the natural resources sector. Resource revenues made up nearly 49 per cent of Africa's tax mix in 2008, just before the impact of the crisis took effect. The huge volatility experienced in the resources sector is also visible in the increased volatility of Africa's revenue base, with resource-related revenues contracting sharply with the crisis. Notably, domestic direct and indirect taxes are also increasing at a rapid rate and with much less volatility, while trade taxes continue to decline (in percentage terms) as a source of revenue, as countries further liberalise trade.

While there is significant variation across countries, domestic tax revenue is already more than 10 times the size of total foreign aid to the region. As seen in Figure 7.4 opposite, total tax revenue in 2010 was US$464 billion, whereas foreign aid to Africa was US$43 billion in the same year, according to OECD-DAC statistics. It is thus helpful to remember that even in the poorest region, the majority of development financing is mobilised domestically.

However, the forces driving revenue mobilisation in Africa is causing a split between countries. For instance, while on the one hand there are those that are mobilising sufficient tax revenues, mainly driven by the presence of natural resources, there are others that, despite significant tax effort (including donor support), are simply working from too shallow a tax base. These countries and their development partners face a double-edged sword. They not only have the weakest

Figure 7.4: Composition of domestic revenue mobilisation in Africa (1996–2010)

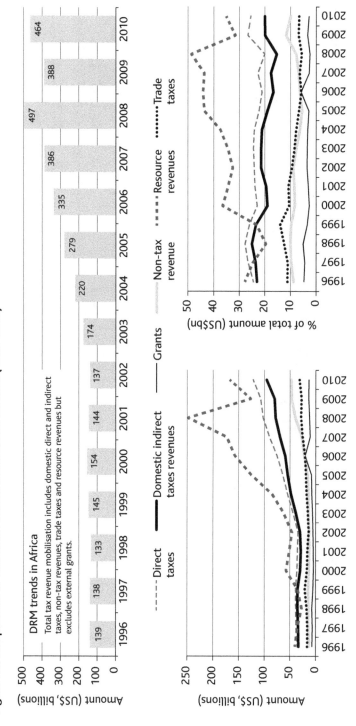

Source: CIPD (2013); Higgins et al (2013)

Figure 7.5: Countries where natural resource related taxes dominate the resource mix

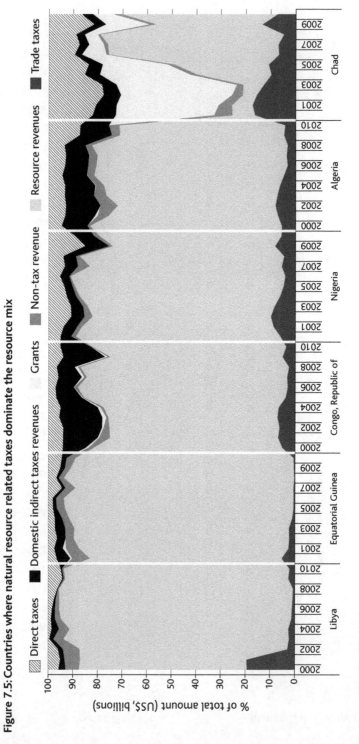

Source: CIPD (2013); Higgins et al (2013)

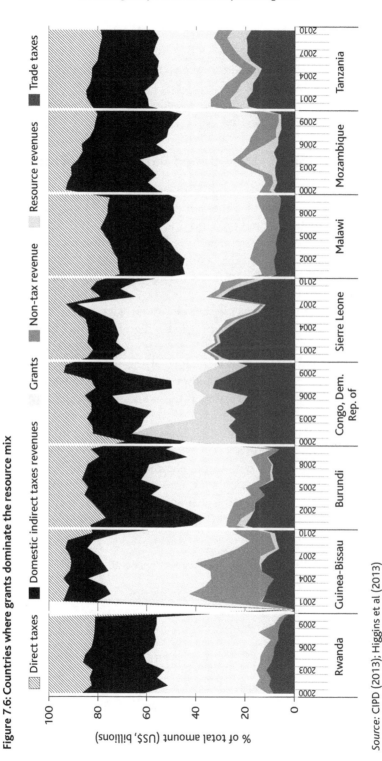

Figure 7.6: Countries where grants dominate the resource mix

Source: CIPD (2013); Higgins et al (2013)

211

DRM capacity and shallowest tax bases, but they also have the weakest aid absorptive capacity.[15] Many of these are fragile states. Aid is already highly concentrated among fragile states, with the presence of aid darlings and aid orphans, and around 38 per cent of global aid goes to fragile states.[16] Strikingly, despite this, in recent years domestic revenue has been as much as five times as large as aid even in the fragile states.

Tax performance, administration and utilisation of tax bases

How does Sub-Saharan Africa compare with other regions on tax performance metrics? This question can be addressed by looking at the cost of tax collection and the ratio of tax authority staff to the overall population. These metrics, while being crude measures, provide a sense of the efficiency of the tax collection system.[17] In addition, we address whether African countries are effectively utilising their existing tax bases.

Tables 7.2 and 7.3 provide data on the average cost of collection and ratio of tax staff to population across regions and income groups. The average cost of collection ('Average cost', in Tables 7.2 and 7.3) is calculated as a ratio of the budget of the tax authority and the total revenue collected by the authority.[18] Similarly, the tax staff ratio ('Average tax staff') is calculated as the number of tax authority staff per 1,000 people in the country.

The data above (for 2011-12) show that Sub-Saharan Africa has one of the most expensive tax collection systems of any region. The ratio of tax authority staff to population is one of the lowest, and despite significant recent reforms, most countries in the region still have inefficient tax collection systems. In Table 7.2, Latin America has almost the same average tax staff, but is more than twice as efficient as Sub-Saharan Africa.

Table 7.2: Tax performance indicators across regions, 2011–12

	Average cost	Average tax staff
East Asia and Pacific	1.19	0.45
Central Europe and Central Asia	1.13	0.99
Latin America and Caribbean	1.26	0.33
Middle East and North Africa	3.17	0.46
South Asia	1.83	0.27
Sub-Saharan Africa	2.93	0.32
Western Europe	0.93	1.19
US and Canada	1.53	0.69

Source: CIPD (2013); Higgins et al (2013)

Table 7.3: Tax performance indicators across income groups, 2011–12

	Average cost	Average tax staff
Low income	3.20	0.17
Lower middle income	1.54	0.43
Upper middle income	1.04	0.81
High income	1.14	1.01

Source: CIPD (2013); Higgins et al (2013)

Research also shows that many African countries are not effectively utilising even their narrow tax bases. A key factor that prevents countries from maximising their revenue potential is the proliferation of tax exemptions. The number of countries in Sub-Saharan Africa offering exemptions of some type (especially in the form of 'free zones', reduced corporate tax rates, tax holidays and investment codes) has risen substantially from 1980 to 2005 (Keen and Mansour, 2009). Exemptions contract the revenue base, complicate tax systems, and open the door to political capture (the party or group in power often uses discretionary exemptions to retain power or undermine businesses linked to the opposition). More importantly, exemptions have a ratcheting effect; once in place they are hard to remove.

Recent research has found that revenues foregone due to exemptions, while hard to estimate, represent a significant share of the revenue base. The IMF estimated that undue exemptions in Burundi cost the Treasury up to 1.5 per cent of GDP in recent years (Girukwigomba, 2010). The highest level was reached in 2006, when 60 per cent of imports entered the country with full or partial exemptions for a total of 10.7 per cent of GDP or 65.5 per cent of tax revenues. In Ethiopia (leaving aside tax holidays of five to seven years), total revenues foregone due to customs exemptions alone were in the range of between 3.7 per cent of GDP (2005) and 4.2 per cent of GDP (2008). Similarly in Tanzania, losses from customs and VAT exemptions range from between 4.5 per cent (2005) and 3.6 per cent (2007) of GDP, and are higher than in the period 2000-04. In Uganda, where select 10-year tax holidays were introduced in 2007-08, key informants suggest foregone revenues amount to at least 2 per cent of GDP. Clearly the level of exemptions relative to the already low revenue bases in these countries suggests the revenue potential is not being maximised, while the impact on investment promotion and other considerations remains unclear (Bhushan and Samy, 2012).

This discussion shows that despite significant recent reforms and a favourable global economic climate (up until the economic crisis in 2008), tax performance in African countries leaves much to be desired.

Tax systems remain inefficient, costly and ineffective. Furthermore, revenue foregone due to tax exemptions (Gaddis, 2013), not to mention tax avoidance (Jordan, 2013), is a significant drain on DRM for many countries in the region. This is often the result of lack of coordination between investment promotion objectives and resource mobilisation needs. Foregone revenues, in addition to large estimates of capital flight from the region, suggest greater DRM potential, even in some of the poorest countries than is being realised (Boyce and Ndikumana, 2012).

Tax effort index for Africa

The tax/GDP ratio is the most widely used taxation indicator because it is easy to obtain and interpret, and provides a quick overview of trends across countries. This measure is best used to analyse tax trends across countries with similar economic structures. As discussed earlier, the tax/GDP ratio is influenced by structural factors such as income levels. Recent literature suggests the tax/GDP ratio has several weaknesses. A low tax/GDP ratio does not necessarily mean bad performance, and a high ratio does not necessarily mean good performance. For example, Lesotho and Swaziland report atypically high tax ratios reflecting a revenue sharing agreement with South Africa, which arguably has little to do with domestic fiscal capacity. Similarly, many oil exporters report high tax ratios when resource-related revenues are counted in (Haldenwang and Ivanyna, 2011; OECD, 2013).

Moreover, research shows that the tax/GDP ratio can go up for all sorts of reasons, including reasons that have little to do with better performance or a better state–citizen compact. During the 1980s and 1990s, Uganda and Burundi, for instance, experienced a marked reduction in donor aid due to conflict or embargo. Despite having been highly aid-dependent, both witnessed an increase in tax revenue during periods of reduced donor support. Instability provides an incentive for the leadership to grab what they can when they can (Sennoga, 2010). In these situations, the tax mobilisation ratio may well rise, but mobilising revenue by imposing punitive costs on the population is hardly what anyone is advocating. DRM ultimately is about building a better state–citizen compact than exists across most Sub-Saharan countries today.

A more sophisticated, yet easy to interpret, approach, is to calculate a *tax effort index* for Africa. While not perfect, this approach helps address some of the weaknesses associated with the tax/GDP ratio. We calculate the index as a ratio between the share of actual tax collection and taxable capacity. For this we first need to compute *taxable capacity*. Following Le et al (2012), we estimate taxable capacity as the predicted tax/GDP ratio calculated using the estimated coefficients of a regression specification, taking into account the country specific characteristics that influence tax mobilisation. In other words, we control for the factors that influence the tax/GDP ratio to predict what individual African countries *should* be collecting, given their structural characteristics.

Tax capacity in this analysis is estimated using a panel dataset of 49 African countries from 1996 to 2010. Using Le et al's specification, we consider the following empirical specification for estimation:

$$\frac{TAX}{GDP} = \beta_0 + \beta_1 GDPPC + \beta_2 TRADE + \beta_3 AGRIC + \beta_4 POP$$
$$+ \beta_5 GOVEFF + \varepsilon$$

where TAX/GDP is tax revenue as a percentage of GDP (tax revenue is the sum of direct, indirect and trade taxes); GDPPC is constant GDP per capita (2000 US$); TRADE is trade as a percentage of GDP; and AGRIC is agriculture value added as a percentage of GDP; POP is the population growth rate; GOVEFF is a measure of government effectiveness from the Worldwide Governance Indicators project of The World Bank. All the estimates are conducted with time and country dummies.

The results that we report below are based on the above equation, but GOVEFF is excluded because the estimated results with this variable did not make theoretical sense. However, it should be pointed out that the various specifications that were tried did not fundamentally change the positioning of countries with regards to their tax capacity and tax effort. In this sense, our results on tax effort are fairly robust to the various specifications adopted. However, we are also fully aware that our tax effort calculations are going to be sensitive to the predicted tax capacity, which, in turn, is going to depend on the specification adopted.[19] In an ideal world, one would like to control for other variables such as exemptions or capital flight, but these variables are lacking for proper panel estimation. Our point in doing the current exercise is to examine the feasibility of mobilising additional resources rather than to provide a measure of actual performance.

A key difference between our analysis and others, such as Le et al (2012), is the data source for the taxation information. We use the African Economic Outlook taxation data. In order to get a more accurate estimate, we limit the revenue sources to those that require significant domestic effort. In other words, we exclude resource-related revenues and aid grants that may skew results. While Le et al (2012) are only able to report findings for 20 African countries, our analysis covers 48 African countries.[20] Other variables are from The World Bank's WDI database. The above equation is estimated using ordinary least squares.

Tax effort for each country and year is estimated according to the definition above, and an average value is calculated over the whole period to derive a single value for each country in the sample. A tax effort index value above 1 indicates 'high tax effort', while an index value below 1 indicates 'low effort'. The correct interpretation of the index is that high tax effort countries are utilising their tax bases well to increase revenues, while low tax effort countries may have relatively substantial scope to increase revenue collection from the existing tax base. In other words, countries already showing high tax effort may not be able to increase revenue mobilisation substantially without affecting other objectives (such as growth and investment).

Figure 7.7 graphs our results. Twenty-five out of the 48 African countries have a tax effort index below 1. However, the lowest index values are for resource-rich countries. While these countries may have the potential to raise further revenue from domestic direct and indirect taxes, it is likely that the prevalence of natural resource-related revenue weakens the incentive to make greater effort in these areas.

Figure 7.7 also indicates that there is a diverse group of African countries that are already making a substantial tax effort and are, in fact, collecting more revenue than would be expected given their structural characteristics. While many of these are small countries, the group also includes more economically advanced African countries such as South Africa, Morocco, Kenya and Ghana, as well as poorer countries such as Liberia, Burundi, Benin and Malawi.

Figure 7.8 plots the tax effort index value for 48 African countries alongside the tax/GDP ratio. Following the same approach as in Le et al (2012), the tax effort index values and tax/GDP ratios are averaged over the period 1996-2010. Using this approach we are able to divide countries into four groups: countries with high tax effort and above median tax mobilisation; high effort but below median mobilisation; low effort and below median mobilisation; and low effort but above median mobilisation. Twenty-three out of 48 countries are already making high tax effort. Tax mobilisation is above the regional median for most of these countries. The tax/GDP ratio was below median in only 6 out of 23 countries. Twenty-five out of 48 countries make low tax effort. The vast majority of these countries, all but five,

Figure 7.7: Tax effort index for Africa

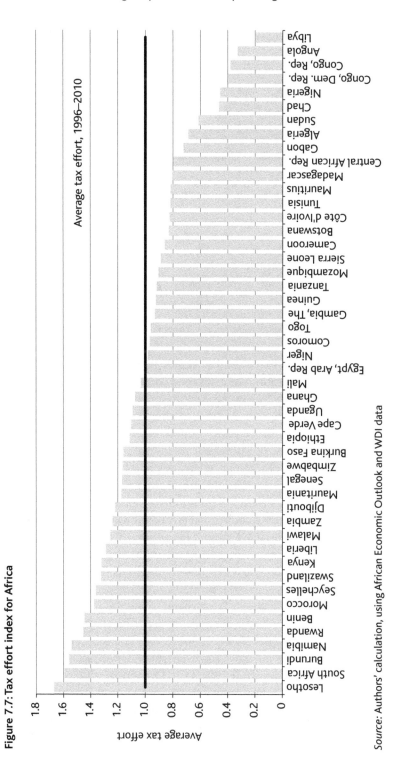

Figure 7.8: Tax effort index for Africa and revenue mobilisation, 1996–2010

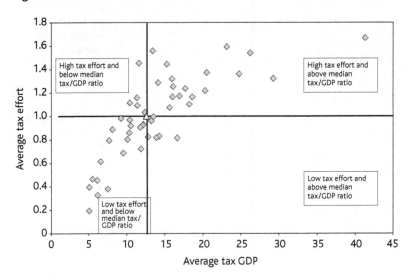

Source: Authors' calculation, using African Economic Outlook and WDI data

have tax/GDP ratios below the regional median. Most of the low effort low mobilisation countries tend to be resource-rich countries.

The general conclusion we can draw from this analysis is that a number of countries in Africa are already making significant tax effort. Most of the low effort countries are resource-rich. These countries may have the potential to increase revenue mobilisation, but the prevalence of resource-related revenues may be weakening the incentive to make a greater effort to capture the domestic tax base.

How does Sub-Saharan Africa compare with other regions on tax effort? To address this question we estimated a tax effort index for all countries, using the WDI data. This approach is similar to Le et al (2012), and our results are consistent with this study.[22] Actual tax collection in Sub-Saharan Africa (at the regional level) is consistently above predicted tax collection or predicted tax capacity. The tax effort index is consistently above 1, especially since the early 2000s (up to the financial crisis). On the other hand, tax effort is lower (below 1) in other developing regions such as South Asia and East Asia. Tax effort has been increasing recently (since the mid-2000s) in Latin America, and is nearly consistently at 1 for OECD countries (Le et al, 2012).

The main finding from our analysis and that of others is that tax collection in Africa remains low despite significant tax effort in many countries. The region as a whole, and many countries within the region, are collecting more through taxes than would be expected given their structural characteristics. A key implication is that structural factors limit how much revenue countries can hope to mobilise before constraining growth, investment and other objectives. Expectations regarding the extent to which domestic revenue can finance ambitious post-2015 goals in Africa, and address huge 'financing gaps', may need to be tempered, especially given that domestic revenue is already more than 10 times the size of aid to the region. While there is significant variation across countries, even in the poorest region, the majority of development financing is already mobilised domestically.

Conclusions: investing in responsible and accountable governments

This chapter has analysed the emerging post-2015 development agenda and the related FFD agenda from the perspective of DRM in Africa. DRM is again gaining prominence as the debate about financing the ambitious post-2015 agenda begins to take centre stage.

The emerging post-2015 FFD agenda has set high expectations surrounding developing country DRM effort. While the role of aid is downplayed in the post-2015 FFD agenda, the role of DRM and foreign private capital is being emphasised. Such an orientation has important implications for poorer countries in the African region, many of which lack substantial experience attracting sustainable foreign private capital, and have shallow tax bases. While the High Level Panel's proposal emphasises big transformative shifts, for all practical purposes the post-2015 FFD agenda may be very similar to the Monterrey Consensus. Yet the emphasis on DRM is so far devoid of any realistic assessment of the financing potential of domestic taxation, non-tax revenue mobilisation or other alternative financing options as they relate to African countries.

We analysed recent trends in DRM in Africa by focusing on taxation and revenue mobilisation. As such, we did not consider other sources of revenue such as remittances, which, while important, are beyond the scope of the current study. The main finding is that while DRM is increasing in the region as a whole, this trend is driven by resource-rich countries and resource-related revenue, which is now the largest component of Africa's revenue mix. Tax ratios for most African countries are below the regional average.

Despite significant recent reforms and a favourable global economic climate (up until the economic crisis in 2008), tax performance in African countries leaves much to be desired. Tax systems remain inefficient, costly and ineffective. Revenue foregone due to tax exemptions, tax avoidance and capital flight is a significant drain on DRM in many countries in the region.

Most of the low tax effort countries in the region are resource-rich. These countries have the potential to increase revenue mobilisation, but the prevalence of resource-related revenues may be weakening the incentive to make a greater effort to capture the domestic tax base.

An important implication of our findings for Africa's development partners is that tax issues cannot simply be reduced to goals and targets aimed at increasing the tax/GDP ratio. Our past research has shown that donor contribution to building tax capacity in the region remains relatively small, and tends to be concentrated in a handful of countries (Bhushan and Samy, 2012). From the perspective of Africa's development partners, DRM, as it features in the post-2015 FFD agenda, should be repurposed to be singularly concerned with investing in responsible and accountable governments. Donors and African governments should not lose sight of the fact that ultimately DRM is about building a better state–citizen compact than exists across most countries in the region today. In terms of future work, it would also be helpful to examine the expenditure side, namely, whether African countries are in fact using taxation revenue to improve development outcomes, for example, by investing in key sectors such as health and education, or to improve productive capacity.

References

African Economic Outlook (2010) *Public resource mobilisation and aid* (www.africaneconomicoutlook.org/theme/public-resource-mobilisation-and-aid/).

African Economic Outlook (2012) *Database on African fiscal performance* (www.africaneconomicoutlook.org/en/database-on-african-fiscal-performance/).

Atisophon, V., Bueren, J., de Paepe, G., Garroway, C. and Stijns, J.-P. (2011) *Revisiting MDG cost estimates from a domestic resource mobilisation perspective*, Working Paper No 306, Paris: OECD Development Centre.

Bhushan, A. (2013) 'Domestic resource mobilization and the post-2015 agenda', *GREAT Insights*, vol 2, issue 3, April.

Bhushan, A. and Samy, Y. (2012) *Aid and taxation: Is Sub-Saharan Africa different?*, Research Report, Ottawa: North–South Institute, May.

Boyce, J.K. and Ndikumana, L. (2012) *Capital flight from Sub-Saharan African countries: Updated estimates, 1970-2010*, Amherst, MA: Political Economy Research Institute, University of Massachusetts.

Brautigam, D. (2008) 'Taxation and state-building in developing countries', in D. Brautigam, O.-H. Fjeldstad and M. Moore (eds) *Taxation and state building in developing countries: Capacity and consent*, Cambridge: Cambridge University Press, pp 1-33.

CIDP (Canadian International Development Platform) (2013) *Tracking post-2015* (http://cidpnsi.ca/tracking-post-2015/).

Clemens, M. and Radelet, S. (2003) 'Absorptive capacity: How much is too much?', in S. Radelet, *Challenging foreign aid: A policymaker's guide to the Millennium Challenge Account*, Washington, DC: Center for Global Development, pp 125-44.

Culpeper, R. and Bhushan, A. (2008) 'Domestic resource mobilization: a neglected factor in development strategy', Background paper prepared for Inception Conference, 27-28 May, Entebbe, Uganda (http://r4d.dfid.gov.uk/Output/185417).

Culpeper, R. and Bhushan, A. (2009) *Reorienting development finance through enhanced domestic resource mobilization in developing countries*, Canadian Development report. Ottawa: North-South Institute.

Culpeper, R. and Bhushan, A. (2010) 'Why enhance domestic resource mobilization in Africa? Trade negotiations insights, ICTSD and ECDPM', Special issue on fiscal implications of EPA and domestic resource mobilisation, *Trade Negotiations Insights*, vol 9, issue 6, July/August.

Cutter, A. (2013) *Financing our future: The Expert Committee on Sustainable Development Financing Strategy* (www.sustainabledevelopment2015. org/index.php/blog/297-blog-finance/1411-financing-our-future-the-expert-committee-on-sustainable-development-financing-strategy).

Dang, H., Knack, S. and Rogers, H. (2009) *International aid and financial crises in donor countries*, Policy Research Working Paper 5162, Washington, DC: The World Bank.

ECOSOC (United Nations Economic and Social Council) (2013) 'Economic and social council has crucial role in promoting dynamic development agenda to foster "transformative change" beyond 2015, says deputy secretary general' (www.un.org/News/Press/docs/2013/ecosoc6567.doc.htm).

European Commission (2013) *Beyond 2015: Towards a comprehensive and integrated approach to financing poverty eradication and sustainable development*, Report No COM(2013) 531, Brussels: European Commission (http://ec.europa.eu/transparency/regdoc/rep/1/2013/EN/1-2013-531-EN-F1-1.Pdf).

Evans, A. and David, S. (2013) *What happens now? The post-2015 agenda after the High Level Panel*, New York: Centre on International

Cooperation, New York University (http://cic.nyu.edu/sites/default/files/evans_steven_post2015_jun2013.pdf).

Gaddis, I. (2013) 'Is Tanzania raising enough tax revenue?', World Bank, Africa Can End Poverty blog (http://blogs.worldbank.org/africacan/is-tanzania-raising-enough-tax-revenue).

Girukwigomba, A. (201) *Domestic resource mobilization in Sub-Saharan Africa: The case of Burundi*, Ottawa: North–South Institute.

Greenhill , R. and Ali, A. (2013) *Paying for progress: How will emerging post-2015 goals be financed in the new aid landscape?*, Working Paper No 366, London: Overseas Development Institute (www.odi.org.uk/sites/odi.org.uk/files/odi-assets/publications-opinion-files/8319.pdf).

Haldenwang, C. and Ivanyna, M. (2011) *Assessing the tax performance of developing countries*, Bonn: German Development Institute.

Herbst, J. (2000) *States and power in Africa: Comparative lessons in authority and control*, Princeton, NJ: Princeton University Press.

Higgins, K. (2013) *Reflecting on the MDGs and making sense of the post-2015 development agenda*, Ottawa: North–South Institute (www.nsi-ins.ca/publications/post-2015-development-agenda/).

Higgins, K. and Bond, R. (2013) *The post-2015 development agenda: Reflections from the High Level Panel Secretariat*, Workshop report, July, Ottawa: North–South Institute.

Higgins, K., Bhushan, A. and Bond, R. (2013) *The North-South Institute post-2015 tracking tool*, Ottawa: North–South Institute (http://cidpnsi.ca/wp-content/uploads/2013/01/NSI-Post-2015-Tracking-Tool-Analysis-July-2013.pdf).

ITC (International Tax Compact) (2010) *Mapping survey: Taxation and development*, Bonn, May.

Jordan, C. (2013) 'Western tax avoidance hinders African development', *The Guardian*, 11 February (www.theguardian.com/commentisfree/2013/feb/11/western-tax-avoidance-restricting-african-development).

Kaufmann, D., Kharas, H. and Penciakova, V. (2012) *Development, aid and governance indicators (DAGI)*, Washington, DC: Brookings Institute.

Keen, M. and Mansour, M. (2009) *Revenue mobilization in Sub-Saharan Africa: Challenges from globalization*, Working paper WP/09/157, July, Washington, DC: International Monetary Fund.

Kharas, H. and Rogerson, A. (2012) *Horizon 2025: Creative destruction in the aid industry*, London: Overseas Development Institute.

Le, T.M., Moreno-Dodson, B. and Bayraktar, N. (2012) *Tax capacity and tax effort: Extended cross-country analysis from 1994 to 2009*, Policy Research Working Paper 6252, Washington, DC: The World Bank.

Mohieldin, M. (2013) 'Financing the next development agenda' (www.project-syndicate.org/commentary/activating-new-sources-of-development-finance-by-mahmoud-mohieldin).

North-South Institute (2013) A roundtable discussion with Dr Jim Yong Kim, President of The World Bank Group's visit to the North-South Institute (www.nsi-ins.ca/events/dr-jim-yong-kim-president-of-the-world-bank-group-visits-the-north-south-institute/).

OECD (Organisation for Economic Co-operation and Development) and AfDB (African Development Bank) (2010) *Public resource mobilization and aid effectiveness*, Paris: OECD.

OECD (2013) *Tax and development: Aid modalities for strengthening tax systems*, Paris: OECD Publishing.

OECD (2014) 'Aid to developing countries rebounds in 2013 to reach and all time high' (www.oecd.org/newsroom/aid-to-developing-countries-rebounds-in-2013-to-reach-an-all-time-high.htm).

Prizzon, A. (2013) 'Show me the money: development finance in the post-2015 era', 28 March, Development Progress (www.developmentprogress.org/blog/2013/03/28/show-me-money-development-finance-post-2015-era).

Roodman, D. (2008) 'History says financial crisis will suppress aid. Views from the center', Blog, 13 October.

Sennoga, E. (2010) 'Political economy dynamics underpinning DRM: Lessons from the EAC and South Africa', Presented by the African Development Bank at the North-South Institute's conference on Domestic Resource Mobilization in Africa (www.nsi-ins.ca/events/enhancing-domestic-resource-mobilization-in-sub-saharan-africa/).

Sheng, A. (2013) *Outlook for global development finance: Excess or shortage?*, High-level Panel Secretariat (www.post2015hlp.org/wp-content/uploads/2013/06/Sheng_Outlook-for-Global-Development-Finance-Excess-or-Shortage.pdf).

Tilly, C. (1975) *The formation of national states in Western Europe*, Princeton, NJ: Princeton University Press.

UN (United Nations) (2003) *Monterrey Consensus on Financing for Development*, New York: UN (www.un.org/esa/ffd/monterrey/MonterreyConsensus.pdf).

UN (2013) *A new global partnership: Eradicate and transform economies through sustainable development*, Report of the High Level Panel of Eminent Persons on the Post-2015 Development Agenda, New York: UN (www.post2015hlp.org/wp-content/uploads/2013/05/UN-Report.pdf).

UN (2015a) Preparatory Process of the 3rd International Conference on Financing for Development, 21 January, Draft (www.un.org/esa/ffd/ffd3/).

UN (2015b) Canada's official comments on the 21 January draft FFD 'Elements' paper (www.un.org/esa/ffd/wp-content/uploads/2015/01/ep-comments-Canada-Feb2015.pdf).

UNTT (United Nations System Task Team) on the Post-2015 UN Development Agenda (2013) *Financing for sustainable development in the global partnership beyond 2015* (www.un.org/en/development/desa/policy/untaskteam_undf/thinkpieces/21_thinkpiece_financing_development.pdf).

USAID (nd) *Collecting Taxes database and full data source*, Washington, DC (http://egateg.usaid.gov/collecting-taxes).

World Bank, The (nd) PovcalNet (http://iresearch.worldbank.org/PovcalNet/index.htm).

World Bank, The (2008) *The growth report, Strategies for sustained growth and inclusive development*, Commission on Growth and Development, Washington, DC: The World Bank.

EIGHT

Economic performance and social progress in Sub-Saharan Africa: the effect of least developed countries and fragile states

Manmohan Agarwal and Natasha Pirzada

Introduction

Economic growth in Sub-Saharan Africa has lagged behind that in other regions over the past five decades (1965-2011). This poor performance contrasts with earlier high hopes, as Sub-Saharan Africa was believed to have the potential for rapid growth (Enke, 1963; Kamarck, 1967). The World Bank has undertaken a number of studies (for example, 1981, 1989; Lele, 1991; Husain and Faruquee, 1994) to analyse the gap between this perceived potential and actual performance. Sub-Saharan Africa has a large number of least developed countries (LDCs) as defined by the United Nations (UN), and also most of the failed fragile states, as defined by the UK's aid agency, the Department for International Development (DfID). The UN lists 48 countries as LDCs, and Sub-Saharan Africa contains 33 of these.[1] While different agencies differ in their definition and classification of a fragile or failed state, there is considerable overlap. Based on the DfID classification, Harttgen and Klasen (2009) and Stewart and Brown (2009) classified 14 countries as failed states and 20 as non-failed states in Sub-Saharan Africa. This chapter explores the extent to which the poor performance of Sub-Saharan Africa is because of the considerable presence of the LDCs and the failed states in the region. For instance, Easterly and Levine (1997) ascribe the poor performance of Sub-Saharan Africa to ethnic divisions, which leads to poor governance and conflict, and so to fragility.

In the next section we compare Africa's economic performance with that of other world regions, highlighting its progress through various indicators describing growth, exports, current account and income inequality. The third section further studies the indicators mentioned, comparing them between failed and non-failed states, and LDCs and non-LDCs. We conclude from this comparison that the distinction between failed and non-failed states and LDCs and non-LDCs is tenuous when measuring economic performance. Furthermore, their performance is influenced considerably by international factors. It is therefore important that the system of international economic governance including the G20 must seek to raise the growth rate of GDP in the developed countries, reform institutions such as The World Bank and International Monetary Fund (IMF) to increase the voice of developing countries, and reverse the trend of the declining importance of aid. And while the score on the economic and political stability index is higher among non-failed states than failed states, a number of anomalies are discussed. All this suggests that further research is needed to develop a classificatory scheme that provides better discrimination between LDCs and non-LDCs, and between fragile and non-fragile states in order to improve policy-making.

In the fourth section we distinguish between countries based on their most important exports. This analysis concludes that the weakest performance is by exporters of manufactured goods. The LDCs have performed better than non-LDCs in the sense that export share in GDP has increased more. Similarly, among the agricultural exporters, the fragile states have performed better than the non-fragile states.

We also compare the performance of countries in Latin America with those in Sub-Saharan Africa by export orientation. Countries in Sub-Saharan Africa have grown more slowly than those in Latin America, even when the export orientation was similar. However, the increase in share of exports of goods and services and of gross fixed capital formation in GDP has generally been greater in Sub-Saharan Africa when countries with a similar export orientation are compared.

We then discuss the progress that Sub-Saharan Africa has made in achieving the Millennium Development Goals (MDGs). We find that in this area of social progress, it also lags behind the other regions. There are two aspects to this relatively poor performance. One is poor growth – growth is very effective in reducing poverty and malnourishment in Sub-Saharan Africa – it is more effective than in the other regions. So poor economic performance has serious consequences for achieving the MDGs. The second aspect can be seen when we examine the effectiveness of growth in reducing mortality rates. Here Sub-Saharan Africa does better than Asia, but worse than Latin America and the Caribbean and the Middle East and North Africa. This shows the importance of governance. Even with the same growth rate, reduction in mortality rates would be less in Sub-Saharan Africa than in Latin America and the Middle East and North Africa. But how governance affects the achievement of MDGs, and how it can be improved, requires deeper analysis. It is unlikely that it is merely a question of failed states or LDCs having poor governance. Since their economic performance has not suffered in comparison to the non-LDCs or non-failed states, it is not clear why their lack of social progress should have suffered.

African economic performance: growth, exports and the current account

In this section we compare the performance of countries in Sub-Saharan Africa with those in other regions. In the last five decades (1965-2011) Sub-Saharan Africa has been one of two regions that has fallen further behind the high-income countries, with the gap in per capita incomes increasing (see Table 8.1).[2] But whereas per capita incomes in Latin America and the Caribbean have grown slightly faster than the world average, those in Sub-Saharan Africa have grown considerably slower. The increase in per capita incomes in East Asia and the Pacific has been spectacular. Growth in South Asia, after lagging in the 1960s and 1970s, has been gradually accelerating so that the gap between per capita incomes in the Asian region and those in the high-income countries is narrowing.[3]

Countries in Sub-Saharan Africa fared particularly badly in the quarter century after the oil price increases in 1973-74, but have

Table 8.1: Average annual growth of per capita income

Region	1965–73	1974–82	1983–1990	1991–2000	2001–05	2006–08	2009–11	GDP per capita 2011 (1965=1)
World	3.3	0.8	1.8	1.2	1.2	2.0	0.2	2.05
High income	4.3	1.6	3.0	1.7	1.5	1.5	−0.4	2.70
East Asia and the Pacific	4.5	4.5	6.3	6.0	7.3	8.6	7.8	14.08
Latin America and the Caribbean	3.6	1.5	−0.2	1.7	0.8	3.7	1.7	2.14
South Africa	0.2	2.0	3.5	3.2	4.6	6.0	5.6	3.85
Sub-Saharan Africa	2.3	0.1	−1.1	−0.4	1.8	3.4	1.3	1.35

Source: World DataBank World Development Indicators (WDIs) and The World Bank (2012)

fared better in this century, although, along with Latin America and the Caribbean, they have seen a worsening performance since the 2008 financial crisis. While growth in all the regions has suffered, the effect has been less in Asia, or in other words, the adverse effect has been more in Latin America and the Caribbean and Sub-Saharan Africa. The economies in Sub-Saharan Africa grew even slower during 2009–11 than they had in 2001-05 (see Table 8.1).

A notable feature of developments in the world economy over the past couple of decades has been the increasing integration of developing countries within the world economy. Restrictions on flow of goods and capital have been reduced. Tariffs have been reduced significantly, and the prevalence of quantitative restrictions on imports considerably lessened.[4] Rules on inflow of private capital have also been liberalised.[5] For instance, inflow of capital was extensively controlled in India in terms of the industries to which it could come, and the share of foreign capital was restricted to 40 per cent. Since 1991 the number of sectors in which foreign capital is allowed has progressively increased, the number of sectors where permission is required has been reduced, and the extent of foreign share of capital has increased. As a result, trade has increased substantially as a percentage of GDP.[6] The aim of trade liberalisation has been to raise the importance of exports, and this has happened (see Table 8.2).[7]

Again, the increase in the share of exports of goods and services in GDP has been the least in Sub-Saharan Africa, perhaps because this region had the highest share during 1965-73. Whereas the share of exports of goods and services in GDP had quadrupled between 1965-73 and 2006-07 for East Asia and the Pacific, and almost quadrupled

Table 8.2: Exports of goods and services (% of GDP)

Region	1965–73	1974–82	1983–1990	1991–2000	2001–05	2006–07	2008–10
World	14.0	18.8	19.8	21.4	26.0	27.4	27.7
High Income	12.8	17.4	17.9	18.8	23.0	29.0	25.8
East Asia and the Pacific	12.4	18.9	23.5	32.8	42.0	50.0	45.9
Latin America and the Caribbean	9.5	11.5	14.8	14.7	22.0	25.2	23.7
South Africa	5.6	7.5	7.9	12.4	17.0	21.6	21.7
Sub-Saharan Africa	23.8	28.1	26.8	28.0	32.0	34.4	29.6

Note: The average for the high-income countries is the average for those countries defined as high income by The World Bank. These are mainly the developed countries, but also include some oil producing and exporting countries and countries such as Singapore and Hong Kong.

Source: World DataBank WDIs and The World Bank (2012)

in South Africa and increased by more than 150 per cent in Latin America and the Caribbean, the share increased by only 50 per cent in Sub-Saharan Africa (World DataBank WDIs).[8]

While exports have grown slowly in Sub-Saharan Africa, the importance of remittances has increased rapidly, which has also happened in South Africa. Remittances, which were 1.8 and 0.8 per cent of GDP in South Africa and Sub-Saharan Africa respectively in the early 1990s, increased to over 4 and 2 per cent respectively by the end of the first decade of the 2000s (see Table 8.3). The increased remittances considerably helped in preventing a large deterioration in the current account in the years before the onset of the financial crisis. Remittances are also particularly important for LDCs – they are larger as a share of GDP for them than for other regions, and may account for their economic performance.

But despite the improved export performance and higher remittances, the current account deficit worsened in South Africa and Sub-Saharan Africa (see Table 8.4) in the years before the financial crisis because of a very high propensity to import goods and services. However, Sub-Saharan Africa still had a surplus, unlike the deficits that had prevailed before the 2001-05 period. South Africa, in contrast to Sub-Saharan Africa, had a substantial deficit before the financial crisis, although the deficit was smaller than those that had occurred in the periods after the oil price increases in 1973-74. The financial crisis has resulted in a worsening of the current account in practically all the developing regions, although East Asia and the Pacific continued to run surpluses; the increased deficit can be potentially damaging to the growth prospects of South Africa and Sub-Saharan Africa.

The current account deficits have been financed mainly by private capital flows rather than aid, although aid has increased in the aftermath of the financial crisis. The importance of aid as a percentage of GDP

Table 8.3: Remittances (% of GDP)

	1991–95	1996–2000	2001–05	2006–08	2009–10	2006–10
East Asia and the Pacific	0.6	0.9	1.4	1.5	1.3	1.4
Europe and Central Asia	1.0	1.3	1.1	1.4	1.2	1.3
Latin America and the Caribbean	0.7	0.9	1.7	1.7	1.3	1.5
Middle East and North Africa	6.0	3.4	4.0	3.3	3.7	3.5
South Africa	1.8	2.5	3.4	4.0	4.3	4.1
Sub-Saharan Africa	0.8	1.4	1.6	2.2	2.4	2.3
Least developed countries	3.4	3.8	5.4	5.7	6.3	5.9

Source: World DataBank WDIs

Table 8.4: Current account balance on goods and services (% of GDP)

Region	1965–73	1974–82	1983–90	1991–2000	2001–05	2006–08	2009–11
World	0.2	0.3	0.4	0.4	0.4	0.8	0.3
High income	0.4	0.2	0.2	0.6	0.6	0	0.1
East Asia and the Pacific	−1.9	−1.2	0.4	1.8	0.2	9.4	4.4
Latin America and the Caribbean	−0.5	−1.5	3.3	−1.1	3.0	0.5	−1.0
South Africa	−1.7	−3.8	−4.4	−3.5	−0.8	−2.2	−2.1
Sub-Saharan Africa	−1.1	−1.5	1.2	−1.3	1.5	0.5	−2.3

Source: World DataBank WDIs

had been diminishing in all the regions in the years before the crisis (see Table 8.5). The decline in the importance of aid reflects in part the slow growth in the sources given to the soft aid agencies such as the International Development Association (IDA), and also the slow growth of bilateral aid, partly because of high deficits in the budgets of the donor governments.

The importance of aid has also diminished when it is measured either as a percentage of gross fixed capital formation or of imports. Correspondingly, there has been an increasing reliance on private capital, particularly foreign direct investment (FDI) (see Table 8.6). The share of official creditors in total capital flows to developing countries has been negative so that private inflows have also had to finance outflows on the official account. However, the flows from The World Bank have been positive. Since the crisis, aid to Sub-Saharan Africa has increased. But it remains to be seen whether this is a temporary response to the crisis, or a more permanent increase.[9]

The rising importance of private capital flows is an indication of the increasing financial integration of developing countries with world financial markets. FDI flows as a percentage of GDP had been increasing until the financial crisis hit in 2008 (The World Bank, 2011). Since then, they have remained strong for East Asia and the

Table 8.5: Aid (% of GDP)

	1991–2000	2001–05	2007
East Asia and the Pacific	0.5	0.4	0.2
Latin America and the Caribbean	0.3	0.3	0.2
South Africa	1.2	0.9	0.7
Sub-Saharan Africa	5.5	5.4	4.5

Source: World DataBank WDIs

Table 8.6: Structure of total capital flows to the regions, 2000–07 (% of total capital flows)

	East Asia and the Pacific	Latin America and the Caribbean	South Africa	Sub-Saharan Africa
Net private	103.9	108.6	88.4	95.4
Net equity	79.4	89.6	54.8	79.2
Net FDI	62.6	78.7	28.6	55.1
Official	−3.9	−8.3	3.1	4.6
World Bank	−0.7	−1.2	2.4	7.7

Source: World Bank DataBank WDIs

Pacific, but have fallen significantly in South Africa and Sub-Saharan Africa (see Table 8.7). However, they had remained strong immediately after the crisis, being higher in South Africa and Sub-Saharan Africa in 2008-09 than in 2006-07, before falling in 2010. The decline in Latin America and the Caribbean seems to be a longer trend as the share has been falling since 2001-05.

The deterioration in the current account bodes badly for the future as, in the past, current account problems often resulted in implementation of contractionary fiscal and monetary policies that at least in the short run had a negative effect on growth. This effect usually operated through a decline in gross fixed investment, as developing countries depended on imports of capital goods. Before the debt crisis of 1982, investment rates in Sub-Saharan Africa are a success story, being the highest among developing country regions (see Table 8.8). However, investment rates had fallen in Latin America and the Caribbean and Sub-Saharan Africa through much of the 1980s and 1990s, and contributed to low growth in those years, whereas investment ratios had been increasing in East Asia and the Pacific and South Africa. But investment rates have held up well since the financial crisis, actually rising further in Latin America and the Caribbean and Sub-Saharan Africa, raising hopes that the crisis may have only a limited adverse effect on growth in developing countries.[10] It is also

Table 8.7: Foreign direct investment inflows (% of GDP)

Region	1991–2000	2001–05	2006–07	2008–09	2010
East Asia and the Pacific	3.5	3.1	4.2	2.9	3.0
Latin America and the Caribbean	2.4	3.0	2.7	2.5	2.4
South Africa	0.5	0.9	2.2	2.8	1.4
Sub-Saharan Africa	1.5	3.1	2.7	3.7	2.3

Source: World Bank DataBank WDIs

Table 8.8: Gross fixed capital formation by region (% of GDP)

Region	1965–73	1974–82	1983–90	1991–2000	2001–05	2006–08	2009–10
World	23.6	23.9	22.5	22.0	21.0	21.7	19.4
High income	24.4	23.8	22.3	21.4	20.0	20.7	18.0
East Asia and the Pacific	28.4	28.5	32.6	35.0	42.0	39.9	–
Latin America and the Caribbean	20.1	22.7	19.2	19.3	20.0	20.3	20.8
South Africa	14.9	17.8	20.0	21.4	25.0	30.3	32.8
Sub-Saharan Africa	21.8	24.0	18.5	17.2	19.0	24.0	24.0

Source: World Bank DataBank WDIs

important to note that the investment share in GDP has recovered in Sub-Saharan Africa to levels that had prevailed in the 1970s, even though in Latin America and the Caribbean it is still lower than it was in the earlier period. In Asia it is considerably higher. The maintenance of investment rates raises the hope that the worsening current account balance may have a limited effect on growth rates. Furthermore, the worsening of the current account may be only temporary if the investment raises the output of tradeables, leading to higher exports and lower imports.

Another hopeful sign is that the capital output ratios have been falling in these regions. Whereas in Asia these have remained at about 4 since the 1970s, they had risen to double-digit levels in the 1980s in the other regions. But currently they seem to vary, from about 4 in Sub-Saharan Africa to 5.5 in Latin America and the Caribbean.[11] The fall in the capital output ratios means that the same investment GDP ratio would lead to a higher rate of growth than it would have in earlier years. Current levels of the investment ratio and the capital output ratios would result in GDP growing at over 5 per cent a year in Sub-Saharan Africa and almost 4 per cent in Latin America and the Caribbean, which would be lower than the growth rates achieved in these regions during 2006-08, but higher than those achieved during 2009-11.[12]

This limited effect on investment is because domestic savings have increased so investment is less dependent on inflow of foreign funds, whether official or private (see Table 8.9). However, the increase in savings rates has been the least in Sub-Saharan Africa, and remains lower than rates achieved in the 1980s. So the region remains vulnerable to negative trends in the current account balance.

In brief, GDP has increased the slowest in Sub-Saharan Africa. There had been higher growth rates in the years before the crisis,

Table 8.9: Domestic savings

Region	1975–82	1983–90	1991–2000	2001–05	2006–08	2009–10
World	21.0	21.5	21.7	21.5	22.1	18.9
High income	20.9	21.0	21.1	20.5	20.4	16.8
East Asia and the Pacific	32.5	34.4	35.1	38.3	45.7	46.3
Latin America and the Caribbean	17.4	18.3	17.5	18.7	22.7	20.0
South Africa	19.0	20.8	23.2	28.8	32.3	32.8
Sub-Saharan Africa	16.3	17.0	15.1	15.6	15.6	16.4

Source: World Bank DataBank WDIs

but Sub-Saharan Africa has been particularly hard hit. Countries in Sub-Saharan Africa have also done less well than countries in other regions in increasing export share, and despite increased remittances, are experiencing a worse current account position than countries in other regions (The World Bank, 2011, 2012). We now examine to what extent the poor performance in Sub-Saharan Africa has been because of the concentration of LDCs and fragile states in Sub-Saharan Africa.

Economic performance of least developed countries and fragile states

The direction of change of many economic indicators is the same in the LDCs and non-LDCs and in the fragile and non-fragile states. In general, there is an improvement in the trends from the 1990s to the years immediately before the financial crisis, 2006–07, and then a worsening after the financial crisis (see Table 8.10). Growth is increased in the years before the crisis and then declined. This is true for LDCs, non-LDCs, fragile and non-fragile states. Similarly, the share of exports of goods and services as a percentage of GDP increases in the years before the financial crisis, as does the share of gross fixed capital formation in GDP. The current account improves in the years before the crisis, and the non-LDCs are even running a surplus. But there is a sharp deterioration in the current account of an average of about 4 per cent of GDP after the onset of the crisis. FDI as a percentage of GDP also has an increasing trend before the financial crisis, although it starts to decline for LDCs and fragile states before the beginning of the crisis.

The similarity of these broad trends may be due to a number of possibilities. One explanation is that these countries were adopting similar policies and the policies had similar effects irrespective of

Table 8.10: Economic performance of least developed countries and fragile states

		LDCs	Others	Fragile states	Others
GDP growth rate	1991–2000	2.4	3.1	2.4	2.0
Average annual	2001–05	4.9	2.9	3.9	3.9
percentage of GDP	2006–07	5.9	3.4	5.2	4.3
	2008–11	4.9	3.4	4.2	3.9
Gross fixed capital	1991–2000	18.8	20.6	17.8	19.7
formation	2001–05	20.6	21.2	18.5	21.5
	2006–07	21.3	22.3	19.1	22.5
Exports of goods and	1991–2000	22.8	42.2	26.6	30.5
services	2001–05	27.6	45.3	31.1	34.5
	2006–07	30.6	48.5	34.4	37.4
Current account	1991–2000	7.4	0.5	5.6	4.8
deficit	2001–05	5.8	2.7	1.7	3.9
	2006–07	5.2	3.0	2.4	2.0
	2008–11	8.7	1.4	6.0	6.0
FDI inflow	1991–2000	3.1	1.4	3.1	2.1
% of GDP	2001–05	5.8	1.7	6.8	3.1
	2006–07	4.7	2.6	5.3	3.2

Source: Authors' calculations based on data from World Bank DataBank WDIs

differences in economic, social and political structures and legal frameworks.[13] An alternative explanation would be that these are small economies all more strongly influenced by international developments than by internal policies and structures. For instance, inflows or outflows of foreign capital will have a large effect on the domestic economy as these are large compared to the domestic money supply. Also, given the large share of exports and imports in GDP, developments in foreign markets for their exports or imports will have a large effect on the domestic economy.

Although the overall trends are similar, the LDCs have in general grown faster than the non-LDCs (Table 8.10), despite having a smaller share of gross fixed capital formation and of exports of goods and services in GDP. The difference is particularly large for the latter indicator, as the share of exports of goods and services in GDP is almost 20 per cent higher in the non-LDCs (see Table 8.10). However, the share has been increasing faster in LDCs than in non-LDCs, and this increase could have provided a boost to growth. The share of gross fixed capital formation in GDP is only about 2 per cent higher in the non-LDCs. The faster growth in LDCs despite a lower investment share suggests either greater efficiency in the use of capital, or investment in more labour-intensive activities in accordance with their comparative advantage.[14] Both groups show a similar increase in the share of gross domestic savings in GDP, about 500 basis points. There is, however, a significant difference in the behaviour of the current account. While the current account improved in the case of both the LDCs and non-LDCs, the latter ran surpluses in the 2000s before the crisis. On the other hand, more FDI flowed into LDCs than into non-LDCs.

There is no such clear difference in the performance of fragile and non-fragile states. The differences between the fragile and non-fragile states are small. The fragile states grew slightly faster than the non-fragile states. But gross fixed capital formation has been smaller as a share of GDP in fragile states as has exports of goods and services. Again, a higher growth rate with a smaller share of gross fixed capital formation in GDP would mean a lower capital output ratio in the fragile states, namely, a more efficient use of capital or investment in more labour-intensive activities. But the difference is not large. The current account deficit has been very similar for the fragile and non-fragile states. Surprisingly, the fragile states have attracted more FDI – it seems that foreign investors are more concerned about the sector they are investing in than in the political stability of the country. Most of the FDI to Sub-Saharan Africa went to just five fragile countries, namely, Angola, Chad, Equatorial Guinea, Nigeria and Sudan, all endowed with rich natural resources (European University Institute, 2009). Presumably since the output is destined for foreign markets they are less affected by domestic conditions. And because these activities earn foreign exchange, foreign investors may have fewer problems in repatriating their profits.

There has been considerable interest in the relation between economic and political stability and economic performance. A study found that the stability index was much higher for the high performing economies of India and China than for the countries of Sub-Saharan Africa (Harttgen and Klasen, 2009).[15] The merits of such a comparison are questionable as India and China are very different from the countries in Sub-Saharan Africa, and outperform African countries in almost every criterion of political and economic stability.

Comparing the performance of failed with non-failed states in Sub-Saharan Africa, the overall average stability index for failed states was approximately 84, and for non-failed states 104, a difference of about 20 index points. While non-failed states are considerably more stable than their failed counterparts, they do not perform much better.

However, one has to take account of the heterogeneity within each group. If we classify those with a score in the range of 50-80 as being of low stability, 81-110 as medium and 111-140 as high, 5 of 14 failed states have low stability while only 3 of 18 non-failed states have low stability. Again, the analytical basis of such a classification can be questioned. Togo, for example, has a low stability index of 71 and is still classified as non-failed by the DfID. Angola, on the other hand, has a stability index of 116, which is a higher value than many other non-failed states, and is still classified as a failed state. It is classified as fragile by the Country Policy and Institutional Assessment (CPIA) and Organisation for Economic Co-operation and Development (OECD) (European University Institute, 2009). Maybe the lack of a relation between fragility and economic performance is a reflection of the weak methodology used to classify the states.

However, we find a suggestive effect of the classification and relation between income inequality and growth. There is no link between the two for both the failed and non-failed states (see Table 8.11), but for LDCs and non-LDCs there is a reversal of the relation between growth and inequality, even though the correlations are weak. For LDCs, higher inequality leads to more rapid growth in the future, whereas for non-LDCs, more rapid growth leads to higher inequality

Table 8.11: Relation between Gini coefficient and growth

Type of country	Time frame as related to the Gini coefficient	Rank correlation
LDC	5 years before	0.165
	10 years before	0.14
	5 years after	0.306
	10 years after	0.241
Non LDC	5 years before	0.28
	10 years before	0.083
	5 years after	−0.05
	10 years after	0.13
Failed state	5 years before	−0.046
	10 years before	0.06
	5 years after	0.12
	10 years after	0.2
Non-failed state	5 years before	−0.015
	10 years before	0.05
	5 years after	0.06
	10 years after	0.003

Source: World Bank DataBank WDIs

in the future.[16] Both the effects are stronger over five years than 10 years. The nature of this difference needs more investigation. It could be that for LDCs the effect of income distribution on savings is stronger. As income increases, even the poor may be able to save, so income distribution has less effect on the savings rate. But the two results together imply a dynamic that may be destabilising. A more unequal distribution in LDCs seems to lead to faster growth, and so these countries would be more likely to become non-LDCs. If they continue to grow more rapidly, the income distribution would further worsen. This suggests that it might be difficult to generate growth that benefits the poor. This would presage a poor relation between economic growth and social progress. Another matter of concern is that increasing income inequality might also increase social tensions.

Classification into failed and non-failed states is problematic from the perspective of explaining economic performance. There is considerable heterogeneity in the economic indicators between countries within each category, whether failed or non-failed, and each country has its own specific historical past and governmental and economic structures. Further research is needed to improve the classification scheme.

Economic performance by export orientation

Another possible explanation for differences in economic performance between countries in Sub-Saharan Africa could be the nature of their exports. We divided the countries by their export orientation, namely, the commodity group that had the largest share. The countries were divided into those exporting final agricultural commodities, agricultural raw material, ores, fuels and manufactured goods. There were 18 countries exporting final agricultural commodities and 8 exporting manufactures. Since there were sufficient numbers in these groups, further analysis in terms of LDCs and non-LDCs and fragile and non-fragile states could be undertaken. We find that growth rates for most of the groups have increased since 1990 (see Table 8.12). Furthermore, exporters of agricultural commodities, whether foods or raw materials, have maintained their good performance after the financial crisis. This might be due to the higher prices of agricultural products in 2007-08 and the maintenance of a favourable price environment. Countries exporting other commodities, particularly manufactured goods, have seen a drop in growth rates. Also, whereas in the 1990s exporters of manufactured goods generally did the best among the different groups, they did the worst in the 2000s. Slower growth since the 2008 crisis seems to have had a particularly unfavourable effect on demand for

Table 8.12: Economic performance by export orientation

		Agriculture	Agricultural raw materials	Fuels	Ores	Manufactures
GDP growth rate	1991–2000	2.6	3.7	2.2	–0.5	3.4
Average annual	2001–05	4.3	8.0	5.4	1.8	2.9
percentage of GDP	2006–07	5.1	3.5	7.6	6.8	4.2
	2008–11	5.0	4.5	5.1	6.2	3.0
Gross fixed capital	1991–2000	16.5	18.8	20.4	11.0	25.2
formation	2001–05	8.6	24.5	20.5	14.8	23.4
	2006–07	20.6	20.2	21.3	20.0	22.8
Exports of goods and	1991–2000	22.4	16.2	42.6	23.1	41.4
services	2001–05	25.0	20.9	49.5	28.2	46.2
	2006–07	28.4	27.05	0.3	33.1	47.6
Current account deficit	1991–2000	6.3	5.4	4.1	2.0	–
	2001–05	5.0	8.1	3.6	1.4	–
	2006–07	4.4	4.9	4.8	1.4	–
FDI inflow	1991–2000	1.8	1.5	2.7	6.4	4.2
% of GDP	2001–05	2.7	6.2	5.6	14.8	3.9
	2006–07	3.2	4.5	7.6	4.8	3.0

Source: Authors' calculations based on data from World Bank DataBank WDIs

manufactures. Most of the groups raised the share of investment as a percentage of GDP from the 1990s; again, the exception was the manufacturing exporting countries. But all groups had higher share of exports in GDP in the period 2008-11 than in the 1990s, except for the fuel exporting countries and manufacturing exporters. This would suggest poor export performance as a possible cause for lacklustre economic growth among the manufacture exporting countries. Their inability to maintain their competitiveness needs further analysis. One possible explanation could be that large retailers such as Wal-Mart find it more economical to meet all their requirements from a large supplier such as China or Bangladesh than form a number of smaller suppliers in Sub-Saharan Africa.

Countries in Sub-Saharan Africa have usually had a deficit in their current account balance. Countries in most groups have experienced an increase in FDI inflows as a percentage of GDP; again, the manufacturing exporting countries are an exception.

Fourteen of the 18 agriculture exporting countries were LDCs, and only 4 were non-LDCs. In the case of the manufacture exporting countries, 3 were LDCs and 5 were non-LDCs. Eight of the agricultural exporting countries were fragile states, but only one of the exporters of manufactures was a failed state. When we contrast the performance of LDCs and non-LDCs we find that the LDCs grew faster than non-LDCs among both agricultural and manufacturing exporting countries.[17] Similarly, fragile states grew faster than non-fragile states among agriculture exporting countries.[18] So once again, the distinction between fragile and non-fragile states seems tenuous at best on the basis of economic performance. The better performance of LDCs could be rationalised on the basis of convergence, namely, the economies of poorer countries grow faster due to initial conditions.

The other region that has lagged in its economic performance in this period has been Latin America. We compare the performance of countries in Sub-Saharan Africa with those in Latin America. For the purposes of the comparison we also divide the countries in Latin America on the basis of export orientation (see Table 8.13), and then compare the relative performance of countries in the two regions according to their export orientation.

The overall trends in Latin America are similar to those in Sub-Saharan Africa. Growth of GDP accelerates for all groups of countries just as it does in Sub-Saharan Africa, and the share of exports of goods and services in GDP increases for all groups, just as it does in the case of Sub-Saharan Africa. The behaviour of investment is different, however. In the case of Sub-Saharan Africa, the share of gross

Table 8.13: Economic performance by export orientation Latin America

	1991–2000	2001–05	2006–07
Growth of GDP (% p.a.)			
Agriculture	3.4	2.9	6.8
Fuels	2.8	5.0	6.5
Ores	3.9	3.4	3.5
Manufactures	3.0	2.3	5.1
Investment (% of GDP)			
Agriculture	22.8	20.5	24.0
Fuels	19.7	20.2	19.5
Ores	24.3	23.6	24.6
Manufactures	18.8	19.9	22.6
Export of goods and services (% of GDP)			
Agriculture	36.8	37.8	43.2
Fuels	31.9	35.6	42.9
Ores	30.0	31.9	40.2
Manufactures	20.2	23.7	25.0

Source: Authors' calculations based on data from World Bank DataBank WDIs

fixed capital formation in GDP increased for all groups except the manufacturing exporters. In the case of Latin America it also increased for manufacturing exporters. However, it was almost constant for exporters of natural resources, fuels and ores. The similarity in trends suggests strongly that the economic performance of these countries is driven by forces in the world economy.

The acceleration of growth for exporters of agricultural and manufactured goods has been greater in Latin America than in Sub-Saharan Africa, and the absolute growth rates have also been higher for these two groups. So in general, countries in Sub-Saharan Africa have performed worse than those in Latin America, even when the export orientation was similar. However, the increase in share of exports of goods and services and of gross fixed capital formation has generally been greater in Sub-Saharan Africa when countries with similar export orientation are compared. This presages well for the future in Sub-Saharan Africa that the gap between countries in Sub-Saharan Africa and Latin America may narrow. It may also mean that countries in Sub-Saharan Africa perform better on the social front as do countries in Latin America and the Caribbean.

Social progress

Poverty has a number of dimensions measured by different indicators, and we examine how some of these indicators have evolved at the regional level in roughly the past two decades. Substantial progress has been made in reducing poverty. At the aggregate level, taking all regions together, the target of reducing poverty by half will be met. All the regions except Sub-Saharan Africa will reach the goal of halving poverty (see Table 8.14).

Table 8.14: Regional poverty and malnourishment (% of population)

	Poverty			Malnourishment		
	1990	2011	% fall	2000	2013	% fall
East Asia and the Pacific*	57.0	7.9	86.2	11.4	5.2	54.4
Latin America and the Caribbean	12.2	4.6	62.3	5.0	2.8	44.0
Middle East and North Africa	5.8	1.7	70.7	8.9	6.0	32.6
South Africa	54.1	24.5	54.7	43.0	32.5	24.4
Sub-Saharan Africa	56.1	46.8	16.6	25.4	21.0	17.3

Note: * This region as used by The World Bank covers East Asia, and South East Asia.
Source: World Bank DataBank WDIs

As far as reducing malnourishment, only East Asia and the Pacific (see Table 8.14) has met the target, and per capita incomes have grown very substantially in East Asia and the Pacific. It seems that Latin America and the Caribbean will just miss meeting the target as malnourishment has declined at the rate of 1.9 per cent a year, so it is unlikely that the remaining 6 per cent can be met in two years. The other regions are far from reaching their targets for reducing malnourishment. In all regions the reduction in malnourishment is considerably less than the reduction in poverty, and the reasons for this need to be explored in order to achieve better outcomes in the post–2015 period.

The targets for mortality rates are to reduce infant and child mortality by two-thirds, and to reduce maternal mortality by three-quarters. East Asia and the Pacific, Latin America and the Caribbean and Middle East and North Africa are on their way to meet the targets for infant and child mortality, although the Middle East and North Africa will have to step up its efforts to reduce infant mortality which must fall further to 17.2. South Africa and Sub-Saharan Africa are unlikely to meet these targets (see Tables 8.15 and 8.16).

In the case of maternal mortality, none of the regions are likely to reach their targets; South Africa seems to be the closest to meeting the target (see Table 8.17).

Table 8.15: Regional infant mortality rates

	1990	2013	% change
East Asia and the Pacific	44.9	16.1	64.1
Latin America and the Caribbean	43.6	15.5	64.6
Middle East and North Africa	51.5	21.3	58.6
South Africa	91.8	44.6	51.4
Sub-Saharan Africa	107.4	61.0	43.2

Source: World Bank DataBank WDIs

Table 8.16: Regional child mortality rates

	1990	2013	% change
East Asia and the Pacific	59.0	19.5	67.0
Latin America and the Caribbean	55.1	18.2	67.0
Middle East and North Africa	67.4	25.5	62.2
South Africa	129.4	56.6	56.3
Sub-Saharan Africa	179.0	92.2	48.5

Source: World Bank DataBank WDIs

Table 8.17: Regional maternal mortality rates

	1990	2013	% change
East Asia and the Pacific	170	75	55.9
Latin America and the Caribbean	150	87	42.0
Middle East and North Africa	160	78	51.2
South Africa	550	190	65.5
Sub-Saharan Africa	990	510	48.5

Source: World Bank DataBank WDIs

Analysis of still longer time trends in maternal mortality (WHO et al, 2012) shows that the rate of decline in maternal mortality had decelerated in the period 2005-10 compared to the period 1990-2005, as rates of growth of per capita income had decelerated, and the elasticity of decline in maternal mortality rates with respect to growth in per capita income had fallen. This could be due to several reasons. Food price inflation has been high in recent years, and this hits the poorest hardest, who spend more of their income on food. The diversion of income to meet food intake leaves much less available for other needs. Healthcare usually takes a big hit because it is expensive and the ill effects of not availing of preventive care are not immediately noticeable, so preventive care is neglected. Food price inflation seems to have added about 4 per cent to the poverty rate (Sobrado et al, 2008). The crisis has also reduced government resources, and governments are reluctant to spend on health if this increases the budget deficit, because with a worsening current account deficit, the prudent policy action would be to reduce government expenditure.

One way to examine whether the targets can be met without special interventions is to see the relation between reductions in these indicators and growth in per capita incomes. This would be particularly relevant for the post-2015 period.

As far as poverty reduction for the Africa region is concerned, growth is very effective, except in the Middle East and North Africa and South Africa (see Table 8.17). It seems least effective in Latin America and the Caribbean, but there is a problem in this estimate. There was a fall in per capita income between 1990 and 1995, leading to a low rate of growth in per capita income between 1990 and 2005. However, there was not a large increase in poverty when income was falling. If one calculates the elasticity with respect to the period 1995-2005, the elasticity is lower, at 1.4, although still higher than in most other regions (see Table 8.18).

Table 8.18: Elasticity of reduction

	Poverty reduction 1990–05	Mal- nourishment 2000–08	Infant mortality rate 1990–2005	Child mortality rate 1990–2005	Maternal mortality rate 1990–2005
East Asia and the Pacific	1.1	0.07	0.4	0.5	0.6
Latin America and the Caribbean	1.4	0.39	2.6	2.8	1.9
Middle East and North Africa	0.6	0.24	2.0	2.2	2.7
South Africa	0.4	0.12	0.6	0.7	1.0
Sub-Saharan Africa	1.9	0.55	0.8	0.9	0.8

Source: Authors' calculations from World Bank DataBank WDIs

Growth is more effective in reducing poverty the lower the inequality (Ravallion, 1997; Bourguignon, 2003; Lopez and Serven, 2006; Perry et al, 2006). Inequality has been falling in Latin America and the Caribbean (Birdsall et al, 2011), and is low in East Asia and the Pacific, so that would explain the fall in poverty. The low elasticity in South Africa may reflect the increasing inequality. The Gini coefficient has increased in South Africa, from 32.5 in 1993 to 37 in 2010 (ADB, 2012). Without this increase, poverty would have been about 10 per cent lower in South Africa, and the elasticity would be somewhat higher. The low efficacy of growth in South Africa also reflects the very low and falling elasticity of employment in organised manufacturing. This declined from 0.63 in the 1990s to 0.51 in the 2000s. The share of wages in manufacturing has also been declining. While per worker output grew by 7.4 per cent a year between 1990 and 2007, the wage rate increased by only 2 per cent a year (Felipe and Kumar, 2010). The low elasticity in India influences the entire South Africa region given India's size, and may also reflect the large population of the 'scheduled tribes' who live in remote areas. These people have often been bypassed by growth as well as government programmes.[19]

The effect of growth on poverty also depends on the nature of growth, which has been very different in Asia compared to the other regions.

In both East and South Asia, value added per worker has increased in agriculture and in non–agriculture, although at a faster rate in East Asia (see Table 8.19). In Asia productivity per worker has also increased more rapidly in non–agriculture than in agriculture, so that the rural

Table 8.19: Nature of growth

| | Value added per worker 2009 (1980 = 100) | | |
	Agriculture	Non-agriculture	Ratio
East Asia	240.5 (3.1)	513.5 (5.8)	0.47
Latin America	187.5 (2.2)	73.5 (−1.0)	2.56
Middle East and North Africa	194.2 (2.3)	75.0 (−1.0)	2.59
South Asia	157.3 (1.6)	240.5 (3.1)	0.65
Africa	119.7 (0.6)	68.7 (−1.3)	1.74
High income	349.4 (4.4)	141.6 (1.2)	2.47

Note: Figure in brackets are the growth rate of the variable. Value added per worker employed in the sector.

Source: Lele et al (2011)

urban gap has increased. This has contributed to increasing income inequality in Asia, which has meant that the decrease in poverty has been less than if there had not been this increase in inequality but growth had remained the same (ADB, 2012). For inequality to remain the same, this would require a faster growth of agricultural output, and it is not so easy to achieve this in Asia because of land scarcity, water shortage and deterioration in the quality of the water and other bad environmental consequences. But the gap in terms of money incomes has not been as large in terms of productivity because the prices of agricultural products have risen in Asia relative to the prices of non-agricultural products, partly because of government intervention by maintaining high support prices for agricultural products (Lele et al, 2011).

The high elasticity for Sub-Saharan Africa is surprising as neither has growth been high nor has it been based on increasing labour productivity that would increase incomes. Furthermore, growth has been particularly low in agriculture.[20] This greater improvement in Sub-Saharan Africa again raises the question of the usefulness of categories such as LDCs or failed states for such analysis. It also questions the perception that governance is poor in Sub-Saharan Africa.

What were likely to be the regional achievements in reducing mortality by 2015 (see Table 8.20)? We use the calculated elasticities. The regions grew rapidly during the period 2006-08, faster than earlier and faster than in the following years. So this might provide the upper range of what could be achieved. Most regions experienced much lower growth rates during the years 2009-10, and these growth rates provided a lower range.[21]

Table 8.20: Reduction in mortality rates (% reduction in 2015 compared to 1990)

	Optimistic case			Pessimistic case		
	Infant	Child	Maternal	Infant	Child	Maternal
East Asia and the Pacific	66	71	79	64	67	76
Latin America and the Caribbean	86	87	85	64	66	69
Middle East and North Africa	69	74	76	63	67	72
South Africa	53	58	75	51	56	73
Sub-Saharan Africa	39	42	43	27	29	31

In both the high and low growth cases, East Asia and the Pacific, Latin America and the Caribbean and the Middle East and North Africa either meet the target for reduction of infant, child and maternal mortality, or are very close to meeting the target (see Table 8.18). South Africa is close to meeting the target for maternal mortality, but far from reaching the target for infant and child mortality. Sub-Saharan Africa will miss all three targets by a wide margin. The performance of Sub-Saharan Africa is particularly lagging in the low growth case because per capita hardly grew during 2009-10, so continued growth until 2015 at this rate means that an increase in income cannot contribute much to reducing mortality. If migration flows and so remittances are adversely affected by the more straitened circumstances, progress in achieving the MDGs will be further retarded.

Conclusions

It is widely believed that rapid progress in social indicators requires both rapid growth and special programmes to reach disadvantaged groups (Bhagwati, 1966). In our analysis of the progress in the different regions, we find that very rapid growth over an extended period in East Asia and the Pacific will lead to the region meeting most, if not all, of the MDG goals. On the other hand, Latin America and the Caribbean has not experienced very rapid growth, but seems to have successfully implemented social inclusion programmes through the mechanism of conditional cash transfers, and this has enabled the region to meet many of the MDGs. The amounts required were well within the fiscal capabilities of the Latin American and Caribbean countries, as the amounts required according to our calculations were considerably less than 1 per cent of GDP, whereas the tax to GDP ratio was over 20 per cent. The South Asia region has also experienced rapid growth, but is unlikely to meet any of the MDGs, except reducing poverty. Various hypotheses have been proposed to explain the relatively poor social performance despite a very good economic performance. These include lack of political will, lack of governance that results in the intended beneficiaries not receiving the service, and lack of resources with the government as the tax to GDP ratio is very low. No analysis has been conducted to assess the contribution of each factor to the poor social performance. The economy of Sub-Saharan Africa has performed poorly,[22] and neither have the African countries been successful in implementing social programmes.

Economic performance over the past more than 40 years in Sub-Saharan Africa has lagged behind that in other regions of the world in that the growth of GDP per capita has been slower. Our analysis above seeks to explain this poor performance. One possible explanation could be the large number of LDCs or failed states in Sub-Saharan Africa.[23] The hypothesis is that LDCs do worse than non-LDCs and that failed states do worse than non-failed states. But we do not find any such systematic difference between the performance of LDCs and non-LDCs and between failed and non-failed states. We therefore raise doubts about the usefulness of these categories for the analysis of economic performance, although we would not deny that these categories might be useful for other kinds of analysis.

The difference in economic performance could be because of internal or external reasons.[24] We then tried to examine the role of external factors by studying what difference the export specialisation of a country made in its performance. We found (i) that the behaviour of countries with different export orientations had the same cyclical pattern, and (ii) that countries that exported agricultural products fared better in this century than countries that exported manufactures, whereas the reverse was the case in the 1990s. We conclude from the observation of similarity of cyclical patterns that international factors played an important role in the performance of these economies. This conclusion is strengthened as we find the same cyclical pattern even across continents when we compare the performance of counties in Sub-Saharan Africa with that of countries in Latin America and the Caribbean. But across export orientation, countries in Latin America and the Caribbean perform better than those in Sub-Saharan Africa, implying the importance of domestic policies and institutions. The similarity of cyclical patterns points to common external factors and the difference in levels we ascribe to differences in domestic policies and institutions.

To conclude, we discuss the role of governance and reduction in corruption. It is tautological to say that better governance and recued corruption would lead to better performance, whether in terms of economic growth or social achievements. The important question to our mind is whether better governance is a 'precondition', in the words of Rostow (1960). Subsequent research has shown that not all of the pre-conditions suggested by Rostow had held in the currently other developed countries (Rostow, 1963). Gerschenkron's analysis (1962) of European development shows that the art of policy-making is not to try to replicate institutions prevalent in other countries, but to creatively import substitutes.[25]

Furthermore, the institutions that exist today in the developed countries, and which are recommended as necessary in developing countries today, did not exist when the currently developed countries were developing (Chang, 2002).[26] Improvement in governance seems to accompany economic development.[27] Furthermore, we find that the improvement of social indicators is usually much greater in Sub-Saharan Africa than in other regions given the growth in per capita income, namely, for the same growth in per capita income the progress in terms of improvements in the social indicators is much greater in Sub-Saharan Africa than other regions. This, again, raises questions about the perception of the lack of governance in Sub-Saharan Africa.

The financial crisis created a less favourable external environment, and this is continuing as growth continues to be slow in the developed countries. Slower growth in the developing countries is likely to have severe adverse effects on their efforts to improve living standards. The post-2015 agenda needs to think of steps that can be taken to lessen the impact of the slowdown in the advanced economies of Europe and North America.[28]

Another aspect of the post-2015 system of international economic governance is suggested by our analysis. The strong influence of international factors implied by our analysis suggests how important reforms of the major international organisations may be. The G20 have agreed on changes in the governance structures of the IMF and The World Bank, but implementation unfortunately has lagged. The G20 summit since the Korean summit and including the recent one in Australia did not lead to any decisions that would improve either economic performance in developing countries or an improvement in social indicators. In particular, attention needs to be paid to reverse the decline in the importance of aid, as the poorer economies may not be able to attract sufficient amounts of private capital.

References

ADB (Asian Development Bank) (2012) *Asian development: Outlook 2012*, Manila: ADB.

Agarwal, M. and Samanta, S. (2006) 'Structural adjustment, governance, economic growth and social progress', *Journal of International Trade and Economic Development*, vol 15, no 3.

Agarwal, M., Mitra, S. and Whalley, J. (2015) 'Indian economic growth: its ups and downs', in A. Manmohan and J. Whalley (eds) *Sustainability of growth: The role of economic, technological and environmental factors*, Singapore: World Scientific, pp 59-79.

Bhagwati, J. (1966) *The economics of underdeveloped countries*, London: Weidenfeld and Nicolson.

Barro, R.J. and Salai-i-Martin, X. (1992) 'Convergence', *Journal of Political Economy*, vol 100, no 2, pp 223-51.

Birdsall, N., Lustig, N. and McLeod, D. (2011) *Declining inequality in Latin America: Some economics, some politics*, Working Paper No 251, Washington, DC: Center for Global Development, May.

Bourguignon, F. (2003) 'The growth elasticity of poverty reduction: explaining heterogeneity across countries and time periods', in T. Eicher and S. Turnovsky (eds) *Inequality and growth: Theory and policy implications*, Cambridge, MA: MIT Press, pp 3-26.

Chang, H.-J. (2002) *Kicking away the ladder: Development strategy in historical perspective*, London: Anthem Studies in Development and Globalization.

Easterly, W. and Levine, R. (1997) 'Africa's growth and ethnic divisions', *Quarterly Journal of Economics*, vol 112, no 4, pp 1203-50.

Enke, S. (1963) *Economics of development*, London: Dennis Dobson.

European University Institute (2009) *Overcoming fragility in Africa: Forging a new European approach*, European Report on Development (http://erd.cui.eu/erd-2009/final-report/).

Felipe, J. and Kumar, U. (2010) *Technical change in India's organized manufacturing sector*, Working Paper No 626, New York: Levy Economics Institute of Bard College.

Gerschenkron, A. (1962) *Economic backwardness in historical perspective: A book of essays*, Cambridge, MA: Belknap Press of Harvard University Press.

Go, D., Nikitin, D., Wang, X. and Zou, H.-f. (2007) 'Poverty and inequality in Sub-Saharan Africa: literature survey and empirical assessment', *Annals of Economics and Finance*, vol 8, no 2, pp 251-304.

Hall, G. and Patrinos, H.A. (2006) *Indigenous people, poverty and human development in Latin America, 1994-2004*, New York: Palgrave Macmillan.

Harttgen, K. and Klasen, S. (2009) *Fragility and MDG progress: How useful is the fragility concept?*, European Report on Development, EUI Working Papers, San Domenico di Fiesole: European University Institute (http://cadmus.eui.eu/bitstream/handle/1814/13585/?sequence=1).

Husain, I. and Faruqee, R. (1994) *Adjustment in Africa: Lessons from case studies*, Washington, DC: The World Bank.

Kamarck, A.M. (1967) *The economics of African development*, New York: Praeger.

Lele, U. (1991) *Aid to African agriculture: Lessons from two decades of donors' experience*, published for The World Bank by Johns Hopkins University Press, Baltimore, MD.

Lele, U., Agarwal, M., Timmer, P. and Goswami, S. (2015) 'Patterns of agriculture and structural transformation in 109 developed and developing countries with special focus on Brazil, China, India and Indonesia', Paper presented at the Conference on Policy Options and Investment priorities for Accelerating Agricultural Productivity Growth, Organised by the Indira Gandhi Institute for Development Research, 9-11 November, New Delhi.

Lopez, H. and Serven, L. (2006) *A normal relationship? Poverty, growth and inequality*, Working Paper Series No IDB-WP-213, Washington, DC: The World Bank and Inter-American Development Bank.

Moreno, V.G. and Patrinos, H.A. (2010) *Poverty in Mexico: Indigenous people*, OPREM Network, Washington, DC: The World Bank.

Perry, G.E., Arias, O.S., Lopez, J.H., Maloney, W.F. and Serven, L. (2006) *Poverty reduction and growth: Virtuous and vicious circlers*, Washington, DC: The World Bank.

Ravallion, M. (1997) 'Can high-inequality developing countries escape absolute poverty?', *Economic Letters*, vol 456, no 1, pp 51-7.

Rostow, W.W. (1960) *The stages of economic growth: A non-Communist manifesto*, Cambridge: Cambridge University Press.

Rostow, W.W. (ed) (1963) *The economics of take off into sustained growth, Proceedings of a conference held by the International Economic Association*, New York: St Martin's Press.

Sobrado C., Demombynes, G. and Rubiano, E. (2008) *Food prices and poverty in Latin America*, PREM Network, Washington, DC: The World Bank.

Solow, R.M. (1956) 'A contribution to the theory of economic growth', *Quarterly Journal of Economics*, vol 70, no 1, pp 65-94.

Stewart, F. and Brown, G. (2009) *Fragile states*, Working Paper No 51, Oxford: Centre for Research on Inequality, Human Security and Ethnicity, University of Oxford (www.crise.ox.ac.uk/).

UNCTAD (United Nations Conference on Trade and Development) (2011) *The least developed countries report*, Geneva: UNCTAD.

Whitfield, L. (2012) 'How countries become rich and reduce poverty: a review of heterodox explanations of economic development', *Development Policy Review*, vol 30, no 3, pp 239- 60.

Williamson, J. (1989) 'What Washington means by policy reform', in J. Williamson (ed) *Latin American adjustment: How much has happened*, Washington, DC: Institute for International Economics.

World Bank, The (1981) *Accelerated development in Sub-Saharan Africa: An agenda for action*, Washington, DC: The World Bank.

World Bank, The (1989) *Sub-Saharan Africa: From crisis to sustainable growth – A long term perspective*, Washington, DC: The World Bank.

World Bank, The (2011) *Global economic prospects: Maintaining progress amid turmoil*, vol 3 (http://siteresources.worldbank.org/INTGEP/Resources/335315-1307471336123/7983902-1307479336019/Full-Report.pdf).

World Bank, The (2012) *Global economic prospects*, July 2012, Washington, DC: The World Bank.

World Bank, The (nd) World DataBank, World Development Indicators (http://databank.worldbank.org/data/views/variableselection/selectvariables.aspx?source=world-development-indicators#s_a).

WHO (World Health Organization), UNICEF (United Nations Children's Fund), UNFPA (United Nations Population Fund) and The World Bank (2012) *Trends in maternal mortality: 1990 to 2010*, Geneva: WHO.

NINE

From regional integration to regionalism in Africa: building capacities for the post-Millennium Development Goals agenda

Cristina D'Alessandro

Introduction

Regional integration, regional cooperation, regional coordination, regional harmonisation, regionalism, alternative/new regionalism, pan-Africanism, African unity.... All are processes, strategies and ideologies aimed at encompassing the current limits, dysfunctions and weaknesses of African states. The vast number and diversity of these approaches concede that these attempts have encountered numerous difficulties. The above list also underlines the fact that two major levels have emerged that remain crucial today: the continental scale and the macro-regional scale, different not only in their size, but also in their aims and instruments. Moreover, they demonstrate the problems associated with bypassing the national scale in Africa. Despite their institutional and technical gaps, African states remain central and key stakeholders in the political arena.

This debate also revives an ancient implicit questioning of the most suitable scale for development and, consequently, for capacity building. From the local to the regional, and through all the intermediate levels, development has been conceived and practised at different levels by different actors during the course of the 20th century. The difference between the most local village-based projects (such as the NAAM projects in Burkina Faso[1] or the CAMPFIRE programme in Zimbabwe[2]), still favoured by non-governmental organisations (NGOs) like Manitese,[3] and the 'trans-boundary conservation and development areas' that contribute to the protection and maintenance of biological diversity, as well as to the promotion of social and economic development (IUCN, nd), is huge.

The current debates on the post–2015 sustainable development agenda also emphasise a regional dimension at the core of the agenda, together with both national and global components. This regional level should be tailored to regional needs, to identify regional trends, obstacles, commonalities, best practices and lessons learned. This regional operating scale should include the various stakeholders and be participatory (UN General Assembly, 2014). There is no doubting the relevance of the regional level for the future of African countries and the continent as a whole. The issue is more about strategies and choices adapted to African contexts. Furthermore, recent security threats (such as Al-Shabab, Ansar Dine and Boko Haram) and health issues (like the Ebola pandemic) increase the need for regional responses and mechanisms to counter security and safety concerns, especially in developing countries. This is confirmed by the Common African Position (CAP) on the post–2015 development agenda, where effective partnerships at the regional and continental level are part of the strategy included in Pillar 5, Peace and security (AU, 2014a).

This chapter aims to investigate macro-regional and continental patterns in Africa, to underline what kind of processes are taking place around the continent, and to establish which of them would be suitable for the future, especially within the context of the post-MDGs agenda.

Progress and challenges toward the Millennium Development Goals in Africa

In 2012, the African Union Commission (AUC), the African Development Bank (AfDB), the United Nations Economic Commission for Africa (UNECA), and the United Nations Development Programme (UNDP) published a joint report assessing the progress made towards accomplishing the Millennium Development Goals (MDGs) in Africa (AUC et al, 2012). The report underlines the important achievements obtained, especially on gender issues, but also on primary education and fighting against diseases such as HIV/AIDS and malaria. Progress is slower in poverty reduction and in the fight against unemployment. Some crucial challenges remain, which explains why most African countries will not meet most of the MDGs. Among the remaining challenges, the report identifies high levels of poverty, especially in rural areas and among women. Although poverty is declining slowly at the continental level, unemployment is still a difficult problem to tackle. In fact, according to World Bank data, the percentage of the population in Africa living on less than US$1.25

a day at 2005 international prices has decreased, from 56.5 per cent in 1990 to 48.5 per cent in 2010 (see http://data.worldbank.org/). Nevertheless, total unemployment in Sub-Saharan Africa remains generally stable with minimal changes (from 7.5 to 7.9 per cent) from 2004 to 2012. Another set of challenges, linked to persistent poverty and high unemployment, is the environmental concern: the declining forest cover has been especially alarming in Africa. In Sub-Saharan Africa, the forest cover has been progressively decreasing over the last decade, with the situation quickly worsening since 2010: from 2010 to 2011, for instance, the forest cover has decreased from 28.2 to 27.4 per cent (see http://data.worldbank.org/).

To help solve these crucial problems, the report focuses on the need for African governments to make fundamental policy and institutional innovations: regional integration is mentioned as a key process (especially to promote and expand trade and investment), but the national level remains central. The report also highlights key investments in terms of capacity building (AUC et al, 2012, p 141). This emphasis placed on individual and institutional capacity building is certainly remarkable, because it is indicative of a shift from a *what* (goals) to a *how* (processes) approach. Concentrating on dynamics also involves giving a peculiar amount of additional attention, beyond national frameworks, to action and the evaluation of results. In fact, the consideration of indigenous voices and homegrown solutions to local problems is fundamental to the post-MDGs agenda (Ezeanya, 2013). This awareness also explains the United Nations' (UN) ongoing efforts to generate grassroots involvement in the post-2015 process, to increase the number and diversity of stakeholders, and to open up online consultations to every person willing to give his/her opinion. This global initiative, called 'The world we want 2015', uses the website created for this purpose (www.worldwewant2015.org/) for wide thematic and national consultations as well as dialogues on implementation processes for the post-2015 agenda. The website is not only a useful tool to encourage participation in discussions and conversations on sustainable development for the post-2015 era, but it can also be used to visualise the results obtained thus far, and to find out more about upcoming events and key dates.

The local scale does not challenge the importance of internationally or globally agreed-on goals, but rather wants to increase their performance and their ability to effectively tackle real problems. To this extent, many actors and sources have emphasised that the regional level is as crucial as the local. Goals should be adjusted region by region to tackle specific challenges. In fact, the focus on the processes and

253

factors driving these problems recognises that some important drivers (such as migrations and cross-border trade) are regional.

> Global governance deficits and failure to implement international legal frameworks have spurred countries to seek regional solutions, including regional trade agreements, regional mechanisms of financial cooperation and informal arrangements to approach regional issues of migration. These arrangements are important in responding to region-specific development needs, but they require coordination to avoid policy fragmentation and incoherence with multilateral regimes and international standards. (UNTT, 2012, pp 18-19)

The MDG Africa Steering Group,[4] created in September 2007, demonstrates once more this emphasis on continental and regional specialised approaches. The regional focus is clearly motivating the recommendations that the Group has published since 2008: 'In many areas improved regional collaboration and integration will need to complement national-level actions to reap economies of scale and address challenges that are too big for any individual country to take on by itself, such as investments in regional power pools and trade facilitation' (UN Department of Public Information, 2008, p 5).

The MDG 2014 report for Africa (UNECA, 2014) and the CAP (AU, 2014a) show that in recent years the regional level has become increasingly central in Africa. Even if the MDGs were not created for meeting regional targets, they are also monitored nowadays at the regional level (UNECA, 2014, p 1). In light of this recent increased interest in the regional level in the African context, this chapter explores, through the regional economic communities (RECs), sectoral arrangements and the results obtained, such as heightened interest and identified recommendations and strategies to improve the current status, especially in terms of capacity building at the regional level. To better portray the current status, it is necessary to briefly revisit the history of formal regional strategies in Africa, and to evaluate their alignment with actual ongoing processes.

Regional processes in Africa: the macro-regional and continental level

The history of official regional integration in Africa has its roots in the pan-Africanist ideology, the idea of a united Africa, which is, in fact, the predecessor for the inspiring idea of regional integration at the continental level and of Agenda 2063 for Africa (AUC, 2014). This explains why the creation of RECs in Africa has been accompanied from the start by the establishment of continental institutions, setting a common framework, organising and coordinating RECs. There are, then, two main and parallel levels of institutions, the continental and the macro-regional, each struggling to complement the other's actions. At the continental scale, official agreements and formal initiatives towards African regional integration, cooperation or coordination are numerous, having increased since the beginning of the new millennium following the Sirte Declaration (see Table 9.1). The Abuja Treaty certainly marked a turning point with the precision of common goals at the continental level (the establishment of the African Economic Community, a common currency, full mobility of the factors of production and free movement of goods and services among African countries) and the establishment of a six-phase calendar whereby 2028 is proposed as the final horizon to complete the process.[5]

This ideology of African unity has been institutionalised by the OAU, later transformed into the AU. In the age of globalisation, the struggle for African unity meets the fight for sustainable development in Agenda 2063, and NEPAD can be seen as the economic contextual tool for regional integration in Africa at the continental level. The APRM, by ensuring accountability, wants to enhance governance and political leadership, and is also part of this regional strategy at the continental level (Adogamhe, 2008).

'The OAU had a limited mandate that was primarily of a political nature ... to achieve the unity and consolidate the political freedom' (Makhan, 2009, p 8). The AU followed this path and emphasised in its Constitutive Act its geopolitical scope, aimed at restoring peace and stability, and preventing genocides, war crimes and crimes against humanity. It is nevertheless a wider vision: 'The AU encapsulates the vision of African leaders for a united, strong, and prosperous Africa that

Table 9.1: Some major steps involved in official integration in Africa

1963	Establishment of the Organization of African Unity (OAU)
1991	Abuja Treaty, establishing the African Economic Community
1999	Sirte Declaration, establishing the African Union (AU)
2001	New Partnership for Africa's Development (NEPAD) and AU Constitutive Act
2003	African Peer Review Mechanism (APRM)
2004	Pan-African Parliament
2007	NEPAD's integration in the AU Commission

takes its rightful place in global economy and polity.... Its approach to Africa's integration and development is holistic, incorporating economic, social and political dimensions' (Makhan, 2009, p 9).

In the Abuja Treaty and in Agenda 2063 (AU, 2014b), RECs serve as building blocs: at least until the fourth phase (ending with the creation of the African Economic Community), which is supposed to finish in 2019. Regional processes of coordination and harmonisation are encouraged in every REC. There are several reasons underpinning the idea of building blocs for Africa's integration, identifying the RECs as the appropriate frameworks for such action. The common colonial legacy, the history of cooperation among countries, and the substantial cost savings between countries adjacent to one another, which shorten the distance for physical and infrastructural linkages, are among the most important reasons. Most RECs were created in the 1980s and 1990s (see Table 9.2), when the continental process was on its way forward.

The AU recognises eight RECs in Africa, all of varying design, scope, objectives and history. These are expected to evolve into free trade areas, a Customs Union and, through horizontal coordination and harmonisation, the African Common Market at the continental level. Nevertheless, RECs are confronted with some limits, slowing down or handicapping their functioning and the entire process. The major problem is certainly overlapping (see Table 9.3): 44 African countries have joined and are part of two, three or even four RECs!

If countries' multiple memberships pose a clear problem for every REC, they also explain the fragmentation of the process and the lack of coordination between the RECs. In fact, besides the free trade areas, the RECs have different goals and priorities, express different current situations, and witness different stages of integration. Some have clear priority areas and they have set their specific goals linked to their development strategies. Others have a generic objective of economic

Table 9.2: Regional economic communities recognised by the African Union and their date of establishment

CEN-SAD (Community of Sahel-Saharan States)	1998
COMESA (Common Market for Eastern and Southern Africa)	1981
EAC (Eastern African Community)	1999
ECCAS (Economic Community of Central African States)	1964
ECOWAS (Economic Community of West African States)	1975
IGAD (Intergovernmental Authority on Development)	1986
SADC (Southern African Development Community)	1992
UMA (Arab Maghreb Union)	1989

Table 9.3: Countries overlapping in regional economic communities

Comoros, Egypt	CEN-SAD, COMESA
Djibouti, Eritrea, Sudan	CEN-SAD, COMESA, IGAD
Benin, Burkina Faso, Cape Verde, Côte d'Ivoire, Gambia, Ghana, Guinea Bissau, Guinea, Liberia, Mali, Niger, Nigeria, Senegal, Sierra Leone, Togo	CEN-SAD, ECOWAS
Kenya	CEN-SAD, COMESA, EAC, IGAD
Central African Republic, Chad, Sao Tomé and Principe	CEN-SAD, ECCAS
Libya	CEN-SAD, COMESA, UMA
Mauritania, Morocco, Tunisia	CEN-SAD, UMA
Somalia	CEN-SAD, IGAD
Burundi	CEN-SAD, COMESA, EAC, ECCAS
Democratic Republic of Congo (DRC)	COMESA, ECCAS, SADC
Ethiopia, Sudan	COMESA, IGAD
Madagascar, Malawi, Mauritius, Seychelles, Swaziland, Zambia, Zimbabwe	COMESA, SADC
Rwanda	COMESA, EAC
Uganda	COMESA, EAC, IGAD
Tanzania	EAC, SADC
Angola	ECCAS, SADC

integration (see Table 9.4). Given this situation at the macro-regional level, it seems difficult to imagine coordination of this scale at the continental level.

The two levels, the continental and the macro-regional, are nevertheless coordinated through the Minimum Integration Programme (MIP). This aims at deepening Africa's integration beyond the single REC's horizon. The meeting of chief executives of the RECs, which took place in Addis Ababa on 12-13 January 2009, mandated the AUC to formulate the MIP, after previous consultations with the RECs, and to define a precise calendar of implementation. The MIP is a mechanism of convergence, based on priority areas to be implemented at the regional level (by every REC) and at the continental level (by the AU/NEPAD African Action Plan 2010-15). Encouraging inter-RECs projects and programmes in key areas, commonly agreed and shared priorities, the MIP implements the Abuja Treaty and is a dynamic strategic framework for the continental integration processes.

The following priority areas have been selected by the RECs: free movement of people, goods, services and capital; peace and security; infrastructure and energy; and agriculture. To these, four additional priorities have been added: trade; industry; investment; and statistics

Table 9.4: Progress of regional processes: Sub-Saharan regional economic communities

---

CEN-SAD is working to build its free trade area.

COMESA has established and is implementing its free trade area since 2009. The common external tariff has been agreed in principle, but it is not yet decided when it will enter into force It has made good progress in creating a Customs Union. The focal areas of integration include trade in goods and services; monetary-integration payments and settlement arrangements; investment promotion and facilitation; and infrastructure development – air, road, rail, maritime and inland transport, information and communications technology (ICT) and energy.

EAC has operationalised its Customs Union and has launched its free trade area. A common market and a monetary union are still under construction. Priority sectors include infrastructure, telecommunications, and energy.

ECCAS has launched its free trade area, but this is not yet fully implemented (and it has not launched the Customs Union).

ECOWAS has launched a free trade area. The monetary union is in progress and the Customs Union is operational (the common external tariff, that is, the key step for a Customs Union, has been operational since January 2015).

IGAD identified three priority areas: food security and environmental protection; conflict prevention, management and resolution; and economic cooperation and integration. It aims to have its own free trade area.

SADC has a free trade area since 2011; implementation of a Customs Union has been delayed. Infrastructure and services are key priority areas, especially energy.

Sources: UNECA, 2012, 2013a; ACBF, 2014 (information prepared by UNECA for the 2015 Conference of Ministers has been added)

(AUC, 2010, p 6). Special attention has been paid to funding the MIP: an African Integration Fund (AIF) specifically devoted to this purpose has been proposed by African Heads of States and governments. An additional constraint that has hindered or slowed the implementation of MIP is lack of effective coordination or compatibility between policies at the national, regional and continental level. The AUC has to effectively strike the needed balance and the AU/NEPAD African Action Plan[6] is an important tool to this extent. After the end of 2015, implementation of Agenda 2063 should take over this process of harmonisation between the different levels (AU, 2014b).

Coordination between the continental and macro-regional levels of integration is also happening through collaborations between different RECs, such as the COMESA-EAC-SADC tripartite agreement. The tripartite cooperation between the three RECs, inspiring the vision and strategy endorsed by the second tripartite summit held in June 2011 in Johannesburg, contains three main pillars: market integration; infrastructure development; and industrial development. The AU/NEPAD African Action Plan and Agenda 2063 share these priorities, facilitating common action. The free trade area is considered to be the first tool for facilitating trade and the free movement of people, goods and business opportunities. A programme on climate change and adaptation and mitigation in Eastern and Southern Africa regions is also included in the tripartite cooperation. This programme, launched in Durban in December 2011, addresses the impacts of climate change, increasing the socioeconomic resilience of communities through climate-smart agriculture. It is intended to promote efficient local agricultural practices and to strengthen linkages between agriculture, forestry and other land uses. It is funded through a multi-donor financial commitment equivalent to US$90 million from the Government of Norway, the European Union Commission and the Government of the UK and Northern Ireland over a five-year period.

Sector-specific integration: a focus on infrastructure, agriculture and industrial development

The difficulties previously mentioned pertaining to the conciliation of the various continental and macro-regional integration initiatives, together with the priority given to different specific sectors by the various initiatives, illustrates in the end that some sectors are widely recognised as high priority sectors for regional processes by different stakeholders, and are already areas in which regional processes are taking place. These sectors and domains of action include agriculture (comprehending climate change adaptation), infrastructure (especially physical transport networks) and industry. Furthermore, the limits of regional processes that are generally mentioned (GTZ, 2009, pp 12-14; AUC et al, 2012, p 2) are often referred to as extensive economic processes of integration. These limitations are certainly more important for broad economic processes than for specific actions. They include country membership to several RECs; lack of political will; shortage of financial and human resources; non-application of the protocols on economic integration; inability to incorporate integration objectives, plans and programmes in national development frameworks; inadequate coordination among RECs and with continental stakeholders; divergent national macroeconomic policies; lack of national mechanisms to coordinate, implement and monitor integration; and limited private sector involvement. Some sector-specific regional initiatives are analysed below, focusing on agriculture, physical infrastructure and industrial development. Their mechanisms, results and effectiveness are underlined to assert that current sector-specific actions of integration could inspire other types of actions in other areas.

Agriculture: a crucial economic and social sector for Africa's development

In their assessment of regional integration in Africa prepared for the sixth AU/UNECA Joint Annual Meetings, held in Abidjan on 21-26 March 2013, the UNECA, the UN Economic and Social Council (ECOSOC) and the AUC present the progress and present status of regional integration related to agriculture and food security (UNECA, 2013b, p 7). The document reports the different SADC initiatives to develop a Regional Indicative Strategic Development Plan (RISDP) on food security and natural resources. The major thrust of the RISDP is, in fact, poverty alleviation through regional integration, with food security as a priority. To improve food security in the region, in 2001 the SADC launched the SADC Seed Security Network (SSSN), willing to increase farmers' access to quality seeds, through the promotion of regulated and collaborative regional seed trade. The SSSN also supports policy harmonisation on agricultural inputs, including improved seeds.

The EAC has taken several initiatives to facilitate and accelerate the development of the agricultural sector. It has developed and approved a Food Security Action Plan for 2011-15, including a detailed action plan aimed at increasing agricultural productivity in the region through improved and appropriate technologies adaptive to climate change and an optimised use of water. Among other goals, it also aims to increase intra-regional food trade and to diversify food production at the regional scale.

The ECCAS is implementing a regional programme on food security and a common agricultural strategy. The overall objective of this strategy is the sustainable development of the agricultural sector by increasing incomes and reducing food insecurity and poverty. To augment the agricultural production in a sustainable way is thus a priority, as well as the sustainable management of natural resources and the reduction of risks and vulnerability. The ECCAS Common Agricultural Policy was adopted in 2003.

The ECOWAS Agricultural Policy (ECOWAP), adopted in 2005, is the most advanced African regional agricultural policy. It is currently implemented to harmonise agricultural policies and to place agriculture at the heart of the development agenda. The major themes are: to increase the productivity and competitiveness of West-African agriculture; to obtain a decent remuneration for those involved in the agricultural sector; and to expand trade on a sustainable basis, both within the region and with the rest of the world. Numerous initiatives have been undertaken in the ECOWAP context, especially putting in place regulatory frameworks for seeds, pesticides, agricultural biotechnologies and biosafety at the regional level; implementing regional thematic programmes on irrigation; adaptation to climate change; and forest resources. ECOWAP is a strategic initiative that will deserve attention in the coming years to follow up on progress, and it will be an inspiring procedure for other African RECs.

Each REC also establishes its own priorities related to the Comprehensive Africa Agriculture Development Programme (CAADP). The CAADP, an African initiative working to boost agricultural productivity in Africa and led by NEPAD, has, in fact, three main levels. The four pillars (land and water management; market access; food supply and hunger; and agricultural research) are part of the continental agreement and engagement, but RECs implement the programme at regional level establishing their own priorities, and national round tables promote growth in the agricultural sector and economic development at country level. If all the RECs are working at various levels towards the CAADP round table processes commenced in 2008, the most notable progress at the regional level has been achieved by COMESA and ECOWAS. COMESA has coordinated regional implementation of the CAADP framework, ensuring policy efficiency as well as monitoring and evaluation of progress and performance. COMESA has also built CAADP partnerships with development partners, researchers, the private sector, farmers and civil society, with the CAADP Multi-Donor Trust Fund created in 2012.[7] The COMESA CAADP Unit is enhancing cooperation in this domain with EAC and SADC in the tripartite context. Since 2006, a regional action plan for the implementation of ECOWAP and CAADP/NEPAD has guaranteed joint implementation. This implementation follows five priority areas: improved management of natural resources; sustainable agricultural development at the farm level; developing agricultural supply chains and promoting markets; preventing and managing food crises and natural disasters; and institution and capacity building in the formulation of agricultural and rural policies and strategies. An ECOWAP/CAADP Donor Working Group is promoting alignment and harmonisation of development partners' support for the ECOWAS region. To address the capacity constraints of the ECOWAS Department of Agriculture and Rural Development, and to facilitate implementation of the ECOWAP/ CAADP, a Regional Agency for Food and Agriculture (RAFA) and a Regional Fund for Agriculture and Food (ECOWADP) were launched in Lomé, Togo on 27 September 2013.

The SADC is harmonising the CAADP with the Regional Agricultural Policy developed in 2008, and is preparing a regional CAADP investment plan, to be presented to the Ministers of Agriculture and Food Security in 2014. ECCAS is setting up a CAADP Development Partners Coordination Group, and is consulting non-state actors to collect their views on the regional policy and investment plan. IGAD is holding similar consultations, and it is developing the CAADP; in 2011 it also set in place the IGAD Drought Disaster Resilience and Sustainability Initiative platform, including member states, development partners, UN agencies and civil society. Through country and regional programming papers, it provides strategic direction and operational frameworks for resilience-enhancing policies and investments, with an emphasis on building the needed capacities at national and regional levels. In 2011, the EAC Secretariat began the regional CAADP process. In August 2012, the EAC Council of Ministers approved a roadmap, including an ambitious timeline (Rampa and van Seters, 2013). National compacts have been signed by EAC member states; the regional compact and investment plan was drafted and reviewed in September 2013, during a meeting in Bujumbura, Burundi, willing to ensure its alignment with existing regional policies (such as the EAC Food Security Action Plan). It was expected that the EAC CAADP compact and investment plans would have been signed in 2014 (Vervaeke, 2013), but process was ongoing by time of going to press.

To encourage Pillar 4 of the CAADP at the continental, regional and national levels through effective research, extension, training and education, The World Bank Africa Regional Integration Programme Active Portfolio finances the Forum for Agricultural Research in Africa Multi-Donor Trust Fund. Its objective is to create an integral agricultural innovation system, along with improved intra-African trade and marketing. The Fund also advocates, catalyses and facilitates strategic reforms and processes, strengthening capacities for agricultural innovation. The pro-agricultural development advocacy wants to convince governments to invest more in agriculture, as strong agricultural innovation systems are key for economic development.

The World Bank also finances a similar project in Eastern and Central Africa (Association for Strengthening Agricultural Research in Eastern and Central Africa Trust Fund, the total project cost being US$50 million). The World Bank regional integration programme, focused on agriculture and fisheries, prioritises programmes related to agricultural productivity in Western and Central Africa (six projects) and West Africa regional fisheries (four projects). For The World Bank, the regional focus is on agricultural research, the establishment of regional centres of excellence, technologies and common regional regulations for genetic materials and pesticides.

The challenge of coordinating these initiatives among them and at different levels confirms the importance of developing regional agricultural value chains, including cooperatives and other peasant organisations as well as agri-businesses ventures: public–private partnerships in agricultural value chains, called agricultural co-entrepreneurship, also guarantee better participation of the various stakeholders. Agriculture is, in fact, a key sector for development, a cross-cutting domain (linked to trade, infrastructure, etc) involving numerous stakeholders.

Infrastructure: a key domain for Africa's development for which the regional level is strategic

Major deficits in transport infrastructure hold back Africa's structural transformation and integration. Transport connections need to be increased (they are often insufficient, damaged by conflicts and natural disasters), but funding is also needed for the basic maintenance of already existing roads as well as the paving of unpaved route networks. If every country is in charge of its national road network, most of the routes and multimodal corridors have to be planned and realised at the regional or at continental scale. Important investments are then needed, but their economic benefits will be greater than the expenses. The World Bank estimates that a 15-year investment project costing US$32 billion in upgrading and maintaining Africa's road network would lead to a US$250 billion dollar increase in trade over the same period, with the biggest gains accruing to the most isolated areas (Deichmann, 2006). Alternatively, the cost of poor roads, in terms of competitiveness, has compelled different stakeholders to invest in African infrastructure. Poor regional roads in particular handicap landlocked countries, as they face more important challenges in getting merchandise into and out of their territories. Conversely, improved road networks have an important impact on trade facilitation: World Bank research (Deichmann, 2006) estimates the benefits if the roads connecting Bangui in the Central African Republic to Kisangani in the Democratic Republic of Congo were improved to a quality level. According to the study, trade volume on this route would expand from the current value of US$15.9 million to US$142 million, with a 793 per cent increase. (Railway networks, ports, maritime and river routes, and air transport are not discussed in this chapter, which refers only to road networks as crucial and exemplar infrastructures.)

Despite the unfavourable conditions, macro-regional and continental projects and investments are driving improvements. 'As a result of this increased rate of investment, the average proportion of paved roads across Africa increased from 35% to 47% between 2005 and 2011. The proportion in low-income countries is significantly less, but still increased from 14% to 17%' (AfDB, 2012, p 16). Numerous initiatives can be reported as recently completed or ongoing, including diverse stakeholders. Besides private investments and public–private partnerships, some major projects have to be mentioned here.

The Euro/African Infrastructure Partnership, as part of the Africa/ European Union (EU) Partnership on Trade, Regional Integration and Infrastructure, explicitly recognises that infrastructure is vital for regional integration. The partnership is also endowed with a EU/ Africa Infrastructure Trust Fund, launched in 2007, that encourages the financing of infrastructure programmes through long-term loans.

NEPAD supports long- and short-term initiatives, among which the Infrastructure Consortium for Africa (ICA) has to be mentioned. This is a platform catalysing donor and private sector financing of infrastructure in Africa. It also works by helping to remove technical and policy challenges and barriers for infrastructure development, and to better coordinate infrastructure finance, including from significant sources of funding, such as China, India and the Arab countries.

Since 2012, the AUC has been involved with the AfDB, NEPAD and the RECs in the Programme for Infrastructure Development in Africa (PIDA), launched in July 2010 in Kampala. PIDA's priorities in the transport sector include the Dobi–Galafi–Yakobi road section of the Djibouti to Addis Ababa (North) Highway; the Mombasa– Nairobi–Addis Ababa Corridor Development Project; the missing links of the Djibouti–Libreville transport corridor; and the missing links of the Dakar–N'djamena–Djibouti Highway Corridor. As PIDA has been estimated by AfDB to cost more than $360 billion by 2040, mobilising funds for its implementation is an ongoing challenge.

Among the 10 World Bank Africa Regional Integration Programmes devoted to trade and transport facilitation, only four pertain to rehabilitation or construction of critical road infrastructure segments, one in the CEMAC, two in West Africa for the Abidjan–

Lagos transport, and the Tema–Ouagadougou–Bamako corridor. Accordingly, road improvement is not a high priority in The World Bank regional integration portfolio. Issues of security and safety, border posts and customs modernisation and harmonisation are included in a larger number of programmes, because they are considered to be an indispensable guarantee of improved trade transactions, crucial within The World Bank vision of regional integration.

RECs are also undertaking road investments and projects. The CEN-SAD Infrastructure Development Plan includes transport projects as part of the strategy to reduce poverty. COMESA is, for example, focusing on the country level, setting up road funds and road development agencies in the different countries in order to maintain both the regional and national road networks. Even the construction and rehabilitation of roads are funded by government budget allocations. ECOWAS is also acting at national level, including private sector stakeholders in the national road transport and transit facilitation committees. IGAD deals with road projects at the bilateral level, but mobilises funds from the AfDB and the EU for a number of projects, mainly focused on facilitation and advocacy for member states in regional priorities. Also, EAC includes some road development projects among its strategic priorities, requiring rehabilitation and upgrading. ECCAS is making progress implementing its blueprint on transport in Central Africa. The SADC Corridor Development Strategy is a testament to the REC's commitment to regional infrastructure development. It is confirmed by the SADC Regional Infrastructure Master Plan, which outlines the different steps to follow. The North-South Corridor Initiative is a good example of collaboration between RECs: it has been approved by COMESA, SADC and EAC. It is expected to build an integrated multimodal corridor across eight countries, facilitating trade and benefiting landlocked countries in particular.

Further efforts to improve infrastructure on the continent should be expected from the private sector, which has played only a modest role thus far relative to its potential. 'Yet infrastructure projects in Africa have been slow largely owing to low private sector investment: at about 15 per cent of GDP, it is estimated at about half Asia's rate' (UNECA, 2012, p 97). To fill this gap, The World Bank encourages public–private partnerships for investments in infrastructure, especially in the SADC region, where a network of public–private practitioners for the SADC has been created and is supposed to accelerate infrastructure development. Other financing options, such as private equity funds, bond markets, diaspora bonds, and the use of sovereign-backed pension funds need to be developed in greater number and more creatively to finance regional infrastructure in Africa.

The example of road projects and programmes is representative of what happens with other types of infrastructure in Africa. It shows that different stakeholders at the macro-regional and continental level need to be involved and collaborate. In fact, infrastructure is recognised as a crucial domain for Africa's structural transformation.

Industrial development: a sector dependent on infrastructure and at the core of regional integration

Considering the limits and difficulties of national industrialisation in so many countries, regional industrialisation is a path to follow in Africa, especially if it goes through policy initiatives. The Action Plan for the Accelerated Industrial Development of Africa, endorsed in 2008 by African states, recommends industrial development to target the value addition of natural resources, and the revenue from these resources to be invested in industrialisation. The AU, the UN Industrial Development Organization (UNIDO), the UNECA, The World Bank and the RECs are all in charge of its implementation. This fundamental document for regional industrial policies recognises the links between industrialisation and natural resources as well as the need to increase FDI to foster local industrialisation. Specialised and technical knowledge and R&D (research and development), together with effective infrastructure and an increased role for the private sector, are at the heart of this plan. Priority sectors are resource-processing industries, such as agro-food, minerals, textile and garments, leather and forestry. The plan includes the AU's Vision Paper on African Industrial Development and the UNIDO-assisted African Productive Capacity Initiative. AU/NEPAD strategic objectives in industry included in the plan emphasise as a first objective 'building productive capacity and capabilities for converting comparative advantage into industrial competitiveness.... Developing small and medium-size enterprises and their linkages to large-scale enterprises for seizing opportunities for industrial expansion.... Fostering public-private partnerships for industrial development' (NEPAD, 2011, p 42). The plan focuses on creating an enabling environment and institutional frameworks promoting private sector-sensitive industrial development, regional economic cooperation and international competitiveness. This is only possible by enhancing supply-side and demand-side capacities for industrial production and trade, which is the aim of the plan.

Compared to what happens in Africa for infrastructure development, regional industrialisation is limited more to policy initiatives, and real industrial development is thus left subject to decisions made at national level. The macro-regional and continental levels are used to set frameworks and to help establish partnerships and collaborations among stakeholders. Regional industrialisation is progressively growing in Africa, but the sector is far from being fully developed. Public–private investment and collaboration (at national and regional level) are, in fact, critical for industrial development: the financial and/or regulatory support given to businesses has to produce 'policy goals' (the results that the policies in the domain target), such as export and/or increased investment. Effective state–business relations are key, as they promote entrepreneurship, enhance government capacities and increase linkages within the domestic economy. In a complementary way, regional integration is critical, as it is the condition needed for robust regional markets (including financial markets) and for reducing the regulatory burden facing African businesses, with the adoption of an appropriate regional exchange rate, monetary and fiscal policies.

Regional integration: from theory to practice in Africa

Although many actors and strategies are involved (or claim to be) in regional integration processes in Africa, regional integration is just beginning, and several limitations and problems continue to slow it down at both macro-regional and continental levels. Certainly, besides the discourse and the acknowledged attention of the widely recognised centrality and strategic role of regional integration for development purposes in Africa, its implementation is time-consuming and problematic. There seems to be a gap between the theory of regional integration and its application to the African continent. If there is a relatively long and continuous history of regional integration in Europe, which is part of the history of the European Economic Community first, and then more recently of the EU, the same cannot be said for Africa. Regional integration in Africa has been affected by Western Eurocentric views and conceptions and attempts to reproduce in Africa what works (not without difficulties) in Europe.

Nevertheless, there is a marked discrepancy between the European and African contexts. In Africa, regional integration has been linked to structural transformation, integrated in the development agenda and part of the broader challenge to improve economic and social conditions for societies and individuals. Europe, for historical reasons, was informed more by the ambition of improving trade conditions and competitiveness, and widening the circulation of goods and people. There is also a second discrepancy in Africa between theory and practice. Even if the various theories linking regional integration to development in Africa acknowledge that this process is not limited to market and trade, as the phenomenon includes very crucial social and political dimensions, in reality, the history of regional integration, through the different agreements and the Abuja Treaty, shows that there is an almost exclusive attention to trade, with the establishment of free trade areas, common markets, customs unions and economic unions at both the REC level and the continental level over the long term (Bourenane, 2002).

> Regional integration in sub-Saharan Africa has been rationalised and pursued within the context of three principal theories, each closely allied to a development theory paradigm. First, it will be argued that modernist conceptions of development promote a market integration approach to regional integration, based on the liberalisation of intra-regional trade designed to abolish discrimination between contracting parties. Second, dependency-led thinking has in the past promoted developmental co-operation and integration, incorporating import-substitution programmes and protectionism.... Finally, the neoliberal Washington Consensus of the past 20 years has prioritised open regionalism, a variant of the market integration approach, as a mechanism to enhance multilateral liberalisation and promote integration in the world economy. (Gibbs, 2009, pp 705-6)

This is evident throughout the historical process, going back to the 1980s, when the link between regionalism and development was progressively established, as Richard Gibbs reiterates (Gibbs, 2009). It is also confirmed by very recent sources, which assess regional integration or propose policy recommendations for the future. Despite some variations, the following examples, taken from an AfDB report, a UNDP programmatic document and a UNECA assessment, follow the same direction. The quotes highlight this focus on markets as drivers of finance as well as many other processes.

> The regional integration agenda incorporates a range of objectives. It is about giving African producers access to regional markets and integrating them into more

productive regional value chains. It includes integrating financial markets, to enable capital to flow more readily among national economies. It also includes promoting the free movement of labour, for more efficient regional labour markets and for improved access to skilled labour for specialist production. (AfDB, 2012, p 3)

The UNDP makes explicit integration an economic process liberalising trade, even if human development and social data are mentioned as strategic.

Regional economic integration is much broader than efforts simply to liberalize trade. It can also include investments in regional infrastructure, harmonization of regulations and standards, common approaches to macroeconomic policy, management of shared natural resources, and greater labour mobility. Human development is about creating the conditions that allow men, women and children to live lives they value by expanding their freedoms and building their capabilities. (UNDP, 2011, p 3)

In the UNECA report, the implicit assumption is that, given that the main actors are RECs, regional integration is an economic process, achieving other results through the MIP.

Deepening Africa's integration goes beyond harmonising RECs memberships and policies. Indeed, the African countries have agreed on a Minimum Integration Programme (MIP). The MIP comprises those activities, projects and programmes that the RECs have selected to accelerate and bring to completion as part of the regional and continental integration process. As a mechanism for convergence of RECs, it focuses on a few priority areas of regional and continental concern, where RECs could strengthen their cooperation and benefit from best integration practices. (UNECA, 2012, p 1)

This attempt to achieve regional integration in Africa through wide and multipurpose economic processes, based on economic policies, with the hope that they could drive processes accordingly, has shown its limits. Even if these are very tangible and crucial procedures that have proven to be successful elsewhere, especially in Europe, where the history is different and where the intersection with development strategies was non-existent (or very different from the African situation, because the entity of the problem is certainly not the same), these have proved not to be effective in African contexts. Considering the fragmentation of the African continent, the historical background and the gravity of development issues, even within the post-MDGs framework (as detailed later), this chapter contends that regional integration in these contexts works better when it is a *sector-specific process*, based on unique, practical, focused issues, that target a precise result in terms of social and economic development. Through programmes and projects interested in agriculture or industrial development or even livestock, fishing, trans-boundary protected areas, natural resource management, etc, regional integration is more likely to be successful and effective in Africa. Accordingly, it becomes an issue that people, social groups and stakeholders can advocate and endorse. It can later meet higher standards of more inclusive market and economic integration, but it should start with focused and sector-specific issues. Some specific guidelines for this kind of approach have to be provided.

The first question is *the scale* of these regional processes. Previous and contemporary regional integration projects and programmes have been based on a fixed scale: the level of the RECs or the AU/NEPAD. This means that, once an agreement is passed, all the states included in the institution find themselves on board to implement the regional policy. Of course, with the precise interests, the situation and the goals differing among even African neighbouring states, the regional integration process is, in the end, slowed down. In fact, their economic conditions and their political systems and leadership vary greatly: a free trade area or a customs union is viewed with a different eye by a less developed country than by a middle-income country, or by a country endowed with commodities versus another without such resources, or by countries with discrepant currencies. Additionally, heads of states and, more generally, African governments tend to be reluctant to accept wide and general regional integration procedures (Makhan, 2009) because they are concerned about being forced to renounce a large part of their sovereignty, the supranational power superseding and neutralising the national. Sector-specific measures could then have an ad hoc size, the one given by the countries interested and concerned by a precise question and measure (for example, seed regulation for agriculture, fishing market and rules, agribusiness development, etc). Sector-specific initiatives would certainly be more difficult to manage compared to previous regional settings, but the ownership and involvement of states, often considered too limited and passive in regular integration procedures, would have a greater chance of being guaranteed by this type of action. These types of programmes would represent *regionalism* rather than real comprehensive *regional integration*, although regionalism could be the first step toward the attainment of wider economic and commercial regional integration. In fact, isn't the EU the latter step of the first European Coal and Steel Community?

Second, stakeholders' *involvement and ownership* are crucial, representing all stakeholders involved in the procedures. With sector-specific programmes, involvement and ownership could be encouraged, especially for the private sector actors that play such a strategic role in any successful regional integration. This is also true for civil society organisations, considering the role that they can and want to have in pushing *alternative regionalisms*, such as the 'People's Agenda for Alternative Regionalism' (Icaza, 2009), taking place not only in Africa, but also in Latin America and Asia.[8] The special issue of the journal *Global Social Policy* published in 2007 and entirely dedicated to alternative regional strategies further confirms this trend. The philosophy and ideology inspiring alternative regionalism is that regional experiences can be promoted by people's strategies and the priority to choose sectors and actions. It is thus a sector-specific approach aimed at broadening the base among key social actors for political debate and action. Frontline stakeholders for this approach include civil society organisations, grassroots organisations and priorities that have, until now, included agro-ecologic farming, infrastructure development and people's access to clean water, education, health services, food and energy. Following Dot Keet (2007), one could also add environmental crises (such as natural disasters), economic and political crises (engendering population migrations) and resource management. Keet emphasises the need for a combination of cooperation, coordination and harmonisation in specific sectoral and issue-based coalitions to advance integration. In Africa, this framework has already been applied in Southern Africa, and SADC has been the natural context for this attempt. Although this is a limitation, it proves that there is room for these experiences that focus on people's needs and demands, and that civil society organisations are crucial both upstream and downstream in advocating and leading groups. This type of action also positions the state at the centre of the process, in line with many regional integration theories, as a fundamental precondition for any successful regional experience. In fact, many sources recognise that regional integration has to be based on state policies oriented towards and inclined to regional integration. This is, of course, the case for alternative regionalisms, because core social issues are more likely to inspire national legislation that answers to a strong social demand rather than regional regulations.

Third, a regional approach such as the one previously outlined would also help to resolve *the discrepancy between formal and informal integration*, often seen as problematic. This is especially the case for informal markets, difficult to quantify but easily reported at the borders between two or three African countries. NGOs have tried to quantify this phenomenon and to track it, but, aside from the difficulties associated with tracking quantities and products that are traded informally, this market is certainly important and sensitive. It includes networks of people, and it is so often intertwined with formal commerce that it is sometimes difficult to separate them. Regional sector-specific procedures do not need to isolate formal and informal dynamics, but can push, prioritise and address issues without their division between formal and informal. This can also be the case for migration as well as natural resource management.

Last, one of the most sensitive questions, common to regional integration and regionalisation, is the issue of *finding the necessary financial resources* to lead these processes. Even if one could imagine that sectoral programmes are less expensive than wide economic processes, certainly expenses are also required for sector-specific projects in a manner proportionate to their ambition. This chapter contends that the needed funding could be derived from already existing tools, frameworks and agreements (the AU/NEPAD African Action Plan and the AU MIP). The post-MDGs agenda is another possible larger framework under which sector-specific regionalisation could be included and funded. The work, the conclusions and the public external financing mentioned by the MDG Africa Steering Group (UN Department of Public Information, 2008, p 32) could be inspiring to this extent. Public–private partnerships, private equity, aid for trade and domestic resource mobilisation are among the creative strategies that will be used and improved for regional initiatives. Macro-regional and continental initiatives have also been given a more central role in the post-2015 sustainable development agenda, compared to the MDG framework: they will be monitored and supported, as well as through Agenda 2063.

Building capacities for regional processes in Africa

Despite the commitment of and action taken by many stakeholders towards regional processes in Africa, progress is slow, partial and disappointing, especially for economic regional integration. As a result, regional integration is often seen as an abstract dynamic, far from the everyday concerns of the large majority of Africans and, as frustration increases, regional integration, although at the centre of rhetoric, publication and debate, remains a distant goal. This situation is mainly linked to the lack of individual and institutional capacities that makes regional processes difficult. This chapter contends that different kinds of capacities need to be built and enhanced, and that many diverse stakeholders need to increase their capacity level to facilitate successful results. Here are some of the most important types of capacities that have to be built:

- *Capacities for advocacy and participation:* a real successful regionalism cannot be only an economic and policy issue. Societies at every level, social groups (including associations, businesses, workers unions and grassroots organisations) and individuals have to be part of it, to help identify the priorities, and to decide how they are going to be handled. Regionalism also has to be advertised, and mobilisation has to be catalysed at all levels. This is, then, a key capacity for which civil society organisations, policy units, universities and research institutions have to be mobilised.

- *Capacities for managing and implementing regionalism:* institutions like the AU, UNECA and NEPAD have to guarantee that regionalism is well managed and that deadlines are met. It is crucial to maintain the elevated involvement of such institutions. For this purpose, a system of sanctions may be useful (Makhan, 2009). Despite the fact that sanctions are hardly implemented by the RECs and the AU, examples of their use exist (Hellquist, 2014). For sectors-specific integration agreements, sanctions could be managed by the AU/NEPAD and be based on a period and/or a degree of exclusion from the specific agreement or on a boycott of a country (Hellquist, 2014). Capacities to make sanctions actionable (including legal capacities, for which the AfDB African Legal Support Facility can be of great help) have to be built.

- *Capacities for knowledge production and management:* universities, policy units and international organisations, have to help produce adapted knowledge, both to further the process and to share experiences among different regions and across sectors. Access to education, specialised training and skills can also be greatly improved at the regional level, as part of regionalism and as a contribution to job creation (Kararach et al, 2011, pp 23-4).

- *Funding capacities:* funding and financial resources remain a constraint for regionalism in African contexts. Innovative financing mechanisms, placing the African business community at the core, have to be established. Public–private partnerships, African private equities and aid for trade mechanisms appear to be promising avenues for the future. Different UN bodies may also play a strategic role to this extent.

- *Monitoring capacities:* the AU/NEPAD, RECs, states and local governments have to develop monitoring capacities in order to track changes and results, and to send back inputs for modification or denunciation if processes are not sufficiently or not rightly implemented.

- *Technical capacities,* in terms of adoption of new technologies, able to introduce regionalism into the priorities of already existing institutions, are also fundamental.

To build these capacities, every stakeholder has to build its specific capacities for regional purposes. This is true for local governments, states, RECs and international organisations, but also for civil society organisations, research and education institutions and the private sector, crucial in building practical and real regionalism through business. The AU/NEPAD also has a central role to play in achieving regionalism in Africa: it has to be the monitoring institution.

To be successful and fully implemented, regionalism should nevertheless be at the core of the post-MDGs agenda. It should be a priority in such a framework, and intertwined with other goals and specific issues. Additionally, it would benefit from its contextualisation within the global framework, where other regional experiences have taken place or are ongoing, especially in other developing regions and contexts. Agenda 2063, recognising the key role of regional processes, could also support sector-specific regional processes compatible with its priorities. Accordingly, regionalism would be ensured, monitored and implemented, both with top-down solutions and with bottom-up inputs.

Regionalism as part of the post-Millennium Development Goals agenda

If the post-MDGs agenda is still an ongoing task, the challenges that remain unmet, the progress that must be made and the urgent expectations in African contexts to improve people's conditions of life are evident and provide a fundamental foundation. The literature that has analysed the MDGs results and progress made in Africa through them is important. It also includes an emphasis on criticism and limits. This is part of the adventure: in fact, the MDGs have been a dream, a first test, and a courageous trial to attempt to solve urgent and common global problems. Considering their ambitious goal (to eradicate extreme poverty at the global scale), complete success was not to be expected. Moreover, the global situation is certainly not the same as it was when the MDGs were conceived and commenced at the beginning of the millennium.

The MDGs did not have an explicit regional dimension because they did not focus on processes, but rather on actual goals. Nevertheless, NEPAD was created in 2001, among other reasons, to follow MDGs achievements in Africa: it has a sound regional focus. To support NEPAD, in 2003 the UN set in place the Office of the Special Adviser on Africa (OSAA): this regional initiative, together with the later MDG Africa Steering Group, highlights that the global agenda needed regional adaptation, especially in Africa, to try to ensure that the specific African problems were tackled to achieve the MDGs. Consequently, for more than a decade regional processes at the continental level have been sustained by global instances to try to achieve global targets in African contexts. Continental and regional adaptations of a global agenda to specific African conditions, given the still high levels of poverty across the continent and the worrying degree of inequality persisting in African societies, should also be included as a fundamental strategy for the post-2015 agenda.

The analysis of major starting points and the identification of priorities to be included in the post-MDGs agenda have already been completed by the UN (UNTT, 2012) as well as by other actors (Ezeanya, 2013). These assessments have pointed out objectives to include and strategies or tools to use. Among the goals, one that is receiving particular attention is the environmental challenge: in light of climate change, natural disasters and risks threatening societies, it is crucial to rethink the relations between societies and their environments. The Sustainable Development Goals (SDGs) have emerged from this assumption. The important environmental focus is linked with the other crucial objective of 'inclusive social development' (UNTT, 2012). Only if people have access to basic healthcare, education and other basic and fundamental services will their relationship with the environment be likely to avoid destruction: many African experiences (in Senegal, for instance) have demonstrated such a relationship. When the environment allows and is used for economic development, social groups are more inclined to respect it. In regards to strategies, it has been emphasised that consensus and awareness comprise the first step towards participation: consultations are, as such, considered to be a key strategy in setting goals that are closer to people's needs and expectations. To this extent, this chapter argues that, besides the global common goals, it is important to find a way to include diversified patterns, taking into account diverse continental and macro-regional situations. This assumption had already been made and developed by the existence and by the work of the MDG Africa Steering Group, willing to assess specific progress on the MDGs, identify challenges in Africa, and propose specific recommendations, as Agenda 2063 does as well.

Regional strategies and adaptations to achieve globally agreed-on goals are one of the major lessons that should be drawn from the MDGs for the post-2015 agenda. This regional focus should be placed on different levels: the continental and the macro-regional levels analysed in this chapter, but also the micro-regional scale which, although it has not been explored here, is equally important for trans-border cooperation and initiatives in trans-frontier regions. In fact, local initiatives (for environmental protection or water management, for instance) have shown to be effective mechanisms of collaboration between neighbouring states, based on sector-specific issues.

Regional processes for the post-2015 agenda have to be multiscale, flexible, paying attention to real and concrete results for African societies and people. For this reason, 'regional integration', an expression generally paying more attention to macroeconomic processes and figures, related to international trade and economic relations between states, does not seem adapted to the vision of regional dynamics highlighted here. For this reason, 'regionalism' is more compatible with the vision presented here of a more flexible, people-oriented regional view, specifically positioned to address African concerns and problems, considering the peculiarity of African situations in their variety.

This is the aim of Agenda 2063 for Africa (AUC, 2014), promoted by the AU, with the UNECA, AfDB and NEPAD. This continental agenda with a global perspective (defined as 'a global agenda to optimise use of Africa's resources for the benefits of all Africans') is based on the participation and inclusion of all stakeholders at every stage, using a results-based approach, with concrete and measurable targets that can be tracked and monitored. Agenda 2063 wants to support an African renaissance: a change of mindsets and attitudes towards values such as honesty, transparency, discipline, integrity and hard work. Agenda 2063 for Africa, although a very welcome initiative of African ownership of global processes and goals, is also a challenge for the post-2015 agenda if the latter is not completely compatible with the former. How would African stakeholders and institutions address the eventual discrepancies?

This new form of pan-Africanism of a united Africa, without forgetting its diversity and complexity, points out that regionalism in Africa is more about cooperation (Olivier, 2010) and collaboration between stakeholders on sector-specific issues than macroeconomic processes and figures. Accordingly, regionalism is also about policy harmonisation as a key premise for regional collaboration. In African contexts, considering the huge capacity gaps at different levels, as emphasised earlier, regionalism has to be about capacity enhancement at every scale as well, from the local to the continental, for institutions and for the various stakeholders. This capacity dimension and a knowledge management oriented towards structural transformation has to be part of the post-2015 agenda for Africa.

The vision of regionalism presented in this chapter is compatible with the literature on new regionalism, acknowledging the shift from state-driven dynamics to diversified stakeholders and coalitions, from mainly economic processes to a wide range of political, economic, strategic, social, demographic, cultural and environmental interactions within regions of various sizes. The new regionalism literature also emphasises a dimension not treated here, but crucial in African contexts: informal regional dynamics (Shaw et al, 2012). It also focuses on regional governance, security threats, and peculiar development imperatives (Grant and Söderbaum, 2003).

Conclusions

Given the views on regionalism presented in this chapter, as well as the need for Africa to be strongly included in the post-2015 agenda, while taking into account its peculiar situations and conditions, this chapter contends that regionalism and regional sector-specific projects and programmes are part of the roadmap for Africa's development, a development focused on improving people's conditions of life and a development that, rather than hiding African differences, asserts that African unity goes through the recognition of diversity and the identification of the right tools to take such diversity into account for the future.

In order to achieve the goals of sustainable development, transforming economies, reducing inequalities, improving service delivery and natural resource management, reducing poverty, and improving people's quality of life requires a global partnership (UN, 2013), as well as regional adaptations, especially in Africa. To this extent, this chapter wishes to emphasise four major recommendations:

- Regional integration has to be replaced by *more flexible multilevel regionalism*, including a variety of formal and informal stakeholders. Regionalism is defined as cooperation on sector-specific initiatives and between the stakeholders interested and concerned by the specific issue.

- Regionalism is based on *policy harmonisation*, considered as an operational tool allowing, facilitating and smoothing cooperation at every level. Without harmonised policies, collaborations are hindered and often not mutually profitable.

- The post-2015 agenda for Africa has to be *results-oriented*, results being practical and visible, promoting a better quality of life for people and society, being easy to measure, track and monitor. Results are better institutions, better basic services, improved educational and training systems, job creation, affordable and quality healthcare systems, etc.

- To achieve results, Africa needs to build 'endogenous/internal' *institutional and individual capacities, and better produce and manage knowledge*, especially for domestic resource mobilisation, to finance as much as possible its own sustainable development.

References

ACBF (African Capacity Building Foundation (2014) *Africa capacity report 2014, Capacity imperatives for regional integration in Africa*, Harare: ACBF (www.acbf-pact.org/sites/default/files/Africa-Capacity-Report-2014.pdf).

Adogamhe, P.G. (2008) 'Pan-Africanism revisited: vision and reality of African unity and development', *African Review of Integration*, vol 2, no 2, July.

AfDB (African Development Bank) (2012) *Development effectiveness review 2012. Promoting regional integration*, Tunis: AfDB (www.afdb.org/fileadmin/uploads/afdb/Documents/Project-and-Operations/Development_Effectiveness_Review_2012_-_Promoting_Regional_integration.pdf).

AU (African Union) (2014a) *Common African Position (CAP) on the post-2015 agenda*, Addis Ababa: AU (www.nepad.org/sites/default/files/Common%20African%20Position-%20ENG%20final.pdf).

AU (2014b) *Agenda 2063. The Africa we want*, Addis Ababa (http://agenda2063.au.int/en/sites/default/files/agenda2063_popular_version_05092014_EN.pdf).

AUC (African Union Commission) (2010) *Minimum Integration Programme 2009-2012*.

AUC (2014) *Agenda 2063. The future we want for Africa*, Zero draft document, Addis Ababa (www.uneca.org/sites/default/files/uploads/zero_draft_agenda_2063_document_19.03.2014_rev1.pdf).

AUC, UNECA (United Nations Economic Commission for Africa), AfDB (African Development Bank) and UNDP (United Nations Development Programme) (2012) *MDG report 2012. Assessing progress in Africa toward the Millennium Development Goals* (www.undp.org/content/dam/undp/library/MDG/english/MDG%20Regional%20Reports/Africa/MDG%20Report2012_ENG.pdf%20%28final%29.pdf).

Bourenane, N. (2002) 'Regional integration in Africa: Status and perspectives', Development Centre Seminars, Regional Integration in Africa, Paris: OECD, pp 17-46.

Deichmann, U. (2006) 'Road upgrading and trade expansion in Sub-Saharan Africa', Research Brief, Washington, DC: The World Bank (http://econ.worldbank.org/external/default/main?theSitePK=469382&contentMDK=22203784&menuPK=476752&pagePK=64165401&piPK=64165026).

Ezeanya, C. (2013) 'Post-MDGs: it's time to listen to the people', ThinkAfricaPress (http://thinkafricapress.com/development/after-2015-then-what-africa-development-agenda-post-mdgs-world).

Gibbs, R. (2009) 'Regional integration and Africa's development trajectory: meta-theories, expectations and realities', *Third World Quarterly*, vol 30, no 4, pp 701-21.

Grant, J.A. and Söderbaum F. (2003) *The new regionalism in Africa*, Aldershot: Ashgate.

GTZ (2009) *Regional economic communities in Africa. A progress overview*, Nairobi (www.g20dwg.org/documents/pdf/view/113/).

Hellquist, E. (2014) *Regional organizations and sanctions against members. Explaining the different trajectories of the African Union, the League of Arab States, and the Association of Southeast Asian Nations*, KFG Working Paper No 59, Berlin: Freie Universitat (http://userpage.fu-berlin.de/kfgeu/kfgwp/wpseries/WorkingPaperKFG_59.pdf).

Icaza, R. (2009) 'Alternative regionalisms and civil society: setting a research agenda', in D. Chavez (ed) *The New Latin American agenda*, Amsterdam: TNI/CordAid (www.alternative-regionalisms.org/wp-content/uploads/2009/07/icaza_alternativeregionalisms.pdf).

IUCN (nd) Global Transboundary Conservation Network (www.tbpa. net/page.php?ndx=83).

Kararach, G., Hanson, K. and Léautier, F. (2011) *Regional integration policies to support job creation for Africa's burgeoning youth population*, ACBF Working Paper No 21.

Keet, D. (2007) 'Alternative regionalisms: why and how?', *Global Social Policy*, vol 7, no 3, pp 255-8.

Makhan, V.S. (2009) *Making regional integration work in Africa: A reflection on strategies and institutional requirements*, ACBF Development Memoirs Series (http://elibrary.acbfpact.org/acbf/collect/acbf/index/assoc/ HASHc31f.dir/doc.pdf).

NEPAD (New Partnership for Africa's Development) (2011) *Revision of the AU/NEPAD African Action Plan 2010-2015. Advancing regional and continental integration in Africa together through shared values*, Johannesburg.

Olivier, G. (2010) 'Regionalism in Africa: cooperation without integration', *Strategic Review for Southern Africa*, vol 32, no 2, pp 17-43.

Rampa, F. and van Seters, J. (2013) 'Towards the development and implementation of CAADP regional compacts and investment plans: The state of play', ECDPM Briefing Note, No 49, March (http://ecdpm.org/wp-content/uploads/2013/10/BN-49-CAADP-Regional-Compacts-Investment-Plans-Development-Implementation.pdf).

Shaw, T.M., Grant, J.A. and Cornelissen, S. (2012) 'Introduction and overview: the study of new regionalism(s) at the start of the second decade of the twenty-first century', in T.M. Shaw, J.A. Grant and S. Cornelissen (eds) *The Ashgate research companion to regionalisms*, Aldershot: Ashgate, pp 3-30.

UN (United Nations) (2013) *A new global partnership: Eradicate poverty and transform economies through sustainable development*, High Level Panel on the Post-2015 Development Agenda, New York: United Nations (www.post2015hlp.org/the-report/).

UN General Assembly (2014) *The road to dignity by 2030: Ending poverty, transforming all lives and protecting the planet*, New York: United Nations (http://www.un.org/disabilities/documents/reports/SG_Synthesis_ Report_Road_to_Dignity_by_2030.pdf).

UN Department of Public Information (2008) *Achieving the Millennium Development Goals in Africa. Recommendations of the MDG Africa Steering*

Group, New York (www.mdgafrica.org/pdf/MDG%20Africa%20 Steering%20Group%20Recommendations%20-%20English%20 -%20HighRes.pdf).

UNDP (United Nations Development Programme) (2011) *Regional integration and human development. A pathway for Africa*, New York (www.undp.org/content/dam/undp/library/Poverty%20Reduction/ Trade,%20Intellectual%20Property%20and%20Migration/RIR%20 English-web.pdf).

UNECA (United Nations Economic Commission for Africa) (2012) *Assessing regional integration in Africa V. Towards an African continental free trade area (ARIA 5)*, Addis Ababa (www.uneca.org/publications/ assessing-regional-integration-africa-v).

UNECA (2013a) *Assessing regional integration in Africa VI. Harmonizing policies to transform the trading environment (ARIA 6)*, Addis Ababa (uneca.org/sites/default/files/PublicationFiles/aria_vi_english_full. pdf).

UNECA (2013b) *Assessment of progress on regional integration in Africa.* Paper prepared for the ECA Conference of African Ministers of Finance, Planning and Economic Development and AU Conference of Ministers of Economy and Finance Abidjan, Côte d'Ivoire 21–24 March 2013.

UNECA (2014) MDG 2014 *report. Assessing progress in Africa toward the Millennium Development Goals*, Addis Ababa (www.afdb. org/fileadmin/uploads/afdb/Documents/Publications/MDG_ Report_2014_11_2014.pdf).

UNTT (United Nations System Task Team) on the Post-2015 UN Development Agenda (2012) *Realizing the future we want for all*, Report to the Secretary-General, New York (www.un.org/millenniumgoals/ pdf/Post_2015_UNTTreport.pdf).

Vervaeke, W. (2013) 'CAADP at the regional level – State of play in the regional economic communities', in S. Bilal and F. Rampa, *GREAT Insights*, vol 3, issue 1, Maastricht: European Centre for Development Policy Management (http://ecdpm.org/great-insights/ family-farming-and-food-security/caadp-rstate-play-regional-economic-communities/).

TEN

Reforming the Development Banks' Country Policy and Institutional Assessment as an aid allocation tool: the case for country self-assessment

George Kararach, Abbi Mamo Kedir, Frannie Léautier and Victor Murinde

Introduction

In Sub-Saharan Africa, The World Bank and the African Development Bank (AfDB) have been the two major players in the arena of multilateral aid. Both have been redefining aid conditionality to Sub-Saharan Africa since the early 1980s, and into the late 1990s. This has implied a move away from an emphasis on structural adjustment, where financing was provided in return for the promise of policy reforms, to disbursement of funds conditional on reforms already achieved. The new practice is known as *aid 'selectivity'* or *performance-based allocation (PBA)*.

Over the last few decades, the aid literature has been engaged with improving the effectiveness of aid, and finding ways of refining the allocation and lending system of major donors such as The World Bank. Whenever aid flows are allocated selectively, donors set conditions or triggers for disbursement according to the achievement of prior policies and institutions. So funds are withheld from countries until they change their policies or institutions to set benchmarks. The World Bank and AfDB base their allocations on an assessment mechanism called the Country Policy and Institutional Assessment (CPIA). This chapter argues that the use of CPIA by the multilateral banks and other donors has significant ramifications for Sub-Saharan Africa and generally for low-income countries to the extent that there is a moral, economic and political imperative for countries to conduct a self-assessment in the event that aid continues to be allocated on the basis of CPIA.

CPIA is produced confidentially by The World Bank or AfDB country economists, and is used as an indicator of the potential effectiveness of the recipients' policies and governance structures in place. Borrowing and lending decisions are made according to the way this index ranks countries. It has been criticised by academics and activists (Kanbur, 2005; van Waeyenberge, 2008; Diarra, 2010; Nissanke, 2013) for being too subjective. Nor is it based on rigorous validation and consensus processes on the part of the aid recipients – especially governments. Thus, by design, it is partial and is not an outcome of widespread public debate and consensus. Countries committed to neoclassical thinking are often given a higher CPIA score by World Bank and AfDB economists, who are the ultimate authority for the computation of the index. In recent years, The World Bank has started a consultation process that engages countries in discussing their CPIA scores. While the countries do not have a say on what their rankings are, they have an opportunity to contest the ratings, and to explain their understanding of the scores they have achieved.[1]

As opposed to The World Bank/AfDB index developed by international experts, country self-assessment CPIA indices, based on the same components, could be more accurate. Such self-assessments, if conducted by independent assessors outside of government, could be subjected to a series of validation and consensus-building processes. Hence, even if they cannot eliminate bias altogether, they could provide a more balanced view of the nature of policies and governance structures.

In this chapter, we work on a set of data generated from such a process of self-assessment. The motivation for this approach is to try to come up with improved sets of indices for a more effective and fairer system of grant and lending allocations by donors, both bilateral and multilateral. Our approach attempts to allay donors' mistrust of African governments' impartiality by combining both donor and government assessments with intensive consultation. Effective country consultations are recommended in the spirit of Paris 2005,[2] and will, through this process, forestall the criticism that 'numbers are what you make of them'. Therefore, as part of the post-2015 development agenda, African countries need to have a greater voice on aid allocation policy if they are to be at the 'table' as equal partners. Our suggestion is an improvement on the existing CPIA rating criteria given the recent changes in the international aid framework with new donors coming into the picture such as BRICS (Brazil, Russia, India, China and South Africa), and other emerging bilateral development partners.

In addition to providing a detailed discussion of the self-assessment index, we also provide econometric evidence linking growth and CPIA, enabling observers to test whether countries with better governance grow better. The CPIA is often criticised for being an implicit conditionality. Consider the efforts by The World Bank Group itself, which include the evaluation made by its Independent Evaluation Group (IEG) suggesting a complete overhaul of the CPIA index. The group questioned the rationale for the existence of the CPIA, insinuating its complete abolition (Alexander, 2010).

In an attempt to make a contribution to the aid allocation literature, this chapter has produced an additional set of CPIA indices, and compares them with ones produced by others. We compare indices produced by The World Bank, ACBF and AfDB. Country self-assessments have been compiled by the ACBF for two consecutive years, starting from 2011. As a contribution to the existing debate, we give the technical and policy implications of the differences highlighted. We are not of the opinion that following neoclassical/neoliberal policies is the surest route to gaining assistance from The World Bank or AfDB. Such policies do not form the bedrock of appropriate institutional systems and economic development in the developing world. Therefore it is vital that alternative policy-making tools are sought, and we attempt to do that in this study.

The key objectives of this chapter are to:

- help the process of transparent policy-making among donors during funding rounds by providing a more rigorous method of constructing the CPIA;
- indicate potential sources of statistical and other errors or subjective biases in the components used to construct the CPIA as well as other problems (for example, comparability across time, sample bias, lack of transparency and underlying motives of assessments made by country economists);
- provide probable explanations for the discrepancies in the indices;
- shed light on the link between the indices and growth performance (for example, are low performers in World Bank indices growing faster or slower than low performers according to the ACBF and AfDB?).

The chapter has seven sections. The following section examines why the use of CPIA is very important for Sub-Saharan Africa, and why its underlying premise needs re-examination. Given the implications the CPIA has for aid allocations by donors (particularly in determining the grant–loan mix in a given aid allocation), and thus on growth, a self-assessment methodology is proposed and discussed in the third section. The chapter examines the findings of the three approaches to the CPIA in the fourth section. The fifth section outlines some of the criticisms of the CPIA methodology, and why countries benefit from self-assessment. In the sixth section, the chapter examines the merit and limitations of doing self-assessment, and proposes how the CPIA method could be enhanced if complemented by other processes such as the African Peer Review Mechanism (APRM) and the Africa Capacity Indicators. It focuses on five fundamental justifications for the superiority of self-assessment to existing CPIA scores generated by the AfDB and The World Bank. The last section concludes the chapter.

What is the Country Policy and Institutional Assessment and why does it matter?

Defining and understanding the Country Policy and Institutional Assessment

To understand the CPIA it is necessary to look at the history of the operations of multilateral banks in Sub-Saharan Africa, particularly The World Bank (Hopkins, 1986). It is necessary to have a sense of how Africa's past affects its present by linking the economic history of the continent to its contemporary development problems and trajectories. The World Bank, as well as the other donors, makes certain assumptions in assessing the current situation in Africa, including interpretations of the relationship between variables such as population, resource use, institutional change and political incorporation. The CPIA is derived from the *subjective* judgement of both The World Bank and AfDB on a country's performance across a set of macroeconomic, structural and social as well as governance criteria. The CPIA has 16 components, grouped in four clusters, as shown in Table 10.1.

Despite The World Bank's attempt to move beyond the fall-out from the structural adjustment periods in Sub-Saharan Africa, the CPIA still embraces well-known neoliberal economic norms that sit uncomfortably with country-level specific social and governance concerns. For example, examined carefully, the economic core of the CPIA reflects a preference for low inflation, a surplus budgetary position, minimal restrictions on trade and capital flows, 'flexible' goods, labour and land markets and the prohibition of directed/ state rationed credit – which were the values advocated during the controversial structural adjustment policies of the 1980s.

Table 10.1: The Country Policy and Institutional Assessment clusters and components

A. Economic management	B. Structural policies
i. Macroeconomic management	i. Trade
ii. Fiscal policy	ii. Financial sector
iii. Debt policy	iii. Business regulatory environment
C. Policies for social inclusion	**D. Public sector management and institutions**
i. Gender equality	i. Property rights and rule-based governance
ii. Equity of public resource use	ii. Quality of budgetary and financial
iii Building human resources	management
iv. Social protection and labour	iii. Efficiency of revenue mobilisation
v. Policies and institutions for	iv. Quality of public administration
environmental sustainability	v. Transparency, accountability and corruption
	in the public sector

Source: The World Bank (2014)

Importantly, the social imperatives are often inconsistent with the economic ones, which pay little attention to the perilous effects on information asymmetry of the market mechanisms. As an example, the market mechanism may not deliver the equity objectives of public resource use and social protection aspired to under the social cluster. The governance cluster reveals its undemocratic tendencies by imposing a one-size-fits-all formula on countries that exhibit a very wide range of sociopolitical and structural characteristics (Kararach, 2011). Arguably, the social and governance priorities are additional to the predetermined economic imperatives (van Waeyenberge, 2008). The CPIA score drives a formula for aid allocations that is 16^3 times more sensitive to changes in policy and institutional set-up in comparison to changes in income per capita (van Waeyenberge, 2008). This is the case because The World Bank attaches 68 per cent of the weight to governance issues (Kanbur, 2005; Tribe, 2013). One immediate consequence of the allocation process is that a developing country scoring in the top performance quintile of the CPIA recently received on average five times as much World Bank aid per capita as countries in the bottom quintile (ACBF, 2012). The differential impact is also evident from the AfDB calculations, which attach less weight to governance than The World Bank.

The other implication is that the quality of a country's policies and institutions, which are based on a set of predetermined norms, is more important than its need for assistance (Rodrik, 2004). Hence, resources are directed to countries where it is expected to be most effective, not necessarily where it is most needed. This deflects interventions away from poverty reduction and the need for sustainable human development.

Table 10.2: Official development assistance (ODA) allocation scenario based on Country Policy and Institutional Assessment calculations of The World Bank and AfDB

Country	CPIA World Bank (AfDB)	Net ODA, US$ million	Net ODA multilateral, US$ million
Uganda	3.9 (4.3)	1785.9	768.8
Benin	3.5 (3.9)	622.9	353.8
Factor	0.4 (0.4)	X3	X2

Source: ACBF (2012)

Diarra (2010) argued that the inequality trap should be considered one of the major under-development issues. De Matteis (2013) shows how pro-poor policies and inclusive governance are critical for aid effectiveness. How relevant is the distinction between inequalities of outcome and opportunity and political, economic or social inequalities? To many, most multilateral and donor organisations are mainly influenced by the liberal approach, which focuses on opportunity inequalities – 'equity' approaches, whereby outcome or income inequalities are sometimes perceived as an incitement factor for investment, risk and effort, for example, as exposed by the Austrian school of economic thought (Kararach, 2011).

Inequalities exist due to persistent differences in power, wealth and status among socioeconomic groups, and are sustained over time by economic, political and sociocultural mechanisms and institutions, leading to efficiency losses and an economic equilibrium that is inferior to alternatives (The World Bank, 2005; Bourguignon et al, 2006; Kararach, 2011). In a state of inequality, the entire socioeconomic distribution remains stable because the various aspects interact to protect the rich preventing the poor from being upwardly mobile (Rao, 2006). But the activities of the multilateral banks seem to be premised on the assumption that, even though some trade-offs between efficiency and equity are unavoidable in the short run, equity restored through market equilibration is likely to be necessary in the long run. Indeed, political and income inequalities lead to inequalities of opportunity, and thus, contribute to inefficiency in resources allocation (The World Bank, 2005). The weak functioning of markets through poor quality institutions plays a crucial role in the creation and persistence of political and economic inequalities, which, in turn, will maintain and perpetuate the trap of harmful institutions. International inequalities are driven by endogenous as well as exogenous factors (Sanderson, 2005). The multilateral banks' approaches perceive inequality and poverty mainly as an endogenous factor related to the problem of marginal effort and productivity of each individual. In this approach, outcome inequalities do not represent a serious problem, and they are even sometimes necessary during the economic development process, as these are outcomes of just-rewards (Thomas, 2001; Basu, 2006; Kararach, 2011).

Other schools of development theory locate international inequalities in the dynamics of the capitalist system through the exploitation of peripheral countries by those coming from the centre (see debates about dependency à la Raul Prebisch and Hans Singer or Samir Amin). The structural weakness and marginalisation of African and other developing countries in the global governance institutions are intertwined with international rules that are detrimental to them, especially in terms of economic liberalisation and international trade (Sarrasin, 1997; Birdsall, 2002, 2003; Jacquet et al, 2002; Beckfield, 2003; Herkenrath et al, 2005; Bourguignon et al, 2009; Diarra, 2010). Indeed, the structural weakness may feed into the unfair assessments of developing countries by multilateral banks and other donors in the process of aid allocation.

Thérien (1999) and Payne (2003) argue that one may identify in international organisations two inequality paradigms about the North and South: the Bretton Woods paradigm (The World Bank, International Monetary Fund [IMF], World Trade Organization [WTO]) and the United Nations (UN) paradigm (UN agencies). In the former, poverty doesn't derive from the asymmetric inequalities in the structure of the world political economy, but results from the temporary disequilibrium of markets. Therefore, poverty factors are driven at the domestic rather than the external level – especially due to poor policies (Diarra, 2010). There is no alternative to the economic liberal order. Poverty should be fought and eradicated through the 'trickle-down' phenomenon with the outcomes of long-term economic growth. The liberal social contract permits diversity in income under the condition that each individual gets the same opportunities at the start (Kararach, 2011).

The multilateral banks' perception of inequality is clearly defined in terms of equity perceived as equality of opportunity. A major factor in the debate about equity and social justice concerns the incorporation of a central role for personal responsibility into the definition of fairness. Diarra (2010) notes that an important strand of the thinking behind inequality is based on the argument that equality of opportunity provides the most appropriate form of justice. Diarra (2010) further argues that this is the case because equality of opportunity eliminates, to the greatest extent possible, inequalities caused by morally irrelevant circumstances, whereas inequality-reflecting differences in personal effort might well be acceptable.

Essentially, at the core of the logic of the International Development Association (IDA) allocation process there is a balance between 'needs' and 'performance'. Needs are represented by gross national income per capita, GNIPC.

This allocation process represents performance by a performance rating, PR, whereby the allocation per capita for a country is a function of GNIPC and PR (Kanbur, 2005). The specific relationship for allocation per capita (APC) with predetermined weights can be written as:

$$APC = f(PR^2, GNIPC^{-0.125})$$

The performance rating is raised to the square power and per capita income to a negative power, −0.125, and these two jointly determine the allocation. The function f(.) reflects the fact that individual country allocations have to add up to the total resources available. The performance rating is weighted higher than the measure of needs (Kanbur, 2005). This is why, among other reasons discussed below, developing countries need to have a greater interest in debating how the CPIA index is developed and used. This is particularly true for the least developed group that is penalised by the CPIA-driven allocation framework.

Country Policy and Institutional Assessment and growth

What is the growth impact of the CPIA index? In a growth accounting framework, we model the growth of per capita GDP as a function of lagged growth of per capita GDP (which captures state dependence or persistence), the CPIA score, foreign direct investment (FDI), population, trade openness, domestic credit and the share of natural resources in the GDP of the country. Due to its relative advantage in improving the precision, handling endogeneity and dynamic nature of the specification, we use a dynamic system-generalised method of moments estimator. Hence, our growth (t) model is given as:

$$GR_{it} = \beta_0 + \gamma GR_{it-1} + \delta CPIA_{it} + \beta X_{it} + u_{it} \qquad (1)$$

where GR is the growth rate of country i, at time t and the lagged value of GR is included to capture persistence and mean-reverting dynamics in growth. We expect past growth (t−1) to be a significant predictor of current growth (t). CPIA is the score of country i at time t and X represents a vector of other relevant explanatory variables. The error term, u consists of country heterogeneity (η_i) and time-specific fixed effects (ε_t) and can be given as $u_{it} = \eta_i + \varepsilon_t + v_{it}$ where v is independently and identically distributed $(0, \sigma^2)$. The main variable of interest is the CPIA score and its disaggregated components such as monetary policy, fiscal policy, debt policy, financial sector, business regulatory environment, regional integration and trade. We examine the effect of the CPIA on growth using the score built both by The World Bank and AfDB. We are not able to estimate the growth impact of the self-assessment score, as data is only available for two years. Thus, linking growth with the score from self-assessments leads to unreliable estimates due to the potential lack of meaningful variation that can be picked by the estimating equation. But with expansion in the sample of observations in the future, it would be interesting to explore the link. Apart from the CPIA score, the AfDB also has a governance score, which we controlled for in the third column of Table 10.3 below.

Table 10.3: Dynamic General Method of Moments estimates of the link between growth, Country Policy and Institutional Assessment and governance scores of the AfDB

Variable	Coefficient (SE)	
Constant	3.903 (0.32)***	3.950 (0.032)***
ln (growth),t–1	0.131 (0.06)**	0.132 (0.06)**
CPIA score	0.112 (0.05)**	
FDI	0.002 (0.001)**	0.002 (0.001)**
ln (population)	–0.028 (0.01)**	–0.024 (0.01)**
Trade openness	–0.0001 (0.00)***	–0.001 (0.00)***
Domestic credit	–0.000 (0.00)	–0.000 (0.00)
Natural resources	0.000 (0.00)	0.000 (0.00)
Governance score		0.014 (0.01)
Monetary policy		
Fiscal policy		
Debt policy		
Regional integration and trade		
Financial sector		
Business regulatory environment		
Wald chi²(p-value)	30.9 (0.00)	27.9 (0.00)
Number of observations	158	158

Source: Authors' computation on our estimation of equation 1 above

Table 10.3 is based on the CPIA and governance scores of the AfDB. Column 2 provides the link between the CPIA score and growth along with other control variables such as FDI, population, trade openness, domestic credit and the percentage share of natural resources in GDP. In column 3, we examine the link between growth and the governance score of AfDB accounting for all the control variables as in column 2. And in the final column, we see the growth impact of the disaggregated components of the CPIA score to shed light on the relative significance of each of the components. According to the estimates reported in column 2, the CPIA score of AfDB, lagged growth and FDI have significant and positive effects on growth at the 5 per cent level, while population and openness have the opposite effect. Replacing the CPIA score of AfDB by its governance score in column 3 did not lead to qualitative changes in our estimates. The results also show that the governance measure of AfDB has no effect on growth. In column 4, taken separately, most of the components of the CPIA score are insignificant for growth. The only component with a positive and significant coefficient on growth is the financial sector variable. Our results suggest that it may be misleading to rely only on the aggregate CPIA score without investigating the relative importance of its components. However, in our setting there is a non-negligible loss of freedom due to the small sample size.

Table 10.4 presents similar results, but is based on the CPIA score of The World Bank and its constituent components. According to the results in column 2, lagged growth is no longer a significant predicator of current growth of GDP, unlike our prior expectation. The CPIA score still has a significant and positive influence on growth. Like the result for lagged growth, FDI and openness do not exhibit a significant link with growth. However, the share of natural resources in the GDP of a given country is positively and significantly linked with growth. As in Table 10.3, population is detrimental to Africa's growth. Column 3 results are based on disaggregated CPIA score components of The World Bank, and they indicate that none of them matter for growth. But on aggregate, the policy and institutional indicators matter for the growth of African countries.

Debating country self-assessments in Country Policy and Institutional Assessment processes

Increasingly, development agencies (including the multilateral banks) are taking cognisance that participation in development will involve broader questions of citizenship, sovereignty and globalisation. In

Table 10.4: Dynamic General Method of Moments estimates of the link between growth and Country Policy and Institutional Assessment scores of The World Bank

Variable	Coefficient (SE)
Constant	4.650 (0.67)***
ln (growth),t–1	–0.020 (0.12)
ln (CPIA score)	0.160 (0.08)**
FDI	0.001 (0.00)
ln (population)	–0.041 (0.02)**
Trade openness	–0.000 (0.00)
Domestic credit	–0.000 (0.00)
Natural resources	0.002 (0.001)**
Macroeconomic management	
Fiscal policy	
Debt policy	
Financial sector	
Business regulatory environment	
Wald chi²(p-value)	51.3(0.00)
Number of observations	**79**

Source: Authors' computation based on equation 1.

recent years, the focus on some of these issues has changed (Mohan, 2001). A growing number of agencies such as the ACBF are seeking to build up the capacity of the state, private sector and civil society to empower all sections of society. This holistic approach to capacity building requires state–society 'synergy' (Ostrom, 1996; Evans, 1997), whereby partnerships aim to produce more lasting development, encourage social inclusion and bolster citizenship in the process (Mohan, 2001). Fowler (1998) argues that non-governmental organisations (NGOs) and other development agencies are yet to form genuine partnerships in which the northern partner does not have disproportionate influence. Greater local involvement in development discourse is seen as paramount. The moral and political imperative is that *local* problems have global causes, so that the most useful thing that a relatively powerful, non-local organisation can do is use its political weight to raise awareness and campaign for the reform of the institutions of global governance (Rayner, 2003). Inclusion of local organisations' views in global policy-making through partnerships may result in ever more complex networks of alliances between NGOs.

The motivations of various actors for encouraging public participation in self-assessment processes are varied. However, each seems to embody a particular idea of the citizen and good governance.

Public participation essentially enhances programme communication by removing resistance brought about by lack of information or understanding about a specific intervention. Public participation offers individuals the opportunity to select from among a limited array of services, but not to play a significant role in setting policy agendas (Gaventa and Cornwall, 2000, 2001).

Effectively, public participation in conducting self-assessments can be defended in terms of extending democratic control. Rayner (2003) argued that participants are socially embedded in a community; locally knowledgeable and intuitively reflexive about society and nature; focus on common good as a core value of public life; and rely on inclusive deliberation to reveal the truth. However, its key assumptions about ideal free speech may mask the indifference, politics and power that characterise real communities (Habermas, 1984; Rayner, 2003).

Indeed, people have multiple, overlapping identities that they are able to mobilise, and reference groups to which they refer for legitimacy and support. Citizenship needs to be redefined, in effect, as engagement through emergent social solidarities, which can be 'increasingly messy and unstable' (Ellison, 1997, p 712). Engagement, involving new processes of social and political interaction, may be directed towards more diverse sets of actors and institutions than those that are derived entirely from the state or even the singular community (Leach and Scoones, 2002). Citizenship as an emergent solidarity mechanism suggests a view of democracy that emphasises the capacity of people to actively participate and engage in the discourses that affect their lives (Pateman, 1970). Participatory management, on the other hand, permits rational debate only within received expert framings as currently propagated by the CPIA processes supported by the multilateral banks (Rayner, 2003). Under democratic governance, citizenship is a dynamic learning process that creates and enhances human capabilities (Sirianni and Friedland, 2000) and, consequently, sustainable development (Rayner, 2003).

Undertaking self-assessment techniques arguably promotes efficiency and transparency through better participation (van Waeyenberge, 2008). The concept of efficiency is used as an explicit value to guide decision-making in the practice of commercial accounting for the stocks and flows of goods as well as when conducting critical performance examinations. In neoliberal thought, the solution that optimises outcomes must also be an efficient solution, since any departure from efficiency, by definition, reduces the amount of goods available for distribution (Rayner and Malone, 1998, p 60). This is embedded in the ethical doctrine of utilitarianism (Rayner, 2003).

Arguably, as in Rayner (2003), there are diverse ethical considerations at play in using the utility principle, which is defined by the capability to measure and monitor stocks and flows of societal good, the proxy for 'good' being wealth in some form. The sense of diversity systematically attenuates decision-maker awareness of alternative ethical considerations. Rayner (2003) further argues that the imperative to provide for societal good at the highest level of aggregation is no guide for securing the happiness of society as a whole. This moral case gives individuals space to interrogate and make decisions on issues that affect their lives with a view to optimise utility and increase efficiency in decision-making. This stance may be considered a good case for individuals and societies to conduct self-assessments in the CPIA process.

Promotion of transparency and accountability is the other justification for the adoption of formal assessment techniques in the CPIA. Moreover, the principle of transparency seems to have been almost universally embraced, and sits easily with other values, such as individual equality or natural rights.

One could argue that CPIA indexing processes are often highly technical, and that most people lack the appropriate background to make sense of the calculations. Besides the technical transparency of assessment techniques themselves, there is the issue of their use in decision-making. Some studies suggest that technical analysis merely provides cover for the implicit exercise of judgement (Rayner and Malone, 1998). However, where numbers are explicitly used, the existence of competing assessments allows decision-makers to select the analysis that most closely conforms to their pre-existing preference. This presents a further case for doing country self-assessment.

Monitoring and evaluation of the performance of public participation in development interventions is problematic. Traditionally, those proposing and implementing the said intervention conduct most evaluations of individual projects and programmes. The focus of evaluation is almost exclusively process-based, for example, looking at how closely the activity corresponds to the stated objectives and goals. There are arguably no credible outcome-based evaluations that have established that the CPIA technique used by the multilateral banks has led to a better outcome than if alternative approaches, such as self-assessments, the APRM or African Capacity Indicators. Self-assessment would open the way for greater public scrutiny of the implementation of development assistance and its effectiveness.

One of the most persistent criticisms of participatory assessment techniques relates to the problem of representation, both in terms of the validity of the participants and their legitimacy to shape decisions for those who were not included in the process. Carson and Martin (2002) argue that sample bias can be overcome by random selection of participants during assessment. However, close examination of their methodology reveals that their citizen juries were far from entirely random (Rayner, 2003).

Although self-assessment may enhance participation, legitimacy concerns may arise due to the exclusion of critical organisations, which may not have been represented in the self-assessment (Rayner, 2003). Essentially, when doing self-assessment and judging the quality of participation, it is important to not only assess who is included, but also which group or perspective was omitted. Agarwal's (2001) study of forestry initiatives in India and Nepal shows how seemingly excluded significant sections of the affected population, especially women, were engaged in alternative and parallel platforms.

As Rayner (2003, p 168) put it:

> Ultimately, the issue of representativeness folds back into the conception of citizenship that one embraces. The perspective that views citizenship in terms of emergent solidarity clearly requires that any forum that is intended to serve as a surrogate microcosm of the wider society must be capable of reproducing or otherwise capturing the emergent properties of that society, which suggests that neither randomness nor categorical representation will do.

Technical perspectives often frame the agenda as inflexible constraints on decisions, while social and cultural perspectives can be corrected by promoting wider understanding of the scientific method. Despite the hegemony of CPIA 'scientific' techniques in aid policy-making, the really thorny issues facing public and private sector decision-makers are more often aesthetic, ethical and political rather than scientific. Complex issues of governance get reduced to issues of scientific uncertainty. This reduction is not merely one of political to scientific, but even further, of science to risk, and its assessment and management (Rayner, 2003). Thus, political economy questions often tend to drive policy formulations, reforms and implementations.

The issues raised in this section put a strong case for Sub-Saharan African countries to conduct self-assessments using the CPIA instrument. Our arguments are also aimed at improving the existing CPIA framework by pointing to critical insights and considerations that should be accounted for in aid allocation. The major philosophical question for the multilateral banks is, in Robert Chambers' own words, '*Whose reality counts?*' The CPIA should, like any other tool, serve to enhance development, which should be about people and the environment, and sustainable wellbeing for all. The policy implications of the self-assessment approach are radical and arguably guided by principles that include: (i) fostering decentralisation, democracy, diversity and dynamism, (ii) managing for diversity and complexity, and (iii) self-critical awareness and admitting and learning from errors.

Evidence from the self-assessment Country Policy and Institutional Assessment processes in Sub-Saharan Africa

Since 2010, the ACBF has supported a number of Sub-Saharan African countries in conducting their own CPIA. The number of countries engaged in the exercise rose from 13 in 2010 (for 2009) to 17 in 2011 (for 2010). An analysis of two years' worth of CPIA data, comparing self-assessments by countries, The World Bank, AfBD and ACBF, was done. The data comparing the different indices assessed is shown in Table 10.5.

Table 10.5 indicates that the AfDB tends to give ratings that are similar on average to The World Bank, but higher than country self-assessments. The variance among ratings is the highest for the AfDB assessments, being twice as high as The World Bank for self-assessment. AfDB's assessments also show more variability than the country self-assessments. The lack of transparency in index construction both at The World Bank and AfDB makes it difficult to compare their CPIA indices, due to the differential weights that have been allocated to the disaggregated components of the CPIA index. For instance, The World Bank attaches a weight of 68 per cent to governance while AfDB uses 50 per cent. Experts may thus disagree on the facts about a country as well as how those facts are to be weighted (Ravallion, 2010).

The differences between ratings are shown in Table 10.6 below. Three countries showed a difference of 20 per cent or more between the country and World Bank assessments in 2009 compared to countries in 2010. In 2009, the major differences related to Côte d'Ivoire, Liberia and Zimbabwe, and in 2010, Côte d'Ivoire, Liberia, Niger, Tanzania and Zimbabwe. Benin had rated itself more severely than The World Bank in 2009, before proceeding to rate itself higher the following year. Dissemination of the 2010 African Capacity Indicator report in the country raised awareness about how ratings are made.

Table 10.5: Comparison of 2009 and 2010 data on Country Policy and Institutional Assessment assessments

Country	CPIA World Bank	CPIA self-assessment
CPIA index based on data in 2010		
Benin	3.5	4.0
Burkina Faso	3.8	4.3
Burundi	3.1	3.4
Cameroon	3.2	3.1
Cape Verde	4.1	4.0
Côte d'Ivoire	2.7	3.5
Ghana	3.9	3.6
Kenya	3.8	4.3
Liberia	2.9	4.0
Madagascar	3.4	3.4
Mauritania	3.2	3.0
Niger	3.4	4.3
Tanzania	3.8	2.7
Uganda	3.8	3.1
Zambia	3.4	3.4
Zimbabwe	2	3.9
CPIA index based on data in 2009		
Benin	3.5	3.1
Burkina Faso	3.8	4.2
Burundi	3.1	2.9
Côte d'Ivoire	2.8	3.5
Kenya	3.7	4.0
Liberia	2.8	3.4
Mauritania	3.2	3.3
Niger	3.3	3.8
Uganda	3.9	4.2
Zambia	3.4	3.4
Zimbabwe	1.9	4.0
Average	**3.31**	**3.63**
Variance	**0.29**	**0.22**
Standard Deviation	**0.54**	**0.47**

Source: ACBF (2012)

Country self-assessments match the AfDB ratings more closely than The World Bank (see Table 10.6), which may be because The World Bank is adjusting for international comparisons and rating African countries on an international scale. On the other hand, the countries themselves, and the AfDB, are closer to the ground, and may have better information on the policy environment.

Table 10.6: Differences between Country Policy and Institutional Assessments from country self-assessments, AfDB and World Bank

Country	Difference ACBF– World Bank (%)	Difference ACBF–AfDB (%)
Differences in the ratings using data from 2009		
Benin	−11.4	−23.6
Burkina Faso	9.6	−1.3
Burundi	−5.3	−5.0
Côte d'Ivoire	23.9	18.8
Kenya	8.6	−4.3
Liberia	22.6	−5.4
Mauritania	1.8	−9.5
Niger	16.3	4.5
Uganda	6.9	−1.7
Zambia	−1.2	−15.4
Zimbabwe	108.9	120.5
Differences in the ratings using data from 2010		
Benin	13.9	2.5
Burkina Faso	13.9	3.8
Burundi	9.6	12.2
Cameroon	−2.0	−16.6
Cape Verde	−1.3	−8.8
Côte d'Ivoire	31.4	19.0
Ghana	−7.9	−12.2
Kenya	14.5	3.6
Liberia	36.2	8.8
Madagascar	−0.2	−0.8
Mauritania	−5.6	−17.4
Niger	27.2	20.1
Tanzania	−28.7	−32.9
Uganda	−18.0	−27.2
Zambia	−0.9	−13.1
Zimbabwe	97.2	106.5
Average	**13.3**	**4.6**
Var	**8.9**	**11.7**

Source: ACBF (2012)

Plotting the data to see the scatter in the differences shows that there is close clustering towards the zero area, which would indicate convergence in the ratings (Figure 10.1). However, we note the outliers mentioned above for both 2009 and 2010. There are as many outliers in the difference between country self-assessments with the AfDB (five) as there are between the AfDB and World Bank (five).

Figure 10.1: Understanding the outliers (%)

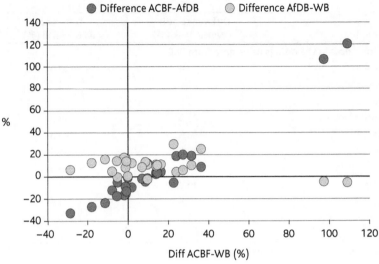

Source: ACBF (2012)

The pattern of outliers indicates that there are a number of systematic biases, especially with respect to the type of country (fragile or non-fragile). This is seen clearly when looking at the percentage agreement/disagreement by country type, as shown in Table 10.7.

The results in Table 10.7 indicate that countries are more reluctant to rate themselves fragile than The World Bank and AfDB. The World Bank rates countries overall more harshly than they rate themselves. These findings indicate that it is very important to use multiple measures by reinforcing their complementarities in classifying countries. A methodology that accounts for systematic biases would largely adjust for this difference, and using a band to classify countries would be more appropriate. Such a band is used to illustrate the range of indicators in Figure 10.2. It is composed of the actual country self-

Table 10.7: Impact of country type on differences in Country Policy and Institutional Assessments

Areas of agreement	Non-fragile states (%)	Fragile states (%)
Country self-assessment and World Bank	74	13
Country self-assessment and AfDB	84	13
World Bank and AfDB	100	63
Country self-assessment, World Bank and AfDB	63	13

Source: ACBF (2012)

Figure 10.2: Variations in the CPIA ratings by source of data

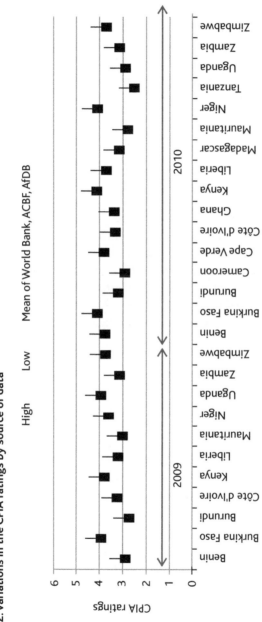

assessment and two measures that are one standard deviation away (that is, +1/−1 standard deviation). The areas of systematic bias are clearly seen in the spread between the low and high ratings in the figure, and can be used during country dialogue or to further examine the sub-indicators to understand the areas of difference.

The CPIA is based on a carrot-and-stick formula. The rewards through IDA resource allocations to 'good performing' countries are also supposed to provide a 'demonstration effect' by encouraging 'poor performing' countries to adopt The World Bank and AfDB's predetermined 'good' policies and institutions. But this approach has, as we have seen earlier in the chapter, a severe impact on low-income countries that remain highly dependent on aid as their main form of external finance as well as overall development financing. This is well documented (see Mosley et al, 1991; Mohan et al, 2000; Woods, 2006).

Alexander (2010) and van Waeyenberge (2008) provide the most comprehensive criticisms of donors and the usage of the CPIA as an aid allocation tool. First, selective allocation of aid based on the CPIA results in a country being locked into a certain policy agenda, with adverse repercussions for growth. For instance, the CPIA persistently precludes the various types of strategic interventions that were successfully deployed by the East Asian tiger economies. (We return to this point later.)

Second, aid selectivity hampers the ability of poor countries to raise their investment rates and/or to protect their pro-poor expenditures. In such countries, aid represents a significant proportion of the national budget. Yet the underlying structural features of such economies mean that they are highly likely to have low CPIA scores. For example, the average per capita income of the countries in the top quintile of the CPIA ranking is at least three times that of the countries in the bottom quintile. The CPIA approach also assumes that national governments have significant control over policy outcomes when other domestic and international factors can have a much more powerful impact. These include a heavy debt burden, declining terms of trade, low productive capacity throughout the economy and a low skill base. Our empirical results shed light on these issues.

Third, CPIA-oriented aid delivery systems can adversely affect the macroeconomic stability of countries with large aid/GDP ratios. Because the allocation formula for aid is sensitive to small changes in CPIA scores, especially for the governance criteria, the uncertainty and volatility of aid flows can be exacerbated. Other limitations include:

- *Baseless premise:* the CPIA advocates a set of policies that advance aid effectiveness, poverty reduction and growth in all countries. There have been many empirical attempts to prove the link between aid and growth (Alexander, 2010; Tribe, 2013). The most famous of these studies have been those of Burnside and Dollar (2000) and Collier and Dollar (2001, 2002).[4] Ideally, the multilateral banks should make attempts to draw country-specific conclusions because 'good' policies vary for each country, its stage of development and its circumstances. Experts and authorities may contest many of the CPIA's 'ideal' policies and institutions. The most critical methodological shortcoming of the aid effectiveness cross-country panel data evidence is the lack of evidence of causality.

- *One-size-cannot-fit-all:* The World Bank's IEG did an assessment of the CPIA at country level, and concluded that some of the criteria, for example, for trade, do not adequately allow for country specificity. The specification of particular tariff rates for different ratings reflects a one-size-fit-all approach to trade liberalisation that is not supported by country experience (The World Bank, 2010). Tribe (2013) considers this as an outcome of the ideology of the neoliberalism encapsulated in the Washington Consensus.

- *Undermining democracy:* by promoting a single set of policies, the CPIA poses a risk to democracy because it shrinks national governments' capacity to respond to the policy preferences of their electorates. Poor responsiveness to citizens' demands creates political instability and builds opposition to governments and the legitimisation process (Alexander, 2010).

- *Insensitivity to Africa's development priorities:* the CPIA does not adequately address itself to Africa's development agenda, including: economic vulnerability to powerful exogenous shocks; Millennium Development Goals (MDGs); agriculture; manufacturing; and environmental/climate challenges. The use of the CPIA results in lower resource allocations for countries with low levels of human development that impaired their policy environment in the first place. The CPIA should focus on achieving important development results and should be outcome-based (Alexander, 2010).

- *Double standards:* even the richest countries in the world have been unable to achieve many of the 'ideal' policies specified by the CPIA, as the 2007/08 global financial crisis demonstrated.

If The World Bank used the CPIA to rate the financial and economic management performance of the US and many European governments, these countries would receive the lowest possible rating (Alexander, 2010).

- *Subjective rating:* the AfDB and World Bank use the same CPIA criteria to assess the performance of the same African countries. Yet the country ratings of the AfDB are generally higher than those of The World Bank for most of the 16 CPIA criteria, and seem to confirm the ACBF survey results, which are based on subjective self-assessment.

- *Aid concentration:* two-thirds of the IDA funding recently disbursed to Africa has gone to only six countries (Nigeria, Ethiopia, Tanzania, DRC, Uganda and Mozambique). Equally, assistance to fragile states remained concentrated in a few countries, creating a significant set of Sub-Saharan African countries that have needs but little support (Alexander, 2010).

- *Complexity and translucency:* the IDA allocation system is complex, translucent, having eight factors (one of them being the CPIA) that determine a country's aid allocation. Given this complexity, and the fact that the CPIA is built on confidential data, this makes it difficult for outsiders to verify the results and to promote buy-in. This undermines the credibility of the allocation process, leaving it discordant with the Paris Declaration, the Accra Agenda for Action and the Busan protocols.

Aid selectivity and its consequent effectiveness depend exclusively on recipient behaviour, to the complete neglect of mitigating structural features of the recipient country or other factors unrelated to aid. Because the core of the CPIA continues to be premised on predetermined neoliberal norms and ideals, the aid practices of the multilateral banks in Sub-Saharan Africa seem to have progressed little in recent years, despite its purported graduation from the Washington Consensus of the structural adjustment period.

Country Policy and Institutional Assessment scores derived via self-assessment as the way forward

Below, we highlight at least five critical issues that may help to improve the CPIA computation from the perspective of self-assessment:

- *Enhanced country ownership:* since the Paris Declaration, there has been a growing consensus that development efforts have to be nationally or otherwise owned to be relevant and sustainable. This was recently re-affirmed in Busan. Local ownership of the process means that policies and interventions become embodied in the context of local priorities and frameworks. For projects/ programmes to succeed, there is a need for political commitment and leadership to demand change, seek performance-orientation and beneficiary participation, all of which redefine the power relationships, for example, in terms of gender and other factors having an impact on inclusion (Acemoglu and Robinson, 2012). Self-assessment becomes a crucial tool for local ownership and buy-in of the CPIA process.

- *Greater accountability for outcomes and results:* one of the criticisms of the existing CPIA scores is their limited focus on results. Countries must be given opportunities for self-assessment to allow for greater inclusivity, as non-inclusivity gives rise to patrimonialism, dictatorship, corruption, mismanagement and conflict. Capacity is eroded and state mandates are delivered on a fragmented 'clientilist' basis. Indeed, competing donor bureaucracies and establishments may undermine coordination and the environment as they occupy space during periods of heightened intervention, leaving the country with disrupted systems after such interventions (Kedir, 2011). This is in sharp contrast with experiences of the developmental states of East Asia. Self-assessment by countries and communities to derive the CPIA would provide greater inclusivity and accountability for development outcomes and results.

- *Strengthening participation and local leadership:* self-assessment by countries would open the way for participation and social inclusion in the CPIA, thus giving greater ownership and credibility not just to the overall process but also the outcomes and results that follow. Countries would also be able to provide the required leadership.

- *Enhancing policy dialogue:* as argued above, self-assessment grants a country and community the opportunity for retrospection and self-reflection. Such a process would considerably enhance the quality of policy dialogue and subsequent programmatic decisions derived from such processes. The quality of policy dialogue in most parts of Sub-Saharan Africa was relatively poor until recently, due to weak governance frameworks and limited engagement in the state by the broader society, thus undermining voice and inclusion.

- *Giving credibility and acceptance to CPIA-related processes:* there are arguably significant principal–agent problems in the CPIA and aid allocation processes have been undermined by the nature of the relationship between donors and recipients, which tend to be largely indirect and distant. This, in turn, leads to a very long and complex chain of principal–agent relationships: donor country taxpayers, parliament, heads of aid agencies, local partners, consultants, etc. In the recipient country, there are similar relationships between citizens, their government and those that actually implement programmes. Consequently, policy objectives, incentives and information available to these agents are not always well aligned with the objectives of either the taxpayers from the donor countries or the beneficiaries. CPIA initiatives must take cognisance of this difficulty in order to ensure aid effectiveness. Self-assessments would arguably cut this rather long CPIA process chain, and grant it greater credibility and acceptance (ACBF, 2011).

Given the systematic biases that are present in all types of assessments, there is a need to be aware that these biases are particularly prevalent in fragile states where the situation is more complex and reality on the ground more difficult to establish. There is need for a combination of measures to remove systematic biases and address data limitations. We propose a measure that reduces this bias by adopting a geometric mean (GM) of the three CPIA scores by the three institutions (that is, The World Bank, AfDB and ACBF's supported self-assessment).

The GM is computed as: $GM = nx^1x^2 \ldots x^n$. We take the nth root of the product of n numbers x^1 to x^n (n is the count of numbers in the set). This approach has the merit of simplicity and is instrumental in reducing measurement error. The result is presented in Table 10.8.

Conclusions

PBA of development aid by donors has been in use since the 1970s. Why do agencies such as The World Bank and AfDB undertake the exercise? And who should be held accountable for the results? There is a broad consensus among development practitioners that 'good' policies and institutions are favourable to growth and poverty reduction, notwithstanding inter-temporal fluctuations arising from internal and external factors or shocks. Two important issues are: (i) development

Table 10.8: Country Policy and Institutional Assessment based on geometric mean

Country	CPIA World Bank	CPIA self-assessment	CPIA AfDB
Benin	3.5	4	3.9
Burkina Faso	3.8	4.3	4.2
Burundi	3.1	3.4	3
Cameroon	3.2	3.1	3.8
Cape Verde	4.1	4	4.4
Côte d'Ivoire	2.7	3.5	3
Ghana	3.9	3.6	4.1
Kenya	3.8	4.3	4.2
Liberia	2.9	4	3.6
Madagascar	3.4	3.4	3.4
Mauritania	3.2	3	3.7
Niger	3.4	4.3	3.6
Tanzania	3.8	2.7	4
Uganda	3.8	3.1	4.3
Zambia	3.4	3.4	3.9
Zimbabwe	2	3.9	1.9
CPIA index based on data in 2009			
Benin	3.5	3.1	4.06
Burkina Faso	3.8	4.2	4.22
Burundi	3.1	2.9	3.09
Côte d'Ivoire	2.8	3.5	2.92
Kenya	3.7	4	4.2
Liberia	2.8	3.4	3.63
Mauritania	3.2	3.3	3.6
Niger	3.3	3.8	3.67
Uganda	3.9	4.2	4.24
Zambia	3.4	3.4	3.97
Zimbabwe	1.9	4	1.8

Source: Authors' calculation based on ACBF, AfDB and World Bank database on CPIA

is driven by local conditions and (ii) there is need to rationalise limited resources. The CPIA is one of the best-known PBA tools. Use of country performance rating ensures that 'good' performers receive, in per capita terms, a higher IDA allocation. A country's overall score is the main element of the country performance rating. The World Bank and other donors also use the scores internally, among other things, to help guide their programming and risk assessment, as well as the research agenda.

We argued in this chapter that the CPIA country rating matters a great deal because it has a significant influence on the allocation of IDA resources, through its role in the IDA country performance rating. There is a need to revisit and overhaul the way the CPIA rating is derived as it has implications for natural justice and democratic practice. Our empirical results show the CPIA is relevant for growth and poverty reduction in the sense that its components sit well with known determinants from the growth literature. Post-Busan developments call into question the current approach of The World Bank and AfDB. The staff of both agencies maintain periodic communication with their counterparts in other multilateral development banks to discuss the criteria and the respective performance-based allocation processes, which does not serve to strengthen country ownership and systems. In fact, the case for alternative aid allocation formulae, reform and support for country self-assessments arise from the fact that the multilateral institutions are accountable for the use of their concessional resources to their shareholders. To entrench development in national strategies, full institutional ownership of country ratings that underpin the allocation of these resources is critical.

The integrity of the policy and of the allocation processes requires that each country carries out an independent assessment and determines its own ratings. With full disclosure of the ratings, the availability of independent assessments by different institutions using the same questionnaire is a useful means of cross-checking those of individual countries. The ACBF has encouraged this approach, as the CPIA can be used more fruitfully as an accountability tool for capacity development. Citizens need voice and inclusivity, meaning that the CPIA should be complemented with other measures of performance such as the African Capacity Indicators and the APRM.

Our proposal calls for the consideration of structural characteristics of countries and their level of development. Equity is not part of the existing performance-based system, and we suggest this to be incorporated in the reformed CPIA given the critical importance attached to inclusion in the post-2015 development agenda. Economic vulnerability and conditions of human capital (for example, education and health) can be detrimentally affected by sudden shocks due to the structural weakness of the poorest of countries (for example, the Ebola outbreak). We suggest that CPIA revision by incorporating these considerations so that their aid allocation is commensurate with their needs and structural features instead of a simple mechanical performance criteria.

No measures are infallible, and each approach introduces some type of bias. Expert-based measures conducted by staff of multilateral organisations may miss local variations and nuances. Self-assessments done by country experts may render the picture rosier than real or harsher for a variety of reasons. There is therefore a need for an approach that mutes the effect of errors. We have shown in this chapter that a rating based on multiple measures with non-correlated sources of measurement error can address such measurement errors. Despite its weaknesses in terms of measurement bias, self-assessment has advantages in terms of context-sensitivity of the results and ownership of the outcomes, which can aid the success in addressing the challenges during implementation. Cross-country and international benchmarking is possible and useful when the assessments are done by multilateral aid agencies, which can, in turn, show accountability to their funders. We have shown that an index created from measures from multiple sources can address the biases in each of the individual measures. All these arguments demonstrate that there is a strong case for reforming the aid allocation tool, as currently enshrined in the CPIA.

References

Acemoglu, D. and Robinson, J. (2012) *Why nations fail: The origins of power, prosperity, and poverty*, London: Profile Books.

ACBF (African Capacity Building Foundation) (2011) *Africa Capacity Indicators: Capacity development in fragile states*, Harare: ACBF.

ACBF (2012) *Africa Capacity Indicators: Capacity development for agricultural transformation and food security*, Harare: ACBF.

Agarwal, B. (2001) 'Participatory exclusions, community forestry, and gender: an analysis for South Asia and a conceptual framework', *World Development*, vol 29, no 10, pp 1623-48.

Alexander, N. (2010) 'The Country Policy and Institutional Assessment (CPIA) and allocation of IDA resources: Suggestions for improvements to benefit African countries', Paper presented at a meeting of the African Caucus of Finance Ministers, Central Bank Governors and Executive Directors of the International Monetary Fund and World Bank, Freetown, Sierra Leone.

Basu, K. (2006) 'Globalization, poverty, and inequality: What is the relationship? What can be done?', *World Development*, vol 34, pp 1361-73.

Beckfield, J. (2003) 'Inequality in the world polity: the structure of international organization', *American Sociological Review*, vol 68, no 3, pp 401-24.

Birdsall, N. (2002) *Asymmetric globalization: Global markets require good global politics*, Working Paper No 12, Washington, DC: Center for Global Development.

Birdsall, N. (2003) *Why it matters who runs the IMF and The World Bank*, Working Paper No 22, Washington, DC: Center for Global Development.

Boone, P. (1996) 'Politics and the effectiveness of aid', *European Economic Review*, vol 40, pp 289-329.

Bourguignon, F., Ferreira, F.H.G. and Walton, M. (2006) *Equity, efficiency and inequality traps: A research agenda*, KSG Faculty Research Working Paper Series, Cambridge, MA: Harvard University (http://ksgnotes1.harvard.edu/Research/wpaper.nsf/rwp/RWP06-025).

Bourguignon, F. et al (2009) 'International redistribution of income', *World Development*, vol 37, issue 1, pp 1-10.

Burnside, C. and Dollar, D. (2000) 'Aid, policies, and growth', *The American Economic Review*, vol 90, no 4.

Carson, L. and Martin, B. (2002) 'Random selection and technological decision making', *Science and Public Policy*, vol 29, no 2, pp 105-13.

Collier, P and Dollar, D. (2001) 'Can the world cut poverty in half? How policy reform and effective aid can meet international development goals', *World Development*, vol 29, pp 1787-802.

Collier, P. and Dollar, D. (2002) 'Aid allocation and poverty reduction', *European Economic Review*, vol 45, pp 1470-500.

De Matteis, A. (2013) 'Relevance of poverty and governance for aid allocation', *Review of Development Finance*, vol 3, pp 51-60.

Diarra, G. (2010) 'Good governance and Samaritan dilemma in multilateral aid allocation: what consequences for inequalities and social protection in Africa?', Paper prepared for the ERD Conference 'New Faces for African Development', 27-30 June, Dakar, Senegal.

Easterly, W., Levine, R. and Roodman, D. (2003) 'New data, new doubts: a comment on Burnside and Dollar's "Aid, policies, and growth', *American Economic Review*.

Ellison, N. (1997) 'Towards a new social politics: citizenship and reflexivity in late modernity', *Sociology*, vol 31, no 4, pp 697-717.

Evans, P. (1997) 'Introduction: Development strategies across the public–private divide', in P. Evans (ed) *State–society synergy: Government and social capital in development*, IAS Research Series No 94, Berkeley, CA: University of California, pp 1-10.

Fowler, A. (1998) 'Authentic NGDO partnerships in the new policy agenda for international aid: dead end or light ahead?', *Development and Change*, vol 29, pp 137-59.

Gaventa, J. and Cornwall, A. (2000) 'From users and choosers to makers and shapers: repositioning participation in social policy', *IDS Bulletin*, vol 31, no 4, pp 50-62.

Gaventa, J. and Cornwall, A. (2001) 'Power and knowledge', in P. Reason and H. Bradbury (eds) *Handbook of action research: Participative inquiry and practice*, London: Sage, pp 70-80.

Guillaumont, P. and Chauvet, L. (2001) 'Aid and performance: a reassessment', *Journal of Development Studies*, August, vol 37, no 6, pp 66-92.

Habermas, J. (1984) *The theory of communicative action: Reason and the rationalization of society*, Boston, MA: Beacon Press.

Herkenrath, M., König, C., Scholtz, H. and Volken, T. (2005) 'Convergence and divergence in the contemporary world system: an introduction', *International Journal of Comparative Sociology*, vol 46, no 363.

Hopkins, A. (1986) 'The World Bank in Africa: historical reflections on the African present', *World Development*, vol 14, pp 1473-87.

Jacquet, P., Pisani-Ferry, J. and Tubiana, L. (2002) *Gouvernance mondiale*, Rapport de synthèse Conseil d'Analyse Economique.

Kanbur, R. (2005) *Reforming the formula: A modest proposal for introducing development outcomes in IDA allocation procedures*, Centre for Economic Policy Research Discussion Paper Number 4971, London: Centre for Economic Policy Research (www.arts.cornell.edu/poverty/kanbur/IDAForm.pdf).

Kararach, G. (2011) *Macroeconomic policy and political limits of reforms in developing countries*, Nairobi: African Research and Resource Forum.

Kedir, A. (2011) 'Donor coordination in fragile states of Africa: capacity building for peace and poverty reduction', *World Review of Science, Technology and Sustainable Development*, vol 7, nos 2/3/4, pp 307-56.

Leach, M. and Scoones, I. (2002) 'Science and citizenship in a global context', Paper presented at Conference on Science and Citizenship in a Global Context, Institute for Development Studies, Brighton, 12-13 December.

Mohan, G. (2001) 'Participatory development', in V. Desai and R. Potter (eds) *The Arnold companion to development studies*, London: Hodder, pp 49-54.

Mohan, G., Milward, B. and Zack-Williams, A.B. (2000) *Structural adjustment: Theory, practice and impacts*, London and New York: Routledge.

Mosley, P., Harrigan, J. and Toye, J. (1991) *Aid and power: The World Bank and policy-based lending*, 2 volumes: vol 1, London: Routledge.

Nissanke, M. (2013) *Managing sovereign debt for productive investment and development in Africa: A critical appraisal of the joint bank-fund debt sustainability framework and its implications for sovereign debt management*, London: School of Oriental and African Studies, University of London.

Ostrom, E. (1996) 'Crossing the great divide: coproduction, synergy and development', *World Development*, vol 24, no 6, pp 1073-87.

Pateman, C. (1970) *Participation and democratic theory*, London: Cambridge University Press.

Payne, A. (2001) 'The global politics of development: towards a new research agenda', *Progress in Development Studies*, vol 1, no 5.

Rao, V. (2006) 'On "inequality traps" and development policy', *Development Outreach*, February, pp 10-13.

Ravallion M. (2010) *Mash-up indices of development*, World Bank Policy Research, Working Paper 5432, Washington, DC: The World Bank.

Rayner, S. (2003) 'Democracy in the age of assessment: reflections on the roles of expertise and democracy in public-sector decision making', *Science and Public Policy*, vol 30, no 3, pp 163-70.

Rayner, S. and Malone, E. (1998) 'The challenge of climate change to the social sciences', in S. Rayner and E. Malone (eds) *Human choice and climate change*, Columbus, OH: Battelle Press.

Rodrik, D. (2004) *Industrial policy for the 21st century*, CEPR Discussion Paper 4767, London: Centre for Economic Policy Research.

Sanderson, S. (2005) 'World-systems analysis after thirty years: Should it rest in peace?', *International Journal of Comparative Sociology*, vol 46, pp 179-213.

Sarrasin, B. (1997) 'Les coûts sociaux de l'ajustement structurel en Afrique subsaharienne: Evolution des critiques externes et des réponses de la Banque Mondiale', *Canadian Journal of African Studies / Revue Canadienne des Études Africaines*, vol 31, no 3, pp 517-53.

Sirianni, C. and Friedland, L. (2000) *Civic innovation in America: Community empowerment, public policy, and the movement for civic renewal*. Berkeley, CA: University of California Press.

Thérien, J.P. (1999) 'Beyond the north-south divide: the two tales of world poverty', *Third World Quarterly*, vol 20, no 4, pp 723-42.

Tribe, M. (2013) *Aid and development: Issues and reflections*, Strathclyde Discussion Papers in Economics No 13-09, Strathclyde: University of Strathclyde (www.strath.ac.uk/media/departments/economics/researchdiscussionpapers/2013/13-09FINAL.pdf).

Thomas, C. (2001) 'Global governance, development and human security: exploring the links', *Third World Quarterly*, vol 22, no 2, pp 159-75.

van Waeyenberge, E. (2008) *After structural adjustment, Then what? Lending selectivity by The World Bank*, Development Viewpoint no 16, London: Centre for Development Policy and Research, School of Oriental and African Studies, University of London.

Woods, N. (2006) *The globalizers: The IMF, the World Bank, and their borrowers*, Ithaca, NY: Cornell University Press.

World Bank, The (2005) *World development report 2006: Equity and development*, Oxford: Oxford University Press.

World Bank, The (2010) *The World Bank's country policy and institutional assessment: An evaluation*, Independent Evaluation Group (www. worldbank.org).

World Bank, The (2014) *CPIA Africa: Assessing Africa's policies and institutions (includes Djibouti and Yemen)*, Washington, DC: The World Bank (http://documents.worldbank.org/curated/en/2014/06/19713179/cpia-africa-assessing-africas-policies-institutions-includes-djibouti-yemen).

ELEVEN

Development and sustainability in a warming world: measuring the impacts of climate change in Africa

Hany Besada,[1] *Fatima Denton and Benjamin O'Bright*

Introduction

In their current manifestation, the Millennium Development Goals (MDGs) are presented as a blueprint to galvanise governments and private actors towards a substantial reduction in extreme poverty levels by 2015 (Sachs et al, 2009, p 1502). While the links between poverty and climate change are unsurprisingly complex, academic research and discourse finds itself approaching these two themes not as interconnected subjects, but rather as variably distinct entities. Cohen et al (1998) argue that even though climate is one symptom of unsustainable development, the two concepts continue to coexist under separate epistemologies, to the extent that climate change has not readily been identified as strongly influencing sustainable development discourse.

Indeed, as emphasised by published data from the National Aeronautics and Space Administration (NASA), the National Climatic Data Center (NCDC) and the European Environmental Agency (EEA), development rarely features in the discussion of indicators for the measurement of climate change and environmental degradation (NASA, 2012; NCDC, 2012; EEA, 2012), despite observations that its impacts fall disproportionately on developing countries and the poor (McMichael and Butler, 2004). Yet it is increasingly rehearsed in the climate change research that in this interface of climate and development, climate policy goals continue to be missed as a priority for many developing countries, as other issues such as poverty alleviation and energy security remain centre stage on the development agenda (Halnaes and Garg, 2011).

In addition, one main observation is that those most deeply affected by changes in global environmental trends seem less to be the beneficiaries of concentrated efforts towards positive progression but rather appear resigned to be left out in the cold. Sachs et al, however, note that by targeting the root causes of development stagnation and regression, particularly embodied by climate change, the international community may achieve complementary positive results in both sectors (Sachs et al, 2009, p 1502). To do so requires issues of climate change being understood and filtered through the empirical lens of sustainable development priorities, which would support the clarification and simplification of related policy avenues.

This chapter follows several avenues of inquiry as a means of unifying research on development issues and related climate change, thereby presenting a critical base on which future study and international action can be undertaken. First, using a variety of sources, this chapter provides a six-fold criteria of observable impact areas of climate change on sustainable development. Second, each of the impacts is evaluated in detail, intrinsically demonstrating argued potential, casual links. Third, this chapter broaches parallel subjects and areas of institutional deficit and sustainability, detailing concerns of strategy derailment caused by a lack of stable, organisational foundations. While institutions themselves have the ability to support adaptation and mitigation processes, many of the impacts of climate change on development find their origins in the absence of robust institutional arrangements that will enable and sustain both adaptation and mitigation processes. Last, looking towards the future, several questions are answered in turn, as a means of enabling the coordination of policy and research responses to climate change and sustainable development: what can be done to mitigate observable effects in the immediate future? What policy targets and partnerships must be developed to achieve a reduction in environmental degradation? And what are the appropriate avenues for education and awareness in regards to climate change that will promote an engaged public?

Developing standardised criteria of climate change effects on development

According to the United Nations Economic Commission for Europe (UNECE), effective indicators of change, as a generalised term, require four distinct characteristics: they must be relevant to the current context; they must be easy to understand; they should be reliable; and they must be based on accessible data (UNECE Expert Group on Indicators, 2005). Indicators should utilise both qualitative and quantitative measurements as complementary means of presenting information, which in this instance is the observable impact of climate change on development (UNECE Expert Group on Indicators, 2005). It is noted, however, that where possible, quantitative demarcations should be given priority due to their evaluative effectiveness and limited scope for potential subjective bias (UNECE Expert Group on Indicators, 2005). In short, indicators point to an issue or condition as a measure of how well a system is working, which can subsequently support the determination of potential solutions for any concerns (UNECE Expert Group on Indicators, 2005). While the indicators forwarded by this chapter may not necessarily be agreed on by all those within the global research community, they can and should be considered as an important foundation for future research.

According to a report by Nicholas Stern, the mitigation of effects caused by a 2°C rise in global temperatures will conclusively cost approximately 1 per cent of the world's total GDP (quoted in *The Economist*, 2009). The World Bank countered that for developing states, including least developed countries (LDCs), the impact of this event will be more severe, with climate change costing upwards of 4 to 5 per cent for some governments (*The Economist*, 2009). The UN Office of the High Representative of the Least Developed Countries, Landlocked Developing Countries and Small Island Developing States indicates that the LDCs are a group of 49 states recognised as the world's poorest and weakest, with extremely low GDP assets, severe economic vulnerability and lack of significant and prosperous human resources (Sem and Moore, 2009). Compared to developed countries, LDCs emit little of the world's greenhouse gases but remain incredibly vulnerable to their resultant effects, particularly due to their inability to adapt (Sem and Moore, 2009). In contrast, for a state to be classified as highly adaptive it must have a stable and prosperous economy; a significant degree of access to technology; well-delineated roles and responsibilities for implementation of adaptive strategies; systems for national and local information dissemination; and equitable access to resources (Sem and Moore, 2009). Yohe and Tol (2002) equally argue that the determinants of adaptive capacity include a range of available technological options for adaptation; a stock of human capital including personal security and education; a stock of social capital including property rights; decision-makers' ability to manage information, their ability to determine which information is credible and their own credibility; the availability of resources and distribution of resources across populations; and the attribution of stress sources and the importance of exposure to its local manifestations (see also

IPCC, 2013, Chapter 18). As such, it is proposed, not only by these authors, that developing countries and LDCs are, and will continue to be, the most vulnerable to climate change and its damaging effects.

In the report *Turn down the heat: Why a 4°C warmer world must be avoided*, The World Bank (2012) outlines several impacts of climate change, emphasising that the most adverse effects will be felt primarily in states that lack adequate infrastructure and support mechanisms to adapt efficiently (Abeygunawardena, 2002; Mizra, 2003; European Commission, 2006). The report notes that the areas that will be adversely affected include: agriculture, as part of generalised economic impacts; water resources; ecosystems and biodiversity, including resultant natural disasters; and human health (McGuigan et al, 2002; The World Bank, 2012). These conclusions are equally reflected by Sem and Moore (2009), which includes the addition of coastal regions, tourism and settlement to this now growing list of affected areas in developing states.

Using the sources above, one can present a tentative and preliminary classification of directly affected development sectors by climate change: economics, particularly agriculture and tourism; water resources; ecosystems and biodiversity, including natural disasters; human health; and coastal region degradation. The following discussion, however, should be viewed within the context of a sustainable development target, which is continually moving and evolving, as strategies for its achievement and analysis of its impact should never remain stagnant. As mentioned above, each of these five sections are evaluated in turn, while attempting to causally link their stagnant and regressive developmental impacts to climate change.

Economics and natural resources

In 2011, The World Bank predicted that if the current rates of poverty reduction continued along similar trends as they have since 2005, headcounts based on US$1 and US$2 earnings per day as the primary indicator may become obsolete as a measure of population wellbeing (Skoufias, 2012). Equally noted was the growing concern that if climate change is not halted, the rise in global temperatures and its resultant effects could slow or even reverse progress on poverty reduction (Skoufias, 2012), effects which include loss of human life, livelihoods, assets and infrastructure through, among other factors, extreme events (Richards, 2003). Indirectly, climate change variation is predicted to slow and alter the origins of economic growth, such as the ability of the poor to engage in non-agricultural sectors while simultaneously increasing both poverty and nullifying any potentially positive macroeconomic policy or private sector investment outcomes (Richards, 2003). These arguments are particularly relevant when taking into account studies that suggest agricultural GDP growth is 2.2 times as effective at reducing poverty as non-agricultural GDP (Hertel and Rosch, 2010).

Indeed, developing countries are more dependent on agriculture and other climate-sensitive natural resources for income and wellbeing (Skoufias, 2012), thereby directly linking climate change effects to potential economic growth and prosperity. Without this primary source of income, which may be ravaged by environmental collapse, development will certainly stall or regress. The United Nations (UN) has predicted that by 2100, parts of Sub-Saharan Africa, considered to be one of the most vulnerable regions of the world, will experience a 2 to 7 per cent loss in GDP due to climatic effects on agricultural production (Sem and Moore, 2009).

More than coins in state coffers, recent estimates showcase that nearly 800 million people around the world continue to be chronically undernourished, with a large portion of them children under the age of five (Hertel and Rosch, 2010) Climate modelling has demonstrated consistent results of negative crop yield impacts worldwide, even with potentially beneficial rises in CO_2 and relative farm adaptation techniques, which have been argued by some to account for a positive political response to environmental change (Parry et al, 2004). In studying this particular climate change–positive yield correlation, all scenarios in Parry et al's work resulted in a dramatic decrease in crop production from between 9 to 22 per cent, thereby increasing the financial disparity among developing and developed states (Parry et al, 2004; Beddington et al, 2013, p 12). In tropical and sub-tropical world regions, areas that include some of the highest hunger levels, climate change could cause crop yields to fall 10-20 per cent or more, between now and 2050 (Thornton, 2012, p 2). Developing countries alone, which account for 90 per cent of irrigated wheat growth worldwide, could see a drop of crop and rice yields by close to 13 and 15 per cent respectively without adaptation measures being put in place, despite demand for these foodstuffs expected to double by 2050 in impoverished global regions (Thornton, 2012, pp 3, 9). Estimates for the African continent are no more positive: warmer temperatures could depress immediate continental harvest rates by between 10 to 20 per cent, placing considerable stress on food security as the world prepares for the near future addition of an estimated 2 billion individuals (Thornton, 2012, pp 9-10).

The above research equally substantiates claims by the Third Assessment Report of the Intergovernmental Panel on Climate Change (IPCC) that argued that crop yields in the most tropical and sub-tropical regions will be significantly reduced due to environmental degradation, as rain-fed crops begin to pass the maximum temperature threshold, beyond which they cannot survive (Richards, 2003, p 5). Field tests have shown that for most crops, surpassing a temperature threshold of 30°C will typically result in decreased yields (Thornton, 2012, p 9). The resultant crop production loss could be up to 30 per cent, although it has also been suggested that states such as China could actually experience a 25 per cent rise in cereal production from the same climate phenomena (Richards, 2003, p 5). The UN has equally advanced more pessimistic numbers, denoting that a reduction of 50 per cent in rain-fed crops could occur by 2020, a 5 to 8 per cent increase in arid land on the African continent, and its complete loss of production ability and capacity for some food stuffs, including wheat (Sem and Moore, 2009).

The question remains, however, as to what impact a lack of available financial and physical resources will have on individual poverty, the reduction of which is primarily linked to an increase in development. According to Hertel and Rosch (2010), since the poor tend to spend the highest share of their limited income on foodstuffs, adverse climate change is expected to have a disproportionately negative effect on them, as economics dictate that reduced production results in higher prices. Without significant improvements in agricultural productivity, through investment and access to new technology, vulnerability to climate change among the poor with continue, adaptation will be unattainable, and poverty reduction, particularly in Sub-Saharan Africa, will be difficult to achieve (Schlenker and Lobell, 2010). As concluded by the Organisation for Economic Co-operation and Development (OECD), 'climate change will compound poverty. Its adverse impacts will be most striking in the developing nations ... [and] within these countries, the poorest, who have the least resources and the least capacity to adapt, are the most vulnerable' (OECD, 2003).

As previously noted, it would be difficult, if not impossible, to discuss the effects of climate change on development without briefly analysing the 30 to 40 per cent of significant natural disasters resulting from carbon emissions (Richards, 2003). In 2000, exceptionally heavy rains in Mozambique were implicated as the primary factor in the destruction of over one-third of the country's staple food (maize) and the deaths of 80 per cent of its cattle herds, having an impact on more than 400,000 people (Mizra, 2003). In 1999, cyclones in

India destroyed 80 per cent of its standing crops and almost half a million head of cattle (Mizra, 2003). In 1998 Hurricane Mitch pushed 165,000 people in Honduras below the poverty line, due in particular to a 29 per cent loss in available crops and a linked 18 per cent loss in assets for the poorest members of society (Richards, 2003). Flooding in previous years has affected between 20.5 and 70 per cent of land in Bangladesh, causing extensive damage to its primarily agricultural-based economy (Mizra, 2003), and Guinea is expected to lose close to 30 per cent of its rice-producing fields as a result of permanent flooding by 2050 (Sem and Moore, 2009). Permanent or semi-permanent flooding itself is characterised by a slow onset of sea level rises and land subsidence, causing overall failure of drainage and water management systems, with a long or indefinite duration (Jha et al, 2012, p 56). While much work continues to be required on the above link between factors, it is seen through these cases, as well as more contemporary disaster events, that climate change can be the spark leading to natural disasters, having a negative impact on the staple economic drivers of developing states, such as agriculture.

In summary, agriculture and other natural resources, which account for a substantial portion of economic momentum and support in developing states, will be adversely affected by climate change. Agriculture and services derived from natural resources support the livelihood structures of 70 per cent of people in Sub-Saharan Africa and represent 40 per cent of export earnings and 50 per cent of total GDP. As such, climate change poses a considerable threat to a sector that as is perceived as a particularly important engine of growth. While there may be certain benefits from warmer temperatures, including longer growing seasons in colder climates, an increase in crop yields for the first 3°C of a global temperature rise, and new opportunities for global shipping through polar regions (*The Guardian*, 2011), it will most certainly create substantial and prevalent negative effects on the world's poorest states, whose dramatic reduction in crop yields are predicted to result in stagnation of development. Approaches to limiting climate change and promoting effective means of adaptation will be necessary if extreme hunger and development regression are to be avoided.

Climate change and water resources

To realise the impact of climate change on water and human security requires first an understanding of the distribution of fresh to salt water on Earth. In 2012, approximately 98 per cent of aqua reserves on the planet were salt water, with the remaining 2 per cent being fresh sources (Mcintyre, 2012). Of those fresh water resources, 70 per cent is in the form of snow and ice, 30 per cent is groundwater and less than 0.5 per cent is surface-based, cradled in lakes and rivers (Mcintyre, 2012). With such a limited portion of global reserves being immediately accessible to low-income populations and states, the impact of climate change on water sustainability is all the more serious. Rapid urbanisation in some developing countries is increasing water demand, and changing industrial uses, including for hydropower. Consequently, the impact from climate change on water resources will have ripple effects on human development and other critical areas.

The following section engages with four broad climate change impacts on water resources, detailing present and predicted difficulties, as well as avenues for adaptation and mitigation: availability and demand; quality; socioeconomic impacts; and extreme events. Within these categories exist many additional direct and indirect impacts of climate change on water resources, which will require additionally comprehensive analysis in the future.

Availability and demand

The IPCC notes that it is very likely that the costs of climate change will outweigh any related benefits when analysed on a global scale (IPCC, 2013, p 44). In particular, the reduction of freshwater availability, facilitated by climate change, has been directly linked to a general increase in worldwide water stress and a decrease in sustainability (Alavian et al, 2009, p 21). While there is substantial variability in projections across studies on levels of water stress, largely dependent on modelling methodology and included external drivers such as population growth and intervening adaptation measures, predictions mark that 2.7 to 4 billion people will be affected by limited freshwater supplies by 2050 (Alavian et al, 2009, p 21; Diop, 2008). Interestingly, using a per capita water availability indicator, the IPCC argues in contrast that climate change could be a facilitator of overall reduced water stress at a global level as increases in run-off are more concentrated in the world's most populous regions, thus demonstrating the potential disparity among research (IPCC, 2013, p 45).

Higher temperatures and increased variability of precipitation are expected to lead to a growth in water demand for personal and industrial use (IPCC, 2013, p 44). It is argued in projections of future water stress that the primary and dominant dependent variable is the growth of domestic water use, as stimulated by rises in income and population (IPCC, 2013, p 45). Particularly in regions termed as having a 'difficult hydrology', which includes variable precipitations and absolute water scarcity (Alavian et al, 2009, p 23), the projected negative effects of climate change-instigated increased variability of precipitation is expected to outweigh any benefits stemming from increased annual water run-off (IPCC, 2013, p 45). While there is high confidence that adaptation can reduce vulnerability and support sustainable development, particularly in the short term, adaptive capacity is intimately connected to social and economic development, which continues to be unevenly distributed across the globe (IPCC, 2013, p 49). In water-insecure regions of the world, characterised by extreme hydrological variability, a poor endowment of water resources, or inadequate capacity, infrastructure and governance institutions, climate change is projected overall to make water security and sustainability harder to both achieve and maintain (Alavian et al, 2009, p 23).

Quality

Water quality affects a wide range of impact areas and is necessary for the continued resilience of human populations. Unfortunately, changes in water quality are primarily the result of human activities on land that generate pollutants, which can subsequently be attributed to the facilitation of an increase in climate change features (Arthurton et al, 2007, p 131). Higher water temperatures, increased precipitation intensity and longer periods of low flows are projected to exacerbate many forms of water pollution, including sediments, nutrients, dissolved organic carbon, pathogens, pesticides and salts (IPCC, 2013, p 43). This is argued to then promote algae blooms, and increase the content of bacteria and fungi in global water resources, thereby having a negative impact on human health (IPCC, 2013, p 43).

The United Nations Environment Programme (UNEP) argues that human health is *the* most important issue related to water quality (Arthurton et al, 2007, p 131). Improving water resource management, increasing sustainable access to safe drinking water and basic sanitation has the capacity to improve the lives of billions (UNESCO, 2012, p 103). As previously noted, however, poor aqua quality and a warmer global climate can lead to a propagation of water and vector pathogens as well as major point and non-point pollutants, including microbes, nutrients, oxygen-consuming materials, heavy metals, persistent organics, sediments and pesticides (Arthurton et al, 2007, p 131). Increasingly intense rainfall, stemming from human-induced climate change, will likely lead to an intensification of these pollutants in water supplies, facilitated primarily by enhanced transportation avenues into surface water and reservoirs for pathogens and dissolved toxins, and increasing levels of erosion leading to an overall deterioration of water quality (IPCC, 2013, p 43). Additionally, an escalated occurrence of lower river flows is argued to lead to a decreased contaminant dilution capacity and thus higher pollutant concentrations, with the issue being compounded in areas experiencing a climate change-induced reduction in run-off (IPCC, 2013, p 43). Lower minimum flows imply less water volume for dilution and hence higher concentrations of pollutants when measured at points of discharge (Whitehead et al, 2008, p v). For example, the River Tame within the heavily urbanised area of Birmingham, UK, has undergone testing to show that there is an increased level of phosphorous concentrations during higher temperature seasons due to reduced flows and decreased dilution capacity (Whitehead et al, 2008, p 26). Indeed, these results are not a localised phenomena: testing by Schneider et al (2013) denotes that changes in global temperatures will result in increased intermittency of river flows for the geographical area around the Mediterranean Sea, such as the Tiber river in Rome, with isolated cases of zero-flows also expanding in number (Schneider et al, 2013, p 336). This situation, caused primarily by climate change, will have a negative impact on water quality as the concentration of pollutants intensifies when flows decrease (Schneider et al, 2013, p 336). Schneider et al predict that in the continental European climate zone, where high amounts of water are extracted for industrial purposes such as electricity generation, climate change is likely to further reduce river flows from spring until autumn (Schneider et al, 2013, p 336), thereby limiting the dilution capacity of water for toxins.

Socioeconomic impacts

The World Bank notes that agriculture is by far the largest user of water, accounting for almost 70 per cent of global withdrawals and 90 per cent of global consumptive water use in 2009 (Alavian et al, 2009, p 26). While an individual may drink between 2-4 litres of water a day, it takes between 2,000-5,000 litres of water to produce an individual's daily food (Alavian et al, 2009, p 26). Over 80 per cent of global agricultural land is rain-fed; this means that productivity in these regions is dependent on precipitation for evaporative demands and soil moisture distribution (IPCC, 2013, p 59). Irrigated agriculture land, representing approximately 18 per cent of production, is directly reliant on the availability and quality of ground-based freshwater resources and associated capacity of natural reserve replenishment (IPCC, 2013, p 59). The IPCC notes that both too little as well as too much water can have disastrous effects on crop production, with each scenario being a plausible outcome of climate change in different regions of the world (IPCC, 2013, p 59). Precipitation shifts, occurring through extreme events, erratic rainfall and seasonal changes in run-off can alter ground nutrient content, leading to extreme soil conditions incapable of sustaining crop growth (Alavian et al, 2009, p 26). Climate-induced pressure on water resource sustainability is also argued to 'lead to increased competition between irrigation needs and demand from non-agriculture sectors, potentially reducing the availability and quality of water resources for food' (IPCC, 2013, p 59). As such, future increases in agriculture production, particularly emphasised by the projected expansion of irrigated crop systems in the developing world, must be matched by the distribution of climate-resilient sustainable adaptation technology such as desalinisation systems, and improved water management and efficient-use programmes.

Extreme events

Water-related extreme events, including flooding and drought, account for 90 per cent of all natural disasters, with some 373 natural disasters killing close to 300,000 people in 2010, directly affecting nearly 208 million others, and costing states almost US$110 billion (UNESCO, 2012, p 115). Although a variety of climate and non-climate processes influence their emergence, frequency and intensity, there are indications that climate change may have already had an impact on a number of occurrences, duration and impact flooding and droughts, with the number of inland flood episodes nearly doubling from 1950 to 2005 (Alavian et al, 2009, p 18). Specific examples of such include the federal Emergency Management Agency's flood risk area being doubled in 2013 for New York City, citing expected tidal surge increases and higher water levels (Buckley, 2013); and two-thirds of coastal locations in the US, including 85 per cent of regions outside the Gulf of Mexico, being predicted to double in their chances of experiencing 'century floods' each year (Strauss et al, 2012, p 4). The latter trend has been associated in studies with an increased frequency of heavy precipitation events, a category of phenomena projected to become more common in most global regions throughout the 21st century (IPCC, 2013, p 41). The rise of flooding is also likely to bring with it an increase of water contamination by chemicals, pathogens, soil and heavy metals, thereby having an impact on regional human health (IPCC, 2013, p 68).

It is equally likely that the global area affected by regular droughts will increase over the next century as a byproduct of a warming world and instigating climate change (IPCC, 2013, p 42). In a single model study of global drought frequency, the proportion of land surface experiencing this extreme event was projected to increase by 10- to 30-fold (IPCC, 2013, p 42). Particularly in regions of the world that rely on glacial melt water for dry season aqua supplies, the increase of drought is likely to be substantial (IPCC, 2013, p 42).

Both flooding and droughts could be tempered by appropriate sustainable infrastructure investments, and changes in water and land-use management (IPCC, 2013, p 74). In 2010, The World Bank reported that government expenditure on disaster prevention is generally lower than overall relief spending, which rises after an extreme event and remains high for several subsequent years (UNESCO, 2012, p 116). Beneficial prevention, however, requires not just an increase in funding but a knowledge-supported targeting and development of sustainable adaptation measures, each of which recognises the above-noted linkages between impact areas, thereby improving the overall effectiveness of financial investment and spending (UNESCO, 2012, p 116).

Climate change and biodiversity

On 13 May 2013, *The Guardian* newspaper reported on new research that suggested that as global temperatures continue to rise, over one-third of common land animals, and more than half of plant species, could see dramatic losses in population numbers by the end of this century (*The Guardian*, 2013). These predictions estimate a loss of more than half of habitat ranges for 57 per cent of plant and 34 per cent of animal life, as a direct consequence of climate change (*The Guardian*, 2013). The largest numbers of plants and animals were likely to be lost from Sub-Saharan Africa, Central America, Amazonia and Australia, with significant plant species reductions also predicted in North Africa, Central Asia and South Eastern Europe (*The Guardian*, 2013). Studies by Bellard et al further add that 35 per cent of the world's bird population, 52 per cent of amphibians and 71 per cent of warm water reef-building corals are also susceptible to even the slightest change in global temperatures (2012, p 372). While a 4 per cent portion of animal species are expected to benefit from climate change, the study's authors predicted that an estimated 4°C temperature rise will result in dramatic global ecosystem collapse, affecting not only state economies and their potential for sustainable development, but agriculture, air quality, clean water access and tourism (*The Guardian*, 2013). These conclusions are also evidenced by researchers at McGill University who argued in a 2012 study that the loss of biodiversity, most particularly plant and animal life, appears to have an impact on the health and sustainability of ecosystems as much as human-originating environmental stresses, including pollution and climate change (Bonnin and Turner, 2012). Therefore, an aggregate conclusion could suggest that climate change-induced biodiversity loss will be critically severe on global ecosystems and development.

Direct effects of climate change on biodiversity

Impacts of climate change on biodiversity do, and will continue to, vary widely in different regions of the world, and will be largely dependent on the ability of plants and animals to evolve their own biological adaptation traits, as well as human-based supportive sustainability measures (Secretariat of the CDB, 2010). At the most basic level of biodiversity, climate change is reported to decrease the genetic diversity of populations due to directional selection and rapid migration, which in turn affects ecosystem function and future resilience (Bellard et al, 2012, p 365). Simply, this means that climate change will cause shifts in a species' geographical range, delimiting boundaries and prompting changes in migratory patterns, thereby allowing previously innocuous, alien species to enhance their reproductive capacity and their competitive power against native plants and animals (Thuiller, 2007, p 550). At a higher level, climate change is expected to directly effect what is termed as biodiversity's 'web of interactions', whereby the response of some species to environmental degradation will indirectly exacerbate difficulties for dependent organisms, many of which exist in a symbiotic relationship with their primaries (Bellard et al, 2012, p 365). Shifts in ecological conditions could support the introduction and spread of animal and plant disease, including parasites and pathogens, into environments that do not possess a natural immunity against them (US EPA, 2013).

Climate change is equally predicted to be substantial enough over the next century to affect complete biomes, or entire regional groupings of distinct plant and animal communities, leading to irreversible tipping points of environmental degradation (Bellard et al, 2012, p 366). The most substantial prediction of all, however, is the continued of loss of entire species, with 'extinction-committed' rates being marked as between 15-37 per cent by 2050 if current climate change trends continue (Thomas et al, 2004). Much of this will derive from ocean and marine life, which are unable to adapt to substantial increases in water acidity and temperature levels derived from carbon dioxide absorption (Secretariat of the CDB, 2010). Additionally, other biodiversity effects of climate change will most likely include changes in genetic richness and an increase in mutation rates; decreased survival rates and disease susceptibility; changes in plant and animal phenology; shifts in interspecies relationships including desynchronisation and disequilibrium; and an overall loss of biological community productivity and ecosystem services (Bellard et al, 2012, p 366).

Sustainable development, biodiversity and ecosystems

The United Nations Development Programme (UNDP) notes that human survival and wellbeing depends on healthy and sustainable biodiversity and ecosystems, as well as the goods and services they each provide (UNDP, 2012, p 13). The loss of biodiversity is a challenge for all, but most particularly for the world's poor, who maintain a substantial dependence on ecosystem goods and services for their livelihoods and subsistence (UNDP, 2012, p 13). Unfortunately, however, the links between biodiversity and ecosystem goods and services, and the role they play in the world's economic progress, are not well understood (UNDP, 2012, p 13). For the most part, environmental goods and services are defined to be a 'public good' and thus do not have a regularly fixed market price, resulting in their rare inclusion in global economic accounts (Conceição, 2012). Despite this, there is evidence that integrating biodiversity and ecosystem management objectives into sustainable development policies and practices, including production sectors, can support overall sustainability (UNDP, 2012, p 21). Termed the 'green economy', future accounting systems can and should internalise the costs and values of natural assets under standardised, global reporting classifications in order to further recognise the indivisible link between economics and biodiversity (UNDP, 2012, p 21).

In simplest terms, a green economy is low-carbon, resource-efficient and socially inclusive, where growth in income and employment are driven by public and private investments that reduce pollution, enhance energy efficiency and prevent the loss of biodiversity and ecosystem services (Ayres et al, 1996). To achieve a green economy is to incorporate broader environmental and social criteria into key economic performance calculations and indicators, such as adjusting GDP to account for pollution, resource depletion, declining ecosystem services and the distributional consequences of natural capital loss for the poor (Ayres et al, 1996). A green economy will recognise that the goal of sustainable development is improving the quality of human life within the constraints of the environment, while equally addressing the concerns of intergenerational equity and eradicating poverty (Ayres et al, 1996). While the transition to a green economy will be different for all states, there are common enabling conditions that will be required, including robust national regulations, policies, subsidies and incentives, as well as an international market infrastructure and accessible technical assistance, mostly directed towards fossil fuel–dependent brown economies (Ayres et al, 1996). A green economy approach has the opportunity to fundamentally change standardised norms of global wealth calculations, thereby including the impacts of climate change on natural capital into the baseline variables of development, which could effectively support the improvement of both mitigation and adaptation efforts.

Coastal degradation and sea level rise

According to *The Guardian*, the people of Newtok, Alaska are poised to become the US' first climate refugees, or individuals who have been displaced from their homes by the impacts of a changing climate (Goldenberg, 2013). Current estimates suggests that the entire town could be washed away by a combination of coastal erosion and rising sea levels within the next five years, with the population requiring resettlement in other cities far from the water (Goldenberg, 2013). Unlike the events of Hurricane Katrina in New Orleans, Newtok is the subject of a slow moving process, and despite this time delay, a report by the US Army Corps of Engineers suggests that nothing that can prevent its destruction, with the town's highest point to be completely submerged by 2017 (Goldenberg, 2013). Indeed, the US federal government has predicted that an additional 180 aboriginal villages dotting the Alaskan coastline face similar risks caused by climate change (Goldenberg, 2013). It is estimated that the relocation of this small, 63-house village could cost upwards of US$130 million, with that total being compounded with an increasing risk of requiring similar responses for other communities (Goldenberg, 2013). If such is the situation being faced by populations in the developed world, what will be the adaptation, mitigation and effectual cost of coastal degradation for the rest of the globe, much of which lacks the available resources to engage similar strategies in face of climate change, as the US does?

Coastal erosion is defined as a natural process whereby wind, waves and tides wear away the coastline, causing it to retreat (Llewellyn, 2012, p 1). The rate of erosion is dependent on a number of factors: coastal geology; height and frequency of waves; connectivity with other coastal systems; the presence of sediment; and changes in sea level (Llewellyn, 2012 p 1). Coastal regions provide a number of important ecosystem services, such as habitats for marine and land plant life, as well as natural protection from flooding (Llewellyn, 2012, p 1). Brought on by human-induced climate change, the rates of coastal erosion are expected to increase over the next century (Llewellyn, 2012, p 1).

The UNEP notes that increased shoreline and coastal erosion, with climate change as a contributing phenomenon, is predicted to have numerous direct and indirect impacts. First, shoreline erosion causes a situation called 'coastal squeeze', whereby coastal habitats are expected to migrate inland so as to keep pace with rising sea levels (Zhu, 2010, p 5). The 'squeeze' occurs when migration is blocked by hard defences on the coastline which prevent a habitat from extending outwards away from the sea, effectively trapping and subsequently forcing a reduction in its own size and that of other habitats already occupying the space (Zhu, 2010, p 5). Second, erosion is likely to reduce the size of sandy barrier islands which effectively dilute the size and force of oncoming waves, thereby facilitating their increased range and impact on land (Zhu, 2010, p 5). Third, a degradation of natural coastal systems, which mitigate the frequency and impact of extreme sea-based events, increases the probability of flooding in coastal zones, causing greater damage to communities along the water whose populations directly rely on natural barriers for defence (Zhu, 2010, pp 5-6). Fourth, cliff failure may be amplified by higher water levels and increased precipitation, dependent on their natural composition, with estimated global averages ranging from long-term losses of 1-2 metres per year (Zhu, 2010, pp 6-7). Fifth, delta regions, which are home to some 500 million people worldwide, provide important environmental services including carrying large quantities of sediment into the sea (Zhu, 2010, p 7). Human-induced climate change is predicted to have a variety of effects on delta regions, including decreasing sediment supplies that are essential for preventing regional erosion; permanent submergence; more frequent flooding; and an increase in tropical storm intensity (Zhu, 2010, p 7). Sixth, as a rise in sea levels will generally lead to erosion, higher water levels and salt water will more frequently intrude into estuaries and lagoons, causing plant and animal life to migrate inland, pressuring already present ecosystems and changing the availability of resultant services for communities (Zhu, 2010, p 8). Seventh, climate change may affect sensitive coral reef systems lying off the coast of areas within the Tropics of Cancer and Capricorn, resulting in a process of coral stress and subsequent 'bleaching' (Zhu, 2010, p 9). There is limited evidence to suggest that corals have a high adaptive capacity, and with the destruction of these ecosystems, wave energy is increasing, leading to greater coastal erosion (Zhu, 2010, p 9). Many countries depend on healthy corals for their income, with the Great Barrier Reef alone contributing over US$5 billion to Australia's economy in 2005 (Cinner et al, 2012, p 12).

While the effects of erosion and rising sea levels will not be uniform across the globe, the consequences of such impacts are expected to be overwhelmingly negative and serious in deltas, coastal areas and small islands (Zhu, 2010, p 11). The International Fund for Agricultural Development (IFAD) predicts that higher rates of erosion are expected in many Pacific Islands as a consequence of projected increases in sea level (IFAD, 2009, p 2). For example, in the Marshall Islands and Kiribati, IFAD estimates that for a 1 metre rise in sea level, as much as 80 per cent and 12.5 per cent of land, respectively, would become vulnerable to coastal flooding and decreased vegetated wetlands (IFAD, 2009, p 2). Estimated impacts of 30-50cm sea level rise on Pacific Island coastal communities were quantified as 77,018km of affected shoreline in 2009, with direct associated costs of US$1.4 billion per year (IFAD, 2009, p 2). Declines in the size of the Pacific Islands, due to soil erosion and a rise in sea level, is expected to reduce the depth of freshwater lens on atolls by as much as 29 per cent by 2050 (IFAD, 2009, p 3).

The IPCC adds that the effects of soil erosion and rising sea levels will equally affect African coastal zones. Much of Africa's population and a substantial amount of industry is located along the sea: for example, an estimated 20 million Nigerians and 66.6 per cent of Senegal's total population live in coastal zones, while Ghana, Benin, Togo, Sierra Leone and again, Nigeria, have positioned much of their industry in the same area (IPCC, 2013). Coastal cities such as Dar es Salaam and Mombasa have been experiencing annual population growth of 6.75 and 5 per cent respectively (IPCC, 2013). For much of the African coastal regions, both East and West, the impacts of climate change-induced sea level rise and coastal erosion have already been felt: coastal erosion has been reported to have already reached 23-30 metres in some parts of West Africa in 1989; Côte d'Ivoire has reported high levels of erosion off the Abidjan Harbour area, thereby reducing its natural defences from storm surges and extreme events; 40 per cent of mangrove areas in Nigeria and 60 per cent in Senegal have been lost since 1980; lagoons, a substantial source of fishery resources, have been substantially polluted in Accra, Lagos and Ebrie; and previous estimates have suggested that for a 1 metre sea level rise, 2,000km^2 of land in coastal areas along the lower Nile delta should be expected to be lost (IPCC, 2013).

So how does the international community engage in appropriate mitigation and adaptation measures, and as a complementary question, what would they look like? Ruckelshaus et al (2013) suggest a five-fold adaptation programme: designing responses based on the value of ecosystem services in the affected region; instituting robust fisheries management policies, including the protection of at-risk stockpiles and identifying alternative and diversified livelihood options for communities; including climate change considerations in sustainability plans for aquaculture; encouraging the use of market-based incentives for companies to cease harmful practices and to encourage support for coastal regeneration projects; and the somewhat controversial practice of relocation as adaptation (Ruckelshaus et al, 2013, pp 156-7). Cinner et al (2012), in contrast, argue for a three-tiered adaptation and mitigation approach: local-scale actions including diversification of industry, encouraging an increased ecological impact knowledge base, and strengthening the power and resources of community groups charged with coastal management; national-level provision of social safety nets for adaptation and investment in alternative energy, new industries, education and carbon-pricing; and, at the international level, the mobilisation of funding for infrastructure and adaptation, as well as the resumption and comprehensive completion of binding climate change mitigation targets and allocation of responsibilities (Cinner et al, 2012, pp 16-17). Last, it is argued that the above could be facilitated and supported by the introduction of 13 adaptive technologies recommended by the UNEP: beach nourishment, artificial dunes and dune rehabilitation, seawalls, sea dikes, surge barriers, closure dams, land claim, flood-proofing, wetland restoration, floating agriculture systems, flood hazard mapping, flood warnings, managed realignment and coastal setbacks (Zhu, 2010, p 20). Evidently, such technologies would require the support of dedicated funding from third party states and international organisations for the developing world, as well as local tailoring to specific circumstances. The above suggests, however, that a combination of knowledge, research, adaptive technology, local empowerment, national policy and international coordination and funding could substantially support the adaptation and mitigation of climate change-induced sea level rises and coastal erosion.

Relevance to the post-2015 development agenda

The post-2015 development agenda will need developed and developing countries to accept their proper share of responsibility in accordance with their resources and capabilities as driven by five fundamental shifts: (i) the eradication of extreme poverty in all forms; (ii) inequality and inclusive economy transformation; (iii) peace and good governance; (iv) forging a new global partnership; and (v) the future of sustainable development given environmental, climate change obstacles (UN, 2013a). Such principles would transform our static understanding of development challenges into a dynamic model for action. Thus, in examining these shifts individually, it is important to recognise the central relevance of environmental sustainability and climate change as a structural change in the post-2015 agenda's vision of human security, cooperation and vulnerability.

The post-2015 agenda now has the opportunity to take a definitive stand against extreme poverty. It should strive to end hunger and extreme poverty in all its forms. This would provide a marked difference from the MDGs target of reducing the levels by half. Similarly, multipronged strategies that address a variety of intersectional factors – such as unemployment, education, natural disasters, healthcare, climate change, infrastructure and local conflict – will be necessary to achieve success in this goal, as well as in completing the others.

In conjunction with other ongoing seminars, such as the UN Climate Change Conference, which is one of the core discussion points of the High Level Panels and the fifth fundamental shift, the issue of environmental sustainability and its potential causal impacts on developmental progress will stress the importance of urgent and collective action required by the public and private sector collectively.

The High Level Panel highlighted that, with climate change being the overarching concern, governments, businesses and individuals 'must transform the way they generate and consume energy, travel and transport goods, use water and grow food' (UN, 2013b). The introduction of new technologies, reduction of unsustainable consumption and mobilisation of the private sector will be crucial. The Panel proposed feasible, cost-effective options, such as the construction of energy-efficient buildings, improved vehicle aerodynamics, recycling waste and soil restoration. In addition, incentives such as taxes, subsidies, regulations and sustainability certification and compliance programmes were proposed to encourage change (UN, 2013b). Powering affordable and consistent *sustainable energy sources* will be fundamental in curbing the effects of climate change and its potential impacts on developmental progress.

The post–2015 development agenda represents a major breakthrough that profoundly puts environmental sustainability at the heart of the development agenda moving forward. It clearly makes the case that poverty is intricately linked to the natural environment, climate change and sustainability issues with respect to natural resources. Equally important, it reflects the need to include all countries in the development debate. Clearly industrialised countries have a fundamental role to play when it comes to tackling poverty and environmental sustainability challenges, both at home and in developing states. It is important to recognise that all major stakeholders have a shared responsibility and joint accountability in advancing the post–2015 development agenda. These include civil society, international institutions, national and local governments, business and philanthropists, among others. The challenge now is to how best shape these bold recommendations and strong aspirations into concrete and tangible actions backed by realistic yet bold targets.

Policy recommendations

We now present several broad categories of policy recommendations, two of which are covered in depth, in support of the continually moving target of sustainable development in the face of climate change difficulties: supported adaptation; increased climate science, and monitoring and evaluation; correcting resource allocation biases; improved governance and capacity building; engaging private actors; and climate change mitigation through infrastructure development, energy technology and a 'green economy'.

Supported adaptation

According to Adger et al (2003), adaptation to climate change is the adjustment of a system to moderate the impacts of environmental degradation, to take advantage of new opportunities and to cope with the consequences. Adaptation strategies, particularly in states that lack the means by which to undergo potential changes efficiently and effectively, are unlikely to be taken autonomously (Adger et al, 2003). As such, support and passive intervention may be necessary to enhance state adaptation capacities to new conditions without becoming more vulnerable (Adger et al, 2003). Indeed, Kreft et al (2010) support this claim by noting a widespread consensus that vulnerable states in general will need more international assistance to meet their adaptation needs. It is argued that the means by which financial support is provided to states must change, defined by new partnerships between donor and recipient governments, as well as horizontally with other private donors; the latter should assume significant responsibility and accountability for their own development processes (Kreft et al, 2010). That being said, continuation of auditing and oversight mechanisms found in institutions such as the Adaptation Fund of the Kyoto Protocol should be a priority, coupled with their enhancement, to ensure that donor governments use funds appropriately (Kreft et al, 2010).

Supported adaptation must equally be wary of tailoring funding packages to the specific needs of states, particularly fragile countries, in order to achieve appropriate results (Kreft et al, 2010). It is also a scalar issue, meaning that sustainability of action is dependent on what level a strategy is deployed, the range of actors involved and their ability to self-organise and innovate. Among the emerging range of adaptation practices, Sem and Moore (2009) note that a diversification of livelihoods, introduction of robust international and domestic institutional architectures, adjustments in farming operations, income generation projects and the move towards non-farm livelihood incomes represent key options. The introduction of new biotechnology and related processes, including investment in water harvesting and irrigation systems, will be required to achieve such diversification (Sem and Moore, 2009). Other measures of resilience to protect against climate change event shocks could include the improvement of early warning systems, maintenance of national foodstuff reserves, enrolment of a population in educational schemes beginning at an early age, and national insurance mechanisms (Sem and Moore, 2009). As consistently argued in this chapter, while analysis can treat each criterion as separate, policy-makers should be encouraged to identify and be cognisant of the linkages between issue areas, ensuring that planning mechanisms are not isolated from one another.

Local institutional arrangements may equally support the means of adaptation to climate change. The introduction of micro-financing schemes, coupled with future-driven education programmes, social safety nets and welfare grants, may aid in offsetting the difficulties of large-scale adaptation by poor governments (Sem and Moore, 2009). By providing states and local populations not only with required funding, but also by arming current and future generations with the knowledge required to support project management and attainment of adaptation goals, the international community may very well encourage poverty reduction as well as the overall mitigation of climate change effects.

International cooperation and institutional deficit

In analysis by the Council on Foreign Relations (CFR), the UN Framework Convention on Climate Change (UNFCCC) is an 'underdeveloped and inadequate system' (CFR, 2013). At the most basic level of this institutional deficit, countries continue to disagree over methods of climate monitoring, rates of financial stipulations and any legally binding aspects of these accords (CFR, 2013). The UNFCCC lacks a substantial process for monitoring emissions from states that themselves lack the domestic capacity to do so, and it is faced with states such as China which argue that any international monitoring represents an infringement on national sovereignty, and is thus incompatible with domestic priorities (CFR, 2013).

The climate change regime equally fails to address issues of financing, particularly where funding streams will come from and how they will be implemented, causing the US and other emitters to move towards a form of à la carte multilateralism characterised by informal, smaller frameworks (CFR, 2013). Outside the UNFCCC, a host of not-for-profit and international organisations have begun designing separate strategies for addressing environmental issues within their own in-house programming, much of which lacks any form of inter-institute coordination, leading to fragmentation and redundancy (CFR, 2013). While the IPCC has been credited with delivering excellent research on environmental degradation, the CFR notes that some of its outputs underplay the risks for developed and developing states alike as a means of garnering rare political consensus and bureaucratic approval (CFR, 2013). Within the UNFCCC governing structure itself, critics note that institutional deficits arise particularly from the variance between commitment by states and resultant action, with those same states failing to adhere to agreements on emission reduction targets (CFR, 2013). Unsurprisingly, the CFR concludes by emphasising that enforcement continues to be relatively non-existent for violating parties (CFR, 2013).

Similarly, Haas (2003) argues that within global environmental policy and organisational management, there continues to be both an institutional and governance deficit (2003, p 5). According to

Haas, there are currently three broad academic arguments in favour of the need to reform: removing redundancy among international institutions; the desire to facilitate less competition among organisations, which would result in increased capacity and efficiency for programme management and implementation; and the need for a stronger environmental presence throughout the international system, and particularly, within the World Trade Organization (WTO) (Haas, 2003, pp 5-6). To rectify what Haas defines as a governance deficit, he proposes the implementation of a new decentralised design principle in global environmental institutionalisation, which would streamline and improve current organisational effectiveness rather than create entirely new institutional bodies (Haas, 2003, p 8). His solution is the improved association of formal and informal activities of various actor levels without an overarching institution, dependent on their current functions and effectiveness: scientists, epistemic communities and government agencies; not-for-profit organisations; media; business and industry; regional development banks; and international organisations (Haas, 2003, pp 8-10). By taking advantage of a decentralised network of actors who already perform individual environmental functions with some degree of efficacy, the overall governance deficit mentioned above could be reduced (Haas, 2003, p16).

There are, therefore, there alternative measures that could be implemented to improve the current institutional and governance deficit in the international system. First, the cracks in the big emitter's 'anti-binding targets barrier' should be rigorously explored (CFR, 2013). For example, China's latest White Paper on energy stresses the need to save energy over developing new production supplies (Boyd, 2012), while the general increase of domestic concern over rising urban pollution could be leveraged as a way to garner increased state support for international environmental regimes. Second, the UNFCCC's Clean Development Mechanism (CDM) could be reformed to ensure that funding is not wasted, but instead directed towards targeted, innovative and potentially successful projects in the developing world, thereby increasing international confidence in the CDM (CFR, 2013). Third, using both executive orders and a marketing programme on improving its comparative advantage, the US must once again be encouraged to take a leadership role in climate change (CFR, 2013). This would require a re-tailoring of the discussion towards the potential economic benefits of the US becoming a global leader in clean energy, rather than focusing on short-term losses. Reframing the debate in terms of climate change as a security issue, or as a resilience effort, could equally yield benefits for the reduction of global institutional deficit via increased US support. Fourth, in a rationalist sense, states will only participate in an international organisation so long as they know that the risk of cheating by others is substantially reduced. As such, it is recommended that a robust, global institution could be created, using the best practices and lessoned learned from the monitoring and enforcement mechanisms of other organisations, such as the WTO and the European Union (EU) in its design (CFR, 2013). Last, institutional deficit could be improved by creating a global culture conducive to climate change mitigation knowledge. By this it is meant that climate change should be included regularly on the agenda of major international groups, such as the G8 and G20 (CRF, 2013). This could increase the salience of this issue, increasing its sense of urgency and linking it directly to the primarily financial discussions, allowing for cost-benefit calculations to be performed by participant governments.

Conclusions

This chapter has presented an evidenced demonstration of the casual linkages between climate change and five affected categories of development, including economics and agriculture; water; ecosystems and biodiversity; human health; and coast regions. In each section, details of the links between development and its stagnation or reversion have been presented, including relevant primary and secondary source material. It was further iterated throughout this chapter that while for analytical purposes the five-presented categories were divided, researchers and policy-makers would do well to recognise that links exist between them.

It should also be noted, however, that while these categories allow the reader to easily classify the impacts of climate change on development, they are by no means a complete taxonomy. Future research would do well to look at other potential impacts, as well as expand on the categories presented above. For example, several authors note that climate change could cause a stagnation or reversal of development by triggering forced migration, political instability and conflict between parties vying for potable water, arable land or regions unaffected by environmental insecurity (Brown et al, 2007; Tadesse, 2010). Future study should examine closely the phenomenon of 'climate conflict', the risk it poses to developing states, as well as appropriate measures to be engaged for its mitigation and adaptation.

We also argue that several other policy recommendations be explored in future study, including the two studied in-depth above.

First, the impact of increased climate science, as well as robust monitoring and evaluation programmes on overall global mitigation actions, should be reviewed. Second, the other side of the climate coin, mitigation, must equally be revisited, emphasising that for adaptation to work, mitigation must be equally viable. Third, the international community must correct biases in resource allocation to the developing world, ensuring that current effective programmes are adequately funded, and new projects are developed. Fourth, the private sector must be seen as a critical partner in not only funding climate change mitigation approaches, but also for developing new technology, innovative approaches, and simply, new ideas to broach this continuing issue.

The shift in the Earth's climate towards warmer temperatures and more difficult weather phenomena is unmistakable. Political dialogue is too often unable to divorce itself from conspiratorial-type positions of uncertainty regarding climate change. We hope that the exploration presented will provide a firm base for the continuing study of climate change, particularly a move towards a definitive remedy for its root causes and its causal relationships with external factors. It is our expectation that the research conducted in these pages will begin the development of innovative means by which poverty reduction, increased development and climate change mitigation can all be equally achieved. Without expanding our understanding of the Earth's current environmental situation, the less we are going to achieve over the long term in our ongoing attempts to protect her.

References

Abeygunawardena, P. (2002) *Poverty and climate change – Reducing the vulnerability of the poor through adaptation*, Paris: Organisation for Economic Co-operation and Development.

Adger, N.W., Huq, S., Brown, K., Conway, D. and Hulme, M. (2003) 'Adaptation to climate change in the developing world', *Progress in Development Studies*, vol 3, no 3, pp 179-95.

Alavian, V., Qaddumi, H.M., Dickson, E. et al (2009) *Water and climate change: Understanding the risks and making climate-smart investment decisions*, Washington, DC: The World Bank.

Arthurton, R., Barker, S., Rast, W. et al (2007) 'Water', *Global Environment Outlook 4*, Nairobi: United Nations Environment Programme.

Ayres, R.U. and Ayres, L.W. (1996) *Industrial ecology: Towards closing the materials cycle*. Cheltenham: Edward Elgar.

Beddington, J., Asaduzzaman, M., Clark, M. et al (2013) *Achieving food security in the face of climate change – Final report from the Commission on Sustainable Agriculture and Climate Change*, Copenhagen: CGIAR Research Program on Climate Change, Agriculture and Food Security.

Bellard, C., Bertelsmeier, C., Leadley, P., Thuiller, W. and Courchamp, F. (2012) 'Impacts of climate change on the future of biodiversity', *Ecology Letters*, vol 15, pp 365–77.

Bonnin, C. and Turner, S. (2012) 'At what price rice? Food security, livelihood vulnerability, and state interventions in upland northern Vietnam', *Geoforum*, vol 43, no 1, pp 95–105.

Boyd, O. (2012) 'The motivations for China's new energy and climate politics', East Asia Forum, 14 August 2012 (www.eastasiaforum. org/2012/08/14/the-motivations-for-chinas-new-energy-and-climate-policies/).

Brown, O., Hammill, A. and Mcleman, R. (2007) 'Climate change as the "new" security threat: implications for Africa', *International Affairs*, vol 83, no 6, pp 1141–54.

Buckley, C. (2013) 'Twice as many structures in FEMA's redrawn flood zone', *New York Times*, 28 January (www.nytimes.com/2013/01/29/nyregion/homes-in-flood-zone-doubles-in-new-fema-map.html).

CFR (Council on Foreign Relations) (2013) *The global climate regime*, 19 June (www.cfr.org/climate-change/global-climate-change-regime/p21831).

Cinner, J.E., Mcclanahan, T.R., Stead, S., Graham, N.A.J., Daw, T.M. and Maina, J. (2012) 'Vulnerability of coastal communities to key impacts of climate change on coral reef fisheries', *Global Environmental Change*, vol 22, pp 12–20.

Cohen, S., Demeritt, D., Robinson, J. and Rothman, D. (1998) 'Climate change and sustainable development: towards dialogue', *Global Environment Change*, vol 8, no 4, pp 341–77.

Conceição, P. (2012) *Africa human development report 2012 – Towards a food secure future*, New York: United Nations Development Programme.

Diop, S. (ed) (2008) *Vital water graphics – An overview of the state of the world's fresh and marine waters*, Nairobi: United Nations Environment Programme.

Economist, The (2009) 'A bad climate for development', 17 September (www.economist.com/node/14447171).

EEA (European Environmental Agency) (2012) *Indicators*, 6 December, 12 December (www.eea.europa.eu/themes/climate/indicators#c10 =&c5=all&c7=all&c13=20&b_start=0).

European Commission (2006) *EU action against climate change – Helping developing countries cope with climate change*, Luxembourg: Office for Official Publications of the European Communities.

Goldenberg, S. (2013) 'America's climate refugees', *The Guardian*, 28 May (www.guardian.co.uk/environment/interactive/2013/may/13/newtok-alaska-climate-change-refugees).

Guardian, The (2011) 'Could climate change be a good thing?', 11 May (www.guardian.co.uk/environment/2011/may/11/climate-change-good-thing-benefits).

Guardian, The (2013) 'Join the debate: America's first climate refugees', 13 May (www.theguardian.com/environment/blog/2013/may/13/join-debate-america-first-climate-refugees).

Haas, P.M. (2003) *Addressing the global governance deficit*, Amherst, MA: University of Massachusetts.

Halnaes, K. and Garg, A. (2011) 'Assessing the role of energy in development and climate policies – conceptual approach and key indicators', *World Development*, vol 39, no 6, pp 987-1001.

Hertel, T.W. and Rosch, S.D. (2010) 'Climate change, agriculture, and poverty', *Applied Economic Perspectives and Policy*, vol 32, no 3, pp 355-85.

IFAD (International Fund for Agricultural Development) (2009) 'Climate change impacts – Pacific Islands', The Global Mechanism (www.ifad.org/events/apr09/impact/islands.pdf).

IPCC (Intergovernmental Panel on Climate Change) (2013) 'Regional impacts of climate change', *Special Reports*, 28 May (www.ipcc.ch/ipccreports/sres/regional/index.php?idp=30).

Jha, A.K., Bloch, R. and Lamond, J. (2012) *Cities and flooding – A guide to integrated urban flood risk management for the 21st century*, Washington, DC: The World Bank.

Kreft, S., Harmeling, S., Bals, C., Zacher, W. and van de Sand, K. (2010) *The Millennium Development Goals and climate change: Taking stock and looking ahead*, Bonn: Germanwatch.

Llewellyn, L. (2012) *Coastal erosion and sea level rise – Quick guide*, Cardiff: Research Service, National Assembly for Wales.

McGuigan, C., Reynolds, R. and Wiedmer, D. (2002) *Poverty and climate change: Assessing impacts in developing countries and the initiatives of the international community*, London: Overseas Development Institute.

Mcintyre, N. (2012) 'How will climate change impact on fresh water security?', *The Guardian*, 21 December (www.guardian.co.uk/environment/2012/nov/30/climate-change-water).

McMichael, A.J. and Butler, C.D. (2004) 'Climate change, health, and development goals', *The Lancet*, vol 364, pp 2004-06.

Mizra, M.M.Q. (2003) 'Climate change and extreme weather events: can developing countries adapt?', *Climate Policy*, vol 3, pp 233-48.

NASA (National Aeronautics and Space Administration) (2012) 'Key indicators', *Global climate change – Vital signs of the planet* (http://climate.nasa.gov/key_indicators/).

NCDC (National Climatic Data Center) (2012) *Global climate change indicators* (www.ncdc.noaa.gov/indicators/).

OECD (2003) *Poverty and climate change reducing the vulnerability of the poor through adaptation*, Paris: OECD (http://www.oecd.org/env/cc/2502872.pdf).

Parry, M.L., Rosenzweig, C., Iglesias, A., Livermore, M. and Fischer, G. (2004) 'Effects of climate change on global food production under SRES emissions and socio-economic scenarios', *Global Environmental Change*, vol 14, pp 53-67.

Richards, M. (2003) *Poverty reduction, equity and climate change: Global governance synergies or contradictions?*, London: Overseas Development Institute.

Ruckelshaus, M., Doney, S.C., Galindo, H.M. et al (2013) 'Securing ocean benefits for society in the face of climate change', *Marine Policy*, vol 40, pp 154-9.

Sachs, J.D., Baillie, J.E.M., Sutherland, W.J. (2009) 'Biodiversity conservation and the Millennium Development Goals', *Science*, vol 325, pp 1502-3.

Schlenker, W. and Lobell, D.B. (2010) 'Robust negative impacts of climate change on African agriculture', *Environmental Research Letters*, vol 5, pp 1-8.

Schneider, C., Laizé, C.L.R., Acreman, M.C. and Flörke, M. (2013) 'How will climate change modify river flow regimes in Europe?', *Hydrology and Earth System Sciences*, vol 17, pp 325-39.

Secretariat of the CDB (Convention on Biological Diversity) (2010) *Global biodiversity, Outlook 3*, Montreal: CDB.

Sem, G. and Moore, R. (2009) *Impact of climate change on the development prospects of the least developed countries and small island developing states*, New York: Office of the High Representative for the Least Developed Countries, Landlocked Developing Countries and Small Island Developing Countries.

Skoufias, E. (2012) 'Disquiet on the weather front: Implications of climate change for poverty reduction', in E. Skoufias (ed.) *The poverty and welfare impacts of climate change: Quantifying the effects, identifying the adaptation strategies*. Washington, DC: World Bank, pp 1-15.

Strauss, B., Tebaldi, C. and Kulp, S. (2012) *Washington, DC and the surging sea: A vulnerability assessment with projections for sea level rise and coastal flood risk*, Princeton, NJ: Climate Central.

Tadesse, D. (2010) *The impact of climate change in Africa*, ISS Paper No 220, Pretoria, South Africa: Institute for Security Studies.

Thomas, C.D., Cameron, A., Green, R.E. et al (2004) 'Extinction risk from climate change', *Nature*, vol 427, no 8, pp 145-8.

Thornton, P. (2012) *Recalibrating food production in the developing world: Global warming will change more than just the climate*, Policy Brief 6, Copenhagen: CGIAR Research Program on Climate Change, Agriculture and Food Security.

Thuiller, W. (2007) 'Climate change and the ecologist', *Nature*, vol 448, no 2, pp 550-2.

UN (United Nations) (2013a) 'Executive summary', *A new global partnership: Eradicate poverty and transform economies through sustainable development*, Report of the High-Level Panel of Eminent Persons on the Post-2015 Development Agenda.

UN (2013b) *A new global partnership: Eradicate poverty and transform economies through sustainable development*, Report of the High-Level Panel of Eminent Persons on the Post-2015 Development Agenda.

UNDP (United Nations Development Programme) (2012) *The future we want: Biodiversity and ecosystems – Driving sustainable development*, New York: UNDP.

UNECE (United Nations Economic Commission for Europe) Expert Group on Indicators for Education for Sustainable Development (2005) *Background paper on the development of indicators to measure implementation of the UNECE strategy for ESD*, The Netherlands: UNECE.

UNESCO (United Nations Educational, Scientific and Cultural Organization) (2012) *Managing water under uncertainty and risk – The United Nations world water development report 4, Vol 1*, Paris: UNESCO.

US EPA (United States Environmental Protection Agency) (2013) 'Ecosystems impacts and adaptation', 22 April (www.epa.gov/climatechange/impacts-adaptation/ecosystems.html).

Whitehead, P., Butterfield, D. and Wade, A. (2008) *Potential impacts of climate change on river water quality*, Bristol: Environment Agency.

World Bank, The (2012) *Turn down the heat: Why a 4°C warmer world must be avoided*, Washington, DC: The World Bank.

Yohe, G. and Tol, R.S. (2002) 'Indicators for social and economic coping capacity – moving towards a working definition of adaptive capacity', *Global Environmental Change*, vol 12, issue 1, April, pp 25-40.

Zhu, X. (ed) (2010) *Technologies for climate change adaptation – Coastal erosion and flooding*, Roskilde, Denmark: United Nations Environment Programme, Riso Centre on Energy, Climate and Sustainable Development.

TWELVE

African development through peace and security to sustainability

Karolina Werner

Introduction

We have reached the deadline for achieving the Millennium Development Goals (MDGs), and debates over the post-2015 development agenda are coming to a close. Following consultations with scholars, practitioners, civil society and other experts, as well as the general public, publications on the way forward have multiplied over the last five years. Critical assessments of the MDGs and achievements have been discussed and weaknesses identified. The meetings early in 2015 finalised the proposal for the new Sustainable Development Goals (SDGs) to present them to the United Nations (UN) General Assembly Summit in September 2015. The negotiations, in which member states decide on new targets, will shape international aid and development policy for the next 15 years. The hope is, that in recognition of the linkages between conflict and development difficulties, they will also address peace and security within the new goals.

While the process of forming the MDGs in the past was one of first presenting a general vision, then developing targets, and only towards the end addressing the means and tools to achieve them (Domínguez, 2013), the lessons of the last 15 years have understandably influenced the current negotiations and resulting framework. Member states are much more conscious of the practicalities of achieving the ambitious goals set out in the new development agenda, especially knowing the scrutiny these achievements undergo. They have also been much more involved in setting the new goals and targets, unlike the MDG process which was largely top-down. Furthermore, one of the criticisms of the MDGs has been that little guidance was provided on how to achieve them, hence, while acknowledging the uniqueness of each case, the new agenda also attempts to provide some general policy guidelines for accomplishing its targets (UN, 2012). It is therefore imperative that the priorities are both actionable and realistic.

As a result, the discussion on including aspects of peace and security in the new development targets is particularly sensitive; on the one hand, because in the mind of many policy-makers, it infringes on the powers of sovereign states, and on the other, because the achievement of 'peace' and/or 'security' is hard to define or measure, and is thus mired in uncertainty and controversy. This is particularly true since some proposals for new goals have included references to good governance as well,1 which may be even harder to measure. Any discussion of good governance, while important, is often taken to mean the implementation of a liberal democracy. When linked with security, the fear is that it could open the door to potential external interventions by the international community in the name of good governance. Although we can probably all agree in principle that peaceful, well-governed and secure environments are an admirable goal, the discussions around the varied definitions of peace, good governance and security foreshadow the complexity of the intergovernmental negotiations that are taking place in 2015.

This chapter adds to the already broad base of literature on the subject by suggesting a potentially constructive, yet balanced, approach, for including peace and security in the development agenda. The hope is to identify options that include peace and security, to which member states will find it hard to object to. Focusing on the critical importance of peace and security, I argue that peacekeeping and peacebuilding[2] are essential elements for successful development in conflict-affected states. Using Somalia as an example, the chapter addresses the issue of conflict as a disruptive influence on the achievement of the MDGs. It further differentiates between fragile and conflict-affected states and, using the example of Burundi, proposes that fragility, unlike conflict, is not, in fact, an obstacle to development. Finally, in the face of the post-2015 agenda negotiations, the chapter suggests a focus on achieving negative peace, the minimum needed to allow for steady progress on development goals, and the incorporation of the principles under the New Deal for Engagement with Fragile States to address issues of peace and security more specifically.

No peace in the Millennium Development Goals

Over the last 15 years, the MDGs have been a yardstick according to which development has been measured. The widely disseminated and iconic eight MDGs[3] formed a list of ambitious and lofty goals to be achieved by 2015. Designed as global targets, they were meant to measure the world's progress toward ending poverty (Salahub, 2013). This was supposed to be a positive aspect, allowing each nation to implement the goals in its own way. In practice, however, they have also been measured at the country level, highlighting the inequalities in development progress between countries around the globe. The MDGs were thus declaimed as 'unattainable' for some countries, and were criticised for making slower, but essential, progress seem like failure (Clemens and Moss, 2005). These discussions identified an important weakness of the MDGs, which is their failure to account for conflict-affected states in which weak governments and/or non-existent governance structures have been disrupting the implementation of development policies and programmes.

While the original Millennium Declaration adopted in September 2000 by the UN General Assembly did address peace and security, the MDGs themselves did not, likely for the same reasons being discussed with relation to the Sustainable Development Goals (SDGs). In fact, an entire section of the Declaration, entitled 'Peace, security and disarmament', affirmed the member states' commitment to the matter, including, but not limited to, making the 'United Nations more effective in maintaining peace and security by giving it the resources and tools it needs for conflict prevention, peaceful resolution of disputes, peacekeeping, post-conflict peace-building and reconstruction' (UN, 2000, para 9).

In reality, the MDGs have been far removed from peacekeeping and peacebuilding, focusing on classic development aid policies, which are unfortunately rarely undertaken in concert with peace and security measures. In fact, most peacekeeping expenditures are not part of official development assistance (ODA) as they are considered military investments. However, there is an ongoing debate within the aid community on expanding the understanding of ODA to include a peace and security dimension.[4] Development has, since the creation of the United Nations (UN), been a collaborative and global concern, especially following the Second World War when the organisation was dedicated to aiding the ailing European population. Issues related to conflict, peace and security, on the other hand, invoke defensive responses by some states that view any detailed international agreements on the topic as possible infringements on national sovereignty (Cox, 2014). The international community in the form of the UN continues to grapple with its approaches to conflict and violence, rarely reacting to crises quickly, as states prioritise national interests, prolonging debates over appropriate responses and setting precedents of interference. This was the case in 1994 in Rwanda, and more recently is visible in the delays in responding to the conflicts in Sudan and Syria, among others, where indecision, past mistakes, rivalries and state foreign policy objectives all compete against each other to delay decisions by the UN Security Council.

Debate on security and the new Sustainable Development Goals

In 2011 The World Bank issued its world development report pronouncing that 'one-and-a-half billion people live in areas affected by fragility, conflict, or large-scale, organized criminal violence, and no low-income fragile or conflict-affected country has yet to achieve [sic] a single United Nations Millennium Development Goal' (The World Bank, 2011, p 1). This oft-cited proclamation has been followed by a number of publications arguing that the post-2015 development agenda should address this glaring gap by including goals related to peace and security. Although The World Bank has since issued a statement in 2013 saying that 26 fragile and conflict-affected states[5] have, in fact, met or were on target to meeting some of their goals in 2015 (The World Bank, 2013), the debate has not subsided. The effect is that, both the UN System Task Team on the Post-2015 Development Agenda (UNTT, 2012) in their report entitled *Realizing the future we want for all*, and the African Union (AU), in their Common African Position (CAP) on the post-2015 development agenda (AU, 2014a), specifically address peace and security as a 'core dimension' (UN, 2012) and 'pillar' (AU, 2014a) of the new agenda respectively. The UN System Task Team identifies peace and security as 'critical for development and a major component of it', and highlights the need to seek 'cultures of peace and tolerance' (UNTT, 2012, pp 31-2, paras 89, 90). The CAP, in turn, notes that peace and security are 'essential for the achievement of the continent's development aspirations' (AU, 2014a, p 14, para 65). It further commits to addressing the root causes of conflict and preventing the outbreak of armed conflicts (p 14, paras 66, 67).

Considering what seems to be the general consensus on the need for establishing peace and security as a precursor to development (The World Bank, 2011; High Level Panel on Fragile States, 2014), and the fact that one-fifth of the world's population lives in conflict-affected or fragile countries (UN, 2012), it is not surprising that there has been much discussion on the inclusion of a goal specifically addressing these issues. However, despite the obvious need for it, the expectation is that member states will have a number of objections to such a goal. The concerns are likely mainly related to the definition of security as a domain of the UN Security Council and Chapter VII[6] of the UN Charter. In addition to the potential infringement on sovereignty, objections could be related to the securitisation of aid, which can syphon funds from poverty alleviation to a focus on donor security; prioritisation of conflict countries in aid donations; or fear of 'punitive and securitised' approaches to fragile states (Kashambuzi, 2013), among others.

Based on the charged meaning of 'security', official UN reports that have followed *Realizing the future we want for all* have avoided using the word, preferring to focus on stability, peace and justice instead.[7] Thus, goal 16 of the 17 goals suggested by the Open Working Group[8] in their proposal for SDGs is to 'Promote peaceful and inclusive societies for sustainable development, provide access to justice for all and build effective, accountable and inclusive institutions at all levels' (UN, 2014a). In his synthesis report on the post-2015 agenda, the Secretary-General identified justice in the form of promoting 'safe and peaceful societies, and strong institutions' as one of the 'six essential elements for delivering on the SDGs' (UN, 2014b, p 20).

Despite this change in rhetoric, peace, security and stability continue to all be important elements, and the hope is that they will be included in the post-2015 framework, even if the actual word 'security' is not. Understanding that such an inclusion will be hotly debated, we propose a stepping-stone for inclusion of peace in the form of negative peace, rather than positive peace, as a means to allow for implementation of development agendas in conflict-affected countries.

Conflict and fragility

The argument that negative peace, defined as the absence of direct violence, is initially sufficient to allow for the development and attainment of MDGs (or SDGs) centres on the premise that only states engulfed in violent conflict are not in a position to sustain development, and are possibly also reversing any development that may have happened previously. Based on studies done by the Geneva Declaration on Armed Conflict and Development Secretariat, violent conflict has been inversely linked to MDG progress (Geneva Declaration, 2010). All the while, in a majority of cases, development aid continues to be delivered in the same way to resilient countries with stronger institutions as to conflict-affected countries (ODI, 2011). Thus, there have been calls for better mechanisms for tracking and monitoring the relationship between violence and development (Geneva Declaration, 2010), while adapting policies for 'best fit' rather than 'best practice'.

Although it is common to find conflict and fragile states grouped together, and the belief is that fragile, non-conflict states were also lagging behind on their MDGs, evidence suggests otherwise. Fragility,[9] a complex and multifaceted concept that continues to amass new definitions, and can be (very) broadly defined as countries that are failing or at high risk of failing (Harttgen and Klasen, 2013), does not seem to be an impediment to development, assuming violence is limited. According to Kenneth Harttgen and Stephan Klasen (2013), while fragile states may have been at a lower level in MDG accomplishments, they were not necessarily exhibiting slower progress. For example, Burundi, as will be shown in more detail below, despite being considered fragile,[10] performed very well on its MDG progress measures. States that have been embroiled in violent conflict on the other hand, such as Somalia, lag far behind. Development is in regression or stagnant as death, violence and extreme poverty abound. Conflict-affected states typically lack government and institutions able to implement broad, long-term development projects. What money flows in is often used for building up the military at the expense of social sectors. Civil wars, due to their centralised nature and longevity, are particularly damaging to development (Stewart, 2003).

The case of Somalia

Somalia, sometimes referred to as the world's most fragile state (Tran, 2013), has recently been emerging from decades of violent and intractable conflict. Divided into two parts during colonial times, British Somaliland and Italian Somalia, the state reunited in 1960 when it gained independence. From 1969 the country has effectively been in a state of conflict. Initially supported by the Soviet government, and later by the US, Somalia amassed arms. After a military coup, the autocratic Major-General Mohammed Siad Barre ruled until 1991 when the military government was overthrown. Violence and clan wars followed, until in 2000 a transitional national government was put in place. After the failure of the government and another attempt at instituting one, the Islamic Courts Union[11] took control of Mogadishu in 2006. In response, Ethiopia, aided and abetted by the US, invaded Somalia, ostensibly to protect and reinstate the transitional national government (UNDP, 2012). In January 2013, Washington recognised the Somali government as legitimate (Goodlet et al, 2015).

The state continued to maintain the top spot in the Fragile States Index for the next few years, in 2014 dropping to number two after South Sudan (Fund for Peace, 2015), and is among the countries with too little reliable data to even qualify for a spot on the Human Development Index (HDI) (UNDP, 2014). In addition to the already insecure environment, the Somali population has experienced severe droughts and famines, and the country is increasingly known for its flourishing piracy. Not surprisingly, it was not expected to achieve any of its MDGs. Over the years of instability, the international community attempted to deliver aid and development funds to Somalia, despite the insecurity and human rights abuses on the ground. In fact, in 2011 official development assistance (ODA) reached over US$1.1 billion, falling slightly to US$1 billion in 2012 (World Bank, 2015). This, however, rather than promoting peace and development, largely ignored the signs of the increasing humanitarian crisis and abuses by the government, and reinforced dysfunction and autocracy by the transitional national government (Menkhaus, 2009).

Aid for Somalia has been far from effective, as it has next to no functional state-level institutions, and few non-governmental organisations (NGOs) are willing or able to work in the failed state. Although it has been internationally acknowledged that fragile states do not lend themselves well to cookie-cutter approaches, with Fragile States Principles (FSPs)[12] explicitly created in 2007 (OECD, 2007), standard operating procedure of the one-size-fits-all type continues to dominate. In fact, a survey in 2011 indicated that donors in 13 fragile countries were either off track or partially off track in implementing 8 of the 10 FSPs (Nussbaum et al, 2012). In the case of Somalia, in particular, it is clear that the usual statebuilding activities have failed, and a more tailored approach is needed to focus funding and capacity building on smaller, local institutions and decentralised government. Local municipalities and hybrid forms of official and traditional methods of governance are increasingly active, and provide some semblance of a rule of law and basic services in the areas of Somaliland and Puntland in particular. Thus, localised aid for smaller municipal governments has had some limited positive influence (Menkhaus, 2014). Ultimately it is this bottom-up approach that might make the difference in the long term.

Somalia epitomises the challenges and complexities inherently involved in aiding conflict countries. While well-intentioned, development funding placed in the wrong hands can further destabilise a country, fuelling the conflict and doing more harm than good (Ahmad, 2012). For example, Somali warlords were routinely hijacking food and medical aid to sell for additional weapons, while millions of Somalis were starving. Thus, innovative, flexible and directed aid is needed to make a difference. Focusing on development targets such as the MDGs in the face of a violent crisis is useless, unless we are able to move beyond violence towards relative stability, security and peace, in which development funding and other efforts can actually address the root causes of conflicts and help high-risk groups move beyond choosing violence to better their situation. Ignoring issues of peace and security in the SDGs renders them useless in the face of conflict and violence, and effectively excludes states in dire need of humanitarian and development aid from the global development agenda. The cost of ignoring states such as Somalia is prohibitive, both to the state itself, as well as the region. In fact, Chauvet et al (2007) have gone as far as calculating the real costs of conflict for both the fragile country as well as the neighbouring states, estimating that the country itself loses around US$39 billion per year, and the neighbouring states US$237 billion per year, through lost growth.

While Somalia's history of protracted conflict has set its development back by years, the country is slowly stabilising as statebuilding progresses, but the security situation remains volatile. According to the most recent UN country progress snapshots, there has either been no data available to measure MDG progress, or where there has, the gains have been negligible (UNSD, 2014). As Somalia slowly prepares for a new constitution and government elections in 2016, continued international support will hopefully translate to better governance and peace (UNDP, 2013). Flexibility, as well as long-term commitment by donors, will be key in reaching those few fledgling local institutions that have taken up the organisation of, and care for, the population in their region. Furthermore, investment in the New Deal, of which Somalia is now a part, may also make an important difference.

The case of Burundi

A former Belgian colony, Burundi achieved independence in 1962. Bearing the scars of the politics of ethnic inequality inflicted by the colonisers, it has been engrossed in violent conflict practically since its independence. Dictatorial military regimes were in power from 1965 to 1993, with ethnic inequalities coming to the fore, including over 80,000 Hutu killed in 1972. Despite attempts at democratisation and successful elections in 1993, the conflict was reignited in 1994, and continued until the signing of the Arusha agreement in 2000, although some rebel factions refused to sign until 2008 (Uppsala Conflict Data

Program, 2014). Like Somalia above, Burundi, after decades of civil war, is still considered a fragile state (Fund for Peace, 2015), and is placed low on the HDI (180 out of 187) (UNDP, 2014). Over the last few years it has entered a phase of relative peace and absence of violent conflict, with an internationally supported power-sharing agreement brokered in Arusha, and successful elections held in 2004. The government made considerable efforts to establish appropriate mechanisms for effective aid handling and disbursement, including creating an interim Poverty Reduction Strategy Paper (PRSP) in 2004 and again in 2006, followed by a five-year plan for 2005-10, and finally in 2005 a National Committee for the Coordination of Aid, among others. Donors, on their part, were implementing the principles of aid effectiveness agreed on both in Paris (2005) and Accra (2008). The approach was holistic, with peace and security goals closely tied to the development agenda (Desrosiers and Muringa, 2012).

Burundi experienced a steady growth of aid from 2004 to 2010, reaching a level of US$630 million of ODA in 2010 (World Bank, 2015). Despite this, intra- and interethnic divisions, low-level violence, such as banditry, proliferation of arms and the resulting general feelings of insecurity, as well as corruption within government institutions, has rendered much of the development aid ineffective (Desrosiers and Muringa, 2012). In fact, according to Desrosiers and Muringa (2012), the principles of aid effectiveness have been detrimental to Burundi in the long run, as the Paris Declaration on Aid Effectiveness clearly noted that the roadmap it produced was not appropriate for fragile states, and urged donors to use a tailored approach in cases of fragility, a warning that was not heeded in the case of Burundi.

Furthermore, ongoing conflicts centred round land continue to unearth the divisions created by the civil war. Unfortunately, while the much anticipated 2010 elections were successful in (re)electing the government, they further destabilised the already fragile country, with accusations of fraudulent results and the new regime exhibiting signs of authoritarian rule as discussions of an unconstitutional third term for President Nkurunziza abound. A new plan for aid priorities has led away from security, to an exclusive focus on development and growth (Desrosiers and Muringa, 2012). As a result, tensions remain, with the current president re-elected following hotly disputed elections in July 2015, and violence increasingly recurred (*IRIN News*, 2014), and violence is increasingly recurring. Despite calls from party members and the international community for the president to abandon his desire for a third term, at the time of writing, it was unclear what decision he would make.

Burundi, in particular, is an excellent example of a fragile state that suffers from classic challenges to aid effectiveness, including low-level violence and insecurity, as well as government corruption, particularly clientelism, whereby connections to high-level decision-makers (patrons) and political support of them provide the targeted 'client' groups with benefits such as services or goods. Yet it has been able to achieve some developmental goals with careful planning, coordination and design of development projects, as well as a focus on achievement of security. In the last decade Burundi was successful in progressing on several MDGs, surpassing the regional average for Sub-Saharan Africa on many targets. The MDGs that were lagging behind included primarily poverty reduction and global partnership (UNSD, 2014). These encouraging results confirm the findings by Hirano and Otsubo (2014), who argue that it is not the initial condition of institutions, but the fact that they are improving over time, both in quality and capacity, that has a positive impact on aid effectiveness.

The strides Burundi made in achieving its MDGs are a clear indication that the country is moving in a positive direction; the international community, however, is retreating much too soon. In line with the recent trend of reducing aid to least development countries, particularly in Africa (OECD, 2014), ODA for Burundi peaked in 2010 at US$630 million, and has been shrinking, with the most recent figure for 2012 being US$523 million (World Bank, 2015). While the international community can and has pressured states to broker a peace treaty, and it is able to engage in peacekeeping to create negative peace, these interventions need to be followed by long-term engagement in development and peacebuilding activities, such as societal reintegration and transitional justice, education, employment creation and institutional reconstruction among others, at consistent levels to ensure that any progress made is maintained and built on. As the situation in the country changes, aid needs to continue, while adapting both donor and local policies to allow for flexibility in addressing key security concerns in concert with development, rather than withdrawing. Otherwise Burundi may return to full-scale civil war, reversing its hard-won achievements and destabilising the region.

The New Deal, peace and the Sustainable Development Goals

According to the 2014 world development report, Sub-Saharan Africa was lagging behind others in meeting all of its MDG targets (World Bank, 2014). Notably, it was conflict and recently post-conflict states that were performing poorest. In fact, these states are four times more likely to be off track compared to stable countries (The World Bank, nd), yet they represent a staggering 1.5 billion people. It is no wonder then that the AU held its own consultations on a CAP on the post-2015 development agenda, and included peace and security as one of its pillars. It has rebuffed any discussion on the difficulties of measuring peace, governance and rule of law, and proposed its own indicators at a meeting held in 2014 (AU, 2014c). The result – an impressive list of indicators related to peace and security – is based on the targets of Goal 16 of the Open Working Group.[13] The UN has also produced a preliminary set of a minimum number of indicators, according to a recent technical report by the Bureau of the UN Statistical Commission (UN, 2015). The UN list is much shorter, and is likely to remain this way as the organisation struggles to reach agreement on each measure.

The AU has also identified peace and security as an important aspiration of Agenda 2063, a blueprint for the continent's next 50 years (AU, 2014b). The Agenda highlights the need for a culture of peace through peace education, the 'silencing of guns', and freedom from terrorism, conflict, extremism and gender-based violence on the continent, calling for a common defence, security and foreign policy (AU, 2014b, pp 6-7, paras 31-39). In addition, the organisation has also supported the work of the g7+[14] group of states in creating the New Deal for Engagement in Fragile States[15] (hereafter, 'New Deal') with its country-owned and led Peacebuilding and Statebuilding Goals (PSGs) and indicators.

The initiative, announced in Busan, South Korea in 2011 as one of the major outcomes of the Fourth High Level Forum on Aid Effectiveness, is aimed at addressing the lack of leadership and trust prevalent in mainstream donor relationships with fragile states, and the need for tailored approaches to aid in fragile environments. It is also a response by the fragile states themselves, supported by the donors, unlike the failing FSPs mentioned earlier, which were created by and for donors (Wyeth, 2012). The g7+, itself a unique grouping, has allowed for an open International Dialogue on Peacebuilding and Statebuilding under the auspices of the fragile and conflict-affected states themselves, and as such fills an important gap, giving these states a united voice in discussions with donors for the first time (Nussbaum et al, 2012). The term 'fragile' has carried a negative connotation for many states what have fallen under this category, as it was seen as a term that would discourage investors and have other negative political and development impacts (Grimm et al, 2014). Thus, the act of creating a group of fragile states and acknowledging the common dilemmas facing the countries is an important step. The New Deal has been generally well received and endorsed by a number of major donors and development organisations.

In recognition of the peace and security gap in the MDGs, and the urgent need for a roadmap to developmental success that begins with addressing and building peace, Somalia is one of the latest countries to launch the New Deal in 2013.[16] Over three years the government will attempt to meet the five PSGs of the agreement: legitimate and inclusive politics; security; justice; economic foundations (jobs); and revenues and services (managing revenue and delivering accountable and fair services). The indicators for achieving these goals are broadly defined, with the New Deal foreseeing tailored approaches to implementation, based on fragility assessments and in-country consultations. These result in national priorities, which are then used to develop plans with donors, aimed at helping the fragile and conflict states to move along the fragility spectrum towards resilience. In Somalia, this has manifested itself in a visible shift in the language of donors to focus around Somali ownership and priorities for development. The process is far from perfect, however; some of the issues identified already include the need for broader confidence building between donors and the country elite, not just the government; balancing the need of donor and government accountability; and aligning existing commitments with new priorities (Hearn and Zimmerman, 2014). According to the latest New Deal monitoring report (International Dialogue on Peacebuilding and Statebuilding, 2014), only three countries have actually signed the compacts, with another four under discussion. Furthermore, TRUST,[17] an important component of the New Deal, highlights the need for lower risk-aversion by the donors and trust in the recipient government's abilities to use the donated funds effectively (International Dialogue on Peacebuilding and Statebuilding, 2014). In light of the complexity of the issues being addressed, the challenges are significant and change and progress is slow, but even small steps are encouraging, if a little sluggish.

In lieu of an agreement on an effective SDG related to peace (and security), it may be that the effort by the g7+ group of states in forming the New Deal and the PSGs will prove fruitful and establish some of the specific goals, guidelines and indicators needed for post-conflict states to address development. These, in turn, can be used by conflict countries as a gradual entry into the more traditionally development-oriented SDGs, thus funnelling any donor funds first into the much-needed peacebuilding and statebuilding activities to stabilise the country. While a similar scheme was envisioned when the PSGs were created under the MDGs, we now have an opportunity to recognise them officially within the SDG framework. The PSGs are already in effect in the UN Development Programme (UNDP) projects for select states who have signed on and have thus been integrated into the UN system somewhat.

Although a thorough discussion of the New Deal is beyond the scope of this chapter, the project is an admirable initiative by fragile and conflict-affected states to secure their own future, and is likely to have an important normative influence on development policy. More research on its implementation and developments is needed as the project progresses. However, the work and experiences that are already available should not be dismissed. Incorporating the principles of the New Deal into the SDGs would provide the development agenda with ready to use (if still in need of adjustments) tools and indicators for peacebuilding and statebuilding issues. This, in turn, would provide the New Deal with the necessary political dimension, in the form of an ongoing dialogue, which is a key component of establishing trust and mutual understanding, which it has recently been criticised for as lacking (Hughes et al, 2014). It would be unfortunate if the SDGs cannot benefit from the work and goals set out in the New Deal, forcing states, particularly the fragile and conflict-affected ones, to grapple with yet another framework.

In creating the SDG framework, peace and security have an important unifying role to play. It has been said that conflict is 'development in reverse' (UN, 2013, p 16), and that insecurity is the 'primary development challenge of our time' (The World Bank, 2011, p 1). Since the hope is that the new development agenda will not only identify goals and targets but also suggest ways of meeting them, it is important to consider what can realistically be achieved through international and national coordination. Despite the diplomatic challenges in finding the appropriate wording, it is clear that the absence of violent conflict is necessary for development to take place. This means that peacekeeping and peacebuilding activities are key considerations in any process related to the achievement of the SDGs.

Conflict is not only undesirable but also unsustainable. From 1990 to 2005, Africa's economy is estimated to have shrunk by 15 per cent, and the cost of conflict on the continent is approximated at US$300 billion (Geneva Declaration, 2008). A similar amount of funds was transferred back to the continent in international aid in the same time period (Geneva Declaration, 2008), although much of it has surely been syphoned off through corrupt practices, and thus did not actually make its way back to the people most affected by conflict. African states, representing the continent with the greatest number of conflict-affected and fragile states, have, through the CAP, emphasised addressing the root causes of conflict, along with the prevention of outbreak of violent conflict as priorities under their peace and security pillar (AU, 2014a).

Thus, in an effort to remain realistic in what can be accomplished in 15 years, and acknowledging the complexities of a negotiation that involves 193 sovereign states, it may be prudent to focus on the achievement of the most basic form of peace – negative peace – followed by a reliance on the already established PSGs. Negative peace is attainable both through peacekeeping and peacebuilding mechanisms already used by regional and international organisations, including the stationing of peacekeeping missions to uphold ceasefire agreements, as well as through transitional justice instruments. In fact, UN peacekeeping operations have been shown to succeed in establishing negative peace, and are relatively effective at extending it (Hoeffler and Fearon, 2014). By contrast, positive peace, understood as the absence of structural violence engendered in social institutions, is more difficult to achieve (Galtung, 1969). In order to establish positive peace, structural changes within the institutions and governance mechanisms of the country need to take place. Positive peace, in turn, leads to sustainable peace. This is where the SDGs come in.

While sustainable, positive peace is, of course, desirable as a long-term goal, negative peace is the bare minimum necessary to achieve some progress on development. Thus, if we are realistic about creating achievable goals, actively supporting conflict nations through peacekeeping to ensure violence is halted and negative peace established may be the first step in allowing them to achieve the SDGs. Longer-term peacebuilding goals are enshrined in the New Deal, and development activities, such as strengthening institutions, lowering the number of people in poverty, ensuring access to safe food and water, and addressing inequalities, as in the MDGs and SDGs, will, in turn, address the very root of conflict in the majority of fragile states. This will fulfil the priorities listed in the CAP under the peace and security pillar, and promote the establishment of positive, sustainable peace. Remaining conscious of the root causes of conflict in forming development programmes and policies in various countries means that these can be tailored to target high-risk groups and promote resilience within the post-conflict communities (Geneva Declaration, 2008).

Conclusions

The discussion on MDG strengths and weaknesses, as well as lessons learned for the SDGs, is ongoing and covers many aspects of global development, including, but not limited to, peace, security, governance, as well as environment, education, poverty and others. This chapter attempts to inform part of the discussion on the inclusion of peace and security in the SDGs in a constructive way. Acknowledging the importance of ending violent conflict and creating a peaceful and secure environment in which over a billion people can live safely, a two-step solution is proposed: an incremental approach of focusing on negative peace through classic international conflict resolution and peacekeeping mechanisms in order to allow for peacebuilding, followed by development funding and programmes, to take place; and second, the incorporation of the New Deal into the SDG framework.

The hope is that the small but significant step of accepting negative peace into the SDGs and creating specific indicators to limit violence is one that the 193 UN member states negotiating the development agenda can readily agree will be an important precursor to meeting other development targets. I posit that establishing negative peace will in turn lead to positive, sustainable peace by addressing the root causes of conflict through long-term development and peacebuilding programmes working in concert. Thus, a target for each country to decrease violence internally,[18] as well as the push for continued peacekeeping efforts and increased development aid for post-conflict countries, particularly in Africa, is key. The long-term aspect of the SDGs allows for programmes and funding to be put to good use, assuming that violence does not subvert the efforts at addressing the core issues of security and development. Hence, while small, it could be a step in the right direction.

As a second measure, the already established New Deal and PSGs can act as the peace and security gateway to the SDGs. When incorporated into the UN-backed development framework, they can act as a stepping-stone for fragile and conflict-affected states, in achieving the SDGs, particularly since the UN Secretary-General has already pledged support for the New Deal (*States News Service*, 2012), and indicated that peacebuilding and statebuilding are 'critical for countries to overcome fragility' (UN, 2014b, p 24, para 79) in his synthesis report on the SDGs. Considering the already identified need for the SDGs to be tailored to the needs of individual countries, and based on the context in which they are implemented, lessons learned from the PSGs could also be useful, particularly on the importance of political dialogue and trust.

And just maybe, after this debate and the negotiations are over, it is time we stop creating new agendas, declarations, goals, targets and indicators, and start focusing on implementing the ones we already have.

References

AU (African Union) (2014a) *Common African Position on the post-2015 development agenda*, Addis Ababa: AU.

AU (2014b) *Agenda 2063: The Africa we want*, Addis Ababa: AU.

AU (2014c) *Towards regional and national statistical capacities for measuring peace, rule of law and governance: An agenda for the post-2015 Sustainable Development Goals framework*, Addis Ababa: AU.

Ahmad, A. (2012) 'Agenda for peace or budget for war', *International Journal*, vol 67, no 2, pp 313-31.

Chauvet, L., Collier, P. and Hoeffler, A. (2007) *The cost of failing states and the limits to sovereignty*, Research Paper No 2007/30, Finland: United Nations University-World Institute for Development Economics Research.

Clemens, M. and Moss, T. (2005) 'What's wrong with the Millennium Development Goals?', CGD Brief, Washington, DC: Center for Global Development.

Cox, J. (2014) 'Embedding peace and stability in the post-2015 development agenda : a civil society view', *Journal of Peacebuilding & Development*, vol 9, no 2, pp 97-103.

Desrosiers, M.-E. and Muringa, G. (2012) 'Effectiveness under fragile conditions? Sociopolitical challenges to aid and development cooperation in Burundi', *Conflict, Security & Development*, vol 12, no 5, pp 501-36.

Domínguez, C. (2013) 'Including security in the post 2015 development goals. Germany could play an active role', *SWP Comments*, December, pp 1-8.

Fund for Peace (2015) *Fragile States Index* (http://fsi.fundforpeace.org/).

Galtung, J. (1969) 'Violence, peace and peace research', *Journal of Peace Research*, vol 6, no 3, pp 167-91.

Geneva Declaration (2008) *Armed violence prevention and reduction: A challenge for achieving the Millennium Development Goals*, New York: United Nations.

Geneva Declaration (2010) *More violence, less development: Examining the relationship between armed violence and MDG achievement*, New York: United Nations.

Goodlet, K.W., Edgar, A. and Sarty, R. (eds) (2015) *Canada in Africa: Addressing insecurity in Somalia and the Horn of Africa*, Waterloo, Ontario: Wilfrid Laurier University Press.

Grimm, S., Lemay-Hebert, N. and Nay, O. (2014) '"Fragile states": introducing a political concept', *Third World Quarterly*, vol 35, no 2, pp 197-209.

Harttgen, K. and Klasen, S. (2013) 'Do fragile countries experience worse MDG progress?', *The Journal of Development Studies*, vol 49, no 1, pp 134-59 (www.tandfonline.com/doi/abs/10.1080/002203 88.2012.713471).

Hearn, S. and Zimmerman, T. (2014) *A new deal for Somalia?: The Somali compact and its implications for peacebuilding*, New York: Center on International Cooperation, New York University.

High Level Panel on Fragile States (2014) *Ending conflict and building peace in Africa: A call to action*, New York: United States.

Hirano, Y. and Otsubo, S. (2014) *Aid is good for the poor*, Policy Research Working Paper 6998, Washington, DC: The World Bank.

Hoeffler, A. and Fearon, J. (2014) *Conflict and violence assessment paper: Benefits and costs of the conflict and violence targets for the post-2015 development agenda*, Copenhagen: Copenhagen Consensus Center.

Hughes, J., Hooley, T., Hage, S. and Ingram, G. (2014) *Implementing the New Deal for Fragile States*, Washington, DC: The Brookings Institution.

International Dialogue on Peacebuilding and Statebuilding (2010) *Peacebuilding and statebuilding priorities and challenges: A synthesis of findings from seven multi-stakeholder consultations* (www.pbsbdialogue. org/documentupload/45454619.pdf).

International Dialogue on Peacebuilding and Statebuilding (2011) *A new deal for engagement in fragile states* (www.pbsbdialogue.org/ documentupload/49151944.pdf).

International Dialogue on Peacebuilding and Statebuilding (2014) *New deal monitoring report 2014*, Fifth International Dialogue Working Group Meeting on New Deal Implementation, Freetown, Sierra Leone.

IRIN News (2014) 'Burundi's troubled peace and reconciliation process', *IRIN Humanitarian News and Analysis* (www.irinnews. org/report/100361/burundi-s-troubled-peace-and-reconciliation-process).

Kashambuzi, E. (2013) *The role of peace and security in the post-2015 agenda: The perspective of African states and LDCs*, New York: Center on International Cooperation, New York University (http://cic.nyu. edu/blog/global-development/role-peace-and-security-post-2015-agenda-perspective-african-states-and-ldcs).

Menkhaus, K. (2009) 'Somalia: "They created a desert and called it peace(building)"', *Review of African Political Economy*, vol 36, no 120, pp 223-33.

Menkhaus, K. (2014) 'State failure, state-building, and prospects for a "functional failed state" in Somalia', *The ANNALS of the American Academy of Political and Social Science*, vol 656, no 1, pp 154-72 (http://ann.sagepub.com/cgi/doi/10.1177/0002716214547002).

Nussbaum, T., Zorbas, E. and Koros, M. (2012) 'A new deal for engagement in fragile states', *Conflict, Security & Development*, vol 12, December, pp 559-87 (www.tandfonline.com/doi/abs/10.1080/14678802.2012.744187).

ODI (Overseas Development Institute (2011) *Getting better results from assiatnce to fragile states*, London: ODI.

OECD (Organisation for Economic Co-operation and Development) (2007) *Principles for Fragile States Principles*, Paris: OECD (www.oecd.org/dacfragilestates/aboutthefragilestatesprinciples.htm).

OECD (2014) 'Aid to developing countries rebounds in 2013 to reach an all-time high', OECD News Release, Paris: OECD (www.oecd.org/newsroom/aid-to-developing-countries-rebounds-in-2013-to-reach-an-all-time-high.htm).

OECD-DAC (Development Assistance Committee) (2014) *Addressing the boundary between ODA and total offical support for development (TOSD) in the field of peace, security and justice*, Paris: OECD.

Salahub, J. (2013) 'MDGs and fragile states: a red herring?', *The Ottawa Citizen*.

States News Service (2012) Secretary-General, at High Level event on peacebuilding, 'Statebuilding, pledges strong, coordinated system-wide support for "New Deal" initiative'.

Stewart, F. (2003) 'Conflict and the Millennium Development Goals', *Journal of Human Development*, vol 4, no 3, pp 325-51.

Tran, M. (2013) 'Somalia the yardstick in new deal for conflict-affected countries', *The Guardian* (www.theguardian.com/global-development/2013/apr/19/somalia-yardstick-new-deal-conflict-countries).

UN (United Nations) (2000) *United Nations Millennium Declaration*, New York: UN General Assembly (www.un.org/en/ga/search/view_doc.asp?symbol=A/RES/55/2).

UN (2013) *A new global partnership: Eradicate poverty and transform economies through sustainable development*, High Level Panel of Eminent Persons on the Post-2015 Development Agenda, New York: UN.

UN (2014a) *Report of the Open Working Group of the General Assembly on Sustainable Development Goals*, New York: UN General Assembly.

UN (2014b) *Synthesis report of the Secretary-General on the post-2015 development agenda: The road to dignity by 2030: Ending poverty, transforming all lives and protecting the planet*, New York: UN.

UN (2015) *Technical report by the Bureau of the United Nations Statistical Commission (UNSC) on the process of the development of an indicator framework for the goals and targets of the post-2015 development agenda*, New York: UN (https://sustainabledevelopment.un.org/content/documents/6754Technical report of the UNSC Bureau %28final%29. pdf).

UNDP (United Nations Development Programme) (2012) *Somalia human development report 2012: Empowering youth for peace and development*, New York: UN.

UNDP (2013) *A new deal for a New Somalia: Somalia annual report 2013*, New York: UN.

UNDP (2014) *Human Development Index 2013*, Human Development Reports (http://hdr.undp.org/en/content/table-1-human-development-index-and-its-components).

UNSD (United Nations Statistics Division) (2014) *Millennium Development Indicators: Country and regional progress snapshots* (http://mdgs.un.org/unsd/mdg/Host.aspx?Content=Data/snapshots.htm).

UNTT (United Nations System Task Team) (2012) *Realizing the future we want for all*, Report to the Secretary-General by the UN System Task Team on the Post-2015 UN Development Agenda, New York: UN.

Uppsala Conflict Data Program (2014) *UCDP conflict encyclopedia*, Uppsala University (www.ucdp.uu.se/gpdatabase/gpcountry. php?id=26&regionSelect=2-Southern_Africa).

World Bank, The (nd) *Stop conflict, reduce fragility and end poverty: Doing things differently in fragile and conflict-affected situations* (www. worldbank.org/content/dam/Worldbank/Feature Story/Stop_Conflict_Reduce_Fragility_End_Poverty.pdf).

World Bank, The (2011) *World development report 2011: Conflict, security and development*, Washington DC: The World Bank (http://elibrary. worldbank.org/doi/book/10.1596/978-0-8213-8439-8).

World Bank, The (2013) 'Twenty fragile states make progress on Millennium Development Goals', World Bank Press Release (www. worldbank.org/en/news/press-release/2013/05/01/twenty-fragile-states-make-progress-on-millennium-development-goals).

World Bank, The (2014) *World Development Indicators 2014*, Washington, DC: The World Bank.

World Bank, The (2015) World Development Indicators (http://data.worldbank.org/indicator/DT.ODA.ODAT.CD/countries/BI?display=graph).

Wyeth, V. (2012) 'Knights in fragile armor: the rise of the "G7+"', *Global Governance*, vol 18, pp 7-12.

THIRTEEN

African development, political economy and the road to Agenda 2063

George Kararach, Hany Besada and Timothy Shaw

Introduction

Since the turn of the millennium, seven out of the ten fastest growing economies in the world have been African, tangible proof of the continent's upward trajectory. Although 10 African countries do still have an African Union (AU) or United Nations (UN) peacekeeping presence, 85 per cent of Africans enjoy peaceful, relatively stable conditions, and these economies generate 95 per cent of the continent's GDP.

Following a 20 per cent decline between 1980 and 2000, average incomes in Africa have risen by 30 per cent since 2005. Strong commodity prices have been central to this turnaround, but other factors such as enhanced governance and macroeconomic management have played a part. Rwanda and Ethiopia, for example, although not blessed with oil or mineral wealth, have become strong performers due to their strategic efforts to galvanise their economies by attracting relevant human capital and investments. Yet significant challenges remain (Kararach, 2014a). Overall, absolute poverty has fallen, but in most places the majority of the population lives in relative poverty due to persistent inequality, which has the potential to destabilise these societies.

While some social indicators such as school enrolment and child mortality have been improving, inequalities remain entrenched, and have, in many instances, worsened. Job creation is a huge challenge in the face of a demographic 'bulge' of educated youth, and the underlying causes are not difficult to discern. There has been limited structural transformation or diversification. Agriculture's share of GDP has declined, but this is not counterbalanced by enhanced value addition or industrialisation. There is a general view that manufacturing growth has been hampered by fragmented markets, while poor infrastructure, particularly a shortage of energy and port capacity, remains acute (AfDB, 2014). There is increasing pressure to develop 'smart' policies and programmes to enhance productivity, sustain economic growth and engender greater social inclusion. Looking beyond the MDGs, the goal of eliminating poverty could be achievable within the coming decade or so, if the right policy and programmatic frameworks are put in place and bottlenecks are eliminated.

Africa is made up of 54 disparate countries in five regions, and is not a single monolithic whole. The 2014 Ebola crisis in three countries in West Africa has once again demonstrated the tendency of those outside the continent to classify it as a distinct entity. Despite the frequent allusion to a new 'scramble for Africa', the continent is planning, managing and starting to finance its own destiny, as it attempts to reclaim the twenty-first century (Shaw, 2014). This chapter attempts to pull together the major threads of this discussion, as Africa anticipates a future that is fraught, not just with challenges, but also with opportunities. Africa's vision for the future as it looks beyond the Millennium Development Goals (MDGs) has recently been endorsed by African heads of states in the name of Agenda 2063.

This chapter is divided into five sections. The second section describes the overall trends and general tenets of Agenda 2063. We argue that any post-MDG targets for development must be situated within the context of socioeconomic transformation, and the resultant political economy or agency issues. We revisit these discussions in the third section. The fourth section outlines some of the major public policies and actions that the continent needs to embark on after 2015 and beyond. Many of these have been outlined by the various contributions to this volume. This amounts to an 'A to Z' listing of what, in our view, are the programmatic actions that are to be recommended. These actions should not be viewed as a long laundry list of 'things to do', but instead are issues that have emerged from the social and historical dynamics as well as the political economy of the continent. It remains for individual countries and regions to prioritise these challenges and to determine the appropriate interventions. The final section concludes.

Africa and the passage from 2015 to 2063

There are five factors that have come to affect Africa's development today (Kararach, 2014a):

- First, the emergence of a multipolar economic world that now includes the global South, a source of new investment opportunities and export destinations, development experience and know-how as well as a new aid architecture.
- Second, demographic changes brought about by a young and increasingly urbanised continent of a billion people – a number which is expected to double to 2 billion by 2050, with two-thirds living in cities. This increased 'human capital' has the potential to revolutionise the productive base of the continent. However, the energy of the young population, if untapped through better employment opportunities, has the potential to become a source of instability and political chaos.
- Third, the continuing discoveries of large amounts of natural resource wealth, and the associated challenges, as well as opportunities, that arise from managing and sharing that wealth.
- Fourth, there is a real opportunity to 'leapfrog' more developed regions through the use of biotechnology and the mobile phone.
- Finally, climate change has the potential to generate significant conflict over environmental assets such as land and water, and can weaken biodiversity and threaten livelihood systems.

Against this backdrop, how can Africa sustain its economic growth and achieve the necessary economic transformation (Amaoko, 2010; ACET, 2014)? A few immediate actions come to mind. First, the continent must achieve real regional economic integration anchored on better connectivity through the building of road, rail and air linkages as well as 'soft' infrastructure – opening up borders and eliminating the needless regulations that currently hinder trade and trans-boundary cooperation. Such actions have to be undertaken by countries individually and collectively in the context of strategic industrial policies that foster economic dynamism, productivity, jobs and social inclusion.

Second, Africa needs better management of its natural resources to ensure that it takes advantage of any strong cycle of commodity prices, thus enhancing intergenerational beneficiation. Commodities should not be sold 'on the cheap', but rather processed in value chains and exported on fairer trading terms. Revenue from these resources must then be invested strategically and wisely (Kararach and Odhiambo, 2016a, 2016b: forthcoming).

Third, we need to address the challenges faced by those African states that are still fragile. Part of their fragility and vulnerability arises from the dangers of climate change (such as desertification, floods and rising sea levels), and immediate practical adaptation and mitigation measures are required.

Fourth, the continent needs to rethink its engagement with the rest of the world in terms of development and multilateral cooperation as an exporter of raw commodities. And finally, the continent must invest in innovation and R&D (research and development), in order to transform its productive systems. Industrial 'leaders', based on economic cluster formations, must be encouraged, who would act as drivers of development in and across strategic sectors (Kararach, 2014c; Howard et al, 2014). We return to many of these issues in the fourth section.

It is generally agreed that the continent needs to get better at mobilising the required resources through improved utilisation of its finances. For example, the continent has to close the US$50 billion annual infrastructure funding deficit, on which it spends at least 2 per cent of annual GDP growth (AfDB, 2013a, 2013b). A collaborative approach to raising finance will become critical where, for example, private capital makes up an important part of the equation, in the form of private equity, debt and the untapped resources of African pension funds and capital markets as well as remittances from the diaspora. The key is to take risk management seriously and to build business confidence. Public actions have to be pragmatic in their approach to policy and regulation, encouraging public–private partnership frameworks, and building the capacity of independent regulators, to avoid agency capture. Risk mitigation instruments – such as credit guarantees – should also be in place, in order to reassure investors. Actions also need to be taken on shadow banking, capital flight and other illicit financial flows, dealing with criminal gangs fostering drug/human trafficking and other organised crime as well as proactive agenda to better the huge 'informal' economy. In other words, Africa's approach to a post-2015 agenda must go beyond 'business as usual'.

Vision 2063: from vision to plan of action in Africa's search for transformation

Agenda 2063 came into being at the 50th Anniversary Solemn Declaration of the heads of state and government of the AU, during the Golden Jubilee of the Organization of African Unity (OAU)/ AU (Addis Ababa, 26 May 2013; see Kiggundu, 2014). Eight pledges were made, as summarised in Table 13.1. The vision of Agenda 2063 reiterates the millennial renaissance theme, which stated that Africans shall work together towards a new beginning, proceeding

Table 13.1: Summary statements of Agenda 2063 50th Anniversary Solemn Declaration by the heads of state and government of the African Union

Agenda 2063 visionary statements
1. African identity and renaissance: accelerate the African renaissance through integrating principles of pan-Africanism in all policies anchored in our belief in common destiny and shared values.
2. Continue the struggle against colonialism and the right to self-determination of people still under colonial rule.
3. Integration agenda: implement the continental free trade area to ultimately establish a united and integrated Africa.
4. Agenda for social and economic development: develop Africa's human capital as the continent's most important resource, eradicate disease especially HIV/AIDS, malaria and tuberculosis; take ownership of the use and development of natural resources, and make development responsive to the needs of the people.
5. Agenda for peace and security: eradicate recurrent conflicts through addressing the root causes of these conflicts.
6. Democratic governance: anchor African societies, governments and institutions on respect for the rule of law, human rights and dignity, popular participation and democratic governance.
7. Determining Africa's destiny: determine Africa's destiny through taking ownership of African issues and providing African solutions to African problems.
8. Africa's place in the world: continue the global struggle against all forms of racism, discrimination, and expressing solidarity with oppressed countries and peoples.

Source: AU (2013, pp 3, 17)

from decolonisation towards self-determination, and calling for greater regional integration, socioeconomic development, peace, security and democratic development, advocating for Africa's destiny and a redefinition of Africa's place in the globalised world. Agenda 2063 acknowledges that Africa needs new institutional and governance arrangements to effectively shape its agenda for development, integration and transformation. However, the exact nature, structure and composition of these 'institutional arrangements' are not defined. It is critical that Africa determines the *how* of developing inclusive political and economic institutions (Acemoglu and Robinson, 2012). Although Agenda 2063 moves beyond the MDGs framework by calling for inclusive and sustainable development, this cannot be achieved unless countries establish institutions that are capable of balancing and resolving competing political interests. The importance of inclusion has been brought home more poignantly by increased activities of Islamic and other fundamentalist groups such as Boko Haram in Northern Nigeria and Al-Qaeda in the Maghreb. Such groups use discontents brewing on the backs of inequalities and exclusion to garner new recruits – especially among unemployed youth.

While many aspects of the statements are forward-looking and reflect current African needs and realities, regional integration, governance, inclusive development and peace and security, and fighting communicable and emergent diseases, others look backwards into Africa's history. By urging a redefinition of Africa's place in the world, Agenda 2063 refocuses on the need for Africa to fight global racism and discrimination, sentiments expressed at the Bandung Conference of 1955 (Kiggundu, 2014). While issues of global human rights deserve serious attention, they do not adequately reflect Africa's contemporary challenges or serve to redefine its place in the world economy (Rotberg, 2013).

Like the MDGs, Agenda 2063 does not refer explicitly to the historical and comparative challenges to economic performance in Africa, which would ensure that maintaining the current growth momentum and economic transformation occupies a pivotal role in the pledges. The silence on this matter may be due to different 'ideological' predispositions, reflecting attempts to reach a consensus, which is a common factor of such 'global', and necessarily broad, political communiqués. Individual economies must strategise on how to leverage their respective advantages to successfully extract benefits from any integration into the global value chain (Kararach, 2014a).

Kiggundu (2014) argues that the challenge for the Agenda's vision lies in whether ordinary citizens imagine a more positive future, while reconciling with historical misdeeds and atrocities, and at the same time coping with the hardship of current realities. This is particularly so for former settler economies (for example, Zimbabwe and Kenya), conflict and post-conflict states (Democratic Republic of Congo [DRC], South and North Sudan), as well as countries with long-serving regimes (Uganda, Cameroon, etc). Two questions are outstanding: what should be done *practically* at the continental level across sectors, stakeholders and countries? And what resources, capacities, capabilities and skills sets can bring forth an effective and sustained implementation of the eight pledges?

It is refreshing that the Agenda drafters explicitly acknowledge new development and investment opportunities for the continent. Africa today is faced with a confluence of factors that present a great opportunity for consolidation and rapid progress, and the Agenda document lists the following:

• unprecedented positive and sustained growth trajectory of many African countries resulting from sound macroeconomic policies and strategies;

- significant reduction in violent conflict, increased peace and stability, coupled with advances in democratic governance;

- prospects for a rising middle class, coupled with the youth bulge, which can act as catalysts for further growth, particularly in the consumer and services sectors; and

- a change in the international finance architecture, with the rise of newly developed countries forming the BRICS (Brazil, Russia, India, China and South Africa) and MINT (Mexico, Indonesia, Nigeria and Turkey), resulting in improved flows of foreign direct investment (FDI) (AU, 2013, p 6).

The Agenda document also notes that success is dependent on unity, transparency, performance and building on successes, placing citizens first, governance and values (AU, 2013). It acknowledges four outcome factors: science, technology and innovation, human development, natural resource management and developmental states.

Kiggundu (2014) warns that previous continental visionary initiatives such as the Lagos Plan of Action and the Abuja Treaty lacked details and a resources plan, resulting in weak delivery and development outcomes. Proponents of Agenda 2063 seem to be aware of this, and have developed a detailed plan of action with specific milestones, deliverables and assigned responsibilities.

The Agenda has three integrated components: the *strategic plan* (spelling out the goals of what to do), the *implementation plan* (how, who, when), and the *monitoring and evaluation framework* (feedback on progress, outcomes and impact). The plan also correctly emphasises the importance of implementation as a core item of action.

However, the Agenda 2063 strategic plan omits to mention resource management. It must spell out the nature, type and amount of resources needed for the effective implementation of the various component parts of the Agenda, a detailed plan for resource mobilisation, development and utilisation, as well as a performance and accountability framework. The plan also lacks an explicit framework for risk assessment, risk management and risk mitigation. These omissions are important, and will affect the implementation of the plan.

Who owns Agenda 2063? Is it the African Union Commission (AUC) and its organs, the heads of states and governments who originated the idea, the AU member states, the regional bureaucrats and technocrats (New Partnership for Africa's Development [NEPAD], African Development Bank [AfDB], United Nations Economic

Commission for Africa [UNECA]), the people and society of Africa, or is it co-owned? This question needs to be clarified because it has implications for commitment and effective and sustained implementation. A related question concerns the implementing agencies for the Agenda's core programmes. These appear to be continent-wide (for example, NEPAD, AfDB, UNECA, African Capacity Building Foundation [ACBF], AfDB), regional economic communities (RECs) (for example, Economic Community Of West African States [ECOWAS], Southern African Development Community [SADC]), national, bilateral (for example, the Forum on China-Africa Cooperation [FOCAC]), drawn from the international/ UN community (for example, the United Nations Development Programme [UNDP], The World Bank Group) as well as African diasporas or combinations thereof. This question has broad implications for the capacity to implement and sustain the Agenda, and for its outcomes (Kiggundu, 2014).

Africa, political economy and the situating of transformation

As James Wakiaga argues in Chapter One (this volume), the MDGs were a strong driving force for national programmes, and formed a rallying point for development in many African countries. We noted earlier that without economic transformation, it is likely that growth will not be sustained, and nor will it be rapid enough to deliver the continent's development agenda after the MDGs. Africa has to build capable developmental states that can proactively promote coherent policies for structural change. Africa must break the link between aid dependence and the MDGs in order to achieve Agenda 2063. Thus the discussion of financing should not focus exclusively on aid. While aid contributed to the investment requirements for the MDGs in Africa, long-term financing modalities for sustained investments have not yet received sufficient attention.

It has been argued that several low-income countries in the sub-region could have met the MDGs by 2015 if their growth rate had been sustained over the period of 10 to 15 years. A number of fragile countries have held back overall growth rates, as well as causing significant weaknesses in Africa's economic structural base. Without coherent policies for structural change, it is inconceivable that growth will be sufficiently rapid and sustained to drive attainment of most of the post-MDGs agenda. Effective developmental states must promote coherent policies for the required structural change. In this regard, governments must:

- formulate long-term frameworks for economic diversification and structural transformation, consistent with respective national resource endowments;
- establish an economic environment to encourage productive investment by using strategic industrial and other related policies for the efficient functioning of the economy;
- modernise the agriculture sector, expand sectoral linkages and invest in infrastructure and support services to fuel productivity and economic transformation;
- increase investments in human capital and ensure effective incentives for enhanced personnel retention;
- enhance institutional reforms to build effective sociopolitical and economic governance; and
- scale up investments in science, R&D and technology, promote diffusion of technologies and innovations to improve productivity, and build Africa's global trade competitiveness.

Africa must build a 'post-donor-assistance' world (Easterly, 2006). Governments must plan to meet their post-MDG-related investment requirements with a decreasing reliance on aid. By this means, governments can become effective catalysts for transformation by establishing the appropriate framework for an expanded private sector role in financing and delivering social services, and for public–private partnerships in support of investments for infrastructure. Similarly, Africa has much to gain from the emerging aid architecture by engaging with other development partners from the South, such as China and India, to direct their expanding economic role in the continent towards transformation-enhancing investments (Shaw, 2014).

Africa has to learn that global averages of socioeconomic progress mask deeper issues of social exclusion that persist at national and regional levels and can breed violent reactions and conflicts. Global monitoring also fails to expose the levels of human deprivation and economic exclusion experienced by various social groups throughout the continent. As we know, MDG indicators failed to capture the underlying policy and institutional determinants associated with such deprivation and exclusion. A redefined post-MDG paradigm must strive to bring these issues to the forefront of any global and continental compacts.

African leaders must recognise the importance of political economy and agency as they chart the transformational agenda of the continent. The MDGs were successful in drawing attention to poverty as an urgent global priority, and they have also led to a reshaping of the idea of development. By reducing the complex challenges of development to a list of eight 'simple' goals, the MDGs redefined the very meaning of development and created a discourse of development as poverty reduction – devoid of agendas for addressing systemic issues in the global political economy, and empowerment of poor people within countries.

It is arguable that the MDG narrative of development appealed to rich country 'publics and parliaments', and led to increases in aid on social spending. However, the goals have had little real impact on fostering economic growth and social justice while addressing poverty, inequality and the fulfilment of human rights. A major challenge for African countries is devising an appropriate inclusive development strategy (Fukuda-Parr, 2011). The MDGs created an international development discourse that was narrow, and overly focused on social investments and social protection. While these are indeed priorities, so, too, is an alternative strategy of national development and global economic reforms that give space for continental transformation (Fukuda-Parr, 2011). The post-MDGs discourse in Africa must also take into account three other broad issues: (i) interpretation of global targets; (ii) reconfiguration of global priorities in the current context of the War on Terror; and (iii) the importance of the political economy in a globalised world.

Issues of interpretation and how global goals are utilised

Fukuda-Parr (2011, p 1) noted that developing countries need to take into account what she termed 'issues of interpretation and how the goals are used', including the following:

Erroneous interpretations in development strategy and the planning of goals: global goals such as Agenda 2063 derive from Declarations – which are broad statements of political commitment by regional and national leaders of their vision of the world by a specified timeline. As benchmarks for achieving normative objectives, such goals are neither scientifically defined planning targets nor new a development strategy. For example, Fukuda-Parr (2011) criticised the MDGs as: (i) low in ambition for countries that had already achieved a minimum of the goals; (ii) unrealistic and overambitious for many countries unlikely to achieve the goals; (iii) misdirected by ignoring the key issues of systemic reforms of the world economy and transformation; (iv) blind to the political dimensions of poverty; (v) inadequately aligned with human rights standards and principles; (vi) having an overly technocratic approach to poverty reduction through resources and technology; and (vii) too narrow in scope by neglecting specific objectives agreed at global conferences.

Erroneous monitoring measure – achieving the targets or making faster progress? History has shown that monitoring reports for globally agreed goals check progress by simply assessing whether the targets have been achieved. This is biased against countries with the highest incidence of the problem being programmed for. More importantly, guidance on how to ensure programme effectiveness is required. The appropriate measure, therefore, is the rate of progress made, not the level of achievement. A focus on the level of achievement may lead to perverse results (Fukuda-Parr, 2011). For example, countries starting from a low base, which make rapid progress, may be seen as off track and failing, while countries that started at low levels of poverty and made very slow progress are assessed as successful (Fukuda-Parr, 2011). Performance should be monitored according to progress rather than level of achievement, and communities must be engaged in determining the M&E (monitoring and evaluation) framework (Kararach, 2004).

Adaptation to national contexts: individual countries should not use global goals as planning tools. Global goals start from different premises and do not acknowledge variations in initial conditions. In the real world, countries face differing constraints and capacities in the financial, institutional and human arenas (Kararach, 2014a). Thus, the MDGs should have been domesticated to allow countries to be ambitious yet able to develop realistic targets (Fukuda-Parr, 2011).

Importance of globalisation in a world characterised by the War on Terror

Africa needs to take account of a number of emerging global issues. First, international economic relations are becoming increasingly defined in a multipolar context. Agreements on major issues today, such as trade, climate change and the War on Terror, must involve a growing number of disparate nations. Second, the African middle class is growing in size (Ncube and Shimeles, 2012), yet millions of Africans are still living in absolute, extreme poverty – many of them in fragile states. Countries have to make a special effort to identify specific policies that will make a difference to the lives of the poor.

Third, the effects of climate change have become increasingly tangible (Kararach, 2014a). Although the poor are not the cause of this threat, they may deplete their immediate environment as they seek to sustain their livelihoods. Africa needs to respond within a context of strategic global cooperation that enhances its chances for transformation.

Fourth, the new reality is that aid is no longer the most important financial flow for most African nations (AfDB, 2013a). Aid has become just one of a mix of capital flows that include private investment, trade, remittances, illicit flows and others. In this respect, African countries should find ways of using development assistance to leverage other capital flows, as they all signal degrees of confidence and form alliances in specific policy regimes.

Finally, since the Marrakech Conference on Managing for Development Results of 2002, the focus has moved from intentions, or money spent, to managing for development results. There is an increasing need to build systems that are much better at measuring and evaluating development results, because the poor people of Africa urgently need results.

What does this mean in practical terms? Four key areas come to mind: (i) there must be an enhanced effort at domestic resource mobilisation (DRM); (ii) skills and human capital must be developed and retained (including tapping the diaspora skill pool); (iii) climate smart development must be emphasised, ensuring green growth; and (iv) there should be a redefinition of the importance of agency and enhanced governance across the board, including in the utilisation of natural resources and prioritising human security.

Rethinking development policy in the context of political economy

The core message of this volume has been that there is a need to rethink African development policy. With the rise of an indigenous middle class, and a political leadership anxious to free itself from the straightjacket imposed by the official development assistance (ODA) regime, there is serious interest in encouraging investments by local entrepreneurs, as well as foreigners, in strategic sectors.

Africa, at the beginning of the 21st century, is ready to redefine its position in the world economy (Hanson et al, 2012). There has been a major turnaround in the past few years. While the rest of the world has struggled with the legacy of the 2008/09 recession and pessimism about the future, Africa has moved ahead, with noticeable growth performance.

It can be argued that pursuing global goals such as the MDGs is like 'placing the cart before the horse'. Countries cannot have sustainable and meaningful poverty reduction unless they first have growth. There has thus arisen a search for 'productive' development policies that accommodate constructive partnerships between the public and private sectors through the use of strategic industrial policies.

Actions for a new development policy

We outline below a number of urgent actions that African countries need to select from and prioritise depending on their individual contexts and associated capacities to respond in the short, medium and long term.

Setting realistic development goals: Agenda 2063 set itself a deadline of ending aid by 2028. This radical measure is a necessary first step towards a new regime that aims to deliver the long-held African dream of self-reliance, bringing to an end the harmful dependency on aid and donor conditionality (Rugumamu, 1997; Moyo, 2009). Such an exit option would compel donors and African recipients to rethink development policy and programming (Hyden, 2010). An aid architecture is beginning to emerge in which Africa can participate as an equal (Hanson et al, 2012). This is not to say – à la Moyo (2009) – that all aid has a deleterious effect on growth, since more robust recent studies show that aid does actually work in particular conditions (Tribe, 2013; Alia and Kouadio-Anago, 2014). Donors need to be made more accountable for and transparent in their aid policies, including how aid resources are allocated to recipients (see Chapter Ten, this volume). As Bhusan and colleagues have noted, all resources need to be mobilised, and, more importantly, used effectively.

Productive approaches to resources: the cessation of ODA payments would not mean ending all resource transfers from rich to poor countries, but rather employing a more productive approach that enables local institutions to have a greater say in how these additional external resources are to be used. The current 'ODA regime has created a grant mentality' in Africa (Hyden, 2010, p 1) that has limited both the appreciation of foreign aid and responsibility for its proper execution (Kamgnia, 2013).

Ending jobless growth: development is more than economic growth, and includes a country's ability to generate jobs as well as greater social inclusion (AfDB, 2014). Poverty reduction must be achieved through an agenda that promotes investment in business and jobs, in turn creating 'more favourable conditions for the growth of organised labour' and wider civic participation in the economy (Hyden, 2010, p 1). By strengthening the formal business sector, jobs would be created that lend themselves to an expansion of the labour movement, to ensure better working conditions. It would also improve collaboration between government and the private sector. Better jobs also create conditions for the reduction of the brain drain, the rise of criminal and fundamentalist groups, and enhanced state legitimacy necessary for the emergence of a developmental state, as noted by Kararach in this volume (see Chapter Five).

Investing in infrastructure: poor infrastructure is a major constraint on Africa's development. Whatever little infrastructure the continent has in terms of roads and railways, for example, has been poorly maintained (Kararach, 2014a). Traditional donors have been only moderately interested in expanding their engagements in infrastructure development on the continent. In contrast, support for infrastructural development, particularly by China and India, in exchange for access to natural resources, is increasing. These countries tend to give contracts to their own companies and jobs to their own nationals, but their contributions have also been enduring, and their aid is therefore greatly appreciated (Bräutigam, 2011). The fact that this aid comes with no political conditionalities has reinforced this appreciation.

Rethinking engagement of the private sector: many projects, particularly in infrastructure, would benefit from the introduction of public–private partnerships (Hyden, 2010; Kararach, 2014b). Infrastructure projects are capital-intensive and have the potential to be politically controversial, as social groups fight over beneficiation; they also require technical expertise that is not available locally (Farlam, 2005). Public–private partnerships can pool resources and managerial skills, as well as helping to forge a better relationship between government and business, thereby institutionalising the social capital necessary for sustaining a national strategy based on investment and a favourable business climate. Equally, there is a large part of the private sector that is either not adequately understood or catered for in development policy and programmes – and that is the informal sector. Countries need to develop proactive approaches with the seemingly rising informalisation of economic activities (AfDB, 2013c), as these tend to be used easily as vehicles for exploitation and criminal operation by unscrupulous operators.

Better understanding of local reality in development planning: context may be even more significant than aid in development. Domestic dynamics in China, Vietnam and India, linked to global trade and finance flows, have achieved stunning results in terms of economic diversification, growth and poverty reduction. Many of the authors in this volume argue that power analysis, drivers of change studies, systems approaches and political economy assessments are critical for understanding the development dynamics of Africa. There has, in recent years, been a search for more 'actionable' and 'practical' approaches to context analyses – sometimes driven by the hope that more refined approaches will reduce the current complexity, restoring traditional linear planning approaches based on simple cause and effect. For whatever reason, this new perspective will redefine the development conversation in Africa after 2015. Issues of capacity will come to the fore of development policy and action (Léautier, 2014), which may lead to a more useful longer-term perspective, ensuring the inclusion of relevant local stakeholders and – fundamentally – to much more modest donor ambitions and engagements in local economies.

The urgency of climate change: since a sharp rise in the use of fossil fuels is incompatible with the objective of limiting climate change, a path of development based on new climate-smart technology is necessary. However, many poor and middle-income countries find it simpler, quicker and often cheaper to use oil- and coal-based power supplies rather than more efficient renewable energy sources such as hydropower or solar and wind power. Greenhouse gas emissions resulting from deforestation and forest degradation in developing countries reportedly account for about 20 per cent of the global total (Solheim, 2010). Therefore, conservation of natural forests is an efficient way of slowing CO_2 emissions, but the costs of preserving forests cannot be carried by the poor countries alone. Large-scale international finance will be needed to compensate for income lost through reducing deforestation. Mitigation and adaptation measures must be incorporated into development policy (Solheim, 2010). In Chapter Eleven (this volume), Besada et al have outlined some novel ways to deal with the challenges of a warming world.

Peace and security as a goal: war and armed conflict continue to be serious challenges for development policy in a number of countries, including the DRC, Central Africa, Somalia, Sudan and South Sudan. In a vicious circle, armed conflict impedes development, and poverty and inequality generate resource conflict, with poor countries running a higher risk of being affected by armed conflict. Meeting specified development goals is particularly hard in conflict areas, for example, in the fields of health and education, where even if funds are available, social infrastructure risks being destroyed. The majority of the 75 million non-school-going children globally live in fragile states (Solheim, 2010). In this regard, peacebuilding must be the top priority. Unlike past wars, more than nine out of ten are now civil conflicts (Solheim, 2010). Human security is a precondition for political, social and economic development, which is in turn a precondition for peace and stability (Solheim, 2010; Hanson et al, 2012). Indeed, peace and security should be seen as part of a wider pro-poor growth strategy – especially in combating the problem of state fragility. Prioritising the fight against the rise of fundamentalist groups such as Boko Haram must be part and parcel of that strategy. Karolina Werner, in Chapter Twelve, notes the importance of security as part of a future African development architecture.

Innovative approaches to development finance: Africa needs to devise alternative types of finance as a core development policy tool that can influence national and local development processes (Kararach, 2014b). The 2008/09 financial crisis resulted in dramatic changes in the economic outlook of both poor and rich countries, thus demonstrating how closely intertwined national and global economic structures have become. Illicit capital flight from developing countries amounts to more than US$750 billion a year, and has a strong negative impact on their growth, with Africa experiencing the greatest proportion of illicit capital flows (Ndukimana and Boyce, 2012). These illicit flows are often linked to criminal activities such as trafficking in drugs, weapons and human beings. Large sums of money also disappear through various types of fraud, corruption, bribery, smuggling and money laundering. Yet the largest share of illicit financial flows is related to commercial transactions, often within multinational companies, for the purpose of tax evasion. Most African countries lack the resources, expertise and capacity to develop an efficient tax collection system. Without proper enforcement, corrupt politicians can more easily exploit the opportunities for economic crime and rent-seeking. This may lead to a desire to weaken such institutions even further. The financial crisis has provided a unique impetus for the fight against tax havens. There is an urgent need to strengthen international rules to prevent assets that are illegally appropriated from developing countries from being concealed or laundered in tax havens. The resurgence of the debate on introducing a Tobin Tax, in the wake of the financial crisis, is thus welcome.

Fostering a knowledge economy: African private sector participants need to improve their ability to solve problems, adapt, evolve to meet changing business environments, and survive disruptive changes such as high staff turnover in the context of a competitive global economy (Kararach, 2014a). Effective knowledge management ensures that organisations, made up of the people that work there, at the same time as the processes, procedures and information systems that drive the activities, are focused on the delivery of the corporate objectives. There is a need for expertise and knowledge on demand in a wide range of private sector operations on the continent, including issues linked to resource mobilisation and the sourcing of financing. In this regard, literacy constraints need to be addressed through appropriate skills development arrangements (Beck, 2013). Knowledge management permits the sharing of lessons learned and the resolution of problems, and incorporates indigenous African knowledge (Hanson and Kararach, 2011).

Building effective R&D platforms: the success of Agenda 2063 rests partially on the extent of the various countries' economic diversity. This diversity may cut across several axes, including systems of innovation, intellectual property rights, governance frameworks and political economy dynamics. The postcolonial legacy has locked most African economies into the natural resource trap. Only South Africa has a national innovation system with a structurally different base from the rest of the continent. South Africa is still a peripheral trader in relation to the world, however, with a competitive advantage in the primary sector, but importing commodities that require a high level of skill and knowledge to produce.

Regional approaches and integration: small, isolated national economies have to cede some independence to strategic alliances that harness knowledge- and-resource-based competitive advantages (Hanson and Kararach, 2011) through integration, as a major tool to protect Africa from shocks (see also Chapter Nine, this volume). Starting with the Abuja Treaty, through to Agenda 2063, Africa hopes to attain economic and monetary union by 2028. Yet effective regional integration and regionalism remain an elusive aspect of Africa's development strategy. The benefits of regional integration and regionalism are obvious, and include (i) greater synergy and symbiosis; (ii) better bargaining in the international arena; (iii) viable size for FDI; and (iv) improved scope for diversification and the resultant benefits of lowering risk in a number of 'shock' areas such as the macroeconomy, food insecurity, climate change and energy. Practical actions must focus on eradicating wasteful or costly duplication and rationalising some overlapping sub-regional blocs as well as pooling resources to finance regional public goods. Commitment by member states beyond political rhetoric, and meticulous and punctual implementation of treaties and protocols, without inefficiencies, lapses or reversals, is paramount. Efforts such as those of the West African Commission on Drugs to combat trafficking and organised crime at a regional level must be replicated and stepped up.

Ensuring equity and inclusion: a defining trend over the last decade has been the increase in inequality within both rich and poor nations across all regions of the world. Only Brazil and a handful of other countries have attempted to buck this trend. For example, the vision of the MDGs was to reduce absolute poverty, but it did not address itself adequately to inequality, except in the case of gender. Of the 60 MDG indicators, only three reflected issues of inequality. Many of the targets that were agreed in the UN development conferences of the 1990s that addressed inequality, marginalisation and the most vulnerable, were omitted from the MDGs (Fukuda-Parr, 2011). Reducing inequality must be a goal in and of itself in future post-2015 development agendas for Africa to reduce alienation and enhance state legitimacy. As Frannie Léautier noted in Chapter Four, one sure way to strengthen inclusion and to defeat inequality is the removal of gender biases in development policies.

Enhancing governance: social scientists are well aware that the reasons for persistent poverty go beyond lack of economic investments, and that poor people remain poor because they are powerless. The multiple dimensions of poverty – poor health and lack of education, resources and access to public infrastructure – all reinforce one another. Poverty reduction strategies therefore require not only new economic and social policies, but also political empowerment of the citizens (Kararach, 2011). Africa needs better governance and nurturing of developmental states that prioritise service delivery. This question has been discussed by George Kararach in Chapters Two and Five (this volume).

Diplomacy and a stronger African voice in the global arena: while African countries have become increasingly assertive in global engagements such as the World Trade Organization (WTO) and the International Financial Institutions (IFIs), there have been no systemic reforms of global economic governance institutions, with the exception of the emergence of the G20, with its concerns about issues of the centrality of supply chains for primary products, governance, regulation, efficiency and human security. The 2008 financial crisis was a harsh reminder of the urgency of building a stable global economy that serves the needs of development rather than speculative capital movements (Fukuda-Parr, 2011). A number of critical and urgent recommendations were made in 2009 by the Commission on the Measurement of Economic and Social Progress (Stiglitz et al, 2009), and Africa needs to work with other partners to ensure these recommendations are implemented as part of the post-2015 agenda. The emergence of a new multilateralism, with Africa as a key player, will be essential to its economic transformation after the MDGs – as noted by James Wakiaga in Chapter One.

Rethinking international aid architecture: most African countries with widespread poverty are aid-dependent; many rely on external aid to finance their entire capital investment budgets (Fukuda-Parr, 2011). This unavoidably weakens states as well as their democratic accountability to their people (Rugumamu, 1997; Fukuda-Parr, 2011). Despite the Paris and Accra agendas for aid effectiveness, aid continues to be a donor-driven process with poor accountability (Fukuda-Parr, 2011). A new aid architecture that enhances democratic accountability is needed.

Prioritising DRM: development aid is unlikely to meet the resource requirements necessary to end poverty in Africa. Several proposals have been made for new sources of development finance – such as taxes on international transactions (Fukuda-Parr, 2011) – as well as factoring and equity, combating shadow banking and illicit flows. There is need to engage the private sector more in these efforts (Kararach, 2014b). Whatever the merits of these recommendations for exploring new funding sources, they can only complement heightened efforts at DRM, as correctly noted by Bhusan and colleagues earlier in the volume, in Chapter Seven.

Adoption of modern approaches and technology: almost all of the most enduring problems of poverty require technological solutions – from higher-performing varieties of crops and new methods of climate-smart agriculture to medicines for endemic diseases. The patent/ intellectual property rights-based model of financing R&D in new technologies is not appropriate for meeting those needs that require innovation as a public good (IDB, 2014), as the introduction of HIV retrovirals demonstrated. Alternative approaches have been proposed, such as prize funds and crowd sourcing, as well as advanced market creation (Kararach, 2014b).

Instituting social protection: the MDGs emphasised social investments and social protection. These are important for education, health, water and sanitation. However, employment and incomes depend less on direct government investments than on inclusive/pro-poor growth (Fukuda-Parr, 2011). In future, more attention should be given to macroeconomic and labour market policies (Fukuda-Parr, 2011); the recent experiences of some Latin American countries are particularly instructive in this regard (IDB, 2014).

Incentives and better usage of skills: the history of economic thought is replete with attempts to understand the dynamics of behaviour in economic systems, that is, the motivations or incentives that drive certain actions on the part of individuals, households or even firms (Laffont and Tirole, 1993). Economic models of compensation treat 'pay' practices as a solution to the incentive problem. High levels of performance require high levels of effort and, beyond some minimal point, providing this effort is costly for firms. Those that are desirous of high levels of performance from their employees therefore link economic rewards closely to an individual's productive contribution. Yet this linkage is not a universal characteristic of pay systems. Firms exhibit enormous variation in the degree to which compensation responds to individual performance (Laffont and Tirole, 1993).

Traditional microeconomic explanations of individual and household poverty concentrate on understanding that an individual's labour (health and energy), human capital (education and skills), and physical and social assets (such as land or access to a social network) determine their ability to earn income both today and in the future. Human capital and assets are critical for two reasons: (i) some assets (such as early childhood nutrition) can only be acquired early in life, and (ii) at low levels of asset wealth, a positive correlation is often observed between wealth and returns to wealth (Dercon, 1996). Path dependencies, and perhaps 'poverty traps', can thus result when levels of human capital and assets are particularly low, as they are for the poorest (Dercon, 1996). Kamgnia and Murinde discussed earlier in this volume (Chapter Six) at length the potential contribution of the extractive sector to use the pool of young people and to fight unemployment in this regard.

Strategic leadership: Africa needs to build the capacity for visionary and strategic leadership (Kararach, 2014a). Without good leadership, all the other excellent initiatives in Africa will remain dormant. Such a leadership would be critical in responding to the political constraints that may obstruct the delivery of economic policies (Tribe et al, 2010).

Risk management and business planning: many businesses in Africa, especially small and medium-sized enterprises (SMEs), fail due to their lack of planning towards an over-arching goal (Gatt, 2012). Without a plan, day-to-day activities can only be haphazard and reactive. Indeed, poor planning may be one of the reasons Africa's private entrepreneurs find finance difficult to source. A business plan is necessary not only to secure funding at the start-up phase, but is also a vital tool for overall business management. A plan allows for considered decisions to chart specific courses of action needed to improve the business. A plan can detail alternative future strategic scenarios and set specific objectives and goals, along with the resources required to achieve these goals. To be able to raise the needed finance, it is necessary to highlight in a plan what opportunities exist for potential investors, including growth prospects. For example, investors may want to see clear evidence of future cash flows to meet debt obligations, while enabling the business to operate effectively (Kararach, 2014b). Besides communicating the intended course of action and using this as a platform for routine management, a business plan provides the firm with appropriate exit strategies. These include initial public offering of stock, acquisition by competitors, mergers, family succession and management buy-outs. Africa's private sector needs to develop the skills to ensure investment decisions are driven by a well-thought-out business plan.

Tackling demographic challenges: given the demographic reality and ever-growing youth population, African countries will have to recognise that finding proper jobs for new jobseekers, especially in cities, will be a challenge, and that it is likely that the informal sector will continue to play a key role for a long time to come (Fox and Gaal, 2008; Kararach, 2014a).

There are increased opportunities in the small scale and export industries for the diaspora to become engaged if the scale of production can be increased using new technology. Second, young people from the diasporas are coming back to their home countries to start businesses in the service sector. This sector provides a key opportunity for jobs, including self-employed, family-owned and small-scale enterprises. Examples of new types of activities led by young people include:

crèches, specialist cosmetic companies for African needs, apparel and clothing companies using local materials and talent, consulting firms, and online shopping companies. Policies specifically targeted at the diaspora could attract them to return to the continent and create jobs that employ young people (Kararach et al, 2011).

Africa has lost significant capacity and skills because of the brain drain (Bond, 2006). The rapid emigration of Africa's skilled professionals to other parts of the world was spurred on by a combination of economic, social and political factors (Adepoju, 1991). Between 1960 and 1987, Africa lost 30 per cent of its highly skilled nationals, mostly to Europe. Between 1986 and 1990, about 50,000 to 60,000 middle- and high-level African managers emigrated due to weakening domestic socioeconomic and political conditions (Adepoju, 2006). It is estimated that about 23,000 African university graduates and 50,000 executives leave the region annually, and about 40,000 PhD holders live outside Africa (Adepoju, 2005). Concrete action needs to be taken to reverse this depletion in human capital by enshrining effective migration and diaspora policies (Kararach, 2014a).

Service delivery: African governments need to enhance their focus and ability to deliver services (Kararach, 2013; and also Chapters Two and Five in this volume). Both the private and public sectors need to develop capacity that is linked to policy engagement and dialogue, including information sharing (Beck et al, 2014). The legislative and policy frameworks in many African countries seem to work against the ease of doing business. In many instances, the private sector is perceived to represent the entrenched and personal interests of business owners. Part of the problem is a lack of community consultation and engagement. For example, there are reports that local frustration with the private sector results from the failure of undertakings such as public–private partnerships to deliver on promises, or the lack of spillover of investment benefits from private sector operations into adjacent community economies (Boylan, 2012). Better service delivery is critical for strengthening social inclusion and statebuilding, both of which are strong antidotes for fighting the rise of extremist and terrorist groups.

Implementation: Africa needs to develop and ingrain in its planning processes the culture of tracking change (see Sumner and Tribe, 2008), and develop the flexibility to deal with it (Kararach, 2014a). The work of scholars including Acemoglu and Rodrik show how strong the links are between cultural and institutional change and socioeconomic development. Institutional adaptation in particular has been shown to be strongly correlated with growth (Acemoglu et al, 2001). Strong institutions are critical for programme implementation, and most development commitments have not been supported by adequate implementation follow-through (Livingstone and Tribe, 1995; Kararach, 2013). There is a tendency among political leaders to derive political mileage at various stages of the project cycle without much focus on results: (i) when a 'project' is first thought of; (ii) again when the preliminary feasibility study is announced; (iii) then again, when the preliminary study is published; and (iv) during project launch, and so on. The public choice literature points out that one of the problems with politicians is that their time horizon tends to be short, due to recurrent elections, and because the amount of time that they spend in any one job is brief (Tanzi and Davoodi, 1998; Persson, 2001). Again, politics and ideology occasionally become confused, so that the politician's 'estimated' decision function is far detached from that of the median voter.

Strengthening the M&E system: in order to enhance programme delivery and optimise resource usage, countries need to develop a culture of M&E development interventions. This means that Africa must invest in data capacity by strengthening the various national/regional statistical systems (Kararach, 2012). Results of evaluations should be used creatively to enhance not just accountability and programme management, but also plough-backs to complete learning loops. In that regard, knowledge and its management must be put at the core of development policy and management.

Conclusions

Africa came a long way towards achieving the MDGs, yet not as far as its leaders had hoped. The link between global development goals and factors that may seem remote from them is becoming increasingly apparent. As an example, the Intergovernmental Panel on Climate Change showed how important climate change is for development, and how interlinked the fights against poverty and climate change are. Equally, the terror attack of September 11, 2001, in the US, increased the focus on global peace and stability. Conflicts in faraway places such as Afghanistan, Syria and Iraq show clearly that there can be no peace without development, and no development without peace. The rise of China as a major source of foreign investment in Africa has altered the picture of financial flows. Aid is no longer the only important source of development finance. And with increased globalisation, much is gained through enhanced trade and transfer of technology, but harmful economic forces also thrive, leading to unbelievably high illicit capital flows from poor African countries as well as 'deindustrialisation'.

Global compacts such as the MDGs will always be important indicators of and frameworks for development. But these can no longer be achieved by aid alone, and other sources of finance such as remittances and private–public partnerships must play their part. In the interim, aid should be combined with global efforts to effectively deal with other critical factors affecting development – climate, conflict and capital. Alternative sources of external finance will only strengthen and become disciplined when they are being reinforced by circumstances and demands from society to collect domestic revenue in a more efficient and effective manner. As Hyden (2010) correctly noted, those best placed to exercise such pressure are the emerging middle class, especially members of the business community who have a vested interest in a predictable and legal-rational environment. With the growing professionalisation of this middle class, the scope for a more influential civil society will also increase and exert additional pressure. The state in Africa has an important role to play in the continent's development, but it will not do so as long as it is weak and artificially propped up by donor funds. Africa needs a developmental state and outcomes that define its development aspirations, as embodied in Agenda 2063, by ensuring effective implementation.

References

Acemoglu, D. and Robinson, J. (2012) *Why nations fail: The origins of power, prosperity, and poverty*, New York: Random House.

Acemoglu, D., Johnson, S. and Robinson, J. (2001) 'The colonial origins of comparative development: an empirical investigation', *American Economic Review*, vol 91, no 5, pp 1369-401.

ACET (African Center for Economic Transformation) (2014) *African transformation report: Growth with depth*, Accra: ACET.

Adepoju, A. (1991) 'South–North migration: the African experience', *International Migration*, vol 29, no 2, pp 205-22.

Adepoju, A. (2005) 'Review of research, data on human trafficking in Sub-Saharan Africa', *International Migration*, vol 43, nos 1/2, pp 75-98.

Adepoju, A. (2006) 'Leading issues in international migration in Sub-Saharan Africa', in C. Cross, D. Gelderblom, N. Roux and J. Mafukidze (eds) *Views on migration in Sub-Saharan Africa: Proceedings of an African Migration Alliance Workshop*, Cape Town: HSRC Press, pp 25-47.

AfDB (African Development Bank) (2013a) *African economic outlook*, Tunis: AfDB.

AfDB (2013b) *An integrated approach to infrastructure provision in Africa*, Statistics Department, Africa Infrastructure Knowledge Program, April, Tunis: AfDB.

AfDB (2013c) 'Recognizing Africa's informal sector', Blog, 27 March, Tunis (www.afdb.org/en/blogs/afdb-championing-inclusive-growth-across-africa/post/recognizing-africas-informal-sector-11645/).

AfDB (2014) *Ending conflict and building peace in Africa: A call to action*, Tunis: AfDB (www.afdb.org/en/documents/document/ending-conflict-and-building-peace-in-africa-a-call-to-action-45113/).

Alia, D.Y. and Kouadio-Anago, R.E. (2014) *Foreign aid effectiveness in African economies – Evidence from a panel threshold framework*, UNU-WIDER Working Paper 2014/015, Finland: United Nations University-World Institute for Development Economics Research.

Amaoko, K.Y. (2010) 'Beyond MDGs – a transformational agenda for Africa', NAI Forum Blog, 10 September (http://naiforum.org/2010/09/beyond-mdgs-%e2%80%95-a-transformational-agenda-for-africa/).

AU (African Union) (2013) *African Union Agenda 2063: A shared strategic framework for inclusive growth and sustainable development*, Background Note, August.

Beck, T. (2013) *Finance, growth and fragility: The role of government*, CEPR Discussion Paper 9597, London: Centre for Economic Policy Research.

Beck, T., Lin, C. and Ma, Y. (2014) 'Why do firms evade taxes? The role of information sharing and financial sector outreach', *Journal of Finance*, vol 69, no 2, pp 763-817.

Bond, P. (2006) *Looting Africa: The economics of exploitation*, Durban: University of KwaZulu-Natal Press.

Boylan, H. (2012) *Public–private partnerships in Africa, Part I – Infrastructure*, CAI Industry and Business Discussion Paper, 16 February, Johannesburg: Consultancy Africa Intelligence.

Bräutigam, D. (2011) 'Aid "with Chinese characteristics": Chinese foreign aid and development finance meet the OECD-DAC aid regime', *Journal of International Development*, vol 23, no 5.

Dercon, S. (1996) 'Risks, crop choice and savings: evidence from Tanzania', *Economic Development and Cultural Change*, vol 44, no 3, pp 485-513.

Easterly, W. (2006) *The white man's burden: Why the West's efforts to aid the rest have done so much ill and so little good*, New York: The Penguin Press.

Farlam, P. (2005) *Working together: Assessing public–private partnerships in Africa*, SAIIA NEPAD Policy Focus Series Report 2, Johannesburg: The South African Institute of International Affairs (http://saiia.org.za/images/upload/PPP-NepadReport-Final9Feb05.pdf).

Fox, L. and Gaal, M.S. (2008) *Working out of poverty*. Washington, DC: The World Bank.

Fukuda-Parr, S. (2011) 'MDGs and the narrative of development – what about pro-poor growth and structural change?', NAI Forum Blog, 11 August (http://naiforum.org/2011/08/mdgs-and-the-narrative-of-development/).

Gatt, L. (2012) *SMEs in Africa: Growth despite constraints*, CAI Industry and Business Discussion Paper, 17 September, Johannesburg: Consultancy Africa Intelligence.

Hanson, K. and Kararach, G. (2011) *The challenges of knowledge harvesting and the promotion of sustainable development for the achievement of the MDGs in Africa*, ACBF Occasional Paper no 12, Harare: African Capacity Building Foundation.

Hanson, K., Kararach, G. and Shaw, T. (eds) (2012) *Rethinking development challenges for public policy: Insights from contemporary Africa*, Basingstoke: Palgrave Macmillan.

Howard, E., Newman, C., Rand, J. and Tarp, F. (2014) *Productivity-enhancing manufacturing clusters: Evidence from Vietnam*, Working Paper Series, UNU-WIDER Research Paper, Finland: United Nations University-World Institute for Development Economic Research.

Hyden, G. (2010) 'Rethinking African development', NIA Forum Blog, 25 August (http://naiforum.org/2010/08/rethinking-development-in-africa-2/).

IDB (Inter-American Development Bank) (2014) *Rethinking productive development – Sound policies and institutions for economic transformation*, Basingstoke: Palgrave Macmillan.

Kamgnia, B. (2013) *Uses and abuses of per-diems in Africa: Political economy of travel allowances*, AfDB Working Paper, Tunis: African Development Bank.

Kararach, G. (2004) 'When do communities know best? United Nations Children's Fund (UNICEF)'s search for relevant social indicators in Zimbabwe', *Development in Practice*, vol 14, no 4, p 10.

Kararach, G. (2011) *Macroeconomic policies and the political limits of reform programs in developing countries*, Nairobi: African Research and Resource Forum.

Kararach, G. (2012) 'Effective states and capacity development for financial governance in Africa: case and agenda for operationalisation', *Capacity Focus*, vol 1.

Kararach, G. (2013) 'Service oriented government: debating the developmental state and service delivery in Africa: are capacity indicators important?', in A. Rosenbaum and W. Liqun (eds) *Studies in administrative reform: Building service-oriented government and performance evaluation systems*, Beijing: Chinese Academy of Governance Press, pp 25-60.

Kararach, G. (2014a) *Development policy in Africa: Mastering the future?*, Basingstoke: Palgrave Macmillan.

Kararach, G. (2014b) 'Capacity, innovative financing and private sector development in Africa's transformation', *Capacity Focus*, vol 4, no 1.

Kararach, G. (2014c) 'Leadership, cluster formations and effects of space on economic development in Africa', PowerPoint presentation at Royal Geographical Society Conference, 28 August.

Kararach, G., Hanson, K. and Léautier, F. (2011) 'Regional integration policies to support job creation for Africa's burgeoning youth population', *World Journal of Entrepreneurship, Management and Sustainable Development*, vol 7, nos 2-4, pp 177-215.

Kararach, G. and Odhiambo, M. (2016a: forthcoming) 'Natural resources, global economic volatility and Africa's growth prospects', in H. Besada et al (eds) *Natural resource governance in Africa*.

Kararach, G. and Odhiambo, M. (2016b: forthcoming) 'Natural resources, volatility and African development policy: some agenda for action', in H. Besada et al (eds) *Natural resource governance in Africa*.

Kiggundu, M. (2014) 'The African Union Agenda 2063: Implications for capacity development and the role of the African Capacity Building Foundation', Paper prepared for the AfDB/IFPRI Conference on Transforming Capacity for African Development, Dakar, Senegal.

Laffont, J.J. and Tirole, J. (1993) *A theory of incentives in procurement and regulation*, Cambridge, MA: MIT Press.

Léautier, F. (2014) *Capacity development for the transformation of Africa*, UNU-WIDER Working Paper 2014/058, Finland: United Nations University-World Institute for Development Economic Research.

Livingstone, I. and Tribe, M. (1995) 'Projects with long time horizons: their economic appraisal and the discount rate', *Project Appraisal*, vol 10, no 2 (www.tandfonline.com/doi/pdf/10.1080/02688867.1995.9726978).

Moyo, D. (2009) *Dead aid: Why aid is not working and how there is a better way for Africa*, New York: Farrar, Straus & Giroux.

Ncube, M. and Shimeles, A. (2012) *The making of the middle class in Africa*, Tunis: African Development Bank (www.afdb.org/fileadmin/uploads/afdb/Documents/Knowledge/AEC%202012%20-%20%20

The%20Making%20of%20the%20Middle%20Class%20in%20Africa. pdf).

Ndukimana, L. and Boyce, J. (2012) *Capital flight from North African countries*, PERI Research Report, Amherst, MA: Political Economy Research Institute.

Persson, T. (2001) *Do political institutions shape economic policy?*, National Bureau for Economic Research (NBER) Working Paper, W8214, Cambridge, MA: National Bureau of Economic Research.

Rotberg, R.I. (2013) *Africa emerges: Consummate challenges, abundant opportunities*, Cambridge: Polity Press.

Rugumamu, S. (1997): *Lethal aid: The Illusion of socialism and self-reliance in Tanzania*. Trenton NJ: Africa World Press.

Shaw, T.M. (2014) 'Conclusion – the BRICs and beyond: new global order, reorder or disorder? Insights from global governance', in L. Xing (ed) *The BRICS and beyond: The international political economy of the emergence of a new world order*, Farnham: Ashgate Publishing, pp 201-18.

Solheim, E. (2010) Climate, conflict and capital – Critical issues for the MDGs and beyond 2015', The Nordic Africa Development Policy Forum, 15 April (http://naiforum.org/2010/04/climate-conflict-and-capital/).

Stiglitz, J.E., Sen, A. and Fitoussi, J.P. (2009) *Report by the Commission on the Measurement of Economic Performance and Social Progress*, New York: United Nations (www.stiglitz-sen-fitoussi.fr/documents/rapport_anglais.pdf).

Sumner, A. and Tribe, M. (2008) *International development studies: Theory and methods for research and practice*, London: Sage Publications.

Tanzi, V. and Davoodi, H. (1998) *Roads to nowhere: How corruption in public investment hurts growth*, Washington, DC: International Monetary Fund.

Tribe, M. (2013) 'Aid and development: Issues and reflections', *Strathclyde Discussion Papers in Economics*, vol 13, no 9.

Tribe, M., Nixson, F. and Sumner, A. (2010) *Economics and development studies*, Oxford: Routledge.

Notes

Introduction

[1] Estimated at 33 per cent and rising, as of 2010 (AfDB, 2011).

[2] Russia, in particular, is reassessing its links with the continent following the end of the Cold War. This is characterised by Putin's aggressive foreign policy agenda following the conflict in Crimea and the Ukraine.

[3] About 4,000 reportedly died in Guinea, Sierra Leone and Liberia from Ebola in 2014, prompting the UN to declare an epidemic. See Cooper et al (2013).

[4] 'Lifestyle' diseases are also reportedly on the rise – for example, the rising incidences of cancer in Africa, due to improved living conditions and disposable income coupled with a poor diet (Besada and Ermakov, 2008).

[5] NEPAD (2009) provides an even longer wish list.

Chapter One

[1] The Rio+20 outcome document, *The future we want*, is a result of the summit of the heads of state and government and high-level representatives, meeting at Rio de Janeiro, Brazil, from 20-22 June 2012, that involved the participation of civil society with a view to renew commitment to sustainable development, and to ensure the promotion of an economically, socially and environmentally sustainable future for the planet Earth. The onus is to accelerate the achievement of the internationally agreed development goals, including the MDGs, by 2015. See Rio+20 (2012).

[2] This is the multilateral agreement resulting from the Fourth High Level Forum on Aid Effectiveness (HLF4), 29 November to 1 December 2011, in Busan, Republic of Korea. It was prepared in consultation with civil society organisations as well as partners' governments, traditional donors, South-South cooperators, BRIC countries (Brazil, Russia, India and China) and private donors. See Busan Partnership for Effective Development Cooperation (2011).

[3] M-PESA is a mobile phone money transfer system that was introduced by a Kenyan mobile network company (Safaricom) and allows people to open accounts and transfer cash, among other transactions, using their mobile phones. Today it has more than 9 million registered users in Kenya, and transfers approximately US$320 million every month. See Mas and Radcliffe (2010).

[4] In July 2012, Secretary-General Ban Ki-moon announced the 27 members of a High Level Panel to advise on the global development framework beyond 2015, the target date for the MDGs. It had three co-chairs: President Susilo Bambang Yudhoyono of Indonesia, President Ellen Johnson Sirleaf of Liberia and Prime Minister David Cameron of the UK. The Panel's report was submitted to the Secretary-General in May 2013 to form part of the ongoing discussion on the world's next development agenda, to succeed the MDGs.

[5] This is an outcome of the High Level Panel UN Conference on SSC held in Nairobi, Kenya, from 1 to 3 December 2009, and declaring how to strengthen and further invigorate SSC.

[6] MINT refers to the emerging countries of Malaysia, Indonesia, Nigeria and Turkey.

[7] Goal 16: Promote peaceful and inclusive societies for sustainable development, provide access to justice for all, and build effective, accountable and inclusive institutions at all levels.

Chapter Two

[1] African political elites now flirt with capital irrespective of the origin, in the name of business first.

[2] We return to this discussion in the context of the African state in the latter part of this chapter.

[3] We highlight later those actions that will support building a truly developmental state in Africa.

[4] These are a number of growth accounting practices that provide a bewildering array of reasons: resource curse, geography, ethnic fractionalisation, poor policies, etc.

[5] By The World Bank classification, around 22 countries qualify as middle income in Africa. See http://blogs.worldbank.org/africacan/africas-mics

[6] A plan developed by the Organization of African Unity (OAU) to increase Africa's self-sufficiency. It was drafted in Lagos, Nigeria, in April 1980, during a conference that included a variety of African leaders as an alternative to the SAPs then being implemented across the continent.

[7] Infrastructure has been a major break on regional economic integration by undermining logistics and the movement of productive factors.

[8] The Logistics Performance Index overall score reflects the perceptions of a country's logistics based on the efficiency of its customs clearance process, quality

of trade- and transport-related infrastructure, ease of arranging competitively priced shipments, quality of its logistics service, ability to track and trace consignments, and frequency with which shipments reach the consignee within the scheduled time. The index ranges from 1 to 5, with a higher score representing better performance. In 2011/12, the figures were: West Africa (2.19), Central Africa (2.27), East Africa (2.49), Southern Africa (2.73), Latin America (3.01), Eastern Europe (3.14), US (3.91) and Western Europe (3.99).

[9] Access to basic health services was affirmed as a fundamental human right in the Declaration of Alma-Ata, USSR, in 1978.

[10] A quick look at Demographic and Health Survey (DHS) data confirms this in most countries.

[11] Few countries have reached the Abuja Declaration target. These are: Rwanda, Liberia, Malawi, Zambia, Togo, Madagascar, Swaziland, Ethiopia and Lesotho.

[12] This is an internationally agreed standard set of recommendations on how to compile measures of economic activity in a coherent, consistent and integrated set of macroeconomic accounts in the context of a set of internationally agreed concepts, definitions, classifications and accounting rules adopted by the UN in 1993.

[13] This is a worldwide statistical partnership to collect comparative price data and compile detailed expenditure values of countries' GDP, and to estimate the purchasing power parities (PPPs) of the world's economies. The AfDB supported many of its regional member countries in joining the partnership.

Chapter Three

[1] The BRICS is comprised of Brazil, Russia, India, China and South Africa. It connects the economic relations between these countries, including the establishment of the BRICS Bank (Shaw, 2015a).

[2] PIIGS was coined in the 1990s to connote the weakened economies of Portugal, Italy, Greece and Spain. Ireland was later added. It is viewed as a controversial and offensive term.

[3] Visit www.naturalresourcecharter.org for further information.

[4] The Dodd-Frank Wall Street Reform and Consumer Protection Act was created in 2010. It mandates all manufacturers to perform supply chain and production audits to ensure there is no use of conflict minerals. Section 1502 makes it mandatory for companies to disclose the use of conflict minerals per annum.

[5] The Lagos Plan of Action was a 1980 African-wide initiative to expand and increase African self-sufficiency through a series of socioeconomic measures that focused on inward-thinking economic solutions. This was particularly noteworthy because it was perceived to contrast the Structural Adjustment Programming of the decade.

[6] The R30 is a set of countries titled as such for their role as key producers, consumers, exporters and importers, of 30 most important resources, as defined by Chatham House.

[7] The 1996 Ottawa Treaty established the Anti-Personnel Mine Ban Convention; the 2003 Kimberley Process created a process through which the location of diamonds would be identified, thus ensuring that conflict diamonds were not used in processing, production, and purchasing. Manufacturers, processors and consumers could now be aware of the origin of their diamond.

[8] Based in the UK, the ISEAL Alliance defines and upholds sustainability standards that are committed to improving environmental sustainability globally. Companies become members by upholding codes defined by the alliance.

[9] REDD is a UN programme founded in 2008 that works to reduce emissions, deforestation, and degradation, particularly through providing assistance and expertise to country's working towards implementing a REDD+ mechanism. These mechanisms ensure that countries meet particular criteria for reducing their emissions, degradation, and deforestation.

[10] Ratified by 61 states and enacted in 2014, the Arms Trade Treaty limits the number of conventional arms internationally traded.

[11] The IGF is a global partnership initiative started in 2005. Governments interested in mining, minerals, and metals have attended the summits to create programmes of action to improve the sustainability of these sectors. Rules and procedures have been created to better ensure sustainability by all member governments.

[12] Greenpeace already publishes a guide to greener electronics (Greenpeace, 2012).

[13] The Maputo Corridor is the trade route that connects the Provinces of Limpopo, Guateng, and Mpumalanga with Maputo, Mozambique. The corridor receives significant attention as there are several mining communities and ports along its geographical barrier.

[14] The T-FTA, created in 2008, an economic agreement between the already-established SADC, EAC, and COMESA. This FTA is a larger market between these three already-existed markets in the southeastern African region.

[15] The ATT came out of IANSA. Both are a conglomeration of civil society actors seeking to stop the manufacturing, distribution, and use of small arms and weapons. Their main aims are to provide awareness of these issues and to represent civil society actors as a larger, collective voice at the global level.

[16] The 'Leading Group' is comprised of 63 actors, including state and non-state actors, including foundations and non-governmental organisations.

[17] The Monterrey Consensus, adopted in 2002 following the Monterrey Conference, captured six key areas of financing for international development, including the mobilisation of resources, international trade and systemic issues.

[18] See www.trademarksa.org and www.trademarkea.org

[19] For more information, please see www.undp.org/content/undp/en/home/ourwork/ourstories/fighting-sexual-violence-in-the-democratic-republic-of-congo.html

[20] This can be seen in West Africa as well, including Sierra Leone, Ghana and Liberia.

Chapter Four

[1] This is usually used to mean the organising, improving and evaluating policy processes so that the perspectives of gender equality are integrated into policies formulated and programmes implemented by a particular organisation.

[2] This is an expert body established by the United Nations (UN) in 1982, composed of experts on women's issues from around the world. It has a mandate to track progress made on women's issues in countries that have signed the Convention on the Elimination of All Forms of Discrimination against Women. It does so by reviewing national reports and offering perspectives and recommendations. For more details see www.un.org/womenwatch/daw/cedaw/committee.htm

Chapter Five

[1] The World Bank has embarked on a project to develop service delivery indicators.

[2] Corrigan (2015) argues that as a voluntary process, the APRM is almost wholly reliant on the perceived credibility and desirability of its processes and reports to remain relevant and attract new member states. Thus, making it a mandatory process will undermine its credibility and be a major mistake.

[3] Subramanian and Roy (2003) argue that this is the sort of Rodrikian industrial policy used in Mauritius to achieve its exemplary development in Africa.

[4] The index is the harmonic mean of the four cluster indices. The rationale for choosing the harmonic mean formula is that none of the capacity development factors as given by the four clusters should be neglected. Weakness in one of the four components should be easily captured by the harmonic mean formula, which is sensitive to small values.

Chapter Six

[1] Extractive industries are taken to comprise mining, quarrying, dredging, oil and gas. *Mining* refers to the extraction of minerals (bentonite, fine clay, kaolin, lignite, quartz crystals, zeolite, or minerals in alluvial form) and solid fossil fuel (oil shale and coal, including their hydrocarbons). In mining, extraction can take place in either an underground mine or in an above-ground mine, known as a surface mine, 'open-cast mine', 'open-pit' or just 'pit'. *Quarrying* defines the extraction of aggregates and industrial minerals above ground. The extraction of marine aggregate underwater is known as dredging, while that of liquid fossil fuel is oil extraction, and that of gas deals with the extraction of gaseous fossil fuel.

[2] See Population Reference Bureau (2012) and UN (2012). This figure has not significantly changed in 2015 given the drags that characterise labour markets.

[3] At the July 2006 summit in Banjul, the Gambia. The initiative basically supported the establishment of national and regional youth networks, including the Pan African Youth Union (PYU), with the aim of channelling youth engagement and promoting youth perspectives to be incorporated into national, regional and continental policies, strategies and programmes (ILO, 2012b).

[4] During the last Executive Council meeting held in Addis Ababa, Ethiopia, in July 2014.

[5] Defined earlier.

[6] 'Artisanal mining is practiced by individuals, groups, families, or cooperatives, using simple, un-mechanized tools and equipment, and usually occurring outside the legal and regulatory framework. Most African artisanal miners excavate gold because it is easy to extract, refine, and transport. In Ghana, gold accounts for two thirds of total artisan and small-scale production, however, artisanal miners also produce about 65 per cent of Ghana's diamond production' (USAID, 2008, p 31).

[7] This led to the adoption of a new mining code in September 2011 (Ministère des Mines et de la Géologie, 2011).

[8] Local content is the development of local skills, using local manpower and local manufacturing. Local content requirements in renewable energy policy serve as either a precondition to receive government support or an eligibility requirement for government procurement in renewable energy projects.

[9] The new mining code that was adopted in September 2011 gave Guinea the opportunity to break from the past by making the mining sector accountable to the Guinean people. Ensuring the successful transfer of benefits to Guinean people is, however, the responsibility of the government in applying the code and in maintaining an open environment with its citizens, creating an attractive environment for investors.

Chapter Seven

[1] Aniket Bhusan is the corresponding author – please email aniket.bhusan@carleton.ca for comments or questions. The authors thank Rachael Calleja and Rebekka Bond for research assistance.

[2] The other five leading actions include: mobilising international financial resources including foreign direct investment (FDI) and other private flows; stimulating international trade as an engine for development; increasing financial (that is, official development assistance, or ODA) and technical cooperation; adopting a sustainable external debt strategy; and addressing systemic issues such as the coherence of the international monetary and financial system.

[3] Some OECD-DAC donors, for instance, Canada (using 2003-04 as the base year), have met this commitment.

[4] This figure is the cost of covering the poverty gap ratio, or the theoretical amount of money it would take to get every person currently below the US$2/day level at least up to the US$2/day level. It is 'theoretical' because it does not mean we have the means to deliver such a result (see Kharas and Rogerson, 2012).

[5] We use the term 'ambitious' here to reflect the idea that much of the post-2015 discussions have been about not only ending poverty, but also going beyond the existing MDGs to address other issues such as inequality, governance, conflict and violence, and climate change.

[6] At the time of writing (2015), it appears that the 17 Sustainable Development Goals (SDGs) (and accompanying 169 targets) proposed by the UN Open Working Group will replace the MDGs at the end of 2015.

[7] This formulation can again be viewed from the perspective of an important shortcoming of the MDGs. Given their emphasis on 'global goals', the MDGs created an odd situation where global targets could be met, even if most countries were worse off. Take, for instance, the MDG 1 target of halving extreme poverty. The global target has been met ahead of schedule, but this is only due to enormous progress in China and India. Meanwhile, the absolute number living in extreme poverty in Sub-Saharan Africa, for instance, has gone up.

[8] We should note that this study is not entirely transparent about the methodology by which these estimates were arrived at. For an alternative study, which does so, see Atisophon et al (2011).

[9] A good example of a recent donor initiative is The World Bank's BOOST initiative. BOOST strengthens public expenditure policy outcomes and accountability by improving the quality of expenditure data, facilitating rigorous expenditure analysis and improving fiscal transparency. See http://go.worldbank.org/UX0PVF5YM0

[10] Similarly, for the most recent year where data is available (2011), WDI only contains tax data for 115 out of a possible 214 countries. By comparison, the USAID Collecting Taxes database used here provides data for 195 countries.

[11] When last accessed in July 2013, WDI carried tax/GDP and other tax data only up to 2010 and in some cases 2011.

[12] For comparison, the latest value for the tax/GDP ratio reported by the WDI for Sub-Saharan Africa is for 2005 (17.7 per cent).

[13] This data includes, and so may be skewed, by resource-related revenues, which can be large, especially in smaller economies and low and low- to middle-income countries as a share of their GDP.

[14] The first experiments with ARA structure go back to Ghana in 1985 following a major economic crisis. Similarly, the Uganda ARA was established in 1991, and the Tanzania ARA in 1996. Both, Uganda and Tanzania, as well as Ghana and Rwanda, initially increased tax mobilisation substantially, but from a low base. However, most countries, with the exception of South Africa and more recently Ghana, have found it difficult to sustain initial performance. For more, see Bhushan and Samy (2012) and ITC (2010).

[15] Research shows that when aid reaches between 15 and 45 per cent of GDP, its effectiveness tends to decline, through effects on the exchange rate, inflation, interest rates and other channels that can heighten macroeconomic volatility (Clemens and Radelet, 2003). There are several African countries that would fall within this group, including Liberia, Burundi, Mozambique,

Malawi, Rwanda, Sierra Leone and the Democratic Republic of Congo (DRC).

[16] Half of this goes to just seven recipients: Afghanistan, DRC, Ethiopia, Haiti, Pakistan, West Bank and Gaza and Iraq.

[17] For example, they fail to account for the widespread existence of tax exemptions.

[18] For instance, if the budget of a tax authority is US$2 million and it collects US$200 million, the cost ratio is 1 per cent – in other words, for every US$1 spent, US$100 is collected.

[19] Neither can this method substitute for in-depth country studies.

[20] However, our findings are entirely consistent with Le et al (2012).

[21] Results for countries such as Lesotho, Swaziland and Namibia may be influenced by the inclusion of trade taxes in our model. However, it can be argued that trade taxes also require collection effort. We do not expect results to change substantially if trade taxes are excluded, although the tax effort index value for some of these countries would be expected to fall.

[22] Le et al (2012) included additional independent variables on demographic characteristics and governance quality in some of their specifications, which we have not included in the results reported here.

Chapter Eight

[1] The list of LDCs is reviewed every three years by the UN Economic and Social Council (ECOSOC), based on recommendations of the Committee for Development Policy (CDP). The UN classifies countries as 'least developed' in terms of their low gross national income (GNI), their weak human assets, and their high degree of economic vulnerability. See www.un.org/en/development/desa/policy/cdp/ldc/ldc_list.pdf. This list also has a footnote that says General Assembly Resolution 68/L.20, adopted on 4 December 2013, decided that Equatorial Guinea would graduate three-and-a-half years after the adoption of the Resolution, and that Vanuatu would graduate four years after the adoption of the Resolution. The UN Conference on Trade and Development (UNCTAD) prepares an annual report on the LDCs, and we have used the 2011 report.

[2] Since we are analysing growth of per capita income, demographics has nothing to do with the analysis. There is no theory or empirical evidence that ties rate of growth of per capita income with rate of population growth.

[3] For an analysis of convergence, see Barro and Sala-i-Martin (1992). See also Whitfield (2012).

[4] Data on reductions in tariff rates and on quantitative restrictions is available in the World Trade Organization's (WHO) annual reports. For instance, the average tariff was reduced between 2001 and 2010 in East Asia and the Pacific, from 11.2 per cent to 7 per cent, in Latin America and the Caribbean, from 11.6 per cent to 8.7 per cent, in the Middle East and North Africa, from 18.8 per cent to 6.7 per cent, in South Africa, from 22.4 per cent to 10.2 per cent, and in Sub-Saharan Africa, from 14.1 per cent to 10.9 per cent (The World Bank, nd).

[5] Liberalisation of capital flows are discussed in the IMF's annual reports.

[6] The increase in the share of trade in GDP is also because of the increase in trade in intermediate goods. Intermediate goods are traded a number of times before they are incorporated in the final product. As a consequence, trade grows much faster than output.

[7] As we know in a two-goods model, a reduction in import duties raises both exports and imports.

[8] As the performance of East Asia and the Pacific shows, there is no particular number at which the share of exports of goods and services in GDP should remain. If exports grow rapidly, then incomes and employment in the export sectors grows, and this has a spillover effect on the rest of the economy. What is important is the change in the share and not the level of the share. The effect of exports can again perhaps be illustrated by the experience of India. India had periodic balance of payments problems with crises in 1966-67, 1979-80 and 1990-91 because of poor export performance – the share of exports of goods and services in GDP was constant at about 5 per cent. These crises disrupted the economic situation, thereby lowering the growth rate. This has changed since liberalisation began in 1991 (Agarwal et al, 2015).

[9] A number of large aid recipients are likely to graduate from IDA in the next few years. If the funds with IDA do not show a proportionate decrease, then more soft aid might be available for countries in Sub-Saharan Africa.

[10] But this hope seems to be belied, as growth rates in Latin America and the Caribbean and Sub-Saharan Africa remain low.

[11] Calculated by the authors from data available in The World Bank DataBank WDIs (nd).

[12] The growth projections for the period 2011-14 of The World Bank (2012) have Latin America and the Caribbean growing at 4 per cent a year, and Sub-Saharan Africa at 5 per cent a year.

[13] This would be a very strong form of economic determinism. It could also be the result of all of them adopting policies strongly supported by the Bretton Woods institutions, the so-called Washington Consensus (Williamson, 1989).

[14] It could also be that since per capita income is lower in the LDCs, we are seeing a slower growth in the higher income countries, as predicted by the Solow model (1956), an example of convergence (Barro and Sala-i-Martin, 1992).

[15] Political stability was calculated by ranking three political indicators obtained from The World Bank's DataBank WDIs (nd). These were: absence of violence, rule of law and government effectiveness, all measured in terms of percentiles from 0-100. The economic indicators were openness of the economy measured by share of exports in GDP, concentration of exports measured by share of IT-related exports in GDP and indebtedness measured by current account balance.

[16] The Spearman rank correlation is calculated between the rank of the growth rate and the Gini coefficient.

[17] It is not possible to compare the performance of different groups among other export groups as there are too few in each category to make meaningful comparisons.

[18] One cannot compare fragile and non-fragile states among manufacture exporters as there is only one fragile state.

[19] In general, reduction in poverty has been lower among indigenous people as compared to non-indigenous people (Moreno and Patrinos, 2010; see also Hall and Patrinos, 2006).

[20] Sub-Saharan Africa is considered to have a high level of inequality, second only to Latin America and the Caribbean in the 1990s (Go et al, 2007).

[21] For South Asia growth in 2009-10 was higher than in the period 2006-08, and has subsequently fallen. So for our calculations we used the growth rate during the period 2001-05, which was lower to calculate the lower band.

[22] Many analysts claim that Sub-Saharan Africa has been performing very well in recent years. While undoubtedly some countries have grown rapidly, this is not true for the region as a whole. The growth rate of per capita income for the region declined from 3.4 per cent during the years 2006-8 to 1.3 per cent for the years 2009-11, and still lower to 1.2 per cent for the years 2008-13 (The World Bank DataBank WDIs, nd). This 1.2 per cent contrasts with 7 per cent for East Asia and the Pacific and 5.2 per cent for South Africa. In the period 2001-05 the growth rate of per capita income in Sub-Saharan Africa was also a mere 1.8 per cent.

[23] LDCs are defined by the UN, and the list is available in UN publications. There are different definitions of failed or fragile states. We have used the definition by some analysts using DfID data. There is considerable overlap between this list of failed states and the one defined by The World Bank.

[24] If external factors did not matter at all, then we would not see any effect of the financial crisis that was in the developed countries affecting the performance of developing countries.

[25] Germany, lacking the institutions that supported British industrialisation, did not try to replicate them but used banks, and Russia used the state.

[26] Anybody familiar with English literature of, say, Jane Austen or Laurence Sterne, say Tristram Shandy is familiar with the level of corruption in England of those times.

[27] The analysis of Agarwal and Samanta (2006) suggests that improved governance follows income growth rather than preceding it.

[28] One possibility that was explored in the background papers to the UN High Level Panel on the post-2015 development agenda was whether and how South-South cooperation could fill in the gap.

Chapter Nine

[1] Born more than three decades ago as a project, the NAAM is now a multilevel federation of more than 5,000 groups. The philosophy and action of this movement is to sensitise local communities to develop themselves while protecting the environment. Promoting local identities and the quest for development strategies adapted to local context and societies, the NAAM do training and cooperation at different levels (http://naam.free.fr/ADSL/FNGN/FNGNAAM.htm).

[2] The CAMPFIRE (Communal Areas Management Programme for Indigenous Resources) has been one of the first programmes to consider wildlife as a renewable natural resource, while addressing the allocation of its ownership to indigenous people.

[3] Manitese is an Italian NGO working in local contexts in various African countries, and is especially concerned with developing rural economies and natural resources, their protection and access to these resources by local communities.

[4] This brought together leaders of multilateral development organisations to identify the practical steps needed to achieve the MDGs in Africa. Chaired by the UN Secretary General, it aims at strengthening international mechanisms

for implementation, more specifically concentrating on health, education, agriculture and food security, infrastructure and statistical data. It also wants to enhance coordination at the national level.

[5] The process includes the progressive establishment of a free trade area, a Customs Union and an African Common Market. Policy harmonisation in key areas is also an important part of the process. Ultimately, the Treaty envisages the establishment of a Pan-African Economic and Monetary Union, the creation of an African Central Bank and the establishment of a Pan-African Parliament.

[6] This is the statement of Africa's current priority programmes and projects related to the promotion of regional integration at both continental and regional levels, anchored in the guiding principles of the NEPAD, and supported by the AU. Its main objective is the development of a roadmap for the implementation of a short-term priority action plan.

[7] This complements existing financial resources, facilitating partnerships among African institutions, partners and donors, targeting specific gaps in financing, and in the end, increasing the efficiency and effectiveness of financial resources around CAADP pillars and thematic priorities.

[8] This initiative promotes alternative regional strategies, opposed to neoliberal export-led integration models. It includes the Southern African People's Solidarity Network (SAPSN), formed in 1999 and including civil society organisations, trade unions, faith-based organisations, student bodies and economic justice networks. The SAPSN mobilises regional solidarity, builds members' capacities and supports people-based cooperation and integration.

Chapter Ten

[1] A workshop conducted in June 2012 in Yaoundé brought together The World Bank and a series of intellectuals and researchers from a number of countries to review the CPIA scores as a group, but also to comment on them as individual researchers. Participants to the workshop included the African Capacity Building Foundation (ACBF) and members of civil society organisations.

[2] The 2005 Paris Declaration on Aid Effectiveness outlined a number of principles for both donors and recipients to optimise the impact of aid.

[3] See the simulation by Kanbur (2005) to this effect.

[4] Further readings: Easterly et al (2003), Guillaumont and Chauvet (2001) and Boone (1996).

Chapter Eleven

[1] Hany Besada is the corresponding author for this chapter. Tel: +1-613-854-6423; Fax: +1-613-241-7435; hbesada@uottawa.ca

Chapter Twelve

[1] For example, the report by the High Level Panel of Eminent Persons on the Post-2015 Development Agenda suggested that Goal 10 be 'Ensure good governance and effective institutions' (UN, 2013).

[2] For the purpose of this chapter, we use the broad definitions of 'peacebuilding' and 'statebuilding' adopted by the International Dialogue on Peacebuilding and Statebuilding: 'In general terms, peacebuilding is about ending or preventing violent conflict and supporting sustainable peace, while statebuilding is about establishing capable, accountable, responsive and legitimate states' (International Dialogue on Peacebuilding and Statebuilding, 2010, p 21).

[3] For more information on the MDGs, see www.un.org/millenniumgoals/

[4] Please see the discussion on total official support for development (TOSD) for more information (OECD-DAC, 2014).

[5] The 20 fragile and conflict-affected states that have met one or more of their goals, according to the 2013 World Bank report, are Afghanistan, Angola, Bosnia and Herzegovina, Comoros, Guinea, Guinea-Bissau, Iraq, Kiribati, Liberia, Libya, Marshall Islands, Federated States of Micronesia, Myanmar, Nepal, Sudan, Syria, Timor-Leste, Togo, Tuvalu, and West Bank and Gaza. The six states on track to meeting some goals in 2015 are Burundi, Chad, Eritrea, the Republic of Congo, the Republic of Yemen, and Sierra Leone (The World Bank, 2013).

[6] This deals with 'Action with respect to threats to the peace, breaches of the peace, and acts of aggression.' It is typically only invoked in extreme cases, and allows for armed intervention by UN forces.

[7] For example, the proposal by the High Level Panel of Eminent Persons on the Post-2015 Development Agenda, entitled *A new global partnership*, suggests 12 goals, of which number 11 is 'Ensure stable and peaceful societies' (UN, 2013).

[8] The Open Working Group, tasked with preparing a proposal on the SDGs, was established on 22 January 2013 by Decision 67/555 of the UN General Assembly.

[9] There has been and continues to be much debate on the exact definition of a fragile state. The Fund for Peace, which produces its annual Fragile State Index, defines fragility as: 'The loss of physical control of its territory or a

monopoly on the legitimate use of force; The erosion of legitimate authority to make collective decisions; An inability to provide reasonable public services; The inability to interact with other states as a full member of the international community.' It further bases its index rankings on 12 indicators. For details please see http://ffp.statesindex.org/

[10] According to The World Bank, Organisation for Economic Co-operation and Development (OECD) and Department for International Development (DfID), among others.

[11] The Islamic Courts Union was a self-organised grouping of Sharia courts that formed in opposition to the transitional national government in Somalia.

[12] The 10 FSPs are: (1) Take context as the starting point; (2) Ensure all activities do no harm; (3) Focus on state building as the central objective; (4) Prioritise prevention; (5) Recognise the links between political, security and development objectives; (6) Promote non-discrimination as a basis for inclusive and stable societies; (7) Align with local priorities in different ways and in different contexts; (8) Agree on practical coordination mechanisms between international actors; (9) Act fast … but stay engaged long enough to give success a chance; (10) Avoid pockets of exclusion ('aid orphans') (OECD, 2007).

[13] Goal 16: 'Promote peaceful and inclusive societies for sustainable development, provide access to justice for all and build effective, accountable and inclusive institutions at all levels.'

[14] This is a voluntary association of 20 countries that are or have been affected by conflict and are now in transition to the next stage of development. For more information, see www.g7plus.org/

[15] For more information on the New Deal, see www.newdeal4peace.org/

[16] Somalia is the ninth state to do so. Others include Afghanistan, Central African Republic, Chad, the Democratic Republic of Congo, Sierra Leone, South Sudan and Timor Leste.

[17] Identified as 'an essential pre-condition for progress', for the New Deal, TRUST means commitment to build mutual TRUST by 'providing aid and managing resources more effectively and aligning these resources for results.' TRUST stands for Transparency, Risk-sharing, Use and strengthen country systems, Strengthen capacities, Timely and predictable aid (International Dialogue on Peacebuilding and Statebuilding, 2011).

[18] For example, some indicators suggested both by the High Level Panel of Eminent Persons and the New Deal specifically list a decrease in the percentage of violent deaths.

Index